REFORMING PUBLIC ENTERPRISES

REFORMING PUBLIC ENTERPRISES

R.K. MISHRA
CH. LAKSHMI KUMARI
J. KIRANMAI

KALPAZ PUBLICATIONS
DELHI-110052

Reforming Public Enterprises

Rs. 1190

ISBN: 81-7835-685-6

Published in 2009 in India by
Kalpaz Publications
C-30, Satyawati Nagar,
Delhi-110052
Phone : 9212729499
E-mail: kalpaz@hotmail.com

Lasser Type Setting by: Rudra Computer Graphics, Delhi
Printed at : G. Print Process, Delhi

Contents

Preface

Public Enterprise (PE) reforms are an important component of economic reforms. Going by the global experience, the reforms should have come much earlier in the overall sequencing of reforms. However, the socio-economic and politico necessity has thus far prevented the Government to initiate PE reforms in a big way. The steps taken between 1991 and 2007 have been far and few between. More importantly, the reforms at the state level in enterprises owned and managed by the State Governments have not received significant attention. In some states where PE reforms were initiated, we are back to the square one. The present volume makes an attempt to study the reform measures at the central and the state levels, examines there adequacy and offers some suggestions that could make reforms a virtuous cycle.

We have immensely benefited from the research experiences relating to PEs through research commissioned by the various state agencies and consultancy assignments completed for several domestic and global organizations. We were privileged to have access to the top brass in executive and PE management.

We hope that the volume would provide new interpretations and insights on PE reforms to the readers.

R.K. Mishra
Ch. Lakshmi Kumari
J. Kiranmai

1

Public Enterprises: Achievements and Challenges Ahead

Abstract

World's largest number of poor people live in India[1]. The present policies of the government aim to create a 'poverty museum' in India by 2020. According to A K Sen[2], 'globalization through trade liberalization, global alliances and strengthing social site of economic operations' could banish poverty by that time. C K Prahlad[3] suggests profits as the way to reach the 'fortune at the bottom of pyramid'. Public Enterprises (PEs) in India can not remain as onlookers in the era of globalization. They are required to seize upon the opportunity and benefit from the process. However, this requires a paradigm shift in policies relating to PEs as also their day-to-day functioning. This paper makes an attempt to portray the achievements of PEs in the recent past, the problems areas clouding their performance and the challenges ahead they face in the era of domestic competition and globalization.

Performance of PEs

Public Sector Enterprises have made a major contribution to the economic growth of the country by creating a diversified industrial base. Some of the PEs have had strong financial results over many years and recently some more have turned the corner. The latest data from the Annual Survey of Industries suggests that manufacturing PEs (including those in the States sector) have outperformed private organized manufacturing in total productivity growth after the mid-1990. A part of this (success) is due to the oil sector performance, but the evidence of superior performance, persists.

PEs suffer from misinformation campaign and adverse publicity. It is surprising that ignorance prevails even in the highest quarters. The slant of discussions on PE performance by the Parliamentary Standing Committee on PEs overbears this generalization. The performance of PEs during 2005-06 contradicts such malicious campaign as could be seen from Table1.

Table 1
Performance of PEs

Indicators	*1991-92*	*2005 - 06*	*Growth (% increase)*
No. of PEs	246	245	
Investment (Rs in crore*)	135445	3,93,057	190%
Turnover (Rs in crore)	1,33,906	8,32,584	521%
Net worth (Rs in crore)	60,330	3,47,032	475%
Net Profit (Rs in crore)	2,356	65,429	2677%
Dividend (Rs in crore)	687	20,713	2915%
Contribution to Central Exchequer (Rs in crore)	19,951	1,10,599	454%
Foreign Exchange earning (Rs in crore)	8,980	42,264	370%
Return on investment	11.6%	18.3%	58%

Source: Public Enterprise Survey 2005-06, Vol. 1 Government of India, New Delhi.

* US $ 1 = Rs 45.00 as on 1-04-07 and US $ 1 Bn = Rs 4500 crore

It is clear from the table that performance was astounding on all fronts. The percentage of increase in net worth, net profit, dividend declared, contribution to exchequer and foreign exchange earned was more than a match to private sector enterprises. The financial performance of PEs has registered a significant improvement over the 15 year period 1990-91 to 2005-06. The growth in the various financial parameters such as turnover, net worth, net profit, dividend declared, contribution to exchequer and foreign exchange earned was far more higher than the growth in total investment

The enterprise-wise details of foreign exchange earning of the CPEs during 2005-06 and 2004-05 for export of goods and services may be shown in Table 2 below :

Table 2

Exports and Foreign Exchange Earnings

(Rs in crore)

Item	*2005-06*	*2004-05*
Export of Goods on FOB basis	42576.48	39927.14
Royalty, know-how, professional and consultancy fees	1093.57	1079.50
Interest and Dividends	880.16	725.19
Other Income	1853.14	518.25
Grand Total	**46403.35**	**42250.05**

Source: Public Enterprise Survey 2005-06, Vol. 1 Government of India, New Delhi.

Export of merchandise was the major source of foreign exchange earnings[4]. Table 3 show the enterprise where the increase in foreign exchange earnings was more than Rs. 50.00 crore during 2005-06 as compared to 2004-05.

Table 3
Increase in Foreign Exchange Earnings

(Rs in crore)

Name of the Enterprises	*2005-06*	*2004-05*	*Increase*
Rashtriya Ispat Nigam Ltd	443.52	259.27	184.25
National Aluminum Co. Ltd	2318.20	2146.87	171.33
National Mineral Dev. Co. Ltd	1185.23	1071.43	113.80
Bharat Petroleum Corp. Ltd	4286.67	1944.56	2342.11
Hindustan Petroleum Corp. Ltd	3271.39	1943.51	1327.88
Indian Oil Corp. Ltd	5617.56	3552.96	2064.60
Mangalore Refinery and Petrochemicals Ltd	11917.19	6191.32	5725.87
Oil and Natural Gas Corp. Ltd	2609.38	1210.49	1398.89
ONGC Videsh Ltd	2037.08	1761.84	275.24
Bharat Heavy Electricals Ltd	1929.40	1608.21	321.19
Cochin Shipyard Ltd	187.51	94.21	93.30
Cotton Corp. Ltd	244.36	35.93	208.43
State Trading Corp. Ltd	929.65	333.32	596.33
STCL Ltd	470.78	87.26	383.52
RITES Ltd	136.50	50.65	85.85
Bharat Sanchar Nigam Ltd	103.11	2.00	101.01

Source: Public Enterprise Survey 2005-06, Vol. 1 Government of India, New Delhi.

PEs contributed to the stability of foreign exchange regime in two ways: (i) in some enterprises the foreign exchange earnings registered an increase, and (ii) in many enterprises the utilisation of foreign exchange decreased. Table 4 shows this phenomenon more explicitly.

Table 4

Decrease in Foreign Exchange Utilisation

(Rs in crore)

Name of the Enterprise	*2005-06*	*2004-05*	*Decrease*
NTPC Ltd	1137.37	1551.87	414.50
Nuclear Power Corp. Ltd	1284.49	924.10	360.39
GAIL Ltd	904.67	956.98	52.31
Madras Fertilizes Ltd	175.82	267.10	91.28
Bharat Electronics Ltd	947.58	1023.35	75.77
Hindustan Shipyard Ltd	83.86	140.56	56.70
Handicrafts and Handlooms Exports Corp. Ltd	996.06	1232.42	236.36
MSTC Ltd	4274.40	4541.89	267.49
PEC Ltd	3123.96	5482.31	2358.35
State Trading Crop .Ltd	4114.77	6942.87	2828.10
Air India Ltd	902.33	3348.71	2446.38
Airport Authority of India Ltd	140.15	203.65	63.50
Shipping Corp. of India Ltd	1152.25	1546.16	393.91
Power Grid Corp. India. Ltd	403.84	455.59	51.75
Telecommunication Consultants India Ltd	183.56	308.99	125.43
India Tourism Dev. Corp. Ltd	7.22	70.98	63.76
Indian Railway Finance Corp. Ltd	85.61	770.32	184.71

Source: Public Enterprise Survey 2005-06, Vol. 1 Government of India, New Delhi.

We discuss below briefly the international operations of some leading PEs :

ONGC

ONGC Videsh Ltd. (OVL), the wholly owned subsidiary of ONGC is engaged in overseas E&P activities. The company secured equity participation in nine oil & gas assets across 7 countries. Besides these, OVL has come to own two highly prospective exploration Blocks in oil reach Nigeria through its joint venture company namely ONGC Mittal Energy Ltd. (OMEL). OVL is currently producing oil & gas from its assets in Sudan, Vietnam, Syria and Russia. ONGC has also got three foreign subsidiaries namely, ONGC Nile Ganga (BV ONGBV) Netherlands, ONGC Narmada Ltd., Nigeria and ONGC Bonny Brahmaputra Ltd., Nigeria.

IOC

Both Indian Oil Mauritius Ltd. (IOML) and Lanka IOC Ltd. (LIOC) are the subsidiaries of IOC. Main activities of these Companies relate to importing, selling and distribution of petroleum products in Mauritius and Sri Lanka. IOC Middle East FZE is a wholly owned subsidiary of IOC operating in Dubai and is also engaged in marketing of lubricants and other petroleum products in Middle East, Africa and CIS regions.

GAIL

As a part of its globalization initiative, GAIL has acquired equity in China Gas Holding Ltd., in China. China Gas, which already has a substantial customer base, holds concession for 47 city/towns of which 24 are already operational. GAIL also formed, a wholly owned overseas subsidiary company, namely, GAIL Global (Singapore) Pte. Ltd.

BHEL

BHEL achieved its highest ever physical export order inflow of Rs. 3348 crore during 2005-06 showing a six fold increase over last year (and more than double the exports order booking ever achieved by BHEL in one year). The year was significant for a string of BHEL's successes in project exports encompassing BHEL's turnkey capabilities in almost all areas. It secured orders for Oil & coal based Steam Power Plants, Gas turbine based Power plants, Hydro Power Plants and for Sub-stations besides orders for loose products like Compressors, Transformers, Solar cells etc. in diverse markets. The company rendered services / supplied equipments etc. to countries like Sudan, Oman, Indonesia, Afghanistan, Ethiopia, Poland, Germany, Singapore, Kazakhstan, Malaysia, Thailand, Srilanka, Bangladesh, Cyprus, Saudi Arabia, Trinidad and Tobogo, etc.

NTPC

It offers a broad range of services, namely, consultancy services in engineering, project management, construction management, operation and maintenance of power plants to clients both within as well as outside India. NTPC is keenly pursuing proposals to increase its presence in the different parts of the world. In order to scout for more business activities in the Middle East NTPC is in the process of setting up a representative office in Dubai.

RITES

RITES is implementing projects in various countries such as Afghanistan, Angola, Bangladesh, Ethiopia, Mali, Malaysia, Muzambique Senegal, Sri Lanka, Sudan. It has also established 2 subsidiaries companies, namely, Rites (Afrika) Pty Ltd, Botswana Rites and Colombia Ltd. for strengthening its overseas operations. Besides these, the company has also entered into joint ventures. The net foreign exchange earnings of the Company for the year 2005- 06 was Rs. 115.4 crore compare to Rs. 39 crore for the previous year.

MECON

MECON is engaged in providing designs and technical consultancy services. The Company rendered services abroad in respect of M/s Dangote Industries Ltd. (DIL), LAGOs, Nigeria, M/s KYCR Colls Industries Ltd., Lagos, Nigeria, M/s Emirates Trading Agency (ETA), Dubai, U.A.E. and M/s Star Steel International, U.A.E.

WAPCOS

WAPCOS is one of the pioneering enterprises providing consultancy services in the field of water resources, power and infrastructure projects. It covers all aspects from, concept to commissioning and operation and maintenance of projects. The Company has entered into a number of joint ventures abroad

Table 5
Top Ten Profit Making PEs (2005-06)

Sl. No.	*Name of the enterprise*	*Rs. in crore*
1	Oil and Natural Gas Corporation Ltd.	14430.78
2	Bharat Sanchar Nigam Ltd.	8939.69
3	National Thermal Power Corporation	5820.20
4	Indian Oil Corporation Ltd.	4915.12
5	Steel Authority of India Ltd.	4012.97
6	GAIL (INDIA) Ltd.	2310.07
7	National Mineral Development Corp.	1827.80
8	Nuclear Power Corp. of India Ltd.	1712.97
9	Coal India Ltd.	1711.66
10	Oil India Ltd.	1689.93
	Total	**47371.19**

Source: Public Enterprise Survey 2005-06, Vol. 1 Government of India, New Delhi.

Table 6

Per capita Emoluments of Public Sector Employees in Relation to increase in Average All – India Consumer Price Index

Year	*Employees (in Lakhs) (excl. casual and daily rated workers)*	*Emoluments (Rs in crore)*	*Per capita Emolument (Rs)*	*% age increase over 1971-72 per capita*	*Average index over 1971-72 in average index*	*% of increase*
1971-72	7.02	415	5920	-	192	-
1981-82	19.39	3133	16158	172.94	451	134.90
1990-91	22.19	10912	49179	730.73	951	395.31
1991-92	21.79	12311	56508	854.52	1079	461.98
1992-93	21.52	13983	64983	997.69	1185	517.10
1993-94	20.70	14913	72043	1116.94	1272	562.50
1994-95	20.62	17015	82517	1293.87	1402	630.21
1995-96	20.52	21931	106879	1705.34	1542	703.13
1996-97	20.08	22219	110662	1769.29	1687	778.65

(Contd.)

(Contd. Table 6)

Year	*Employees (in Lakhs) (excl. casual and daily rated workers)*	*Emoluments (Rs in crore)*	*Per capita Emolument (Rs)*	*% age increase over 1971-72 per capita*	*Average index over 1971-72 in average index*	*% of increase*
1997-98	19.59	25385	129582	2088.89	1803	839.06
1998-99	19.00	26254	138179	2234.10	2039	961.98
1999-00	18.06	30402	168339	2743.56	2109	998.44
2000-01	17.40	38223	219672	3610.67	2190	1440.62
2001-02	19.92	38556	193554	3169.49	2284	1089.58
2002-03	18.66	42169	225986	3717.33	2375	1136.98
2003-04	17.62	43919	248481	4097.31	2467	1184.89
2004-05	17.00	48629	286053	4731.97	2561	1236.98
2005-06	16.49	45625	276683	4573.70	2674	1292.71

Source: Public Enterprise Survey 2005-06, Vol. 1 Government of India, New Delhi.

Table 7
Cognate Group-wise Women Employment during 2005-06

Commodity Group	*Managerial and Supervisory*	*Non-Executive*	*Total*
Enterprises under construction	151	124	275
Steel	1080	7981	8998
Minerals and Metal	418	1900	2318
Coal and Lignite	2547	27991	30538
Power	1175	2386	3561
Petroleum	3762	3277	7039
Fertilizers	311	600	911
Chemicals and Pharmaceuticals	104	546	650
Heavy Engineering	1107	1446	2553
Medium and Light Engineering	1704	10275	11976
Transportation Equipment	725	1646	2371
Consumer Goods	188	707	895
Agro-based Industries	12	196	208
Textiles	90	1149	1239
Trading and Marketing Services	831	1756	2587
Transportation Services	1878	1715	3593
Contract and Construction Services	289	447	736
Industrial Dev. and Tech Consultancy Services	794	622	1416
Tourist Services	175	347	522
Financial Services	373	338	712
Telecommunication and Information Technology Services	926	10104	11030
Section 25 Companies	104	208	312
Total	**18744**	**75698**	**94440**

Source: Public Enterprise Survey 2005-06, Vol. 1 Government of India, New Delhi.

namely, Salma Dam Project, Afghanistan; Tata H.E. Project, Bhutan; Construction of Tubewells in Nimro Province, Afghanistan; Rehabilitation of West Baray Irrigation Project, Cambodia; Technical Assistance for feasibility study for Electrification and Irrigation Development in Lesotho; Amir Ghazi Dam and Quargaha Reservoir.

During the year 2005-06 shares of MTNL (ADR) were listed in New York Stock Exchange and GAIL and SAIL (GDR) were listed on London Stock Exchange.

The top ten profit making PEs did extremely well in terms of profit earnings and in no way there performance was inferior to the performance of their counterparts. Oil and Natural Gas Corp. Ltd led the pack followed by Bharat Sanchar Nigam and the National Thermal Power Corp. Ltd. However the profit earnings in the case of the Oil and Natural Gas Corp needs to be adjusted against the price push brought about by the changes in international petroleum prices.

The wage and employment behavior of PEs could be discerned from Table 6. It is interesting to note that the per capita emoluments have registered higher rate of growth than the growth in the price index. That PEs are competitive on the employment and the wage fronts could be known from the facts that the wage costs as a part of cost of production was a mere 6.3 per cent in 2005-06

The gender bias in PEs is declining as compared to gender representation in organized employment in private sector. The women employment is about six per cent of the employed managerial and labour force in PEs.

Problems and Challenges Ahead

There are many areas where PEs could make a substantial headway providing scope for making these enterprises as the national jewels and market leaders.

Corporate Governance, Vision and Mission and decentralized decision making

The Sarbanes Oxley Act on Corporate Governance has once again reasserted the need for instituting robust internal management systems and disclosure requirements. The initiation of the process of corporate governance in PEs is likely to result into a series of important benefits. Firstly, the flip-flop about owning of the responsibility about the low performance of these enterprises would come to an end, as the PE board would have to own up the moral responsibility for their good or bad performance. This would result into goal and role clarity. These enterprises would become mission and vision-driven organisation in which their top management would work for creating their own culture, leading to their transformation from government entities to corporate entities, from state sponsored and financed organisations to self-sustained organisations. The formulation of vision will impel them to think as to what they should be in the next 25 years and evolution of mission will help them in defining the business they should be in during the next 15 years. The process of arriving at the vision and the mission will integrate the personnel with the enterprise which ultimately will lead them to cultivate their own culture and ethos. It has been found that many-a-PE are not able to distinguish between the objectives listed in their Memorandum of Association (MoA) and the mission that an enterprise should have. The toning up of the corporate governance function could help them a great deal in brand building and relating well to society, business, employees, legal institutions and accounting world. The application of Clause 49 of the Securities Exchange Board of India (SEBI) Code is a point in reference. Although approved by SEBI in 2004, many PEs have not been able to appoint 50% of the board strength as independent directors. In turn, they asked for relaxation to 33%. The corporate governance could tremendously improve as could be seen from the operations of the Audit, Compensation and Appointments

Committee reports in many PEs. The Government directors could add more value by making enterprise specific contribution. There is no evaluation system in place for the independent directors and other directors including the Chairman-cum-Managing Director. PEs need to benchmark their targets, output, process, procedures and market orientation. The issue of clarity of organizational mission and vision, and corporate governance induced culture is better handled by an effective board. Table 8 shows that PEs have to go a long way in resolving the boards related issues as there is not enough clarity on formal and informal roles of the board.

Table 8
Role of Board of Directors

Name of the Enterprise	*Role of the BoDs Formal and Informal*
BCPL	Over all policy guidelines : to help the company to prepare long range plans, appointment of key managers.
BDL	Board will have to Be cohesive and play a progressive role in shaping the destiny of the company
BEL	Setting corporate machine, objectives, goals, reviewing the performance, framing corporate policies and conducting SWOT analysis.
BPCL	Setting the companies strategic aim, providing leadership, supervising management of the business, reporting to shareholders on Board's / stewardship.
CMPDL	Advising and guiding the Board, cautioning the board about pitfalls.
ECL	To provide directions for growth of the company and monitor progress in constructive manner.
GRSE	Board must be the supreme policy making body to manage the company in the best interest of the enterprise. Govt.

(Contd.)

(Contd. Table 8)

Name of the Enterprise	*Role of the BoDs Formal and Informal*
	should not try to do backseat driving through nominated directors.
GSYL	Chairman should take the decision with informal / formal advice from the Board.
HAL	Policy formulation and updating review, monitor implementation of plans, ensure compliance of laws, guide in technology updation, give fillip to R&D effort, monitor progress of new projects / diversification programmes.
HFCL	Give their view points and benefit of their experience in taking major policy decision.
HLL	BoD should be able to give professional guidance to the corporate body.
HPCL	Directors should meet in Board meetings to approve various growth oriented agenda with pragmatic views in regard to size, nature and tough external competition.
HVOC	As under Memorandum of Association and Articles of Association.
ITI	Formulation of policy guidelines, superintendence, formation of JVCs, foreign collaboration.
MAPL	To manage business of the company by exercising all such powers within the frame work of the Companies Act.
MECL	To guide the company towards growth in today's competitive market, lay down policies and monitor its implementation.
MTNL	BoD should give a feedback on the performance of the company based on the knowledge and interaction with the members of the public.

(Contd.)

(Contd. Table 8)

Name of the Enterprise	*Role of the BoDs Formal and Informal*
MDL	Role of the Board should be confined to setting up targets of production in terms of quantity and value; review of actual production vis-à-vis targets; assessment of under utilisation of capacity by determining attainable production vis-à-vis firm orders / projected demand; prescription of standards of equipment utilisation, broad targets of inventory levels.
MFL	Board should monitor executive management; should present a balanced and understandable assessment of company's position; should establish an audit committee; should devote time and effort to attend meetings.
NALCO	To set goals, to set over all policies, to decide strategies for future.
NEPA	To guide senior level management on policy matters; interact with ministries in government and other agencies to further development of the organisation. General image building for the company in different flora.
NHPC	Board should guide the organisation in the short and long term plans. Extend advice and assistance in technical, financial, administrative and organisational matters to ensure best performance. Board should be a vocal mouth piece to project corporation's achievements and aspirations and protect the same from adverse actions and reactions from various quarters.
NPC	BoD should be mainly concerned with formulation of policy and to review the performance of the on-going projects, performance of the operating stations and exercise the powers which are vested in the BoD with regard to sanctions and approvals.

(Contd.)

(Contd. Table 8)

Name of the Enterprise	*Role of the BoDs Formaland Informal*
NSC	More concentration on practical operational aspects. Free and frank brain storming discussion. Each and every director should be heard.
NSICL	Board should be available to visualise the future scenario and direct accordingly the future activities. Monitor aspiration of the service user, general economy and employees to give proper policy direction. Adopt techniques of successful managerial practices of private sector boards.
ONGC	Develop a long lasting vision of the company. Provide strategic direction, promote business and ensure long term growth, add value in large investment decisions, encourage creativity, technology up-gradation and value based business.
RCFL	BoD is the pivotal authority created by the company. Role is mainly in laying down policies and to ensure strategic and long term plans are carried out. Role is insignificant in the field of development and creation of core competence.
SIIL	Assist company through their inputs in strategic planning provide support in controlling external environment. Provide guidance and bridge in the knowledge gap in areas like technical / marketing. Finance / HR / Operations.
STC	Formulation of corporate plan / policies / strategies. Fixation of targets and laying down of control / monitoring mechanism.
TCIL	To evolve strategic plan, its implementation monitoring.
WPCS	The directors in the respective professional field apart from dwelling on board proceedings shall also share the

(Contd.)

(Contd. Table 8)

Name of the Enterprise	*Role of the BoDs Formal and Informal*
	responsibility to develop strategies and plan for business development and to be proactive in resolving key issues in the implementation process. This interaction shall be through a sub-committee which shall function under the CMD and report to the Board from time to time.

Source : Mishra, R K, Public Enterprise Boards in India, Institute of Public Enterprise, Mimeo, 2006.

The decentralized decision making acts as a pivotal force in the functioning of successful firms. To reap benefits of the decentralized decision making, the organisational structure has to be suitability evolved. Budgeting, strategic business groups, MIS, and business rules decide the degree of decentralisation in an enterprise. Organisationally, many PEs have become monolithic. Large enterprises such as the ONGC Ltd and the SBI are the cases in point. Restructuring these organisations is essential to take them forward in the global scenario. The formulation of corporate plans is necessary in both letter and spirit.

Inter-corporate Coordination

The inter-corporate coordination in PEs holds a great hope for their future. Such coordination could bring together this PEs to facilitate exchange of their strengths for eliminating their weaknesses. In each area e.g., marketing, finance, personnel, strategy, international business, customer relationship management, corporate social responsibility, productivity, value engineering, research and development, purchases and inventory management, public accountability, board practices, these enterprises could exchange their knowledge and strengths which would provide them a rare opportunity of creating a competitive edge to walk through the markets.

Autonomy and Accountability

Autonomy is the key issue remaining in the state of limbo at the hands of the Government which has shied away from taking some concrete decisions such as the removal of Article 12 from the Indian Constitution which hinders the autonomy of PEs in terms of recruitment, promotion and day to day business. Like the private sector enterprises, there is a need to have a level playing field for PEs and going by this assertion we could easily make out a case for exempting PEs from Article 12 of the Indian Constitution. The Comptroller and Auditor General (CAG) audit is under thorn in the flash. Till 1954, as pointed out by Ashok Chanda, there was no CAG audit for PEs. Later, in 1956 on the pretext of the Government funding, this PEs was brought under the control of the CAG. The business acumen of the CAG auditors' need a pep up in the absence of which there are not able to discern the difference between the action of the Government and the action of a commercial entity. The influence of the institution of the Chief Vigilance Commission (CVC) has not helped public sector in any way. The appointments at the board level got delayed because of too much time being taken by the CVC. Then, for each appointment of the same person, the CVC has to be approached time and again. The CVC takes about six months to one year in clearing the names for the consideration of the Cabinet Committee on Appointments. The Public Enterprise Selection Board (PESB) needs time to put top managerial personnel in PEs in their respective positions. The salaries offered are not competitive and tagging the salaries to the officers of the IAS would not take PEs anywhere as there is resource crunch of good managers even in private sector. The Public Investment Board requires the enterprises to go through it in case the investment proposals are beyond a threshold limit although to some extent the Navratnas and the Miniratnas do not come under its purview. The investment decisions in PEs should be subjected by the same norms as those applied in the case of private enterprises plus PEs should get a credit for the social content of their project appraisal. The Optimum Performance Through Internal Management Action (OPTIMA) could usher in a new era of sound working of PEs as it could take care of budgeting, pricing, management information system, internal audit, transfer pricing, management by objectives and higher performance through consensus.

Improved Resource and Programme Management

It is common knowledge that the productivity in PEs is very low and the quality of programme management is not above the mark. The productivity as measured in terms of Value Addition per Employee (VAPE), growth in VAPE and Return on Capital Employed (ROCE) is medium to poor in PEs. The asset utilisation ratios have been very low as the capacity utilisation has tremendous potential to increase. The inventories are a major culprit in this regard. As on March 31 2004, the CPSEs had total inventories worth Rs 59,754 crore, which was equivalent to 42 days of cost of production / services rendered. The stores and spares inventories are very high in terms of absolute value and relative parameters. The sensitisation about supply chain management has not made the required dent. The private sector firms have taken on supply chain management as the principal area of the managerial attention. The cash management is feeble. The cash on float is still very high and cash balances are not giving appropriate mileage. The receivables management is not very sound as the collection period needs to be shortened to bring it on par with the aggregate ratio. The earning power is imbalanced on the asset turnover side. The cost management also does not present an encouraging picture. The standard costs have not been developed. The per unit costs are not controlled through inter and intra firm comparisons. The cost manuals have not been prepared by many enterprises. Pricing is not done on the basis of costs in many enterprises. The difference between the marginal and full costs is not made for the purposes of pricing by many enterprises. The internal audit systems are not in a good shape as test checks are preferred to concurrent internal audit. The use of information technology is yet to make deeper in roads. The enterprise resource planning (ERP) is still a dream in the case of many large and medium PEs. The project management is tardy as the time and cost overruns are legion. The incremental capital output ratio (ICOR) is a good measure to evaluate the resource use efficiency in business enterprises. PEs are credited with an increasing ICOR implying the fact that the resource use efficiency is very low in the case of these enterprises. Excessive investments in land, building, plant and machinery, and working capital are responsible for this phenomenon.

Regulation

In the marketized world when we talk of a new world economic order, the commanding heights could not be left to private institutions and business. Regulation could alone ensure a happy co-existence of public and private sectors; developed and developing world; and consumer and producer. Some examples of regulatory bodies in India include the Telephone Regulatory Authority of India (TRAI), Insurance Regulatory and Development Authority (IRDA) and Securities and Exchange Board of India (SEBI). PEs need to be provided a level playing field by these regulatory authorities. The behaviour of private sector has been adverse to the interest of the consumer as proved by the power supply disaster during the Mumbai floods in 2005 and super-cyclone of Orissa where private sector defaulted in fulfilling its obligations to the local consumers and burden alone PEs which stood like Gibraltar rock in the service of consumers.

The Central Electricity Authority and the State Electricity Regulatory Authorities have found the behaviour of private sector power generation, transmission and distribution firms very inappropriate in terms of working out profits on capital employed, accounting systems, control on T&D losses, and modernization of their functions.

Upgraded work efficiency

Enhance productivity of the work force holds the key to the success of PEs in future. The salaries and wages as a percentage of cost of production in the CPEs is about 12 per cent as compared to about eight per cent in private sector. PEs suffer from labour hoarding. There is a need to upgrade the work efficiency of PE personnel through job cataloging, performance appraisal, counseling, job rotation, job enlargement, job enrichment, training and management development. The recruitment policies will have to undergo a change which need to provide a greater weightage to computer literacy, familiarity with information technology and expertise in the use of internet. Sadly, PEs lack multi-skilling. There is a bunching of a large number of employees at the lower levels. These happen to constitute about 75 per cent of the total workforce in sectors like steel, coal, textiles, transport, etc. Multi-skilling will keep them fit for the changing work needs of PEs. The factory layout, rearrangement of production facilities and shift from traditional and outmoded methods of production to batch manufacturing, computer aided design, computer aided manufacturing and digitalized production will have to find a place for upgrading the efficiency of the workforce. The flexi hours, work from home and employee centered output approaches providing enough cushion to give need to the family problems of employees would go a longway in upgrading the efficiency. The focus need to shift also to employees stock ownership plan whereby the integrity and loyalty of the personnel could be ensured for the well being of the PEs.

Proactive and Competitive market strategies, Customer satisfaction benchmarks and complaint resolution mechanism

Marketing is the weakest link in the chain in PEs. The output orientation and captive market have kept PEs alienated from the market. The globalized world is dominated by market force which requires an enterprise to have its deeper understanding in terms of product, place, channel, and price. PEs will have to differentiate between 'selling' and 'marketing'. The former requires traditional strategies to push the products whereas the latter requires proactive strategies. In terms of pricing, PEs may have to vary the line and length from time to time choosing from a basket of pricing policies such as marginal pricing, incremental pricing, full cost pricing, dual pricing, domestic and international pricing. Discounts may have to be offered to win market share. The product line may have to undergo a change to suit the requirements of the customer. Access to global markets will have to be ensured. The concept of 'cross selling' will have to be introduced. The idea of 'brand ambassador' need to be explored. Product innovations should become the normal feature. The Boston Consulting Group (BCG) matrix may have to be adopted to differentiate the products in terms of competitive market strategies. The 'cash cows' and 'stars' need to be preferred to 'dogs' and 'question marks'. In so far as international selling is concerned, appropriate transfer pricing systems will have to be evolved to acquire competitive market edge.

Customer loyalty has become an integral part of competitive market strategies. In fact, customer loyalty is giving way to customer delight. PEs have had a peripheral aquitance with customer loyalty as they operated in the regime of sheltered markets. In the case of PEs operating in the field of public systems, customer satisfaction is a key determinant of their overall success. PEs hardly classify their customer accounts, dissect their needs and strategize their marketing plans. There are not many PEs following the balance card approach of measuring their performance especially the customer satisfaction. PEs in different cognate groups in the category of producing and service rendering enterprises do not benchmark the customer satisfaction with their counterparts in private sector and multinational firms. In fact, there are good benchmarks achieved by PEs in each cognate group but in the absence of 'knowledge management', the other enterprises remain ignorant about such successors. The complaint resolution mechanism is not effective as it hardly provides solution on the real time basis and at times functions in such a way that the problem is shielded by ineffectiveness. PEs have to attach a great significance to this aspect in there scheme of operations. Even enterprises such as the Bharat Heavy Electrical Ltd, State Trading Corporation of India and the Steel Authority of India have shown lax reflexes in the complaint resolution. For proactive and competitive marketing strategies, it is

Table 9
Impact of NEP on Working System in PEs

Working Systems	*Change*	*No. of Enterprises*	*No change*	*No. of Enterprises*
Recruitment	34%	12 / 35	66%	23 / 35
Terms & Conditions	43%	15 / 35	57%	20 / 30
Interface relationship with the company	29%	16 / 35	71%	25 / 35
Accountability	34%	12 / 37	66%	23 / 35
Budgeting	29%	10 / 35	71%	25 / 35
Auditing	23%	8 / 35	77%	27 / 35
Market position	37%	13 / 35	63%	22 / 35

Source: Mishra, R.K., *Op.Cit.*

required that PEs transform their working systems. A survey of 35 PEs shows that working systems have not changed much even after the onset of economic liberalization.

Conclusion

To conclude, PEs in the era of economic liberalization have done extremely well much against the prophesies of the prophets of doom who had expected them to wind up and disappear. They have performed well in the market based regime. They could have done much better with superior internal management systems, enterprise oriented government policies, improved resource use, upgraded labour efficiency and honing their competitiveness through building up enterprise specific ethos and culture and decentralized method of work supported by knowledge based systems, innovations and technological backup. More autonomy need to be imparted to these enterprises by clothing them with more relevant form of organisations and shunning the plain vanilla approach of organizing them as government companies. The introduction of MoU provides an evidence that given the suitable autonomy, these enterprises could leap forward to unscaled peaks. The Korean, French and Singaporean examples provide a good framework to develop the Indian model. These enterprises could perform better by superior inter-PE collaboration, Optima, lack of bias in regulation, improved corporate governance and strong interface with national and international capital markets. There is a need to empower PEs for self- sustained and organic growth in future.

Notes and References

1. 35% of world's poor live in India. The number of people living less than \$ one a day is 1,016 million.

See : *Times of India*, Special Report : End of Poverty, Hyderabad, December 17, 2006, p. 11.

2. *Ibid.*
3. *Ibid.*
4. Government of India (Department of Public Enterprises, Ministry of Heavy Industries & Public Enterprises), Public Enterprises Survey: 2005-06, Vol. 1, New Delhi, pp. 2-3.

2

Public Sector Reforms in Global Perspectives: The Indian Case

Abstract

Public sector in India comprises government departments, autonomous public enterprises and departmental undertakings. Public sector controls a quarter of the Indian economy. Public sector contributes 25% to the Gross Domestic Product (GDP) in India. Despite the mega, macro and micro rollback of the Indian State, public sector continues to occupy commanding heights of the Indian economy. 45% of the capital formation in the Indian economy takes place in public sector. The public investments continue to play a strategic role in the acceleration of the rate of growth of the Indian economy and also act as a catalyst for accentuating the development of private sector in India. The Indian economy is getting integrated with the rest of the world. The process of such an integration has necessitated to shun seclusion and embrace competitiveness embodying leadership in quality, in product range, service delivery, citizen centricity, productivity, financing, organizing and strategizing. In order to be globally competitive, public sector in India has to set new

terms for its functioning which will help it in acquiring the competitive edge resulting in offering value for money to the citizens of the country and the world at large. While the government departments will do well to exploit the ICT (information and communication technology), PPP (public-private-partnership) and agency approach to organizing its activities, autonomous public enterprises are required to take recourse to the OPTIMA (Optimum Performance Through Internal Management Action) and improved government – public enterprise interface. The departmental enterprises will have to go in for conversion into the non-departmental enterprises. Both the non-departmental and the departmental enterprises have to introduce new techniques of performance evaluation including the balance scorecard, share holders value creation and economic value added. This may require management development and training programmes on restructuring covering physical, financial, manpower, organisational and technology restructuring.

Public sector at all the three levels is required to create a new breed of leaders. The leadership role has to be donned not only by people at the top but also by people at the middle and lower levels of the organisation. Public sector will have to create leaders all the way from top-down to the bottom.

Ushering in global competitiveness in public sector in India is no easy task. It requires a cultural change through training and management development. The contents of the general and the functional management development and training programmes have to undergo a complete change as the public sector organisations have to be now outward looking. The focus of the programmes has to shift to the generic and the specific concepts of restructuring. The multiculturalism and multilingualism have to make inroads in the contents of the programmes designed and implemented. The challenges thrown by the global organisations and multilateral trading blocks such as WTO (World Trade Organisations), WB (World Bank), Asian

Development Bank, International Monetary Fund, European Commission, ASEAN (Association of South East Asian Nations), etc need to be factored in the management development and training programmes.

India with a population of more than one billion people having acquired the distinction of being the back office of the world depends a great deal on public sector. There is a need for public sector to acquire global competitive edge which, among other things, is expected to come through customized management development and training programmes for the employees in this sector operating at all the levels.

The purpose of the paper is to discuss the scope and expanse of public sector in India, measures taken to make it globally competitive, steps that are required to boost the global competitiveness, and the implications of making it globally competitive in terms of education and training.

Scope

Public sector is defined in myriad ways by various experts. Some include only the government departments as a constituent of public sector whereas others include the commercial activities of the government organized as separate arms also within the scope of public sector. There have been exceptions made even to the liberal interpretation of the scope of public sector as some experts include the autonomous enterprises carrying out the various commercial activities as a part of public sector. There have been situations where some countries are organized on unitary basis and in such case the autonomous enterprises fall within the ambit of the working of the central government. However, there have been situations when countries are not organized on unitary basis and are run as federation of states or regions. When countries are organized on federal basis with provinces under its control / or as a union of states, the sub-national enterprises of autonomous character are set up which by their very nature qualify to be a part of the public sector.

This is true of the countries which are organized on the basis of 'regions'. However, both in the case of a country organized on the unitary basis and also when it is organized on the federal basis operating through 'regions' or 'provinces / states', the local level administration might set up some enterprises in the departmental form or as autonomous enterprise which also qualify to be considered as a part of public sector. In other words, public sector includes government departments, departmental enterprises and non-departmental / autonomous enterprises within the scope of its operation.

Expanse

Public sector occupies a very important part in the economies of nations. This can be gazed from the national budgets and the activities which are managed, owned and controlled by the governments. The plan outlays, in case indicative / centralized planning is done, could also throw light on the extend and importance of public sector. The data at our disposal point out very clearly that public sector commands a great strength in the Indian economy and that it would continue to wield a great influence in the Indian economy. It may be noted that the local administration in India holds a microscopic importance in terms of financial dimensions and therefore the data discussed relate only to the public sector at the central and the state levels.

The net effect of the efficiency of public sector could be seen by combined surplus/ deficit of the state governments.

Table 1 shows that public sector plan outlay from 2000-01 to 2005-06. During 2005-06, the public sector outlay was about 11 per cent of the gross domestic product (GDP). The public sector outlay is widely dispersed in the areas of agriculture &allied activities, rural development, special area programmes, irrigation and flood control, energy, non-conventional sources of energy, industry and minerals, transport, communications, science, technology & environment, general economic services,

Table 1
Public Sector Plan Outlay (at current prices)

(Rs in Crore)

Year	*Agriculture & allied services*	*Rural development and special areas programmes*	*Irrigation and flood control*	*Energy*	*Industry and minerals*	*Transport*	*Education*	*Health including medical*	*Others*	*Total*
2000-01	7577	10897	13529	36613	6866	25734	11691	14450	37122	164479
2001-02	8248	15154	14552	37145	7942	29918	11556	13814	47986	186315
2002-03	7655	20819	11965	44710	8776	35244	12585	16143	52306	210203
2003-04 (RE)	9436	23839	15817	57926	7698	38145	15169	18831	56689	243550
2004-05 (RE)	10875	24093	20505	60144	10196	38986	18672	11056	74738	269267
2005-06 (BE)	13840	28477	26957	77356	15303	59992	24651	14891	9972	361239

(Source: Handbook of Statistics on the Indian Economy, Reserve Bank of India, 2005-06, p. 180)

RE : Revised Estimates BE : Budget Estimates.

social services and other services. It may be noted that the public sector outlay is only slightly lower than the private sector outlay. Table 2 shows the position of public sector in organized employment in India as compared to the organized employment in the private sector. The table clearly points to the strong position of public sector as private sector provides only 25 per cent of the organized employment in India as compared to 75 per cent of the public sector. However, the public sector has to become more efficient and globally competitive the need for which could be seen from Table 3 which gives the combined deficit of central and state governments. Although this deficit is no more spiraling, it continues to be alarming and is about 10 per cent of the gross domestic product. As per the fiscal norms this should be around three per cent of the GDP. The persistent fiscal deficit leads to deficit financing, resultant unbridled inflation, depreciation and devaluation of the domestic currency, uncertain trade scenario, halting foreign domestic investments, inequitable distribution of income, and socio-political instability in the economy. The persistent fiscal deficit in India is the result of oversized government, ineffective governance, loss making public enterprises and inefficient functioning of departmental enterprises at both the central and the state levels. The national

Table 2

Employment in Public and Organized private sector

Year	*Public Sector*	*Private Sector*	*Number of persons on the live register*
2000-01	19.14	8.65	42.00
2001-02	18.77	8.43	41.17
2002-03	18.58	8.42	41.39
2003-04	18.20	8.25	40.46
2004-05	-		39.35

(*Source*: Handbook of Statistics on the Indian Economy, Reserve Bank of India, 2005-06, p. 44)

economies are tending to converge to the world financial order. India can not be a silent observer watching this transition and ultimately left behind in the exercise. It has to seize the opportunity. This points the need of making the public sector in India globally competitive in the absence of which its entire economy will lose the global advantage.

Table 3

Combined Deficits of Central and State Governments

(Rs in crore)

Years	*Gross fiscal deficit*	*Gross primary deficit*	*Revenue deficit*
2000-01	199852	75035	138803
2001-02	226425	84039	159350
2002-03	234987	75927	162990
2003-04	234502	56701	159406
2004-05	234719	42407	114761
2005-06	263195	57234	109105
2006-07	257088	30488	86513

(*Source*: Handbook of Statistics on the Indian Economy, Reserve Bank of India, 2005-06, p. 187)

Initiatives

India is in the throes of rapid economic development. The rate of economic growth of India is only second to that of China's. Not only the government and governance but also its domestic business is deeply involved in transformation to attain the global competitiveness. India has taken a wide array of initiatives to transform the public sector. Some of the major initiatives include downsizing public sector, introducing technology up-gradation, making it customer friendly and citizen centric, public-private partnership and delegation and decentralization.

Downsizing public sector

India is working towards a public sector which is lean and mean. Since, the independence, the public sector has fattened itself through allocating unjustifiably large resources, employing too many un-required people, indulging in uneconomic spending and entering non-core areas of social and economic activities. During the last 20 years as a part of economic and administrative reforms, the government at both the central and the state levels and also through its departmental and autonomous commercial organizations, has come down heavily on the size by imposing restrictions on the creation of new posts, curtailing the number of existing posts, offering voluntary retirement scheme to those employees who would like to opt out of the services, effecting cuts on the sanctioned budgets, adopting zero-based budgeting and discouraging the growth of defence out lays. Multi-tasking, multi-skilling and outsourcing have become the principal techniques of downsizing. The non-core activities have been hived-off. Such non-core activity include maintenance, cleaning, canteen and gardening, etc.

Technology up-gradation

The government at the administrative and commercial levels has, among other things, gone in for e-Governance which has brought under its scope the citizen related activates, commercial and enterprise related activities. As a part of e-Governance, many states in India and also the central government has set up e-Seva (Service) which enables a citizen to avail all the citizen centric services at one roof at a given price which is very moderate for longer hours and for longer number of days in contrast to what it used to be when the services were rendered manually. This step has increased India's global competitiveness through enhanced public sector effectiveness tempting even foreign direct investment to get attracted to India in increasing volume and also the investors having enormous private equity.

Customer friendly and citizen centricity

The public sector in India is shedding its old style of treating people with askance and as captive crowd. The public sector official used to convey the signal to people: 'take it' or 'leave it'. There is a sea change today in the attitude of the same official. Culture building is no more a preserve of corporates. It has permeated with full throttle in the government at different levels and layers. This change of attitude has resulted in treating people as customers. Now the government officials are being re-designated as managers and people satisfaction is being equated to customer satisfaction. The grievance redresseal departments in the government are being renamed as customer relationship departments. The citizens centricity is reflected in the citizen charters which are modeled as MoUs between the citizen and the government. The score cards for each department are prepared to evaluate their performance. Such score card also provides the basis for identifying the areas for corrective action. An efficient web management / portal management is the medium used for improving the government competitiveness in the area of customer relationship management.

Public-private-partnership

The public sector in India is doing its every bit to improve its effectiveness to make it globally comparable and competitive. Public-private-partnership is tending to become the most preferred technique in realizing this goal. The public sector is faced with resource crunch and managerial ability of high order. Further, its competencies suit the old economy industry and government and are quite unsuited to the new economy industry and the government. Public-private-partnership provides an opportunity to garner resources and also hire / avail managerial talents from the private sector. In partnering with private sector, the public sector stands to gain by minimizing the risk and improving its image and thereby tap the international capital markets. Almost all the ministries in India at the central and the state levels and also at the enterprise level are engaged in public-private-partnership to improve their performance and achieve their objectives. Public-private-partnership has picked up well in railways, road transport, infrastructure and health sectors.

Delegation and Decentralization

Public sector of yester years was bereft of delegation and decentralization. The expert committee reports by Paul H Appleby and A D Gorwala for the first time argued about ample delegation and decentralization. This was supported later by V K Krishna Menon and Ashok Chandra. The first Administrative Reforms Commission (1966) and the second Administrative Reforms Commission (2006) have been much more vocal about the need for greater delegation and decentralization. Similarly, public enterprises which form a part of public sector have been allowed generous delegation and decentralization of financial powers. These enterprises are categorised as nine champions, mini champions, profit making, mixed performance, loss making and sick enterprises. There has been an extensive delegation of powers to these enterprises by the government in 1996 and again in 2006. The process is on. The principal objective behind empowering these enterprises is to enable them to be globally competitive.

Implications to Education and Training

The implications of making public sector in India globally competitive are far-fetched in terms of education and training as it is nothing short of revolutionalising them in terms of curricula, pedagogy, teaching aids, evaluation and faculty backup.

The in-house training establishments in public sector have to be outward looking. The in-breeding has to go. Those who are not good at work and also good for nothing should not be pushed as resource persons in training programmes. The training function deserves a greater attention. The training budgets have to be increased as also the physical facilities for training resulting in a good ambiance. The post-training effectiveness appraisal has to have a greater element of seriousness. The impact of training in terms of increased productivity and a better fit between the employee and employer needs to be measured in a business-like way. The training programmes have to undergo a radical change in terms of content and the approach. For the training for officials in the top rung, it is necessary that intellectual input on concept related issues is provided. This may relate to international markets, regional trading blocks, management education, computer and information technology and behavioral sciences. So far as duration is concerned, for top level personal, there could be short duration programmes and seminars. For the middle level officials / executives, a one week course could be ideal whereas for junior executives a two to four week course is desirable on the workshop mode. For education, the implications are phenomenal. The government could start distance education programmes on global competitiveness for public sector entities. It may outsource the post graduate programme teaching and organisation to universities in India. Even good universities from abroad be invited to jointly sponsor such programmes with Indian universities or institutes of higher learning. In case of both education and training, the course contents have to be related to the context, they may have to undergo frequent revision, new courses may have to be introduced and teaching methodology and materials have to be properly matched with the requirement. The entire effort has to be woven around the global competitiveness.

New Horizons for Research

Although public sector in India is making a great march towards global competitiveness, such a movement requires continuous support through relevant research that could point out the areas that need to be probed further. One such area is productivity, its measurement and link with wages and wage revisions. The other area that need to be research is coordination that should take place between two departments and among departments, the reasons obstructing such coordination and the policy revamp. There is a need to even look into the total policy frame governing public sector and its soundness in relation to similar policy frame for private sector and multinationals.

Conclusions

Public sector forms the backbone of the Indian economy. It is a crucial determinant of the success of the private sector in India. Over the years, the public sector did not function effectively resulting in its deterioration on the indicator of global competitiveness. However, during the last 15 years a series of measures have been initiated to make the Indian public sector globally competitive. These have ranged from downsizing the government to public-private-partnership and delegation of financial powers. The outcomes have been quite impressive. Public sector in India is turning out to the competitive not only in the domestic markets but also globally. The training and education could further fuel this change and make it a lasting gain. To enhance global competitiveness, public sector in India has to adopt new methods of performance evaluation. No more it has to depend on confidential reports. It has to move to globally accepted techniques of performance evaluation such as the balance scorecard and economic value added. It could be shareholder value creation in the case of its autonomous public enterprises.

3

Performance of Public Enterprises in the Era of Economic Liberalization

Abstract
This paper proposes to analyze the performance of the Public Enterprises (PEs) in the era of economic liberalization against the backdrop of trenchant criticism of their non-performance and argument about their folding up in the wake of the development of private sector and private initiative. In doing so, the paper portrays the Government policy on PEs, performance of PEs during the era of economic liberalization, salient features of functioning of PEs, and the scope for improvement in their future performance.

PE Policy

PE policy in India has changed from time to time. The economic liberalization has brought about a radical transformation in PE policy which is explained as below:

- "Portfolio of public sector investments will be reviewed with a view to focus the public sector on strategic, high-tech and essential infrastructure.

- Public enterprises which are chronically sick and which are unlikely to be turned around will, for the formulation of revival / rehabilitation schemes, be referred to the Board for Industrial and Financial Reconstruction (BIFR), or other similar high level institutions created for the purpose. A social security mechanism will be created to protect the interests of workers likely to be affected by such rehabilitation packages.
- In order to raise resources and encourage wider public participation, a part of the government's shareholding in the public sector would be offered to mutual funds, financial institutions, general public and workers
- Board of public sector companies would be made more professional and given greater powers.
- There will be a greater thrust on performance improvement through the Memorandum of Understanding (MoU) system through which managements would be granted greater autonomy and will be held accountable.
- To facilitate a fuller discussion on performance, the MoU signed between Government and the public enterprises would be placed in Parliament. While focusing on major management issues, this would also help place matters on day-to-day operations of public enterprises in their correct perspective
- The Government will commit itself:
  (i) To devolve full managerial and commercial autonomy to successful, profit-making companies operating in a competitive environment
  (ii) Not to generally privatize
  (iii) To modernize and restructure sick public sector companies and revive sick industry
  (iv) To chronically sell / close down loss-making companies
  (v) To induct private industry to turn-around companies that have potential for revival

(vi) To use privatization revenues will be used for designated social sector schemes

(vii) Public sector companies and nationalized banks will be encouraged to enter the capital market to raise resources and offer new investment avenues to retail investors.

Although, the PE policy leans towards a balanced approach, the behaviour of the Government at times has been inconsistent with the professed policy[2]. During the period 1999-2004, PE privatization and disinvestment was attempted on imprudent basis. The sale of Bharat Aluminium Company Limited (BALCO) and the transfer of property of the Hotel Airport, Mumbai are the cases in point. The sales were transacted at un-remunerative prices to the Government without a proper social safety net to the employees and disregarding the well established principles of preventing the creation of monopoly. The Airport privatization has been opposed not only by the Labour Unions and the Left but also by a bidder on the ground of administrative sanctity. During the period of economic liberalization, the Government has shown a bias in favour of reducing the involvement of PEs through their sale / disposal / disinvestment – partial or full, based not on a rational basis but under the pressure of the ideology that markets are efficient, and such efficiency is greater when PE element is minimal. There have been suggestions on setting up a general asset fund on the pattern of China which has a State Asset Holding Ministry. As an alternative, the Government has been toying with the idea of setting up a Special Purpose Vehicle (SPV). A general consensus about the PE policy has been sadly lacking even in the United Progressive Alliance (UPA) Government. The Left is completely opposed to the idea of removing the profitable PEs from the portfolio of PEs of the Central Government. This is supported by their stand on the disinvestment of the BHEL and the sale of the leftover stake of the Government in BALCO.

Performance

As the public enterprises are expected to run on commercial lines, the financial appraisal continues to be an important yardstick to measure the performance of these enterprises. An analysis of performance of these enterprises with reference to some important ratios such as profit before

Table 1
Trend Analysis

(Rs. In crore)

Particulars	*1995-96*	*2004-05*
No. of operating Enterprises	239	227
Capital employed	173948	504826
Profit before dep, int, tax & EP (PBDITEP)	40161	142606
Depreciation	12574	33132
Interest	27587	108491
Profit before Tax & EP (PBTEP)	13966	22428
Tax provisions	13621	86063
Net Profit before EP	4047	21661
Net profit making PSEs	-	-1027
Loss of loss incurring PSEs	9574	65429
Loss of loss incurring PSEs	14763	74432
Profit making PSEs	5188	9003
Loss incurring PSEs	132	143
PSEs Making no profit / loss	102	73
Dividend	-	10
Dividend tax	2205	20713
Retained profit	-	2851
Financial Ratio %	7369	41865
PBDITEP to Capital employed	23.1	28.25
PBITEP to Capital employed	15.9	21.49
Dividend payout	23	31.66

**US $ I billion = Rs.4500 crore as on June 1, 2006.*

Source: Government of India (Department of Public Enterprises, Ministry of Heavy Industries and Public Enterprises), Public Enterprises Survey: 2004-05, Vol. 1, New Delhi.

interest and tax to capital employed, sales to capital employed, etc has been attempted. Considering the fact that the public sector has to discharge a number of socio-economic obligations, the performance appraisal also covers items like internal resources generation for financing the Plan Outlay, contribution to the public exchequer, management development, development of backward regions, employment generation, employees welfare measures, foreign exchange earnings, import substation effort and such other related matters, so as to present a comprehensive picture.

Table 1 depicts many brighter aspects of the financial performance of PEs:

(i) The various profitability indicators are on rise
(ii) The number of loss making enterprises is on decline
(iii) The relative ratio of profits of profit making enterprises is increasing faster than the losses of the loss making enterprises
(iv) There has been an appreciable increase in the dividend cover
(v) The retained profits have sky rocketed

The character of financing in PEs has undergone a complete transformation. Under the liberalized economic regime, these enterprises have followed the 'ABC' dictum. They started with complete assistance from the Central Government in the form of grants taking the route of equity or debt. Then they moved to the budgetary support under which the equity or debt had to come on the basis of project justification. However, with the onset of economic liberalization during 1985, they moved to capital markets for mobilizing resources. Table 2 shows the resource mobilization by PEs in relation to plan investment. The budgetary support declined from a high of 50.57% in 1985-86 to 19.14% in 1991-92, and dropped to a low of 12.75% in 2004-05. PEs made it possible by exploiting new financial instruments such as commercial paper, bonds, public deposits, Global Depository Receipts and American Depositary Receipts. The

European Commercial Borrowings also played an important role. The suppliers' credit assumed an important proportion. The foreign bonds raised in the Japanese capital market and the Luxemburg capital market helped these enterprises substantially. Some enterprises accessed moneys successfully through floating rate debentures. The State Bank of India is a case in point. Public deposits have also yielded adequate finances to these enterprises especially in the present era when the interest rates are heading southwards. The working capital financing has drastically decline from the Government of India and the dependents of PEs has substantially increased on the commercial banks and capital markets. It may be noted that PEs has established themselves so firmly in the capital markets that they have been able to raise resources through taxable bonds. The proportion between taxable bonds to tax-free bonds is increasing in the favour of former. This is least to say that PEs did not resort to the traditional sources of financing such as the inter-corporate deposits. These were of vast magnitude amounting to Rs.10986.29 crore during 2003-04 which turned

Table 2
Resources Mobilization and Plan Investment

(Rs in Crore)

Year	*Net Internal Resources*	*Extra Budgetary Resources*	*Budgetary Support*	*Plan Outlay*
1985-86	3333.05 (33.68)	1559.19 (15.75)	5005.38 (50.57)	9897.62 (100.00)
1990-91	6180.57 (33.68)	7696.74 (41.94)	4474.17 (24.38)	18351.48 (100.00)
2004-05	32222.46	26006.52	5090.24	63319.22

Source: Government of India (Department of Public Enterprises, Ministry of Heavy Industries and Public Enterprises), Public Enterprises Surveys for the years 1985-86 to 2004-05, Vol. 1, New Delhi.

Table 3

Public Sector's Contribution in Total Industrial Production

Item	*National Production (NP)*		*Public Sector's Production (PSP)*		*PSP to NP (%)*	
	1968-69	*2002-03*	*1968-69*	*2002-03*	*1968-69*	*2002-03*
Fuel (Million Tonnes)						
Coal	71.40	341.25	12.61	325.40	17.66	95.36
Lignite	3.98	26.02	3.98	26.02	100.00	100.00
Petroleum (Million Tonnes)						
Crude Oil	6.06	32.04	3.08	28.95	50.83	87.62
Natural Gas	NA	31.40	NA	25.99	NA	83.73
Refinery Crude	16.55	112.56	8.09	74.76	48.88	66.42
Basic Metal Industries (Million Tonnes)						
Finished Steel	4.58	33.63	2.55	10.97	55.68	32.62
Non Ferrous Metals (000 Tonnes)						
Aluminium	125.3	689.19	Nil	244.71	Nil	35.51

Source: Public Enterprises Survey, (Government of India, New Delhi) 2004-05: Volume 1, 2006.

out to be 12.94% of the total financing of these enterprises in that year.

The economic liberalization much against the professed belief has not resulted in the decline of contribution of PEs to total industrial production. The public sector's contribution to the quantum of production of Coal, Lignite, Crude Oil, Natural Gas, Refinery Crude, Finished Steel and Aluminium has increased over the period 1968-69 to 2004-05.

The contribution of PEs to the Central Exchequer has been rising year after year. The contribution can be in the form of dividends, interests, excise duty, custom duty, corporate tax, dividend tax, sales tax and other duties and taxes. During 2004-05 the contribution stood at Rs. 61037.48 crore which was Rs. 62865.53 in 2003-04.

Salient Features of PE Functioning

During the period of economic liberalization, PEs has had certain special features of their functioning which were mostly the result of their own initiatives.

Memorandum of Understanding (MoU)

The MoU was patterned on the French model of evaluating the performance of an enterprise based on the vision and mission, objectives, targets and performance score on the part of enterprise and the obligations of the Government to the enterprise. During 1991-92, as a part of economic liberalization policy, the Government decided to extend the system to as many PEs as possible which resulted in 99 PEs signing MoU with the Government during 2004-05 as opposed to 4 PEs signing MoU in 1987-88. The introduction of MoU has given a rare opportunity both to the Government and PEs to negotiate certain measure of performance and compare the ex post performance with the ex ante performance. Most of the MoU signing enterprises have shown a great deal of appreciation for the MoU system which distinguishes the managerial performance in PEs with the enterprise performance. The MoU system also presents an objective solution to the problem of conflicting interests of principals with the agent. The Arjun Sengupta generation of MoUs has undergone a drastic change with the current generation of MoUs based on the scrutiny of the Cabinet Secretariat of the expert committee report prepared by the National Council of Applied Economic Research. The revised system relies more on dynamic indicators as compared to the static indicators that formed the base of the first generation MoUs.

Navratnas / Miniratnas

Taking a cue from the Korean concept of Chaebols, the Government of India decided to elevate some highly successfully enterprises to the special status of Navratna wherein they were delegated enhanced financial powers in relation to committing capital expenditure, starting joint ventures and providing incentives to their employees. Comparatively smaller enterprises that did not meet the stringent norms for qualifying as Navratna but were way above the rest of the enterprise were accorded the status of Miniratna which also benefited from the Government policy with regard to Navratna, albeit on a smaller scale. The concept has been applauded by PEs who have consistently shown better results year on year. The Navratna / Miniratna enterprises have proved that given the sufficient freedom of operation and non-interference from the Government, they could not only excel in their field in India but also take on the multinationals and could snatch the market share from private sector enterprises in India and their competitors abroad. It is said that the extension of this concept would enable the rest of the successful enterprise in unlocking previous value by way of investment in physical and financial assets. The positive aspects of the Navratna concept have forced the Government to consider conferring this status upon the Coal India Ltd and Rashtriya Ispat Nigam Ltd. The Navratna /

Miniratna concept has received a shot in the arm from the Arjun Sengupta Committee Report on Autonomy of PEs set up by the Government of India. The report advocates for greater autonomy to Navratnas in the matters of policy and day-to-day functioning.

PEs in Market

Much before the onset of the economic liberalization, Mr R Venkataraman, the then Finance Minister, Government of

Table 4
Percentage of Investments by Institutional Investors during 2004-05

(In Percentage)

	2004-05
Bharat Petroleum Corporation	29.49
Chennai Petroleum	24.86
Hindustan Petroleum Corporation	39.96
IBP Limited	31.32
Kochin Refineries	20.92
Naveli Lignite Corporation	8.12
National Mineral Development Corporation	9.10
Bharat Earth Movers Limited	21.40
Bharat Electronics Limited	17.20
Bharat Heavy Electricals Limited	30.29
Cement Corporation of India	34.08
Shipping Corporation of India	13.57
ITI Limited	39.21
Hindustan Organics & Chemicals Limited	5.16
Life Insurance Corporation	48.94
State Trading Corporation	3.00
Tamil Nadu Newsprints Limited	44.62

Source: Institute of Public Enterprise database on Public Enterprises.

India, pleaded for the PE interface with the capital market. The Krishna Menon Committee report on autonomy of PEs in 1959 made a strong case in favour of autonomous PEs. The economic liberalization is promoting this interface very intensively. As a result, a large number of PEs and banks have entered the capital markets. More than 50% of the market capitalization belongs to PEs which has also added so much of liquidity and credibility to the capital markets. The Oil and Natural Gas Corporation leads 33 Indian companies on Forbes

Table 5
Percentage of Investments by General Public during 2004-05

(In Percentage)

	2004-05
Bharat Petroleum Corporation	2.86
Chennai Petroleum	5.43
Hindustan Petroleum Corporation	6.66
IBP Limited	12.34
Kochin Refineries	13.24
Naveli Lignite Corporation	1.53
National Mineral Development Corporation	3.81
Bharat Earth Movers Limited	12.31
Bharat Electronics Limited	4.3
Bharat Heavy Electricals Limited	0.89
Cement Corporation of India	1.83
Shipping Corporation of India	4.43
ITI Limited	3.22
Hindustan Organics and Chemicals Limited	28.6
Life Insurance Corporation	9.93
State Trading Corporation	4.69
Tamil Nadu Newsprints Limited	13.1

Source: Institute of Public Enterprise database on Public Enterprises.

list of top 2000 corporate titans across the world. The wealth engines of PEs had a market capitalization of Rs. 579,242 crores as on March 31,2006[3]. The market capitalization of these wealth engines was Rs. 3,78,922 crores as on March 31, 2005. The wealth engines included Oil and Natural Gas Corporation Ltd, NTPC Ltd, Indian Oil Corporation Ltd, Bharat Heavy Electricals Ltd, State Bank of India Ltd, Steel Authority of India Ltd, Gail (India) Ltd, National Aluminium Company Ltd, Punjab National Bank Ltd and Bharat Petroleum Corporation Ltd. The capital market interface through the Institutional investors has made a good dent and is a precursor to the future success of PEs as seen in Table 4.

Table 5 gives the percentages of investments in PEs by general public during 1998-99 to 2004-05. A perusal of the table shows that the general public has started finding in PEs a good investment channel. It is expected that PEs would be a greater hit with the general public in future.

Encouraged by the market interface, more PEs proposed to benefit from it. The Government on its part is considering to make listing of PEs on stock exchanges compulsory – may be in the initial run only on the enterprises which have consistently a good record of profit making and are also competitive in nature.

Disinvestment

One of the major elements of the PE policy in the economic liberalization era relates disinvestment therein through the sale of equity and trade sale. The policy has lacked consistency, continuity and well thought out reasoning.

Table 6 provides the quantum of actual disinvestments in PEs and methodologies adopted during the era of economic liberalization. The targets barely exceeded a mark of 50% of the planned exercise. The methodologies had a wide swing from bundling of shares to bidding, strategic sale and wholesale transfer of assets. There has been a trenchant criticism of the disinvestment moves during 1991-92 to 1999; between 2000 and

2004; and during the period 2004-06. Although many administrative innovations were done to make disinvestment a logical exercise, the doctrinaire approach could never delivered the goods as it lacked pragmatism. Two of the oft raised questions against the disinvestment in India has been as to what was the motivation of the Government in neglecting the restructuring exercise prior to such an effort which is a globally accepted practice and the bias against IPOs as a method of sale

Table 6

Actual Disinvestment and Methodologies Adopted

(Rupees in crore)

Year	*Target receipt*	*Actual receipts*	*Methodology*
1991-92	2,500	3,038	Minority shares sold by auction method
1992-93	2,500	1,913	Shares sold separately for each company by auction method
1993-94	3,500	Nil	Equity of 7 companies sold by open auction
1994-95	4,000	4,843	Sale through auction method
1995-96	7,000	168	Equities of 4 companies auctioned
1996-97	5,000	380	Global Depository Receipt (GDR)
1997-98	4,800	910	GDR
1998-99	5,000	5,371	GDR and Domestic Cross purchase
1999-00	10,000	1,860	GDR
2000-01	10,000	1,871	Strategic sale
2001-02	12,000	5,632	Strategic sale
2002-03	12,000	3,348	Strategic sale
2003-04	14,500	15,547	Public offer of shares to retail investors
2004-05	4,000	2,765	Public offer of shares to retail investors
2005-06	5,000	1,567	Sale of stake to development banks
Total	**96,800**	**49,213**	

Source: DPE Survey (GoI, New Delhi) and Ministry of Finance, GOI, Economic Survey, 2006.

of shares despite high ranking of many PEs in capital market in India as assessed by the credit rating agencies.

Reconstruction of PEs and Social Safety Net Programme (SSNP)

The Washington Consensus of 1983 as reflected in the economic liberalization programme of 1992 was based on the sole premise that the wellbeing of people could be increased by disposing of the public assets owned by PEs. The global experience of disinvestment has relied on the restructuring of PEs prior to their sale as also their reconstruction for their rehabilitation. The Common Minimum Programme (CMP) of the UPA Government makes a mention of rehabilitation of PEs through the Board for Reconstruction of Public Sector Enterprises (BRPSE). 20 cases have been referred to BRPSE of which it has considered 17 cases and is in the process of giving its mind to the remaining three cases. BRPSE is implementing the plans for the rehabilitation of seven PEs including Bridge & Roof Co Ltd, Hindustan Salts Ltd, BBJ Construction Co Ltd, Praga Tools Ltd, HMT (Bearings) Ltd, Heavy Engineering Corpn Ltd and Braithwaite & Co Ltd. It is interesting to mention that as a part of restructuring exercise and to fight fit for successful existence in the global market, the merge of Air India and Indian Airlines, Rashtriya Ispat Nigam Ltd and Steel Authority of India Ltd and Oil Group Companies is being considered. The Indian Post is an excellent example of undergoing restructuring to come back with a big bang to take on private sector couriers and couriers from abroad such as DHL. The Indian Railways are not lagging behind and giving a tough fight to the private sector Airlines. Many PEs are going for diverse types of restructuring such as manpower, operations, strategic, financial and organizational restructuring including setting up of joint ventures. Hindustan Machine Tools Ltd, State Bank of India, Hindustan Shipyard Ltd, Rashtriya Ispat Nigam Ltd is some of the cases in point.

The SSNP to project the human face of the Government was started with a great fanfare during 1993-94. The programme was supported by the National Renewal Fund for five years. Thereafter a programme of counseling, retraining and redeployment was launched. The first five years of the programme covered by and large the surplus workers of the National Textiles Corporation. The later programme had some financial support and also the organizational backup of a large number of well established institutes and centres. However, looking to the labour forces employed in PEs, it could be said that the SSNP did not cover a large chunk of people under the programme. Moreover, the stress of the programme is on only retraining and redeployment and that too partially. The insurance component of the SSNP has not received any attention at the hands of the Government. The SSNP abroad has insurance as the mainstay of the programme.

Scope for Improvement

There are many areas where PEs could make a substantial headway and which posses the potential of making these enterprises as the national jewels and market leaders.

Inter-corporate Coordination

The inter-corporate coordination in PEs holds a great hope for their future. Such coordination could bring together this PEs to facilitate exchange of their strengths for eliminating their weaknesses. In each area e.g., marketing, finance, personnel, strategy, international business, customer relationship management, corporate social responsibility, productivity, value engineering, research and development, purchases and inventory management, public accountability, board practices, these enterprises could exchange their knowledge and strengths which would provide them a rare opportunity of creating a competitive edge to walk through the markets.

The toning up of the corporate governance function could help them a great deal in brand building and relating well to society, business, employees, legal institutions and accounting world. The application of Clause 49 of the Securities and Exchange Board of India (SEBI) Code is a point in reference. Although approved by SEBI in 2004, many PEs have not been able to appoint 50% of the board strength as independent directors. In turn, they have asked for relaxation to 33%. The corporate governance is not working well as could be seen from the operations of the Audit, Compensation and Appointments Committee report in many PEs. The Government directors continue to swell in strength and block the progressive moves in these enterprises. There is no evaluation system in place for the independent directors and other directors including the Chairman-cum-Managing Director. In many PEs, the officers of the Indian Administrative Services perpetuate their existence in the name of the public-ness of the enterprise.

Autonomy

Autonomy is the key issue remaining in the state of limbo at the hands of the Government which has shied away from taking some concrete decisions such as the removal of Article 12 from the Indian Constitution which hinders the autonomy of PEs in terms of recruitment, promotion and day to day business. Like the private sector enterprises, there is a need to have a level playing field for PEs and going by this assertion we could easily make out a case for exempting PEs from Article 12 of the Indian Constitution. The Comptroller and Auditor General (CAG) audit is under thorn in the flash. Till 1954, as pointed out by Ashok Chanda, there was no CAG audit for PEs. Later, in 1956 on the pretext of the Government funding, this PEs was brought under the control of the CAG. The business acumen of the CAG auditors' need a pep up in the absence of which there are not able to discern the difference between the action of the Government and the action of a commercial entity. The influence of the institution of the Chief Vigilance Commission (CVC) has not helped public sector in any way. The appointments at the board level get delayed because of too much time being taken by the CVC. Then, for each appointment of the same person, the CVC has to be approached time and again. The CVC takes about six months to one year in clearing the names for the consideration of the Cabinet Committee on Appointments. The Public Enterprise Selection Board (PESB) takes too long a time to put top managerial personnel in PEs in their respective positions. The salaries offered are not competitive and tagging the salaries to the officers of the IAS would not take PEs anywhere as there is resource crunch of good managers even in private sector. The Public Investment Board also impairs the autonomy of PEs, although to some extent the Navratanas and the Miniratnas do not come under its purview. The investment decisions in PEs should be subjected by the same norms as those applied in the case of private enterprises plus PEs should get a credit for the social content of their project appraisal

Regulation

In the marketized world when we talk of a new world economic order, the commanding heights could not be left to private institutions and business. Regulation could alone ensure a happy co-existence of public and private sectors; developed and developing world; and consumer and producer. Some examples of regulatory bodies in India include the Telephone Regulatory Authority of India (TRAI), Insurance Regulatory and Development Authority (IRDA) and Securities and Exchange Board of India (SEBI). PEs have been voicing their grievance against these regulatory authorities as private sector counterparts have been benefited more by the policies adopted by the regulatory agencies. The behaviour of private sector has been adverse to the interest of the consumer as proved by the power supply disaster during the Mumbai floods in 2005 and super-cyclone of Orissa where private sector defaulted in fulfilling its obligations to the local consumers and burden alone PEs which stood like Gibraltar rock in the service of consumers. The Central Electricity Authority and the State Electricity Regulatory Authorities have found the behaviour of private sector power generation, transmission and distribution firms very inappropriate in terms of working out profits on capital employed, accounting systems, control on T&D losses, and modernization of their functions.

Conclusion

To conclude, PEs in the era of economic liberalization have done extremely well much against these prophesies of the prophets of doom who had expected them to wind up and disappear. They have performed well in the market based regime. They could have done better but for the waywardness of the Government in terms of the policy regime for these enterprises which has never been consistent and to some extent anti-PE. These enterprises are expected to perform better by superior inter-PE collaboration, Optima, lack of bias in regulation, improved corporate governance and strong interface with the national and the international capital markets.

References

1. Government of India (Department of Public Enterprises, Ministry of Heavy Industries & Public Enterprises), Public Enterprises Survey: 2004-05, Vol. 1, New Delhi, pp. 2-3.
2. Institute of Public Enterprise, Spot Light: Central and State Public Enterprises, May, 2006, p. 2.
3. Standing Conference of Public Enterprises, KELEIDOSCOPE, New Delhi, April, 2006.
4. Institute of Public Enterprise, Spot Light: Central and State Public Enterprises, May, 2006, p. 1.

4

Restructuring Public Enterprises in India

Abstract

The paper provides theoretical backdrop to restructuring and the need for restructuring public enterprises (PEs) in India. The paper describes the forms of restructuring and the institutional arrangements for restructuring in PEs. Two case studies of restructuring related to the Central PEs viz., Electronics Corporation of India Ltd (ECIL) and Rashtriya Ispat Nigam Ltd (RINL) have been discussed to highlight the process and drivers of restructuring and the fallouts. Finally, the paper offers the following suggestions which may enable PEs to move from a lower point of restructuring continuum to its optimum point in a given matrix:

(a) Constantly examine the activity portfolio in financial and marketing terms (Boston Consultancy Group matrix)

(b) Constantly look at the organisational set up and make an effort to keep it lean and mean

(c) Continuously revisit the financial paradigm maximizing profits through volume, leverage, differential pricing, strategic costing, quality improvements and growth in 'other income'

(d) *Constantly increase the market share through better CRM and brand equity, and go in for mergers and acquisitions, joint ventures and collaborative arrangements to boost the market share*

(e) *Constantly rightsize the labour force, motivate employees, create superior employer-employee relationship, and improve labour productivity*

(f) *Constantly look out for technological upgradation and internalize it through a series of appropriate measures resulting in IPRs, improved R&D practices and manufacturing systems*

Restructuring Public Enterprises has become an integral part of their strategic management in the context of the New Economic Policy enunciated in 1991, the adoption of the National Common Minimum Programme by the United Progressive Alliance (UPA) Government at the centre and the globalization. Public Enterprises (PEs) in India are an important component of the public sector and such enterprises operate at both the central and the state levels. As an instrument of public policy, these enterprises are involved in a wide spectrum of socio-economic activities and act as a countervailing force against private sector. The investments in PEs are enormous and run into about Rs 10 lakh crore. However, these enterprises have not yet achieved the status of 'net savers'. This point to the need of unlocking the value in these enterprises which is possible only through restructuring which is a constant phenomenon in the case of a healthy enterprise. The absence of this condition is a sure way to make an enterprise fall terminally sick.

Restructuring is an omnibus term including in its ambit re-engineering the organisational structure, technology, operations, financial management, human resources, mergers and acquisitions, and disinvestment and privatisation. Restructuring is essential for increasing market share, technology up-gradation, deriving benefits from size and scale of operations, rightsizing the organisation, enhancing competitiveness in domestic and global markets, and maintaining and increasing the return on investment. Restructuring is more than turnaround, industrial rehabilitation and formulation of packages by the Board for Industrial and Financial Reconstruction (BIFR) and the Board for Reconstruction of Public Sector Enterprises (BRPSE) in that restructuring is an ongoing exercise and not a one-off activity. PEs in India could look to restructuring as a continuum and a wealth creation strategy.

The purpose of this paper is to discuss the various forms of restructuring, their relevance to PEs, the role played by BIFR and BRPSE in PE restructuring, and present two specific case studies on restructuring. Finally, the paper offers suggestions which may enable PEs to move from a lower point of restructuring continuum to its optimum point in a given matrix.

Forms of Restructuring

Restructuring can take diverse forms.[1] However, the principal forms of restructuring have been discussed as below:

1. Organisational restructuring: This concerns the restructuring of organisation in terms of its activities, design, location, hierarchical levels, manpower, training and management development systems, quality and customer service, technology upgradation, merger and acquisitions and information flow. Organisational restructuring makes the firm stronger to face competition and ensures the composition of an educated workforce that is compatible with the new environment. Formation of result oriented teams, faster response, higher degree of empowerment and attainment of quality systems are the positive effects of organisational restructuring. However, organisational restructuring may lead to retrenchment and disruptions in the organisational design which may create an environment of fear, mistrust and

discontent resulting in a decrease of loyalty quotient to the organisation. The various steps involved in this are as follows:

(a) Establish the right size for the organisation on the basis of pre-determined production and marketing strategy of the rationlised enterprises

(b) Determine the leadership style, to be adopted, based on an understanding of the prevailing organisational culture, and the environmental constraints

(c) Make the enterprise receptive to change at all levels, through workships and meeting, elucidating the financial status of the company and the need pressure for change, the benefit of change and the safeguards contemplated to take care of negative aspects of change

(d) Tackle opposition and unions by devising appropriate strategies

(e) Redefine roles and responsibilities to rationalize reporting and decision making levels, to build flatter and more efficient organisations

(f) Evolve a training policy. train and motivate staff at all levels to acquire the necessary skills and loyalty for implementation of organisation missions as a team

(g) Improve personnel policies – rationalization of pay and promotion structure processing of routine establishment matters such a leave, increments efficiency, pensions, disciplinary procedures

(h) Improve evaluation procedures, to make evaluation of tool for human resource development

(i) Introduce systems of rewards and incentives

(j) Provide channels for vertical and horizontal information flow, to keep all levels informed and involved, with the total achievement, of the organisation.

(k) Define the roles of the other components in the system. Simplify and clarify the linkages and improve operating systems

(l) Consider and decide upon possible variants of the public enterprises systems:

   (i) Divesting or diluting government ownership or direct involvement by transferring the ownership of an enterprise

   (ii) Reducing the extent of government ownership by a partial sale of the government shareholding to potential investors,

   (iii) Negotiating joint venture agreements, with potentioal investors or corporation and limiting government interest to a minority shareholdings

   (iv) Negotiating management contracts with a private management group to manage the enterprise as agents for government

2. Financial restructuring: Financial restructuring[2] is the most fundamental reorganization, the enterprise must go thorough, to ensure that the right financial structure is in place. This exercise eliminates those activities, proven to be unsustainable and putting in place those which ensure the success and are inline with the changed environment. The first and foremost change which must be accepted, is that the enterprise will now operate as a purely profit oriented entity and therefore must be self-sufficient, a careful assessment of the existing operations is called for at this stage to determine the viability of each activity. Those which are proven to be making losses, must be closed down and resources be utilized efficiently in those activities providing the entity with a return. The organisation also needs to do an inventory of their resources/assets available, as well as their existing commitments. This information is required to determine the need for further investment. If there is a need for more funds, which is in most cases the norm, then examine whether it is feasible to source it internally or externally. Revaluation of all existing assts is a must, to lessen the

distortion in the balance sheet, due to outdated methods of recording used. Also accounts receivable need rationalization with elimination of those amounts, unlikely to be recovered. The issue of whether it is to the firm's benefit, to write off some of its debts, must be raised at this stage. This decision will make the values of shares of PE more attractive is prospective buyers, when they are floated on the stock market. The number of shares to be sold to the public, would depend on the level of ownership to be retained by the government, as well as the amount of capital needed for expansion / upgradation. Having done all these, a system is then put in place, to support the daily running of the activities. This can be done by creating cost centers, each being responsible for particular aspects of the functions undertaken. These cost centers must in turn have objectives and a structure defining specific lines of responsibilities. They are responsible for their own operations and an appropriate reward system, must be put in place and implemented to boost morale, performance and productivity. It must also be recognized at this stage, that now that the organisation is operating in a free and open market it must cater to the changes in the environment. This may necessitate alliances and joint ventures with other companies and the development of more efficient ways to cater to the changing needs of customers. Continuous success can be achieved by means of developing, profit making business interests. Other related measures to be adopted are

(a) Limiting production to high demand products and core competence areas

(b) Cutting administrative and all other possible extra costs

(c) Adopting no-cost / low cost innovative marketing strategies – services oriented rather than capital oriented

(d) Price and discount strategies

(e) Very strict, detailed and constant inventory control. Bulk sale of old and dead inventory

(f) Aggressive debt recovery policies

(g) Extension of supplier credit periods

(h) Tight control on working capital, to maximize value addition from scarce resources

3. Marketing restructuring: Since the marketing function is what ultimately brings in the money and profits, marketing systems have to be well researched and clearly directed towards maximizing customer satisfaction. The typical steps involved in restructuring of the marketing activity are as follows:

(a) Analyze market behaviour, customer preferences and product demand.

(b) Formulate and implement a strategy for capturing the targeted market segments/niche markets. Here the place, product and price would be crucial factors. Depending on customer concentrations and preferences, location of retail outlets, product mix at different outlets, product promotion through publicity and packaging, pricing in tune with purchasing power as well as seasonal/clearance discounts, incentive and bargains would have to be planned.

(c) Make the cutting edge – customer friendly and customer focused. The environment, behaviour of sales staff, facilities and conveniences offered, should aim at securing customer delight and developing customer loyalty.

(d) Provide constant feedback to production division, for improving the product, rationalizing the distribution and controlling the inventory, so that the right product reaches the right place, in optimum volumes at the right time.

(e) Establish effective systems of sales reporting and monitoring, so that, immediate corrective measures may be initiated, as soon as required.

(f) Establish strategic marketing alliances – sharing of retail/distribution networks, joint publicity, package deals and bargains should be struck for mutual advantage.

(g) Analyze and manage competition – highlight functional advantages of your own product, exploit competitor weakness, pursue aggressive initiatives where affordable, and exploit strategy of alliances when competition becomes mutually detrimental.

4. Production restructuring: Once the enterprise portfolio has been defined, the production lines and process have to be restructured, to deliver the goods or services, as the case may be, to the desired level. Typical steps at this state of restructuring would be follows:

(a) Analyze productivity and efficiency and arrive at the most cost-effective plan, for achieving the desired level of production or service, including changes in technology and need for other resources, where necessary

(b) Effect the required changes for facilitating implementation of revised production plan.

(c) E.g. technology change, agreements with suppliers, infrastructure and manpower requirements, etc.

(d) Establish benchmarks and production targets/ schedules and ensure they are understood at all levels.

(e) Implement the production plan with regular monitoring and strict quality control.

(f) Devise systems and exercise strict control over inventories in the work-in-progress and finished goods.

(g) Establish smooth delivery systems, for example chain of go-downs, transportation, distribution mix and network.

(h) Establish systems for effective utilization / disposal of by-products and waste.

(i) Establish effective maintenance systems for smooth running of production facilities.

(j) Make research and development and design cells, responsive to feedback from marketing, for constant market-led product innovation.

Role of BIFR and BRPSE in Restructuring PEs

The Sick Industrial Companies Act (SICA), 1985 amended in 1991 brings industrial public sector enterprises under its purview. A company is termed sick if at the end of any financial year, it has accumulated losses equal to or exceeding its entire net worth. Such industrial company is required to be referred to the Board for Industrial and Financial Reconstruction (BIFR) for formulation of rehabilitation/ revival plan. As per Department of Public Enterprises[3], a company is considered 'sick' if it has accumulated losses in any financial year equal to 50% or more of its average net worth during 4 years immediately preceding such financial year and/or a company which is a sick company within the meaning of Sick Industrial Companies (Special Provisions) Act, 1985 (SICA). The BIFR decides the viability and sanctions the rehabilitation schemes for sick industrial PEs under the provisions of SICA. For other PEs, the concerned administrative Ministries/ Departments explore various options for restructuring/ rehabilitation of the enterprises under their control on case-to-case basis in consultation with all stakeholders including employees. The problem of sickness in PEs is addressed by the administrative Ministries/ Departments in the Government by evolving appropriate need based strategy concerning a particular PSE. 74 industrial PEs were registered with BIFR up to 31.3.2006 for formulation and sanction of revival schemes. Some of the strategies for restructuring / revival of PEs including sick units on long-term basis include:

- Revival through the process of BIFR;
- Financial restructuring;
- Formation of joint venture by induction of partners capable of providing technical, financial and marketing inputs; and
- Organizational restructuring and manpower rationalization through approved Voluntary Retirement Scheme (VRS).

The National Common Minimum Programme envisages a strong and effective Public Sector whose social objectives are met by its commercial functioning. The endeavour is to restructure and revive sick PEs. Only chronically loss making PEs may be closed down or sold off after all the employees are paid their legitimate dues.

The Government constituted a Board for Reconstruction of Public Sector Enterprises (BRPSE) in December 2004 as a part-time advisory body to address the task of strengthening, modernization, reviving, and restructuring of PEs and advise the Government on strategies, measures and schemes related to them. The Board comprises a Part-time Chairman, three Non-official Members and three official Members. In addition, Chairman, Standing Conference of Public Enterprises (SCOPE), Chairman, Public Enterprises Selection Board (PESB) and Chairman, Oil and Natural Gas Corporation Ltd. (ONGC) are permanent invitees. The Secretaries of the Ministry/Department of those PEs whose proposals are considered by the Board are invited to attend those Board meetings as Special invitees when the proposals of the concerned PEs are considered. The Board is serviced by the DPE.

While Board for Industrial and Financial Reconstruction (BIFR) is a statutory body created by an Act of Parliament, i.e., Sick Industrial Companies (Special Provisions) Act, 1985 (SICA), under the Ministry of Finance, the BRPSE is an advisory body created by a Resolution of the Government to address the task of strengthening, modernizing, reviving and restructuring of Public Sector Enterprises and advise the Government on strategies, measures and schemes related to them. The jurisdiction of BIFR is larger as it covers both public and private sector enterprises, but the BRPSE only deals with PEs. BIFRs role is restricted to only industrial enterprises while BRPSE can deal with non-industrial PEs also. Advice of BRPSE is also sought by the Government in case of PEs which have already been referred to BIFR for firming up Government's view on revival/rehabilitation of PEs. An incipient sick PE may also be referred to the BRPSE, as its advice may help the enterprise to avoid reference to BIFR. The concerned administrative Ministry/ Department identifies the sick enterprises and makes a reference to the BRPSE through DPE for its consideration and making recommendations to the Government. The Board is expected to make its recommendations within two months from the date of receipt of complete proposal from the administrative Ministry/ Department. BRPSE will also fix reasonable time limit for implementation of the recommended package. Thereafter, based on the recommendations of the BRPSE, the concerned Ministry/Department submits their proposal for the approval of the Government. Based on the definition of sick companies, 81 PEs have been identified as sick for making reference to BRPSE (See : Department of Public Enterprises, Public Enterprise Survey; Vol. 1; 2003-04, 04-05, 05-06,Government of India, New Delhi). As there was single proposal of revival of National Textiles Corporation Ltd. and its subsidiaries, the NTC group has been treated as only one company.

The Board, being a part-time advisory body, normally meets twice in a month. The Board held 46 meetings, considered 51 cases and made recommendations in respect of 43 cases. The remaining cases are remitted to the concerned administrative Ministries/Departments for further examination. The aggregate cost of revival to Government in respect of 41

PEs recommended by BRPSE is Rs.1705 6crore involving cash support of Rs. 3249 crore and non- cash support of Rs.13809 crore. The cash assistance normally is in the form of equity/loan/grant. The non cash assistance comprise of waiver/ write off of loans, interests, guarantee fee, conversion of loan and interest into equity/bonds/debentures, and provision of Government guarantee for loans to meet capital investment or working capital needs.

Case Studies

There have been a plethora of cases of restructuring in PEs. We propose to take up the cases of two central enterprises viz. Electronics Corporation of India Ltd. (ECIL) and Rashtriya Ispat Nigam Ltd (RINL) to show as to how restructuring could change the face of a PE, make it vibrant and infuse the element of competitiveness to enable it to become a 'leader' in the domestic and global markets. The two case studies throw light not only on the process but also on the final outcomes.

Electronics Corporation of India Ltd. (ECIL)

ECIL, a fully owned central PE under the Department of Atomic Energy was set up to create facilities for manufacture of specialized nuclear components. However, over a period of time ECIL extended its activities to the fields of computers and information technology, defence, instrumentation, antennas, scanning equipment, television, etc. This resulted in investing heavily in new divisions, creating new facilities, recruitment of manpower and reinforcement of service centers through regional offices. The company incurred a loss of Rs. 100 crore in setting up main frame computers. The companies fortune faced rough weather after two decades of its setting up due to sever competition for low -tech and consumer items, out sourcing becoming much cheaper, prohibitive input costs with low volumes, un-remunerative prices, high financing and manpower costs. As a result net worth was eroded by 50 per cent, company was referred to BIFR and flow of finance faced obstructions at the hands of banks and creditors. This led to the coming together of the management and the workers both of whom showed their determination to bring the company out of the dumps. The enterprise set up a management committee comprising employees and management, nominated the Union President and Secretary as members of the committee, began treating suppliers as strategic partners, built the trust relationship with the suppliers and streamlined financial discipline. A number of strategic measures were initiated including reconstitution of price strategy committee, converting production centers into strategic business units (SBUs) and their full empowerment and intensive training to the SBU leaders and senior executives in accounting and financial management techniques. The company appointed ICICI to carry out a diagnosis study, closed the television division and sought the government approval for writing-off the total losses of the Main frame computer unit, capital reorganization and assistance of VRS. The company initiated financial restructuring which led to conversion of debt to equity, write-offs and rescheduling debts, moratoriums, closures of un-economic activates, embargo on introducing new business lines, products and systems. The Government of India was supportive of the exercise. It granted the write-off of losses concerning the mainframe division, permitted the conversion of loans into equity and extended grants for the VRS. The outcomes were as expected. The company had a very healthy turnaround. The company reduced its staff by 1200 employees and also its accumulated losses. It obtained the requisite support from suppliers and bankers. Its share in defence projects improved substantially. Its order book registered significant improvement with a welcome change in the nuclear power policy. It received major orders for manufacturing electronic voting machines. The loss making position of 1998 -99 and 1999-00 underwent a 360^0 change to paying dividends, huge income tax, positive net worth and becoming debt free and cash rich during

2000-01 and 2001-02. The company has been receiving the MoU excellence award consecutively from the year 2001. CRISL has awarded the highest credit rating to the company. The company has become a favoured account for the banks.

Rasthriya Ispat Nigam Ltd (RINL)

RINL is one of the largest PE in India in terms of investment. The study of its turnaround presents an outstanding example as to how a PE could successfully face the vicissitudes in the corporate world. The company was written off and was to be taken to the BIFR. The company has managed a turnaround from near bankruptcy to being in the pink of financial health of high profit making. The turnaround of the company will result in achieving the following guideposts :

(a) Expand plant capacity of 5 Mt by 2007-08 with the mission to attain 10.0 Mt capacity in two subsequent phases
(b) Wipe out accumulated losses by 2006-07
(c) Be amongst top five lowest cost liquid steel producers in the world by 2006-07
(d) Achieve customer satisfaction levels on par with world class organization by 2006-07
(e) Make RINL the employer of choice by caring for employees. Develop people as knowledge workers by 2005-06 and achieve an improvement of 5 percentage points in employee's satisfaction levels every alternate year.
(f) Be ranked as an excellent business organization by 2006-07

This long gestation period of almost 22 years from concept to commissioning, let to escalation of capital cost of the plant. Original estimate in the year 1979 was Rs. 2256 crore which increased to Rs. 3897 crore by 1982 and further increased to Rs. 6849 crore in 1986. Under the rationalized concept after dropping certain facilities, the total capital cost finally stood at Rs. 8594 crore, when it was declared fully commissioned in August 1992. Out of the total cost of Rs. 2674 crore. Borrowings were resorted to with the interest rate ranging from 13 to 21% to meet part of the project cost due to inadequate budgetary support and release of funds by GOI. As a result this company has to bear high interest and depreciation burden resulting in continuous losses year after year. In fact the company even before commencing its operations had incurred a loss of over Rs. 2000 crore.

In this scenario, Government of India came to the rescue of the plant through two stages of capital restructuring in 1993 and 1998 converting all its loans into equity and preferences shares. By this Government of India (GOI) converted Rs. 3330 crore of its loan and Rs. 791 crore of interest on GOI loans into equity / preference shares thereby bringing the total investment of GOI in the form of share capital with zero GOI Loans. This resulted in lowering the interest burden on VSP by Rs. 521 crore annually.

After careful consideration and through consensus across the RINL has identified five key areas for restructuring which include technological up gradation and re-engineering, cost reduction, environment and safety, expansion and quality.

One of the primary objectives to the Company is to develop a well-knit personal policy and a comprehensive personnel programme that will be result-oriented and to develop an organizational culture, which motivates employees to contribute their best towards achievement of organizational objectives. In accordance with this objective, RINL has given considerable emphasis on development of human resources, as well as formulation and implementation of progressive personnel policies, systems, rules, and procedures to synchronize organizational needs with individual aspirations. Since inception, RINL has laid emphasis on effective man management as it subscribes to the belief that effectiveness and success of the organization depend largely on the skills and commitment of the people. The human resources restructuring is focused on Identification of Competence needs providing training inputs, monitoring the effectiveness of training, creating learning environment, facilitating self-development, innovativeness and self-expressions and enabling employees to assume higher responsibility. Some of the innovative practices introduced in the of human resource restructuring include Six sigma, S B G, profit centre concept, MOU concept, 7-S, value engineering, 360 degree appraisal, business process, re-engineering, TQA, TQM, balance score card, MBO, process management, corporate business systems, ISO certification, knowledge management and competency mapping, etc. Establishing and sustaining a productive work culture has been considered of crucial important in RINL. Several initiatives have been taken towards this end. RINL has adopted a multi-skill and multi-trade pattern of working with emphasis on flexibility in job deployment for ensuring optimum utilization of its human resources. Productive work culture has been ensured by well-planned and timely stress on attitudinal changes and positive work ethics through tailor-made human resources development programmes.

RINL, by following a strategy of education and persuasion of the employees and with the firm handling of indiscipline has been able to establish by and large a cordial industrial relations climate. This has seen concerted efforts for a fuller utilization of manpower, stabilization of multi-discipline approach to work, elimination of restrictive and wasteful work practices and inculcation of strict discipline in the organization. A constructive industrial relations climate has been evolved through a conscious policy of combining 'firmness' with 'fairness'.

The overall Industrial Relations scenario in RINL/VSP is peaceful, cordial and healthy. A host of proactive IR measures which inter-alia include Confidence Building Measures between Union-Management, extensive communication, continuous interaction with Unions were taken for building Harmonious Industrial Relations.

To sustain the spirit of the participative culture, a total of 66 Participative Committees are being functioning with participation both from the Management and the workers.

Approximately 15% employees are given an opportunity of participation in these forms at RINL including the quality circles and suggestion schemes, etc. These have helped the organization in accomplishing the organizational goals through the active employee's involvement.

Suggestions

PEs in India will do well to accept and make restructuring an integral part of their functioning. To move from lower point to higher point in the value chain, PEs may consider examining the following suggestions :

(a) Constantly examine the activity portfolio in financial and marketing terms (Boston Consultancy Group matrix)

(b) Constantly look at the organisational set up and make an effort to keep it lean and mean

(c) Continuously revisit the financial paradigm maximizing profits through volume, leverage, differential pricing, strategic costing, quality improvements and growth in 'other income'

(d) Constantly increase the market share through better CRM and brand equity, and go in for mergers and acquisitions, joint ventures and collaborative arrangements to boost the market share

(e) Constantly rightsize the labour force, motivate employees, create superior employer-employee relationship, and improve labour productivity

(f) Constantly look out for technological upgradation and internalize it through a series of appropriate measures resulting in IPRs, improved R&D practices and manufacturing systems

To sum up, restructuring holds an olive branch for the success of PEs in the times to come. PEs would do well to seize upon this opportunity to become vibrant, strong, internationally competitive and organic entities.

References

1. Morton Davis, el.al, Privatisation A Global Perspective, Vikas Publishing House Pvt. Ltd., 2004, New Delhi.
2. Mishra, Financial Restructuring of Public Enterprises, Institute of Public Enterprise Journal, 1997, Vol. 3, p. 120.
3. *Department of Public Enterprise, Government of Indian, New Delhi, Resolution dated 6.12.2004.*

5

Scope and Modalities for Restructuring SLPEs in Sikkim

Abstract

The State Level Public Enterprise (SLPEs) are an important component of the economy of the State of Sikkim. The finances of the State of Sikkim need strengthening in terms of their allocation and productive deployment. The re-engineering of the state finances has to de done with a human face. The social and economic consequences of the re-engineering have to be kept in the backdrop while designing the strategies for this purpose and implementation of such strategies. The investments in the SLPEs in the State of Sikkim have been increasing over the years. The performance, however, has not kept pace with the expectations. This divergence has adversely affected the state finances. The time is ripe for the policy makers to have a fresh look about the portfolio for retention of the SLPEs. The purpose of this paper is to discuss the typology, classification, market structure, models for identifying the candidates for disinvestment / privatisation and list out the SLPEs in Sikkim for disinvestment / privatisation and retention. The paper also attempts to evolve a framework for the modalities of restructuring and privatization of SLPEs in the State of Sikkim. It may be noted that 22 SLPEs have an investment of Rs. 726 crores employing 6036 personnel.

Typology

A study of the categorization and objectives of the SLPEs shows that the government company, public corporation, co-operative society and the departmental forms have been used in setting up these enterprises. Most of the enterprises have been established after the integration of Sikkim in the Union of India. The enterprises that existed with the state before integration were Sikkim Nationalized Transport, State Energy and Power Department, State Bank of Sikkim, State Trading Corporation, Sikkim Fruit Preservation Factory, Tea Board of Sikkim Ltd and the Denjong Agricultural Co-Operative Society Ltd.

The all-India pattern enterprises were established soon after the integration of Sikkim. These included Sikkim Jewels, Sikkim Times Company (SITCO), Sikkim Industrial and Investment Development Corporation Ltd (SIDICO), Sikkim Consumer Co-operative Society, Sikkim State Co-operative Supply and Marketing Federation Ltd (SIMFED) and Sikkim Co-operative Milk Producers Union Ltd (Sikkim Milk Union). The 1990s have seen a spurt of activity with regard to the setting up of the SLPEs. In this decade the enterprises set up included Sikkim Tourism Development Corporation Ltd, Sikkim Handloom and Handicrafts Development Corporation, Sikkim Poultry Development Corporation Ltd., Sikkim Hatchery Ltd, Sikkim Precision Industries Ltd, Sikkim Scheduled Castes, Tribes and Other Backward Classes Development Corporation Ltd (SABCCO), Sikkim Power Development Corporation Ltd. and Sikkim State Consumer Co-operative Bank. The following Table 1 provides the details with regard to forms of organization of the SLPEs.

Table 1
Typology of SLPEs

Typology	*No. of Enterprises*
Government Company	11
Public Corporation / Boards	4
Co-operative Society	5
Departmental Enterprise	2
Total	22

(Source: On the spot visit of SLPEs in Sikkim).

The Government Company form was the most preferred method of setting up the SLPEs. It is, however, important to note that the State of Sikkim continues to have its own Companies Act which was earlier promulgated by the Chogyal in 1961 titled as the Registration of Companies Act.

Classification

A peep into the objectives of the SLPEs points out that the major purposes of their creation related to undertaking in the state sector manufacturing, trade and services, financial, promotional, welfare and utility sector activities. The manufacturing enterprises dominated the overall number, followed by trade and service, utility, welfare and promotional

Table 2
Classification of SLPEs

Classification	*No. of Enterprises*
Manufacturing	8
Trade and Service	4
Financial	3
Promotional	3
Utility	3
Welfare	1
Total	22

(Source: On the spot visit of SLPEs in Sikkim).

enterprises. Table 2 provides the details with regard to the classification of the SLPEs.

Market Structure

The SLPEs operated in markets varying from competitive to monopoly conditions. Some enterprises enjoyed captive market conditions initially but due to the liberalization policies adopted by the Government of India they are compelled to operate in competitive markets currently. Even in the field of utilities monopoly markets are assuming competitive character

Figure 1
Market Structure

Competitive	*Non- Competitive*
• Sikkim Precision Industries Ltd • State Trading Corporation • Government Fruit Preservation Factory • Sikkim Consumers' Co-operative Society • Sikkim State Co-operative Supply and Marketing Federation Ltd • Sikkim Jewels Ltd • Sikkim Hatchery Ltd • Sikkim Poultry Dev. Corp. Ltd • Sikkim Times Corp. Ltd • Sikkim Co-operative Milk Producers Union Ltd • Sikkim Power Dev. Corp.	• Sikkim Industrial and Investment Development Corp. Ltd • Sikkim State Co-operative Bank • State Bank of Sikkim • Tea Board of Sikkim • Sikkim Tourism Development Corp. Ltd • Sikkim Nationalized Transport • Sikkim State Energy and Power Department • Sikkim Scheduled Castes, Tribes and Other Backward Classes Development Corp. Ltd • Khadi and Village Industries Board • Denjong Agricultural Co-Operative Society Ltd • Sikkim Handloom and Handicrafts Dev. Corp. Ltd

(Source: Discussions with the Chief Executives of the SLPEs in Sikkim).

due to unbundling / strategic business group approach being adopted in power sector and cold privatisation being followed in the public transport corporations. However, this may not be true of the promotional, welfare and co-operative SLPEs as they have a specific mandate of helping the weaker sections of the society and foster the growth of given activities, on the one hand, and protect the interest of the co-operators, on the other. In terms of market structure, the position of the SLPEs is shown in Figure

Conceptual Models

Figures 2 and 3 present the conceptual models that could suit the requirement for identifying the SLPEs in the State of Sikkim for the purposes of disinvestment, privatisation and retention. The first model is known as the Three Dimensional Matrix and the second one is know as the Two –by - Two Matrix[1]. It may be noted here that no such exercise has been undertaken in the case of the Central Public Enterprises (CPEs), wherein the disinvestment has become a matter of intense dissension.

Three Dimensional Matrix

The Three Dimensional Matrix based on factors such as (1) public purpose, (2) mobilization of resources from external sources, and (3) profitability could be applied to rank public enterprises as high or low. The enterprises being high on all three dimensions merit retention in the public enterprise portfolio. On the other hand, the enterprises being low on all

Figure 2
Three Dimensional Matrix

Factors	*High*	*Low*
1. Public Purpose	H1	L1
2. Resource Mobilisation from Financial Institutions	H2	L2
3. Profitability	H3	H3

three dimensions need to be transferred to the private sector. The enterprises falling in intermediate categories need to undergo restructuring.

Two - by - Two Matrix

The second model is based on financial performance and market structure. The SLPEs may have a positive or negative financial performance. In terms of market structure, they may constitute a single source of supply or constitute to multiple sources of supply. The enterprises registering good financial performance and having multiple sources of supply emerge as clear candidates for privatization. On the contrary, the enterprises characterized with good financial performance but belonging to single source of supply need to be retained in the public enterprise portfolio. The SLPEs in the other categories need to be restructured.

Figure 3
Two-by-Two Matrix

Market Structure	Financial Performance		
	Good		Bad
	Single Source	A	B
		Non-Competitive Successful PEs	Non-Competitive Unsuccessful PEs
	Multiple Source	C	D
		Competitive Successful PEs	Competitive Unsuccessful

Identifying SLPEs for Restructuring

The data for the year 2003-04 pertaining to the SLPEs have been considered for the application of the three dimensional matrix and the Two – by – Two Matrix. Public purpose is considered high if the enterprise is involved in core activities which can not be totally executed by the private sector. Resource mobilisation is considered high if 20 per cent or more of the resources have been raised externally. Profitability is considered high if the net profits earned are more than ten per cent of the investment.

Table 3
Three Dimensional Matrix and SLPEs

Name of the enterprise	*Public Purpose*	*Resource Mobilization*	*Profitability*
SIDICO	High	High	Low
State Bank of Sikkim	High	High	Low
Sikkim State Co-operative Bank	High	Low	Low
Sikkim Jewels Ltd	Low	Low	Low
Sikkim Hatchery Ltd	Low	Low	Low
Sikkim Poultry	Low	Low	Low.
Sikkim Precision Industries	Low	Low	Low
SITCO	Low	Low	Low
Tea Board of Sikkim	High	Low	Low
Sikkim Milk Union	High	High	Low
Govt. Fruit Preservation Factory	Low	Low	Low
Sikkim Tourism	High	Low	Low
Sikkim Handicrafts and Handlooms Development Corporation	High	Low	Low
Khadi and Village Industries Board	High	Low	Low
State Trading Corp.	Low	Low	High
Sikkim Consumer Co-operative society	Low	Low	Low
SIMFED	High	Low	High
Denjong Agricultural Co-Operative Society Ltd	High	Low	High
Sikkim National Transport Corp.	High	Low	Low

(Contd.)

(Contd. Table 3)

Name of the enterprise	*Public Purpose*	*Resource Mobilization*	*Profitability*
State Energy and Department of Power	High	Low	Low
Sikkim Power Dev. Corp.	Low	Low	Low
SABCCO	High	High	Low

Source : Prepared on the basis of the discussions with Chief Executives of the SLPEs and Policy Makers, Government of Sikkim.

As per the Three Dimensional Matrix, there is no SLPE in Sikkim qualifying for straight retention. However, there are nine SLPEs requiring privatisation / closure. These enterprises include Sikkim Jewels Ltd, Sikkim Hatchery Ltd, Sikkim Poultry Dev. Corp. Ltd, Sikkim Precision Dev. Corp. Ltd, Sikkim Time Corp., Sikkim Trading Corp., Sikkim State Consumer Co-operative Society, Government Fruit Preservation Factory, and Sikkim Power Dev. Corp. Ltd. Though Sikkim Consumer Co-operative Society and State Trading Corp. have been profit making ventures, their privatisation / winding up has been suggested in view of the duplication of activities with SIMFED and the Denjong Agricultural Co-operative Society. The rest of the enterprise (namely, SIDICO, State Bank of Sikkim, Sikkim State Consumer Co-operative Bank, Tea Board of Sikkim, Sikkim Milk Producers Union; Sikkim Tourism Dev. Corp. Ltd, Sikkim Handloom and Handicrafts Dev. Corp. Ltd, Khadi and Village Industries Board, SIMFED, Denjong Agricultural Society, Sikkim Nationalized Transport, Sikkim Energy and Department of Power and SABCCO) need to be restructured as per the suitably designed modalities.

Figure 4 shows that three enterprise viz., Sikkim Precision Industries Ltd, State Trading Corporation, Government Fruit Preservation Factory qualify for privatisation as they are profitable and are also competitive. The table shows that five

Figure 4

Two –by – Two Matrix and SLPEs

Financial Performance		*Competitive*	*Non- Competitive*
	Profit Making	1. Sikkim Precision Industries Ltd 2. State Trading Corporation 3. Government Fruit Preservation Factory	1. Sikkim Industrial and Investment Development Corporation Ltd 2. Sikkim State Co-operative Bank 3. Tea Board of Sikkim 4. Sikkim Consumers' Co-operative Society 5. Sikkim State Co-operative Supply and Marketing Federation Ltd
		First Quadrant	**Second Quadrant**
	Loss making	1. Sikkim Jewels Ltd 2. Sikkim Hatchery Ltd 3. Sikkim Poultry Dev. Corp. Ltd 4. Sikkim Times Corp. Ltd 5. Sikkim Co-operative Milk Producers Union Ltd 6. Sikkim Power Dev. Corp.	1. State Bank of Sikkim 2. Sikkim Tourism Development Corporation Ltd 3. Sikkim Nationalized Transport 4. Sikkim State Energy and Power Department 5. Sikkim Handloom and Handicrafts Dev. Corp. Ltd 6. Khadi and Village Industries Board 7. Denjong Agricultural Co-Operative Society Ltd 8. Sikkim Scheduled Castes, Tribes and Other Backward Classes Development Corporation Ltd
		Three Quadrant	**Fourth Quadrant**

enterprises, viz Sikkim Industrial and Investment Development Corporation Ltd, Sikkim State Co-operative Bank, Tea Board of Sikkim, Sikkim Consumers' Co-operative Society, and Sikkim State Co-operative Supply and Marketing Federation Ltd are profitable but non- competitive. These enterprises need to be made competitive and in course of time required to be shifted to the first Quadrant making them amenable, if necessary, for privatisation. There is a need to introduce policy and managerial reforms to shift these enterprises to the first quadrant. Quadrant three shows viz., Sikkim Jewels Ltd, Sikkim Hatchery Ltd, Sikkim Poultry Dev. Corp. Ltd, Sikkim Times Corp. Ltd, Sikkim Co-operative Milk Producers Union Ltd and Sikkim Power Dev. Corp.. There is a need to introduce policy and managerial reforms to shift these enterprises to the first Quadrant. Quadrant four shows that eight enterprises viz., State Bank of Sikkim, Sikkim Tourism Development Corporation Ltd, Sikkim Nationalized Transport, Sikkim State Energy and Power Department, Sikkim Handloom and Handicrafts Dev. Corp. Ltd, Khadi and Village Industries Board, Denjong Agricultural Co-Operative Society Ltd, and Sikkim Scheduled Castes, Tribes and Other Backward Classes Development Corporation Ltd are loss making and non – competitive. There is a need to make these enterprises competitive and then introduce managerial reforms in order to shift them from Quadrant four to Quadrant three and eventually to Quadrant one.

The application of the two models provides the same choice for the portfolio for retention of the SLPEs in the State of Sikkim which facilitates our task of outlining the modalities for restructuring and privatisation.

Modalities of Restructuring

The SLPEs are ranked as high or low on various parameters of the three dimensional matrix. By placing them on the three dimensional matrix, we obtained 2x2x2 i.e. 8

categories containing 22 enterprises. No enterprise was high on all the parameters. Eight enterprises were low on all the parameters. 14 enterprises belonged to the other six categories. State Trading Corporation has also been identified for privatisation / closure due to its presence in non-strategic area of operation. Table 4 provides the details in terms three dimensional matrix of category-wise listing of the SLPEs in the State of Sikkim.

Table 4
Categorization of SLPEs as per Three Dimensional Matrix

Category Name	*Name of the enterprise*
Category 1 : Public purpose high, resource mobilization high, profitability high	#
Category 2 : Public purpose low, resource mobilization low, profitability low	• Sikkim Jewels Ltd • Sikkim Hatchery Ltd • Sikkim Poultry • Sikkim Precision Industries • SITCO • Govt. Fruit Preservation Factory • Sikkim Consumer Co-operative society • Sikkim Power Dev. Corp.
Category 3: Public purpose high, resource mobilization low, and profitability low	• Sikkim State Co-operative Bank • Tea Board of Sikkim • Sikkim Tourism • Sikkim Handicrafts and Handlooms Development Corporation • Khadi and Village Industries Board • Sikkim National Transport Corp. • State Energy and Department of Power

(Contd.)

(Contd. Table 4)

Category Name	*Name of the enterprise*
Category 4: Public purpose high, resource mobilization low, profitability high:	• SIMFED • Denjong Agricultural Co-Operative Society Ltd
Category 5: Public purpose high, resource mobilization high, profitability low	• SIDICO • State Bank of Sikkim • Sikkim Milk Union • SABCCO
Category 6: Public purpose low, resource mobilization high, profitability low	#
Category 7: Public purpose low, resource mobilization low, profitability high	• State Trading Corp.
Category 8: Public purpose low, resource mobilization high, profitability high	#

\# *No enterprise classified in this category.*

The modalities for restructuring category-wise are discussed below:

Category 1:- Public purpose high, resource mobilization high, profitability high: The SLPEs in this category should be continued since they are good performers. They should be freed from government control on operational issue matters. The Memorandum of Understanding (MoU) should specify support to be extended and financial returns expected by the Government. The Governing Boards of these enterprises should not have more than one government nominees. All measures under cold privatisation could be adopted for enterprises in this category. The enterprises in this category should be provided autonomy and become financially viable. The term cold privatisation refers to optimum performance through internal management action which calls for introduction and strengthening of financial and management systems such as budgeting, costing, pricing, internal audit, manpower planning, recruitment, performance appraisal, training and management development, supply chain management, technological up-gradation, computerisation and restructuring of varied kinds, viz., organisational, financial, human resources, operations and technological restructuring. No SLPE has been ranked as high - high – high.

Category 2:- Public performance low, resource mobilization low, profitability low: The enterprises in this category are a fit case for liquidation or total divesture, if possible. This would lead to avoidance of further investment thereby reducing the burden on the State exchequer. Sikkim Jewels Ltd, Sikkim Hatchery Ltd, Sikkim Poultry Ltd, Sikkim Precision Industries, SITCO, Govt. Fruit Preservation Factory, Sikkim Consumer Co-operative Society and Sikkim Power Dev. Corp. come in this category of the three dimensional matrix.

Category 3:- Public purpose high, resource mobilization low, and profitability low: These enterprises should be continued in the state sector. The accent on resource mobilization and profitability should be increased and then partial / cold privatization could be attempted. Sikkim State Co-operative Bank, Tea Board of Sikkim, Sikkim Tourism Dev. Corp. Ltd, Sikkim Handicrafts and Handlooms Development Corp., Khadi and Village Industries Board, Sikkim National Transport Corp., State Energy and Department of Power, form a part of this category.

Category 4:- Public purpose high, resource mobilization low, profitability high: The enterprises in this category could be continued in the State sector. The accent should be on improving the resource mobilization increased borrowings on commercial terms. The profitability improvement measures could also be introduced to improve the market standing of the enterprises. The enterprises in this category then be partially privatized. SIMFED and Denjong Agricultural Co-Operative Society Ltd form a part of this category as enterprises.

Category 5:- Public purpose high, resource mobilization high, profitability low: While enterprises in this category could

Table 5

Anticipated Benefits of Modalities

Categorization of SLPEs			*Names of SLPES and No. of SLPEs*	*Suggested Action*	*Anticipated Results*
Public Purpose	*Resource mobilization*	*Profit ability*			
H1	H2	H3	#	Continue in the state sector with greater autonomy	Better service to consumers
L1	L2	L3	• Sikkim Jewels Ltd. • Sikkim Hatchery Ltd • Sikkim Poultry Ltd • Sikkim Precisions Industries Ltd • SITCO • Govt. Fruit Preservation Factory • Sikkim Consumer Co-operative Society and • Sikkim Power Development Corp. Ltd	Closure or Liquidation or total divestiture	Saving of Govt. Resources

(Contd.)

(Contd .Table 5)

Categorization of SLPEs			*Names of SLPES and No. of SLPEs*	*Suggested Action*	*Anticipated Results*
Public Purpose	*Resource mobilization*	*Profit ability*			
H2	L2	L3	• Sikkim State Co-operative Bank • Tea Board of Sikkim • Sikkim Tourism Dev. Corp. Ltd • Sikkim Handicrafts and Handloom Dev. Corp. Ltd • Khadi and Village Industries Board • Sikkim National Transport and • State Energy and Department of Power	Continue in the state sector with increased accent on resource mobilisation and profitability	Improved fulfillment of public purpose
H1	L2	H3	• SIMFED • Denjong Agricultural Co-operative Society Ltd	Increased accent on the resource mobilisation / partial disinvestment	Better Revenues or reduced budget support

(Contd.)

(Contd.Table 5)

Categorization of SLPEs			*Names of SLPES and No. of SLPEs*	*Suggested Action*	*Anticipated Results*
Public Purpose	*Resource mobilization*	*Profit ability*			
H1	H2	L3	• SIDICO • State Bank of Sikkim • Sikkim Milk Producers Union • SABCCO	Disinvest	Additional resource to Govt.
L1	H2	L3	#	Introduce financial adjustments and then of in for disinvestment	Long term Improvement in service to consumers
L1	L2	H3	• State Trading Corp. Ltd	Introduce financial adjustments and then go in for disinvestment	Long term Investment in service to consumers
L1	H2	H3	#	Disinvest	Reduced Govt. support

#No enterprise classified in this category.

be continued in the State sector, there should be total reorganization of internal management and profitability elements concerning these enterprises. SIDICO, State Bank of Sikkim SABCCO and Sikkim Milk Union form a part of this category of enterprises.

Category 6:- Public purpose low, resource mobilization high, profitability low: Such cases should go in for disinvestment. Total divestiture could also be attempted. Although, no enterprise falls in this category, any enterprise established in future, qualifying for this category, should be taken up for disinvestment or total divestiture.

Category 7:- Public purpose low, resource mobilization low, profitability high: In such cases the government fund could be withdrawn by borrowing more from the market and institutions in view of the good profitability. The enterprises in this category could be considered initially for partial divestiture leading to full divestiture in the final course. State Trading Corporation is the cases in point concerning this category.

Category 8:- Public purpose low, resource mobilization high, and profitability high: These form appropriate cases for total disinvestment resulting in capital accretions for the State government. No SLPE qualifies for inclusion in this category.

The anticipated benefits of the modalities suggested are given in Table 5.

Privatisation Method

An enterprise could be privatised with or without divestiture. The divestiture could be full or partial. The privatisation without divestiture could be positive or negative. The choice of methods would be determined by the characteristics possessed by each enterprise in terms of being strategic or non-strategic in nature. Both the strategic and non-strategic enterprises creating fiscal pressures by continued loss making need to be removed from the portfolio for retention of the SLPEs. However, between the strategic and non-strategic enterprises, it is easier to privatise the non-strategic enterprises.

Requirement for restructuring

In order to affect restructuring for privatisation, disinvestment and retention, some legal, accounting and financial requirements need to be fulfilled besides pledging the political commitment. The legal requirements include the settlement of claims of employees, fulfillment of the provisions of the companies act and corporatisation of the departmental enterprises. The accounting requirements comprise the updation of accounts, assessment of contingent liabilities and settlement of claims. The financial requirements include the changes in the debt - equity ratio, broadening of capital structure, introduction of financial systems and valuation of the enterprise. The socio- political requirements include the creation of pro-restructuring / privatisation climate, transparency in restructuring / privatisation, setting up independent machinery for the purpose and strong political commitment ensuring the successful functioning of the post-privatised enterprises. The setting up of regulatory bodies, wherever required, is also necessary for the success.

Characteristics of SLPEs in the State of Sikkim

We explain below the characteristics relating to the activities, financial status, physical performance, total employment, social purpose, financial system and management, interface with government, performance improvement plan, Strengths, Weakness, Opportunity and Threats (SWOT) analysis, problems encountered, and strategic initiatives of the SLPEs in Sikkim. A majority of the enterprises have been incorporated in the company form. All the manufacturing enterprises excepting Sikkim Co-operative Milk Union have been registered as the Government Company. The social purpose of these enterprises (excepting Sikkim Co-operative Milk Union) is very low. They qualify for full privatisation. The Sikkim Power Development Corporation, although an enterprise in the utility category, has also a low social purpose and qualifies for full privatisation. SABCCO and Sikkim Tourism Development Corporation have a high social purpose. In their cases, cold privatisation could be introduced through Optimum Performance Through Internal Management Action (OPTIMA).

- The utility enterprises are large sized. They operate as departmental enterprises. There is a need to corporatise these enterprises, make them competitive, and commercially and financially viable. Partial / full privitisation could follow thereafter.
- Out of four public corporations, two corporations, viz., State Bank of Sikkim, Khadi and Village Industries Board, and Tea Board of Sikkim have a high public purpose, and State Trading Corporation has a low public purpose. Whereas, the first three need to be retained in the public sector, the last one needs to be privatized. However, in both the cases, partial/ full privatisation or cold privatisation could be considered as per the need of each case.
- In the case of co-operative enterprises, public purpose being high, the retention is the only option presently available with the government. However, in their case also, there is a possibility of merger and OPTIMA.
- The size of the SLPEs in the State of Sikkim is small in terms of both the turnover and the volume. This makes them amenable for restructuring and privatisation.
- The financial position of the enterprises is very discouraging as most of the enterprises completely depend for share capital on the government, have not garnered debt, are characterized by receding or negative net worth due to accumulated losses, and are incurring losses. Some of the enterprises have either low or negative working capital.
- The wage costs are very high as non-managerial staff far exceeds the managerial staff in number. The overstaffing has taken place through the muster roll, work-charged

and casual employment routes. Some enterprises have tried to go in for labour adjustments through VRS but the success has been minimal and a lot more remains to be done.

- The revenues earned / turnover of the enterprises is very low and is about 15 per cent of the total investment. The capacity utilisation in manufacturing enterprises ranges from 10 -30 per cent.
- The enterprises have perennially continued with same activities without any R&D and innovations.
- The financial and management systems such as budgeting, costing, pricing, internal audit, management information system (MIS), project appraisal, recruitment, manpower planning, supply chain management, appointment of professional directors, excessive presence of government directors on the board have encouraged non commercial culture and bureaucratisation. The enterprises are not board-led ones.
- The SWOT analysis points that strengths are far less as compared to weaknesses and so is the case between opportunities and threats.

  Most of the enterprise did not formulate performance improvement plans and are not internally funded. Further, many enterprises lack the government support in that there interaction with government is very low.
- The problems faced by these enterprises are galore ranging from operations related, market mix, location, over aging of plant and machinery to strategic issues such as settlement of debts, diversification, finding new markets, innovating new sources of finance, increase in employee productivity, unwarranted internal competition and neglect of technology, to mention a few.
- The SLPEs have shown a very poor appreciation for strategic initiatives including the rationalization of manpower and modernization of plant and machinery. The

issues in organisaitonal, financial, human resource development and industrial relations, operational and technological restructuring have not been attended to by them.

Summing up

Restructuring business enterprises is the order of the day. Restructuring effects suitable changes to align the current business practices in tune with the changed requirements. Restructuring brings about a long term change and renders the business fit to match the changing business requirements. Restructuring includes in its gamut organizational, financial, human resource, operational and strategic re-alignment. The privatisation, disinvestment and closer constitute a part of such restructuring. The GoS has formulated a comprehensive policy with regard to privatisation and disinvestment. By and large, the GoS proposes to privatize/ disinvest the SLPEs which are not strategic in nature. It is expected that such disengagement would lead to the development of private sector and freeing resources which are unwarrantedly locked up in the public sector. The GoS proposes to carryout the entire restructuring exercise on case-to-case basis in a transparent manner without hurting the interest of workers. The SLPEs are encouraged to formulate their VR schemes to minimize the social consequences of labour adjustments. The GoS has also formulated some criteria for disinvestment to avoid subjectivity in the selection of candidates for disinvestment and pre-empt formation of monopolies. However, these criteria need an analytical formulation to identify the candidates for privatisation, disinvestment and retention. This alone could indicate as to what should be the SLPEs portfolio for retention by the GoS and as to which modality could be followed for privatisation / disinvestment of the left over SLPEs. The application of the restructuring models clearly point out a vast scope for policy and managerial reforms for the SLPEs that are required to be retained in the medium and long term by the GoS and privatisation/ disinvestment of un-strategic SLPEs.

References

1. Mishra, R.K. and Bhar K.S. Privatisation, Vikas, New Delhi, 2003, pp. 1-7.

4. Mishra, R.K., et.al., Economic Liberalisation and Public Enterprises, Concept, New Delhi, 2006, pp. 13-16.

6

Privatization Challenges for Good Governance: A Case of India

Abstract

Privatization is considered as an important technique for enhancing the rate of growth in India through unlocking the idle and depreciating wealth in the public sector and reduction of fiscal deficits. Privatization is intended to alleviate poverty at a faster rate through the roll back of the State in India in sectors where its presence is not required and the private initiative from within the country or abroad is available to take up areas of the economic activities where the public sector is present. India is a Union of States. The economic activities in the Country have been taken up both by the central and the state governments which have launched privatization programmes to prop up the tempo of economic development. The process of privatization needs to be managed effectively which requires the presence of good governance as a pre-requisite.

This paper brings out the commonalities and distinguishing features of privatisation of the State Level Public Enterprises

(SLPEs) in the various states. The paper presents the quantitative dimensions of privatization at the central and the state levels. The quantitative dimensions of privatization at the central level include parameters such as the no. of companies in which equity sold, target receipt for the year, actual receipts and methodology of disinvestment / privatization. The quantitative dimensions of privatization of the SLPEs include total number of enterprises, no. of SLPEs privatized, no. of SLPEs proposed to be privatized, no. of SLPEs closed / under closure and the no. of profit making / loss making SLPEs. The paper provides a comparative view of privatization of the Central Public Enterprises (CPEs) and the SLPEs. Besides bringing out the commonalities, the paper deals with the differentiating features of privatization of the SLPEs and the CPEs. Finally, the paper outlines the issues that confront privatization programme relating to the SLPEs and the CPEs in India. The paper presents a matrix of interactions between privatization and poverty, and applies the matrix in the case of some enterprises which have been privatized in Orissa.

1. Some Dimensions of Privatization

The quantitative dimensions of privatization provide an insight into the happenings and progress of privatization both at the central and the state levels. These dimensions vary as between the centre and the states and further between one state to another state. Any study of the issues in privatization needs to precede a discussion on the quantitative dimensions of privatization. Table 1 provides the state-wise details of privatization of the SLPEs in India.

Table 1 shows that, Kerala, Karnataka and U.P. topped the list in terms of the number of SLPEs. As on March 31st 2007, Orissa, Assam, Bihar clearly emerged as the privatization leader. U.P., Karnataka and West Bengal also propose to take a big action in this direction.

Table 1

Status of SLPEs as on March 31, 2003

State	*Total Number of Enterprises*	*No. of SLPEs Privatized*	*No. of SLPES Proposed to be privatized*	*Close / under closure*	*No. of Profit making enterprises*	*No. of Loss making enterprises*
Andhra Pradesh	56	1		3	11	9
Tamilnadu	69	-	-	8	25	14
Arunachal Pradesh	7			2	2	3
Assam	49	2	6	18	16	25
Bihar	55	4	-	17	17	10
Delhi	12	-	-	-	6	2
Goa	17	-	-	-	3	11
Gujarat	57	-	4	5	18	6
Haryana	28	1	-	-	7	9
Himachal Pradesh	21	2*	-	1	7	9
Jammu & Kashmir	23	1	-	2	8	10
Karnataka	82	-	31	5	38	18

(Contd.)

(Contd. Table 1)

State	*Total Number of Enterprises*	*No. of SLPEs Privatized*	*No. of SLPES Proposed to be privatized*	*Close / under closure*	*No. of Profit making enterprises*	*No. of Loss making enterprises*
Kerala	114	-	-	12	16	45
Lakshadweep	1	-	-	-	-	-
Madhya Pradesh	44	-	-	4	4	10
Maharashtra	76	-	1*	10	4	10
Manipur	15	-	-	1	3	-
Meghalaya	10	-	-	1	8	8
Mizoram	7	-	-	4	1	4
Nagaland	15	-	-	-	0	3
Orissa	64	3	-	15	29	13
Pondicherry	13	-	-	-	2	5
Punjab	46	1	4	8	10	4
Rajasthan	29	-	-	1	4	4
Sikkim	15	-	-	2	2	7
Tripura	10	-	-	-	-	-
U.P.	95	-	27	10	32	21
West Bengal	86	-	22	18	28	23
Total	**1116**	**12**	**94**	**147**	**301**	**298**

(Source: Database on SLPEs, Institute of Public Enterprise, Hyderabad)

2. Commonalities

In main, the following are the commonalities in the privatization practices of the SLPEs in the various states:

(i) Most of the states explicitly or implicitly realized the need for privatization of the SLPEs. The fiscal crunch pressed them hard to go in for privatization.

(ii) Many states formulated a public enterprise policy to consider afresh the retention of their SLPE portfolio.

(iii) Some states set up a mechanism to deal with privatization of the SLPEs whereas many others were in the process of imparting a thinking to this issue.

(iv) Manufacturing SLPEs found a greater appeal for privatization.

(v) Social Safety Net emerged as an important issue in privatization exercise.

(vi) Trade Sale was the preferred modality for the transfer of ownership.

3. Distinguishing Features

The following are the main distinguishing features:

(i) Whereas states such as Andhra Pradesh, Karnataka, Punjab, Maharashtra Orissa, Uttar Pradesh, Manipur and Assam showed a clear preference for privatization, states like West Bengal, Kerala, Tamil Nadu, Madhya Pradesh and Meghalaya prefer restructuring.

(ii) Punjab, Maharashtra, Karnataka and Kerala set up the privatization mechanism through independent enactments. Rajasthan, Haryana, Madhya Pradesh, Orissa, Andhra Pradesh, Assam and Tamil Nadu have either set up separate departments or used the existing mechanisms to handle the issues related to privatization.

(iii) Andhra Pradesh, Orissa, Kerala and Karnataka prepared phase-wise programme for privatization of their SLPEs.

(iv) The privatization programmes of Andhra Pradesh , Orissa and Uttar Pradesh received the support of DFID and have been carried out with the support of foreign consultant. The Madhya Pradesh and Gujarat programmes received the support of Asian Development Bank and have also been carried out with the support of foreign consultants.

4. Process of Privatization

The due diligence process for privatization of the CPEs and the SLPEs is as follows:

Step-1: Government approval for privatization/sale of an enterprise.

Step-2: PE Department invites 'expression of interest' (EoI) through open advertisement, for selection of advisor to assist in the implementation of the disinvestment decisions. Concurrently, valuation of the SLPE is undertaken in accordance with the standard national and international practices.

Step-3: Appointment of the Advisor with the approval of the Restructuring Committee.

Step-4: Advisors assist the Department of Public Enterprise (DPE) in issue of advertisement for EoI from prospective buyers.

Step-5: Short-listing of the prospective buyers using the pre-qualification criteria set out in the EoI advertisement.

Step-6: Preparation of the Information Memorandum by the Advisors in consultation with the concerned SLPE, which is given to the short listed prospective bidders, after they enter into a confidentiality agreement.

Step-7: The draft sale agreement and other legal agreements are prepared by the Advisors and given to the short listed bidders to elicit their response.

Step-8: The prospective bidders undertake due diligence of the SLPE and hold discussions with the Advisors/the Government/ the Management of the SLPE for any clarification.

Step-9: Based on the response received from the prospective bidders, the draft sale agreement and other legal

Implementation Mechanism

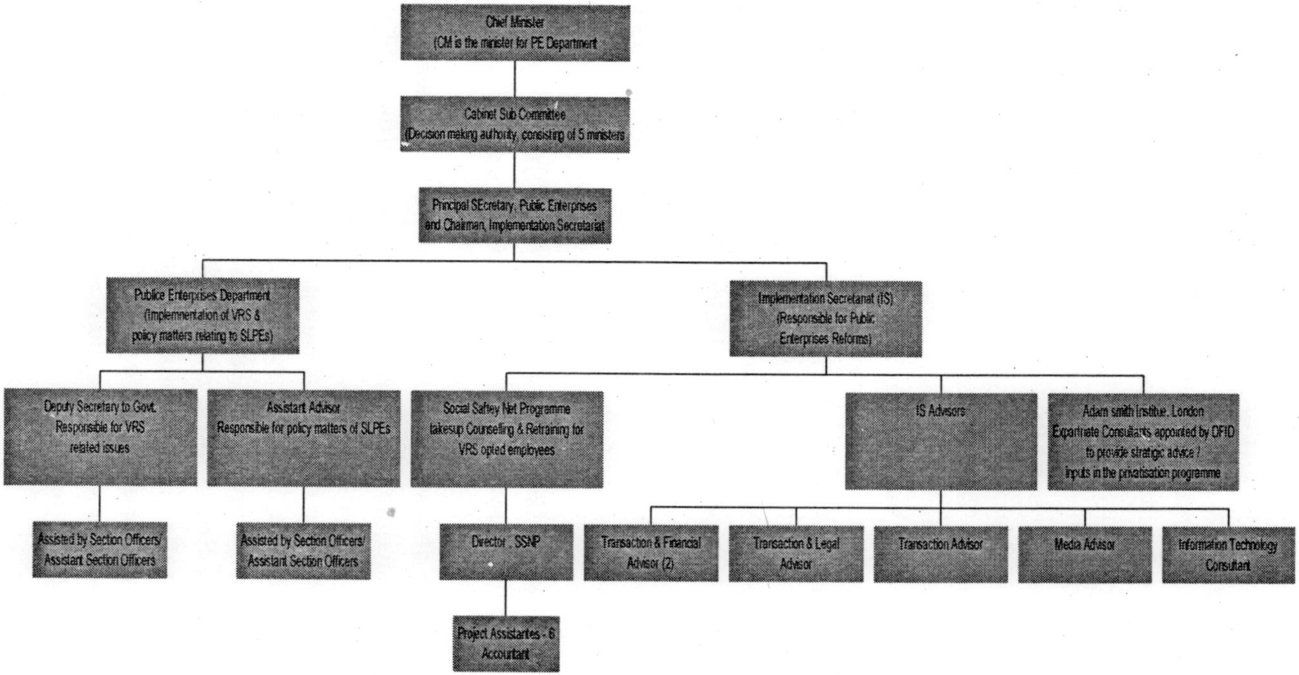

agreements are finalized, vetted by the Law Department, approved by the Cabinet Committee on Disinvestment (CCD) and then sent to the prospective bidders for inviting final binding bids (Technical & Financial).

Step-10:After examination, analysis, evaluation and further negotiation, if necessary, the recommendations of the Inter-Departmental Core Group (IDCG) are placed before the CCD for final decision regarding selection of the preferred bidder, signing of necessary legal agreement and other ancillary issues.

It is clear that the privatization process is very tardy and cumbersome. The implementation mechanism is too complex at the central level whereas some state governments have modified the mechanism adopted by the centre as per their requirements giving due considerations to the factors such as transparency and speed. The cumbersome privatization process adopted by the central government and the various state governments in India have delayed the implementation of privatization programme and undermined the revenue potential from privatization. The following diagram depicts the implementation mechanism for privatization in Andhra Pradesh – the *privatization leader* in India.

5. Comparative View: Centre versus States

The following are the chief comparative features of privatization relating to CPEs and SLPEs.

(i) The disinvestment/privatization of CPEs began since the launching of New Economic Policy in July 1991 whereas privatization of SLPEs was resorted to much before in the case of the states e.g., Allwyn Nissan, in Andhra Pradesh, Uttar Pradesh (U.P) Auto Tractors Limited in Uttar Pradesh and Charge Chrome Plant in Orissa.

(ii) The States preferred Trade Sale as the modality of privatization as compared to the partial disinvestment and strategic sale by the Central Government.

(iii) There is a trend in the States to prefer an independent legislation to execute privatization programmes as compared to the executive action in the case of the central government.

(iv) The privatization exercise in the state governments is not target based whereas the Central Government laid down the targets of money to be mobilized through disinvestment/privatization.

(v) The Central Government prefers to use the term "disinvestment" to ward off any ideological/political problem whereas the State Governments do not refrain themselves from revealing their preference for privatization. However, some states such as West Bengal, Kerala and Tripura have rejected the use of both the terms viz., privatization and disinvestment.

(vi) The privatization of SLPEs, barring the State Electricity Boards (SEBs) turned out to be an easier exercise as compared to the central PEs because of their size and appeal.

(vii) The privatization of both the CPEs and the SLPEs was confounded by the problem of transparency and valuation.

(viii) Both the speed and the mechanisms for privatization posed governance challenges at the central and the state levels in terms of socio-politico-administrative issues.

(ix) The cultural factors were also responsible for the success or failure of privatization.

6. Poverty and Privatization

Does privatization alleviate poverty ? In this section, we present a matrix of interactions between poverty and privatization and relate it to some enterprises that have been privatized in Orissa.

Orissa was one of the first State to initiate the process of disinvestment even before the Government of India announced its policy of liberalisaticn in 1991. The fist unit divested was the Charge Chrome Plant of the Orissa Mining Corporation (OMC) Alloys Ltd. which was sold to TISCO (Tata Iron & Steel

Table 2

Matrix of Interactions between Privatization and Poverty

	Indicators of assessment	*Type of change*	*Overall growth impact*	*Impact on distribution*	*Impact on poverty*
Distribution of assets	Assets ownership	Nil	Depends on whether transfer of assets and changes in conditions of ownership are pro growth or not	depends on terms of sale and distribution of (-) assets	Poor gain if they benefit from redistribution of assets or access to assets and services
	Financial performance	Improvement in financial performance	Inpotentially (+) eg. if the increased profits are reinvested to expand productive capacity	(+) for the new owner (+) for government if tax revenues increase as result	The poor gain if (+) growth and distributive impact enhance their welfare
		Deterioration in financial performance	Potentially negative	(-) for the new owner, (-) for government tax revenues increase as a result of privatization	The poor gain if (+) growth and distributive impact stifle their welfare

(Contd.)

(Contd. Table 2)

	Indicators of assessment	*Type of change*	*Overall growth impact*	*Impact on distribution*	*Impact on poverty*
	Output	Increase in output	Positive	Could be neutral, regressive or progressive	Positive if growth is pro (-) poor
		Decline in output	Negative		Negative if it leads to reduced consumption employment etc. for the poor
	Prices	Prices increase	Depends on the extent and interaction between (-) multiplier effect ((+)) profitability effect for new owners, (-) profitability effect for input users	Loss for consumers and input users, gain for new owner.	(-) potentially more so if the output is a basic commodity consumed by the poor

(Contd.)

(Contd. Table 2)

	Indicators of assessment	*Type of change*	*Overall growth impact*	*Impact on distribution*	*Impact on poverty*
Impact on Efficiency		Price decline	Depends on the extent and interaction between (+) multiplier effect (-) profitability effect	Gain for consumers and input users; loss for new owners	(+) potentially. More so if the output is a basic commodity consumed by the poor
	Quality	Improvement	(+) if it leads to market expansion	(-) for consumers and input users without price increase; (+) for new products if markets expand and price increase more than the cost of quality improvement	(+) potentially without price increase. More so it the output is a basic commodity consumed by the poor
		Deterioration	(-) if it leads to market contraction	(-)for consumers and input users,(-) for new producers if markets contract	(-) potentially. more so if the output is a basic commodity consumed by the poor

(Contd.)

(Contd. Table 2)

	Indicators of assessment	*Type of change*	*Overall growth impact*	*Impact on distribution*	*Impact on poverty*
	Access	Improvement	Positive	(+) for new users and the new provider	(+) only if the new users are amongst the poor
		Deterioration	Negative	Loss of disconnected users	(-) if disconnected users are amongst the poor or are made poor
	Employment	Redundancy/ retrenchment	(+) if productivity is increased and (-) through reverse multiplier effect	Loss for the households of redundant workers gain for new owners; existing workers may lose if more flexible employment contracts are used after privitisation	Potentially (-). Depends on; who are made redundant, their skills and wealth, compensation package etc.
		Increase in employment	(+) multiplier effect if unemployment goes down	Gain for the newly employed	Only positive if the new employment opportunities benefit the poor and unemployed

(Contd.)

(Contd. Table 2)

	Indicators of assessment	*Type of change*	*Overall growth impact*	*Impact on distribution*	*Impact on poverty*
Impact on Labour Market	Wages	Decline	Could be (+) through increased competitiveness. (-) through reverse multiplier effect	Workers lose ; new owners gain	Some households may fall below poverty line
		Increase	Opposite to what is said above	Workers gain ; new owners lose	Some households may be lifted above the poverty line.
	Work conditions	Improvement	Depends on the nature of improvement. (+) if there are incentive effects (labour productivity may rise) (-) effect on the cost of production of any	Workers gain, new owners lose if cost of production rises, they gain if labour productivity improves	Depends on the extent to which the poor benefit from these improvements
		Deterioration	Ambiguous	Loss for the workers, ambiguous for employers	(-) if poor are affected

(Contd.)

(Contd. Table 2)

	Indicators of assessment	*Type of change*	*Overall growth impact*	*Impact on distribution*	*Impact on poverty*
Fiscal impact	Sale proceeds	(+) sale proceeds	(+) if used for growth promoting purposes (e.g investment) or for eliminating obstacles for growth (e.g. debt reduction, skill development)	Natural for tax payer, revenue gain for government, revenue loss for buyers the size of these depends on the extent to which sale proceeds reflects the true value of the SOE assets	The poor gain only if the sale proceeds are used for poverty reduction directly or indirectly
		(-) sale proceeds	(-) revenue impact on growth , the size of impact depends on whether the (-) sale process are borne by growth enhancing sectors	Loss for taxpayer; loss for government and gain for buyer if the values of privatized assets are underestimated or discounted	The poor lose if negative sale proceeds leads to a shift of resources away from poverty reducing spending. Negative growth impact may further aggravate the circumstances.

(Contd.)

(Contd. Table 2)

	Indicators of assessment	*Type of change*	*Overall growth impact*	*Impact on distribution*	*Impact on poverty*
	Tax revenues	Increase in tax revenues	Potentially positive	Gain for the government and those who benefit from the rise in tax revenue	The poor gain if increased revenues are used for poverty reduction or pro-poor growth is hampered
		Decline in tax revenues	Potentially negative	Loss for the government and those whose welfare deteriorated as a result	
	Return on assets	Foregone SOE profits	(-) if profits before divestiture were larger and or they were used more productively under public ownership	Loss for tax payer and government , gain for buyer if enterprise remain profitable	(-) if SOE profits contributed to Poverty Reduction

(Contd.)

(Contd. Table 2)

	Indicators of assessment	*Type of change*	*Overall growth impact*	*Impact on distribution*	*Impact on poverty*
		Riddance of SOE losses	(+) revenue impact	Gain for tax payer and government , loss for the buyer	(+) if the released revenue release is used for poverty reduction and or pro-poor growth
	Administrative accost of privitisation		(-) revenue impact	Loss for tax payer and government	(-) if there is a resource shift away from poverty reduction. Further adversities if pro-poor growth prospects are reduced.

Source ; Dagdeviren, Hulya, and Fine Ben, "The Macroeconomics of Poverty Reduction : Thematic summary Report Privatization", United National Development Programme, p.8.

Company). The plant, which had started commercial production in 1957, made a loss of Rs. 56 lakhs in 1988-89 and was facing difficulty in meeting its working capital requirement and in obtaining packing credit. Therefore, the Board passed a resolution in 1989 to sell the unit. There were 543 regular employees who were all taken by TISCO. The sale price of Rs.156 crore was much higher than the project cost. TISCO has in-

Table 3

Comparative Analysis Of The Pre And Post Privatisation Of OMC

Benefit	*OMC Period*	*TISCO Period*
Average monthly salary paid to employees	Rs.2,600/-	Rs. 9,800/-
No. of houses provided to	158	190
Recreation facilities provided	Nominal facilities	New multi-channel T.V. connection. Sports facilities and library with 2000 new books.
Conveyance allowance	No conveyance allowance	Rs. 106,000 being paid as conveyance allowance per month.
LTC	Very nominal	Rs. 106,000 being paid as conveyance allowance per month
LTC	Very nominal	Rs.7,500/- per employee in every block of two years.
Protective clothing	No protective clothing	160 technical staff provided with protective clothing

creased the capacity utilisation from 75% to 100% in the second year after acquisition and then gradually to 120%. The fear that the privatization would affect the interest of the employees has been proved wrong, as the following Table 4 shows:

Another case of successful privatization has been the case of Gangapur Weavers Co-operative Spinning Mills at Sundergarh. The mill which had sustained loss of over Rs.16 crore, was declared locked out in August 1991 and closed in June 1992. The mill was sold to Ashoka Synthetics Ltd. in 1993 at a bid price of Rs.1316 crore (against an original investment of Rs. 11 crore). The performance of the mill has substantially improved as the following Table 4 show:

Table 4
Performance of Gangapur Weavers Co-operative Spinning Mills

	Prior to privatization	*After privatization*
Maximum capacity utilisation	65%	90%
Payment of salary etc.	Had been totally s stopped	Regular payments are being made
Profit	Making losses	Earning 12% return on investment
Revenue for Government of Orissa	Nil	Rs. 15 crore per year
Exports	Nil	Foreign exchange earned through exports

The only objection to the privatization of Gangapur Mills's privatization has been the loss of jobs as the total staff strength has been reduced from 1,500 to 500. However, it is also felt that had the mill continued in its previous condition, the loss would have been far greater and probably the employees would have lost their jobs.

The next important case of disinvestment was in the power sector, which absorbed nearly 70% of the total public sector investment of the State. The Orissa State Electricity Board (OSEB), which had become monolithic and unmanageable, was suffering from problems of adverse capital structure, uneconomic tariff, high T&D losses, weak billing and collection system, over-staffing and mismatch of manpower and skills. Continuous losses were eroding the capital loss of the SEB and it was not in a position to pay its creditors and suppliers. It was unable to invest in modernisation, which was an urgent requirement. To respond to this problem, the Orissa Electricity Reforms Act was passed in January 1996 and it came into effect on 1st April, 1996. The reforms involved restructuring of the sector through unbundling of generation, transmission and distribution. It also included privatization of generation and distributor, competitive hodding for new generation, transparent and independent regulating agency, and tariff reforms both at bulk power level and retail level which have been the key components of reforms. The State Government has been the pioneer in privatization of the power sector. As part of the process, 49% of Orissa Power Generation Corporation (OPGC) was sold to a strategic investor – AES Corporation of USA – in 1997 for Rs. 603 crores (fetching a premium of 155% over the book value of equity). Likewise, 51% of equity shares of the four distribution companies were sold to private companies in 1999-2000 for Rs. 159.01 crores against a book value of Rs.114.72 crores. The reform was supported by a World Bank loan of US $350 million and DFID grant of UK £ 65 million.

The salient benefits of disinvestment/restructuring have been that:

(i) TIPS after being taken by National Thermal Power Corporation (NTPC) is now operating at a PLF (Plant

Load Factor) of 75 per cent whereas it had never operated previously beyond 30 per cent.

(ii) OPGC is consistently maintaining a high PLF of 70 to 80 per cent, a performance level comparable to NTPC.

(iii) Disinvestment of 51 per cent of government share in distribution and also 49 per cent in OPGC has unlocked substantial funds, and helped the Government reduce its fiscal deficit by 2 per cent.

(iv) The quality of power supply is improving and there are fewer interruptions.

(v) Studies have been stopped and generating companies are distributing dividend.

(vi) The system loss has been reduced from over 50 per cent to 43 per cent.

(vii) Losses in distribution are now shared with private investors.

7. Issues in Privatization

The privatization experiences of the central and the various state governments point out very clearly that an effective governance could go a long way in speeding up the implementation of the privatization programmes which could yield considerable finances for poverty alleviation programmes. Some important issues in privatization as revealed by the privatization experience are as follows :

(i) It is easier to privatize the smaller enterprises.

(ii) The manufacturing enterprises possess a greater appeal for privatization.

(iii) Effective due diligence expedites privatization.

(iv) The SLPEs organized under the Companies Act could be taken to market with a greater ease and comfort as compared to the SLPEs organized as public corporations.

(v) Valuation should be considered as an important element of the privatization process. The entire valuation exercise should be made transparent.

(vi) In the case of loss making enterprises with multiple subsidiaries and product groups/SBUs (Strategic Business Units), restructuring should precede privatization.

(vii) It is always helpful to establish a dialogue with the employees before any action is initiated to privatize an enterprise.

(viii) Sole reliance should not be placed on any particular method of privatization. Depending on the nature of the SLPE and market conditions, a combination of methods of divesting the SLPEs should be employed to achieve the objectives of privatization.

8. Conclusion

The central governments as well as most of the states explicitly or implicitly realize the need for privatization of the SLPEs to mobilize finances for poverty alleviation programme, implement the philosophy of the roll back of the State and diminish poverty levels through creation of larger number of jobs in the privatized public enterprise. However, whereas states such as Andhra Pradesh, Karnataka, Punjab and Orissa show a clear preference for privatization, the states like West Bengal, Tripura and Kerala indicated their disenchantment with the term 'Privatization' and opted for restructuring. The privatization pattern of the central and the state governments differ in many regards especially in relation to the method of sale. The Central Government prefers partial disinvestment and strategic sale as compared to the trade sale modality popularly adopted by the state governments. The privatization experiences of the state governments point to a number of lessons to be learnt for the future. Instead of depending on a specific modality, it would be beneficial to depend on a mix of methods. The smaller enterprises specially the manufacturing ones could be preferred for privatization. There is a need to simplify both the privatization process and privatization mechanism. The governance dimensions such as transparency and accountability should have a trade off against the efficiency and the speed dimensions. The matrix of interactions between poverty and privatization as related to the privatized enterprises very clearly convey about healthy outcomes dispelling the existing belief that privatization results in job losses.

7

Regulation in India: Conformance and Performance

Abstract

India joined the club of reformists in 1991 when it launched New Economic Policy to ensure economic stabilisation and bring about structural adjustments in its highly volatile economy. The government initiated an exercise of having a fresh look of its public enterprise portfolio to only find as to which activities it had to retain in the public sector and which one it was required to privatize. It was realized that a new public-private mix had to be innovated to provide a new stimulus to the economy. In this new regime the government could not have continued both as the producer and controller of the various sectors of the economy. The economic liberalization saw the emergence of private enterprises in the various services sector including telecommunication, power and passenger road transport.

This paper proposes to describe the evolution of regulation in India, its spread to the various sectors of the economy, legal backdrop of regulation, mechanisms and effectiveness of regulation, and its comparability in the international context. Corruption has been a central issue concerning all matters pertaining to good governance. The paper will make an attempt to examine as to whether the present regulatory practices have acted as an effective deterrent to corruption. The paper will examine in detail the regulation of power and telecom sectors. In doing so, an attempt will be made to study the impact of regulation on the development of these two sectors in terms of growth of the services provided, spatial distribution of the facilities, trends in costs and tariffs, and their accessibility to the poor. The state of customer relationship management (CRM) will be studied to ascertain the aspect of co-value creation. The models of regulation pertaining to these two sectors as related to the central government and the state governments will also be discussed to reveal the extent of both the convergence and divergence. One issue that the paper will highlight is the autonomy and independence of the regulators. Instances of 'Regulator Capture' have been legion in the liberalized economies. Following this, the paper makes some suggestions to strengthen the regulatory framework in India

Backdrop

India joined the club of reformists in 1991 when it launched New Economic Policy to ensure economic stabilization and bring about structural adjustments in its highly volatile economy. The government initiated an exercise of having a fresh look of its public enterprise portfolio to only find as to which activities it had to retain in the public sector and which one it was required to privatize. It was realized that a new *public-private mix* had to be innovated to provide a new stimulus to the economy. Whereas, the extinction of the entire public sector was not possible, its continued domination was also not felt necessary in order to step up the rate of economic growth for the country and thereby reduce the levels of poverty and enhance the competitiveness of the Indian economy. In this new regime the government could not have continued both as the producer and controller of the various sectors of the economy. The economic liberalization saw the emergence of private enterprises in the various services sector including telecommunication, power and passenger road transport. In the field of financial services, the denationalization of banks gave a fillip to the setting up of the private sector banks. The transactions in the capital market received a big boost both due to the deregulation and globalization. The availability of food grains constituted the life line of the country. With the success of the green revolution initiated in 1970s, it became imperative on the government to assure an economic price to the farmers and also to a large sector of society which was below poverty line. All this impelled the government to introduce regulation in the various sectors of the Indian economy to ensure a level playing field for the public and the privates sector in India and Indian industry as opposed to its counter parts globally.

Scope

This paper proposes to describe the evolution of regulation in India, its spread to the various sectors of the economy, legal backdrop of regulation, mechanisms and effectiveness of regulation, and its comparability in the international context. Corruption has been a central issue concerning all matters pertaining to good governance. The paper will make an attempt to examine as to whether the present regulatory practices have acted as an effective deterrent to corruption. The paper will examine in detail the regulation of power and telecom sectors. In doing so, an attempt will be made to study the impact of regulation on the development of these two sectors in terms of growth of the services provided, spatial distribution of the facilities, trends in costs and tariffs, and their accessibility to the poor. The state of customer relationship management (CRM) will be studied to ascertain the aspect of co-value creation. The models of regulation pertaining to these two sectors as related to the central government and the state governments will also be discussed to reveal the extent of both the convergence and divergence. One issue that the paper will highlight is the autonomy and independence of the regulators. Instances of 'Regulator Capture' have been legion in the liberalized economies. The regulator capture takes place mostly through the appointments of retired civil servants or people belonging to party in power. There have been cases when a top ranking jurist has been appointed as chief of a regulatory body but in protocol he is placed below the permanent secretary of a specific government department. Following this, the paper makes some suggestions to strengthen the regulatory framework in India.

Evolution of Regulation in India

India has been a highly regulated State. There has been hardly any economic activity which was left unregulated during the period 1960-1990. India became an independent country in 1947. The first flush of regulation came in 1951 when the Indian Planning Commission was setup to guide the allocation of economic and financial resources for the central and the state governments in terms of the national priorities laid down by the National Development Council –NDC- headed by the Prime Minister of India and its membership composed of Chief Ministers of some of the provinces and some of the Cabinet Ministers of the central government. Of the 25 per cent of the public expenditure incurred by the central and the state governments, about 12.5 per cent is disbursed through plan grants by the Planning Commission and similar bodies set up by the various states in India. The public utilities have had a long history of regulation in India. The power sector was been controlled by the Electricity Supply Act, 1948 and the Indian Electricity Act, 1910. The Department of Telecommunications regulates the telecomm sector under the Wireless Telegraphic Act, 1933 and the Indian Telegraphic Act, 1885; the central government, state governments, Directorate General of Shipping, and dock labour boards regulate the port sector under the Ports Act, 1908, the Major Port Trusts Act, 1963, the Merchants Shipping Act, 1958, and the Dock Workers (safety, health and welfare) Act, 1986. The commercial banks were controlled by the Indian Banking Companies Regulation Act, 1948. The Indian Railways were regulated by the Indian Railways Act, 1934. The Reserve Bank of India Act, 1934 was passed to regulate the financial sector in India.

The regulatory framework created during the period 1960-1990 was based on the premise that public sector is above board in terms of its efficient operations, that private sector needed to be heavily regulated and that the government was not coming in conflict with the interest of people at consumer and user of the services by acting both as the provider and the regulator. There was also the implied belief that accountability to the government and through the government to the Parliament or the legislature was adequate to ensure transparency and that no objectivity in regulation or disclosure to the public was necessary. This form of regulation or control resulted in one or more of the following :

- unlimited discretionary powers to the service providers
- operational inefficiency and poor quality of service
- lack of transparency in the decision-making process and of accountability
- high barriers to entry and negligible flow of private capital
- financial mismanagement and laxity
- lack of protection of consumer interest with non-competitive prices and restricted consumer choices.

The introduction of new economic policy (NEP) in July, 1991 seriously looked at the deficient regulatory framework and established the need for separating the 'provider state' from the 'regulatory state'. This encouraged the government to setup the Central Electricity Regulatory Commission and the State Electricity Regulatory Commissions (SERC) through an Act in 1993. The Telecom Regulatory Authority of India (TRAI) was set up in 2000. Earlier as a part of economic liberalization, the Securities and Exchange Board of India (SEBI) was set up in

1989 to regulate the functioning of the stock exchanges in India, primary market and secondary market, and merchant bankers. The Non-Banking Finance Companies Act was enacted in 1996 to regulate the working of financial institutions which performed financial services other than the commercial banking. The insurance sector was brought under the umbrella of the Insurance Regulatory and Development Authority (IDRA) through an Act of 1996. The Indian Airports Authority was set up in 1992 to oversee the functioning of the airports. In many states, the move is afoot to set up State Transport Authorities to regulate the passenger road transport. A Board has been set up to control prices of drug and pharmaceuticals companies. There is a move to set up a regulatory authority in the field of iron and steel. A petroleum regulatory authority and the tariff authority for major ports is also in the offing. The central purpose behind setting up these regulatory bodies is to be even handed with both the public and private sector firms providing common services and producing similar goods in order to protect the consumer interest by motivating well intentioned competition. It is important to note that India is tending to become a regulatory state in future.

Objectives of Regulation in India

The objectives of regulation in India comprise promoting competition, preventing profiteering, providing universal services, preventing self destructive price competition, and protecting customers, employees and environment from unjustifiable behavior of firms. The regulation has three main aims in India: to protect consumers from abuse by firms with substantial market power, to support investment by protecting investors from arbitrary action by government and to promote economic efficiency.

Sectoral Coverage of Regulation in India

The sectoral coverage of regulation in India extends from regulation of tariff, ensuring quality of services, improving efficiency and productivity, ensuring fair competition in the sector to protect consumer interest, resolution of disputes between different players, and preventing cartelization.

Attributes of Regulation in India

An important issue relating to the functioning of the regulatory authorities is independence. In this context the term independence has been subject to different interpretations, whereas, some experts use it interchangeably with autonomy others perceive greater or lesser difference in meaning between the terms. The independence for regulators is expected to consist of three elements: arm's – length relationship with regulated firms, consumers and other private interests, arms-length relationship with political authorities, and specific organizational autonomy such as earmarked funding and exemption from restrictive civil services salary rules, necessary to foster the requisite expertise and to underpin those arm's – length relationship.

Safeguards for Regulation in India

The various legislations embody a number of formal safeguards for the functioning of regulators independently. These safeguards provide regulators a distinct legal mandate freeing them of ministerial control, prescribe professional criteria for appointment of regulators, involve both the executives and the legislative wings in the appointment process, appoint regulators for fixed terms and protect them from arbitrary removal, exempt the regulators from civil service salary rules that make it difficult to attract and retain well qualified professionals, and provide the regulatory bodies with a reliable source of funding usually earmarked levies on regulated firms or consumers.

Functional characteristics of Regulation in India

Some of the functional characteristics of regulatory institutions are outlined as below:

Functional Characteristics of Regulating Authorities in India

Regulatory Authority	*Appointment, removal of members*	*Funding*	*Regulatory process*
Telecom Regulatory Authority of India (TRAI 2000)	5 Members, appointment by GoI, and removal by GoI	TRAI general fund	Consultative
Tarrif Authority for Major Ports (TAMP 1997)	3 Commissioners appointment by GoI, and removal by GoI	Ministry's budget	Consultative
Central Electricity Regulatory Commission (CERC 1998)	5 Members, appointment by GoI through selection committee, removal by president on recommendation by supreme court	Consolidated fund of India (charged)	Public hearing, central advisory commission

(Contd.)

(Contd. Table)

Regulatory Authority	*Appointment, removal of members*	*Funding*	*Regulatory process*
State Electricity Regulatory Commissions (SERC under ERC Act 1998)	3 Members appointment by state government through selection committee and removal by the state government following a report by high court	State consolidated fund (charged)	State advisory commission, public hearing
OERC (Orissa Electricity Regulatory Commission (1996)	3 members appointment by State government through selection committee and removal by the state government following a report by high court	State consolidated fund (Charged)	State advisory commission public hearings

Independence and Accountability : The Twin aspects of Regulation in India

The conflict between independence and accountability is assuming serious dimensions in so far as the functioning of regulators is concerned. The issue is complex and there can not be any final word on it. However, the following measures need to be taken to reconcile independence with accountability: independence needs to be reconciled with measures to ensure that the regulator is accountable for its action, checks and balances are required to ensure that the regulator does not stray from its mandate, engage in corrupt practices or become crossly inefficient, striking the proper balance between accountability and independence in difficult but the following measures have been adopted by a ground number of countries, mandating rigorous transparency including open decision making and publication of decisions and the reasons for those decisions, prohibiting conflicts of interest, providing effective arrangements for appealing the agency's decisions, providing for scrutiny of the agency's budget usually by the legislature, subjecting the regulators conduct and efficiency to scrutiny by eternal auditors or other public watchdogs, and permitting the regulators removal from office in cases of proven misconduct or incapacity. Only TRAI and IRDA have been allowed to levy fees and charges, and have their own funds. The CERC, SERCs and TAMP are wholly dependent on the government for funding. The CERC also requires the approval of the government for the creation of posts. Although this requirement has not been specifically mentioned for TAMP, it is evident that government approval is necessary as the government has to approve TAMP's budget. In the cases of most of the regulatory authorities the decision to supersede them is left to the discretion of the government which could be a threat to their autonomy. The relationship between the government and the relevant authority has also not been defined in most of the enactments giving birth to these authorities in the absence of which disputes have arisen between the government and such authorities compelling them to proceed to the appropriate court. The acts are also silent on the issue of transparency of the regulatory authorities. Excepting CERC, SERCs, TAMP and TRAI which have been directed to ensure transparency while excising their powers and discharging their functions through open public hearings, accessibility of proceedings and formal discussions, the other regulatory authorities are not mandated to comply with any such provisions. So far as, powers are concerned, the position of the various regulatory authorities is not the same TRAI is a civil court, the CERC is not, although it is a quasi-judicial body with the powers of the civil court for certain limited purposes. The IRA and TAMP have not been given any of these powers. TRAI has been declared a civil court and given powers under Section 195 and Chapter XXVI of the CrPC 1973, whereas the powers of the CERC have been restricted under Sections 345 and 346 of Chapter XXVI of the CrPC 1973. Thus, TRAI has full powers to prosecute for contempt of lawful authority of public servants, offences against public justice, and offences relating to documents given as evidence, whereas the CERC does not have these powers and can only summarily proceed in the matter of contempt. As pointed out earlier, TAMP has no powers even to access documents, call for attendance, etc. Again as regards penal provisions for non-compliance of orders, the provisions in the TRAI Act are more rigorous than those in the ERC Act while there are no such provisions in the case of TAMP and the IRDA.

The relation between regulators at the centre and in the states is another crucial issue in autonomy. It is interesting to note that the mechanism for interaction between the central and state regulatory authorities has not been structured in India especially keeping in backdrop the fact that it is a union of states. While the CERC Act has provisions which are more in the nature of guidelines, for the setting up of the SERCs the Act does not address the relationship between the central and state bodies in dealing with interstate transmission issues. The role of TAMP has been restricted to the major ports, without any thought being given to the need for regulation of tariff in the minor or private ports and implication of tariff regulation in one category of ports without any regulation in the other category.

Regulation of Telecom and Power Sectors in India

The telecom and the power sectors have become the growth engine in India. The information technology and software sector is another driver of growth. Incidentally, the information technology and software sector is not regulated formally by a body appointed under enactment. However, a voluntary association known as National Association of Software and Service Companies (NASSCOM) which is recognised by the government acts as a regulatory organisation for this sector. The telecom, power, and software sectors have registered an unprecedented growth in terms of the volume of business, contribution to the gross domestic product, profitability, competitiveness, quality, salaries to employees, value addition and customer delight. The prices of telecom services and products have registered an amazing decline. The TRAI is considering to introduce a uniform charge for local and subscriber's trunck dialing(STD). The rates of STD have already decline to 1/15 as compared to the charges in vogue in 1991. The charges for international subscriber's dialing (ISD) have decline to 1/5 during the same period. A host of services are being extended without any extra charge (eg., call forward facility, voice mail, group dialing, etc.). The mobile telephoning has caused a great revolution in India which has now more than ten million mobile phone holders and 50 million landline phone holders. India expects this number to touch 120 million by 2010. The sector has participation from not only public and private sector firms but also foreign firms. The sector has been allowed to have 75 per cent foreign direct investments (FDI). The power sector has undergone a similar revolution. Just after the independence in August 1947, India was generating 1500

MW of power. Since the introduction of the new economic policy, India now generates 1,40,000 MW of power. The Electricity Act, 2003 provides for open access and participation of both the domestic and global firms in the generation, transmission, and distribution of power. The transmission losses are been curbed, financial losses are being reduced, downsizing of manpower is being undertaken, and modernization of the sector is progressing to make it globally competitive. The sector was thrown open for FDI in 1991 itself.

The introduction of regulation in the telecom and power sectors has changed the focus of work from production (output) to customer. These two sectors have become customer centric. The complaints are attended to very promptly. The people's courts have been setup for grievance redressal. The production, transmission and administrative processes are being revisited to make them customer friendly. The partnership of the customers in different processes is being ensured to improve constantly the customer satisfaction.

Future concerns

The regulation had made a good mark in India but it has to go a long way in future. Some of the regulatory concerns for future are mentioned below:

1. The effectiveness of regulation is being impeded by the multiplicity of regulatory bodies and enactments. Is it desirable to have an overreaching legislation across various sectors with sector – specific differences being covered under subordinate legislation
2. Should such an overreaching legislation specify details on the various facets of regulation?
3. How could the regulatory bodies discharge more effectively the task of consumer protection, consumer education and consumer grievances?
4. How should regulation keep pace with economic environment? Who will initiate changes in regulation?

5. How should regulator assess the firms under its control?
6. Should there be a permanent forum for the regulatory bodies to share their experiences?
7. How should government be encouraged to shed their powers and leave regulation to authorities with the necessary objectivity and expertise?
8. What changes in the regulatory framework should be brought about to take care of the conflict interests of these centre and the states?
9. How should the regulatory bodies promote the cause of the knowledge management to improve the working of various institutions in their ambit?

To conclude, the regulatory frame work in India is in line with its socio-economic- politico requirements. However, there is a need to make the framework more compatible with international practices.

8

State Level Public Enterprises in Assam: Performance Problems and Prospects

Abstract

Assam is socially, politically and economically a strategic state of the Indian Union in the north-east. The performance of the State Level Public Enterprises (SLPEs) is crucial in attaining the goals of the socio-economic policy for the State, on the one hand, and setting a trend for financially vibrant performance of the SLPEs in the other states of the region, on the other. The purpose of this paper is to discuss the genesis, growth, objectives, financial and budgetary profile, and forms of organization, activity classification, problems and prospects for the SLPEs in Assam. The paper also incorporates the initiatives that have been taken to reform and restructure the SLPEs. Finally, the paper presents a futuristic framework for the successful functioning of the SLPEs in Assam.

Genesis, Growth and Objectives

Assam, including the present-day Meghalaya, Mizoram and Nagaland, had no SLPEs during the pre-Independence era as compared to Karnataka, Kerala, Tamilnadu, Rajasthan and

Table 1
Plan-wise Enterprises

Sectors	Five-Year Plans										
	I	*II*	*III*	*IV*	*V*	*VI*	*VII*	*VIII*	*IX*	*X*	*Total*
Manufacturing	0	1	4	7	1	1	2	2	0	0	**18**
Trading & Services	1	2	0	0	0	0	0	0	0	0	**3**
Financial	1	0	2	0	0	0	0	0	0	0	**3**
Promotional	0	0	0	1	2	1	1	4	0	0	**9**
Welfare	0	0	0	0	3	0	0	0	3	0	**6**
Utilities	0	0		1	1		1	2		5	**10**
Total	**2**	**3**	**6**	**9**	**7**	**2**	**4**	**8**	**3**	**5**	**49**

Source: IPE Database on SLPEs in India.

several other states which had some SLPEs on the eve of their formation. The total dependence on agriculture and lack of education about the benefits of industrialization was responsible for this phenomenon. The policy makers in the State as a part of their plan of placing it on the all-India map of industrialization and development, set up the Assam State Financial Corporation as the first SLPE in 1954. Table 1 shows the growth of SLPEs during the Five-Year Plans. Table 1 reveals that the maximum numbers of SLPEs were set up during the Fourth and Eighth Five-Year Plans. Most of the enterprises set up during the two

Table 2
Financial Profile of SLPEs in Assam

(Rs in crore)

Items / *Years*	*2002-03*	*2003-04*	*2004-05*	*2005-06*
1. Total no. of SLPEs	42	42	43	49
2. No. of Working SLPEs	32	32	33	39
3. No. of Non-Working SLPEs (i) Under liquidation (ii) Under Closure (iii) Under Merger (iv) Others	10	10	10	10
4. Total Equity	1828.84	1829.37	1786.91	1230.25
5. Total Debt	2351.06	624.73	2556.07	753.93
6. Total Investment	4179.90	2454.10	4342.98	1984.15
7. No. of Profit making enterprises	6	6	7	7
8. No.of Loss making enterprises	33	34	32	32
9. Net Profit/Loss	-691.61	-727.47	-670.94	-1035.94
10. Accumulated Loss (-)/Profit	4944.40	4503.01	5268.40	-6465.55

Source: Reports of the Comptroller and Auditor General of India (Commercial), on Assam for 2002-03 to 2005-06.

plans were in the nature of manufacturing and promotional enterprises which were required to provide fillip to the use of local resources and strengthen private sector development. The entities in power sector dominated the setting up of new SLPEs in Assam during Ninth Plan. As a matter of fact, the new entities were carved out of the Assam State Electricity Board.

Profile of SLPEs in Assam

Table 2 presents the profile of the SLPEs in Assam in terms of working and non-working SLPEs and their total equity, total debt, total investment, profit/loss making, and accumulated losses / profit.

The table shows that the non-working enterprises form a significant chunk of the total number of the SLPEs. It is clear from the table that the total investment is on decline both because of decline in debt and equity due repayment/adjustment of equity and loans on account of restructuring of the Assam State Electricity Board into five companies. The net losses are on increase resulting in a heavy buildup of accumulated losses in these enterprises which are about three and a half times of their total investment.

Budgetary Support to SLPEs in Assam

The budgetary support is steadily increasing. The budgetary support has been extended through the route of subsidies. It is worth noting here that the guarantees outstanding against the SLPEs were to the tune of Rs. 407.29 crores during the year 2005-06.

Sectoral Analysis of SLPEs in Assam

The sectoral analysis of SLPEs in Assam has been undertaken by classifying the SLPEs into 6 cognizant groups viz., Manufacturing, Trading and Services, Financial, Promotional, Welfare and Utilities. Sector-wise SLPEs list is

Table 3

Budgetary Support to SLPEs in Assam

	2003-04				*2004-05*				*2005-06*			
	Companies		*Corporation*		*Companies*		*Corporation*		*Companies*		*Corporation*	
	No	*Amount*	*No*	*Amount*	*No*	*Amount*	*No*	*Amount*	*No*	*Amount*	*No*	*Amount*
Equity Capital from Budget	-	-	-	-	-	-	-	-	-	-	-	-
Loans Given from Budget	2	23.38	3	701.39	1	3.02	3	775.23	2	122.78	1	1053.46
Grants towards Projects, Programmes/Schemes	-	-	1	0.10	-	-	-	-	-	-	-	-
Subsidy	-	-	1	0.10	-	-	-	-	-	-	-	-
Total outgo	2	23.38	4	701.49	1	3.02	3	775.23	2	122.78	1	1053.46

Source: Reports of the Comptroller and Auditor General of India (Commercial), on Assam for 2003-04 to 2005-06.

given in Annexure 1. The Planning Commission and 8th, 9th, 10th and 11th Finance Commissions have formulated optimal rates of return that the SLPEs should yield in each group of these enterprises on the basis of the framework developed by the Institute of Public Enterprise (IPE) in its studies[4]. As per the yardstick rates of return, the Manufacturing Enterprises, Trading and Services, Financial, Promotional, Welfare and Utilities should earn rates of return of the order of 12 per cent, 10 per cent, 8 per cent, 5 per cent, 4 per cent and 12 per cent, respectively. The sectoral position of the SLPEs shows that on the whole their profitability was dismal. Broadly the classification suggests that the enterprises involved in manufacture of products come under manufacturing sector. The enterprises such as the Handlooms and Handicrafts Development Corporations and the State Trading Corporation can be brought under trading and marketing enterprises. The enterprises such as the Industrial Development Corporations and the State Finance Corporations can be classified as financing institutions whereas enterprises like Small Scale Industrial Development Corporations, Mineral Development Corporations and Fisheries Development Corporations can be classified as promotional enterprises. The welfare enterprises are those which have as their mission the task of improving the welfare of some targeted group of people or area. The Backward Classes Corporations and the Scheduled Castes Corporations come under this category. Annexure-2 gives Sector-wise financial data.

Manufacturing Sector SLPEs in Assam

Table 4 shows that despite increasing total investment, the SLPEs in manufacturing sector have been incurring losses in the backdrop of the fact that during 1997-98 and 1998-99, they were making profits. The accumulated losses have been of the order of about 20 per cent of the total investment. The capital employed has not been used productively.

Table 4
Financial Performance of Manufacturing Sector SLPEs in Assam

(Rs. In Crore)

Year	*Total Investment*	*Net Profit / Loss*	*Reserves and Surplus*	*Accumulated losses*	*Net Worth*	*Capital Employed*
1997-98	235.66	18.36	0.5	45.16	29.77	119.33
1998-99	226.25	21.11	0.71	53.62	5.48	111.54
1999-00	220.07	21	0.93	-65.62	5.72	144.24
2000-01	218.05	21.77	1.19	-53.63	6.04	174.77
2001-02	231.74	22.33	1.46	-67.41	6.3	199.29
2002-03	236.14	22.36	1.76	-63.95	4.59	185.85
2003-04	191.42	16.06	1.76	-63.95	152.18	207.37
2004-05	287.72	29.78	1.76	-63.95	67.81	226.57

Source: IPE Database on SLPEs in India.

Trading and Service Sector SLPEs in Assam

The enterprises in this category are highly profit making in the other states due to their unique feature of faster turnover and minimal capital employed. Table 5 shows that the net worth of these enterprises was less than the total investment and the capital employed indicating an absence of vigilant financial supervision.

Table 5
Financial Performance of Trading and Service Sector SLPEs in Assam

(Rs. In Crore)

Year	*Total Investment*	*Net Profit*	*Reserves and Surplus*	*Accumulated losses*	*Net Worth*	*Capital Employed*
1997-98	17.86	-0.21	0	3.7	9.76	21.26
1998-99	16.27	-0.21	0	-2.38	0	13.51
1999-00	16.32	-0.21	0	-2.38	0	12.32
2000-01	16.9	-0.21	0	-3.14	0	16.91
2001-02	16.9	-0.21	0	-3.14	0	16.91
2002-03	16.9	-0.21	0	-3.14	0	16.91
2003-04	17.77	0.05	0	-3.14	15.74	19.58
2004-05	19.97	-0.04	0	-3.14	10.21	16.35

Source: IPE Database on SLPEs in India.

Promotional Sector SLPEs in Assam

The promotional enterprises were set up to foster economic activity in the various regions of Assam and attend to the needs of certain sections of society. However, these enterprises did not take care of their well being and incurred net losses to erode the net worth. Table 6 shows the financial position of the enterprises in the promotional sector.

Table 6
Financial Performance of Promotional Sector SLPEs in Assam

(Rs. In Crore)

Year	*Total Investment*	*Net Profit*	*Reserves and Surplus*	*Accumulated Profits / losses*	*Net Worth*	*Capital Employed*
1997-98	38.91	0.05	9.51	3.32	0.57	35.69
1998-99	39.93	0.05	10.07	3.32	-0.15	30.05
1999-00	89.61	-0.24	10.11	-8.83	-0.13	77.89
2000-01	90.7	-0.34	10.12	-75.8	-0.67	75.04
2001-02	90.85	-0.23	10.12	-10.98	-1.01	60.57
2002-03	91.19	0.03	10.12	-10.95	-0.81	60.91
2003-04	95.89	-1.633	10.12	-10.95	7.9	62.16
2004-05	96.2029	-1.49	10.12	-10.95	10.38	62.14

Source: IPE Database on SLPEs in India.

Financial Sector SLPEs in Assam

The enterprises in this sector are involved in promoting the entrepreneurship to step up the development of small and medium industrial units. Table 7 shows that the total investment in these enterprises is on decline possibly because of the drawl of the equity support of the central financial institutions in the event of non-payment of dues. The counterparts of these enterprises in Andhra Pradesh, Uttar Pradesh, Rajasthan and Karnataka have been doing well.

Table 7
Financial Performance of Financial Sector SLPEs in Assam

(Rs. In Crore)

Year	*Total Investment*	*Net Profit*	*Reserves and Surplus*	*Accumulated Losses*	*Net Worth*	*Capital Employed*
1997-98	220.08	-12.48	53.16	-100.86	114.73	135.72
1998-99	223.44	-11.25	53.16	-68.57	109.95	136.25
1999-00	221.23	-9.66	53.16	-72.53	106.87	137.15
2000-01	222.52	-9.09	62.34	-77.9	105.73	138.44
2001-02	224.81	-8.73	62.34	-82.97	100.69	140.73
2002-03	225.03	-4.33	62.34	-83.12	100.54	140.95
2003-04	170.19	-5.42	62.34	-13.45	231.67	193.04
2004-05	191.52	-0.96	62.34	-62.62	145.05	75.52

Source: IPE Database on SLPEs in India.

Welfare Sector SLPEs in Assam

The financial performance of the welfare sector enterprises was in cloud. Although they have been set up to cater to the needs of the depressed classes of society, their well being was endangered by continuous loss making and equity erosion.

Utility Sector SLPEs in Assam

The utility SLPEs comprise the Assam State Road Transport Corporation, Assam State Power Development Corporation, Assam State Electricity Board and the various distribution companies. In the case of all these enterprises the total investment is predominated by debt which resulted in a sub-optimal debt-equity ratio leading to incurrence of heavy

Table 8
Financial Performance of Welfare Sector SLPEs in Assam

(Rs. In Crore)

Year	*Total Investment*	*Net Profit*	*Reserves and Surplus*	*Accumulated losses*	*Net Worth*	*Capital Employed*
1997-98	11.27	2.22	0	0.31	0	2.22
1998-99	11.27	2.22	0	0.31	0	2.22
1999-00	12.27	2.74	0	-0.62	0	2.74
2000-01	21.79	4.02	0	-0.73	0	4.02
2001-02	11.27	2.22	0	0.31	0	2.22
2002-03	11.27	2.22	0	0.31	0	2.22
2003-04	31.02	9.69	0	0.3	-9.55	9.69
2004-05	38.99	3.11	0	0.3	-24	3.11

Source: IPE Database on SLPEs in India.

losses by these enterprises. Table 9 depicts the financial performance of these enterprises.

Problems

An intensive study of the working of the SLPEs in Assam suggests the following as the major problem areas:

(i) Incidence of Sickness: About half of the SLPEs have been incurring cash losses. Of these the major losses have been incurred by the Assam State Electricity Board, Assam Tea Corporation, Cachar Sugar Mills and Assam Fertilizer and Chemicals Ltd. A decision will have to be taken to attempt the restructuring and revitalization of these enterprises. The predominance of the social responsibilities has also caused a

Table 9

Financial Performance of Utility Sector SLPEs in Assam

(Rs. In Crores)

Year	*Total Investment*	*Net Profit*	*Reserves and Surplus*	*Accumulated losses*	*Net Worth*	*Capital Employed*
1997-98	3147.94	-28.26	10.6	126.74	19.65	2126.61
1998-99	3163.53	-31.77	10.68	96.64	5.22	2111.89
1999-00	3033.34	-35.56	10.68	-2175.1	-15.55	1985.18
2000-01	3049.21	-42.05	10.68	-2765.2	-40.06	1631.14
2001-02	3091.71	-35.69	10.7	-2799.2	-31.54	1639.14
2002-03	3149.07	-23.47	10.9	-2821	4.2	1682.41
2003-04	1793.31	-722.08	10.9	-2821	607.31	882.9
2004-05	3725.74	-682.04	10.9	-2820.4	-1516.3	691.73

Source: IPE Database on SLPEs in India.

great burden in the case of these enterprises and it will have to be seen as to what could be done to overcome this paradox.

(ii) Ineffective Management: The improper selection of top level executives, frequent transfers of their chief executives and lack of management expertise in the areas of Finance and Marketing have emerged as the major bottlenecks confronting these enterprises. The surplus manpower has added fuel to the fire. Despite this, these enterprises even then have not been able to keep pace with their production schedules. The administrative personnel are overstaffed whereas there has been inadequate staffing of the shop-floor.

(iii) Operational Snags: These include unscientific inventory management, raw materials and marketing problems and power shortages. The power problems have hit these enterprises hard during the last 10 years. Frequent load shedding and breakdowns have resulted in heavy losses. The Assam State Electricity Board and the carved out entities have not been able to rise up to the expectations. The inventory problems are of dual nature. There has been overstocking of materials unrelated to business operations. On the other, there has been an acute shortage of certain critical spare parts. Transport costs have inflated the prices and the best prices for the products have not been obtained on account of an aggressive marketing management. It is interesting to note that same raw-materials were procured by the different enterprises at different prices.

(iv) Absence of Professionalism: The reflection of the general backwardness of Assam has linkages with the management systems of the SLPEs. The business like work-culture is yet to penetrate into most of the SLPEs. This situation is epitomized in the fact that professionalisation of management is still a distant goal in Assam. Most of the Managing Directors are deputationists from the State Administrative Services who may not have any previous experience in management of enterprises and they are frequently transferred. Distinction between financial management and book-keeping is yet to be recognized in most of the SLPEs. Management Information System is still an unknown development in the SLPEs in Assam. Only few SLPEs have cost and chartered accountants on their rolls. The job of Personal Manager in most SLPEs is performed by the junior rank administrative officers. It is worth mentioning here that Assam faces the dearth of professionally competent workforce for its SLPEs. The SLPEs have not prepared training plans to enhance the human resource potentials. Perhaps a mention of Internal Audit system may be made as an illustration. It is a known technique and many SLPEs utilize it. However, the system is designed to serve only accounting purposes but not financial management purposes.

(v) Boards of Management: The power of appointing the Boards of Management in Statutory Corporations and Government Companies vests in the Government. This power as regards the SLPEs in the Cooperative sector has also been taken over by the Government. The number of members of the Boards in case of each SLPE is determined as per provisions of the articles of association or relevant rules of the SLPEs. The Board of the Assam State Electricity Board consists of 3 to 7 members. In other cases, broadly speaking, around 11 members constitute the Boards. There has been no fixed tenures of the Boards. In some cases, the Boards have been reconstituted frequently. There are no norms about the frequency of holding meetings of the boards. Even ministers and Civil Servants are appointed as members of the Board.

(vi) Monitoring and Evaluation: A negotiated performance evaluation system did not exist for the SLPEs in the State. The objective of the SLPEs, their corporate mission, their annual plans and targets were not being formulated by these enterprises. The targets for different stages of the project implementation were not quantified in terms of time and cost. All these factors combined together made the problem of monitoring and evaluation very complicated. However, the MoU system found its place in the monitoring and evaluation during the fiscal 2006-07. The system operates in form but lacks spirit.

(vii) Social Consideration: The public aspect has overtaken the enterprises considerations in the case of many SLPEs. The Assam State Electricity Board has incurred huge losses on account of rural electrification. The Assam State Transport Corporation has piled up losses due to extension of its services to remote and hilly routes and also on account of Guwahati city services.

(viii) Financial Crisis: Many SLPEs are faced with mounting overdues to financial institutions and banks. Non-payment of salaries and deposition of Provident Fund (PF) due to resource crunch is another problem in this realm. The debt-equity ratio of many of these enterprises is adverse. Working capital crisis has crippled their day-to-day operations.

(ix) Non-Finalization of Annual Accounts: Like the SLPEs in other states of the Indian Union, the SLPEs in Assam also suffered from this acute problem. As many as 16 out of the 49 SLPEs had not finalized their annual reports and accounts for 11 to 20 years as on August 8th, 2005. The SLPEs having their accounts in arrears between 6 and 10 years numbered 10 as on the same date. The main reasons responsible for the non-finalization of accounts include improper records, lack of sufficient accounts personnel, improper accounting systems, extension of accounting year pursuant to the change in the Income Tax Law and delay in Statutory Auditors appointment by the Company Law Board.

Reforms

The SLPEs reforms have attracted the attention of the Government of Assam from time to time. Several reviews on the performance of the SLPEs were conducted at different levels during the period 1999-2000 to 2004-05. These include the high level reviews conducted by Public Enterprises Department, Government of Assam, (July-August, 2001 and subsequently), Committee on Fiscal Reforms (2001), Committee on State Public Sector Enterprises (2003), Asian Development Bank (2004), Chief Secretary Government of Assam (2004), Chief Minister, Government of Assam (2005), the Committee on State Public Sector Enterprises (April, 2005). As a part of reform measures, besides the acceptance of the recommendations emerging from these high level reviews, the Government of Assam has introduced the system of execution of Memorandum of Understanding (MoU), between the administrative departments and selected SLPEs from 2005-06, set up an empowered committee to rationalize the human resource in the SLPEs and take up a social safety net programme for the employees released under the voluntary retirement scheme and introduce the concept of Chairperson-cum-Managing Director in selected SLPEs through the public enterprise selection board.

The thrust of the suggestions of many of these studies is about closure of the SLPEs that are neither capable of being privatized nor being revived, privatization of SLPEs that cannot or are not required to be revived and creation of fund for payment of liabilities in respect of the SLPEs that are to be privatized and for paying working capital margin money and other requirements for SLPEs to be revived. The reviews have suggested the tenure for the CEO has three years. The reform measures dealing with accountability issues suggest introduction of bottom-up accountability structures through workers participation and interest group representation. The reviews have also dealt with enterprise- specific remedies. It has been suggested that the Assam State Electricity Board should reduce T&D losses, Assam State Transport Corporation may improve its fleet utilization and reduce he bus-staff ratio, Assam Gas Company Limited may exploit further potential. Assam Industrial Development Corporation Limited and Assam Financial Corporation may go in for restructuring and intensify recoveries, Assam State Textile Corporation may offer one-time settlement to financial institutions and handover the mill by transfer of shares. Cachar sugar mill Limited may be put up for out right sale and Assam Fertilizer and Chemicals Limited may be revived. The reviews further suggest that the Assam State Housing Board should go in for commercial housing schemes.

Annexure- 3 provides the enterprise-wise problems identified and recommendations to deal with the identified problems by the review meeting held by the Government of Assam on September 4, 2003. Annexure-4 provides the summary of recommendations of the report on state public sector enterprises submitted on July 17, 2003.

Conclusion

The losses incurred by the SLPEs in Assam were about 38 per cent of the state's own tax revenue. The Gross Fiscal Impact on the state finances could be seen from the fact that the losses incurred by the SLPEs in Assam were about 115 per cent of the state's own tax revenue. It is high time that an action oriented approach is initiated to make the SLPEs a vibrant part of the economy of Assam.

Annexure-1

Sector-wise List of SLPEs
Assam

Financial

1. Assam Financial Corporation
2. Assam Industrial Development Corporation Limited

Manufacturing

3. Assam Seeds Corporation Limited
4. Assam Agro-Industries Development Corporation Limited
5. Assam Livestock and Poultry Corporation Limited
6. Assam Tea Corporation Limited
7. Assam Gas Company Limited
8. Assam Petrochemicals Limited (Subsidiary of AIDC Ltd.)
9. Ashok Paper Mills (Assam) Limited
10. Assam Conductor and Tubes Limited
11. Assam Electronics Development Corporation Limited
12. Assam State textile Corporation Limited
13. Assam Mineral Development Corporation Limited
14. Assam Police Housing Corporation Limited
15. Assam Government Construction Corporation Limited
16. Assam State Fertilizers and Chemicals limited (Subsidiary of AIDC Limited)

17. Assam State Text Book Production and Publication Limited
18. Industrial Papers (Assam) Limited (Subsidiary of AIDC Limited)
19. Amtron Sen Electronics Limited
20. Assam Spun Silk Mills Limited
21. Assam Polytex Limited (Subsidiary of AIDC Ltd)
22. Assam Syntex Limited (Subsidiary of AIDC Limited)
23. Assam State Weaving and Manufacturing Company Limited (Subsidiary of AIDC Ltd)
24. Assam & Meghalaya Mineral Development Corporation Limited
25. Cachar Sugar Mills Limited
26. Fertichem Limited
27. Assam Power loom Development Corporation Limited
28. Assam Plantation Crop Development Corporation Limited
29. Assam Plains Tribes Development Corporation Limited
30. Assam Tanneries Limited

Promotional

31. Assam State Minor Irrigation Development Corporation Limited
32. Assam Fisheries Development Corporation Limited
33. Assam Hills Small Industries Development Corporation Limited
34. Assam Small Industries Development Corporation, Limited
35. Assam Tourism Development Corporation Limited
36. Assam State Film (Finance and Development) Corporation Limited

Trade and Service

37. Assam Government Marketing Corporation Limited
38. Assam State Warehousing Corporation

Utility

39. Assam State Electricity Board
40. Assam State Transport Corporation

Welfare

41. Assam State Development Corporation for Other Backward Classes Limited
42. Assam State Development Corporation for Scheduled Cases Limited.

Annexure -2

Sector-wise financial Data of Enterprises in Assam

Assam Financial Corporation						
Financial Year	*Total Investment*	*Surplus Reserves*	*Accumulated losses*	*Net Worth*	*Capital Employed*	*Net Profit*
1997-98	87.18		53.16	-37.55	88.71	0
1998-99	90.01		53.16	0	88.9	-6.05
1999-00	86.9		53.16	0	88.9	-6.05
2000-01	86.9		62.34	0	91.88	-3.66
2001-02	86.9		62.34	0	91.88	-3.66
2002-03	86.9		62.34	0	91.88	-3.66
2003-04	31.54			69.67	87.79	-0.35
2004-05	82.24			20.5	89.32	-0.3
Assam Industrial Development Corp. Ltd.						
1997-98	132.9	0	-63.31	26.02	132.9	-12.48
1998-99	133.43	0	-68.57	21.05	133.43	-5.2
1999-00	134.33	0	-72.53	17.97	134.33	-3.61
2000-01	135.62	0	-77.9	13.85	135.62	-5.43
2001-02	137.91	0	-82.97	8.81	137.91	-5.07
2002-03	138.13	0	-83.12	8.66	138.13	-0.67
2003-04				143.88	190.22	-5.07
2004-05				55.73	72.7	-0.66

(Contd.)

(Contd.Annexure-2)

Assam Seeds Corporation Ltd						
Financial Year	*Total Investment*	*Surplus Reserves*	*Accumulated losses*	*Net Worth*	*Capital Employed*	*Net Profit*
1997-98	5.35	0	12.23	-10.77	-0.26	-1.75
1998-99	5.35	0	12.23	0	-0.26	-1.75
1999-00	5.56	0	-6.66	0	4.78	-1.13
2000-01	5.56	0	-8.03	0	6.01	-1.36
2001-02	11.46	0	-10.43	0	7.79	-0.82
2002-03	11.46	0	-10.43	0	7.79	-0.82
2003-04				2.32	7.07	-1.15
2004-05				2.32	7.07	-1.01
Assam Apex Wavers and Artisans Co-operative Federation Ltd.						
1997-98	7.8	0.5	0	5.27	3.03	0.25
1998-99	11.03	0.71	0	5.48	3.86	0.21
1999-00	14.68	0.93	0	5.72	4.93	0.22
2000-01	18.71	1.19	0	6.04	21.06	0.25
2001-02	22.81	1.46	0	6.3	25.24	0.27
2002-03	30.9	1.76	0	6.88	3.55	0.3
2003-04	30.9	1.76	0	6.88	3.55	0.3
2004-05	30.9	1.76	0	6.88	3.55	0.3

(Contd.)

(Contd.Annexure-2)

Financial Year	Total Investment	Surplus Reserves	Accumulated losses	Net Worth	Capital Employed	Net Profit
Assam Livestock and Poultry Corporation Ltd						
1997-98	2.19	0	0.001	0	0.01	0
1998-99	2.19	0	0.001	0	0.01	0
1999-00	2.19	0	0.001	0	0.01	0
2000-01	2.19	0	0.001	0	0.01	0
2001-02	2.19	0	0.001	0	0.01	0
2002-03	2.19	0	0.001	0	0.01	0
2003-04	0	0	0	-0.09	0.01	-0.009
2004-05	0	0	0	-0.09	0.01	-0.009
Assam Tea Corporation Ltd						
1997-98	59.67	0	48.84	-21.3	11.61	8.81
1998-99	60.45	0	48.84	0	11.61	8.72
1999-00	59.67	0	-30.75	0	42.89	8.24
2000-01	60.45	0	-30.75	0	42.89	9.21
2001-02	60.45	0	-38.67	0	69.7	9.21
2002-03	60.45	0	-38.67	0	69.7	9.21
2003-04	0	0	0	13.15	37.92	2.78
2004-05	0	0	0	5.67	37.92	2.78

(Contd.)

(Contd.Annexure-2)

Financial Year	*Total Investment*	*Surplus Reserves*	*Accumulated losses*	*Net Worth*	*Capital Employed*	*Net Profit*
Assam Gas Company Ltd						
1997-98	27.44	0	0	22.34	41.16	5.41
1998-99	14.46	0	6.26	0	31.68	8.49
1999-00	20.38	0	7.32	0	34.34	8.23
2000-01	16.69	0	10.78	0	42.59	8.23
2001-02	20.38	0	7.32	0	34.34	8.23
2002-03	16.69	0	10.78	0	42.59	8.23
2003-04	17.2261	0	0	94.0939	94.41	14.44
2004-05	110.5	0	0	21.68	115.27	23.46
Assam Petrochemicals Limited						
1997-98	20.08	0	0	29.58	41.52	6.92
1998-99	18.56	0	18.59	0	37.68	6.92
1999-00	18.56	0	3.68	0	43.14	6.92
2000-01	15.24	0	19.09	0	37.97	6.92
2001-02	15.24	0	19.09	0	37.97	6.92
2002-03	15.24	0	19.09	0	37.97	6.92
2003-04	9.1215	0	0	37.2385	37.24	6.75
2004-05	9.12	0	0	39.18	39.18	10.36

(Contd.)

(Contd.Annexure-2)

Financial Year	Total Investment	Surplus Reserves	Accumulated losses	Net Worth	Capital Employed	Net Profit
Assam Electronics Development Corporation Ltd						
1997-98	8.47	0	2.45	5.9	8.51	0
1998-99	9.06	0	-0.61	0	8.51	0
1999-00	9.06	0	-0.87	0	8.7	0
2000-01	9.64	0	-0.87	0	8.7	0
2001-02	9.64	0	-0.87	0	8.7	0
2002-03	9.64	0	-0.87	0	8.7	0
2003-04	12.28	0	0	6.37	9.39	-0.51
2004-05	15.86	0	0	-1.54	4.86	-0.44
Assam Mineral Development Corporation Ltd						
1997-98	7.39	0	2.49	2.39	4.89	0
1998-99	7.38	0	0.16	0	5.96	0
1999-00	7.38	0	-0.74	0	5.06	0
2000-01	7.38	0	-1.48	0	5.43	0
2001-02	7.38	0	-1.48	0	5.43	0
2002-03	7.38	0	-1.48	0	5.43	0
2003-04	7.38	0	0	2.38	4.88	-0.67
2004-05	5.5	0	0	3.88	4.5	-0.15

(Contd.)

(Contd.Annexure-2)

Financial Year	Total Investment	Surplus Reserves	Accumulated losses	Net Worth	Capital Employed	Net Profit
Assam Police Housing Corporation Ltd						
1997-98	0.04	0	-3.41	-3.38	-3.38	-0.79
1998-99	0.04	0	-0.66	0	1.58	-0.79
1999-00	0.03	0	-0.41	0	0.44	-0.79
2000-01	0.03	0	-0.28	0	0.31	-0.79
2001-02	0.03	0	-0.28	0	0.31	-0.79
2002-03	0.03	0	-0.28	0	0.31	-0.79
2003-04	0	0	0	-0.04	-0.04	-0.62
2004-05	0	0	0	-0.04	-0.04	-0.62
Assam State Fertilizers and Chemicals Ltd						
1997-98	8.7	0	7.26	-4.21	-1.8	-0.69
1998-99	9.2	0	-7.25	0	-2.13	-0.69
1999-00	9.68	0	-7.78	0	-1.22	-0.69
2000-01	10.01	0	-7.78	0	-1.22	-0.69
2001-02	10.01	0	-7.78	0	-1.22	-0.69
2002-03	10.01	0	-7.78	0	-1.22	-0.69
2003-04	10.68	0	0	-7.75	-0.82	-1.01
2004-05	10.68	0	0	-7.85	-0.92	-0.26

(Contd.)

(Contd.Annexure-2)

Assam State Text Book Production and Publication Corporation Ltd						
Financial Year	*Total Investment*	*Surplus Reserves*	*Accumulated losses*	*Net Worth*	*Capital Employed*	*Net Profit*
1997-98	1	0	0	3.95	3.79	0.2
1998-99	1	0	0.76	0	2.79	0
1999-00	1	0	1.02	0	2.87	0
2000-01	1	0	1.02	0	2.87	0
2001-02	1	0	1.02	0	2.87	0
2002-03	1	0	1.02	0	2.87	0
2003-04	0	0	0	6.23	6.23	1.3
2004-05	0	0	0	7.64	7.64	0.91
Assam Conductor & Tubes Limited						
1997-98	4.65	0	-0.8	0	0.28	0
1998-99	4.65	0	-0.8	0	0.28	0
1999-00	5.85	0	-0.8	0	0.28	0
2000-01	5.85	0	-1.17	0	0.61	0
2001-02	5.85	0	-1.17	0	0.61	0
2002-03	5.85	0	-1.17	0	0.61	0
2003-04	5.85	0	0	-2.54	1.78	-0.06
2004-05	5.85	0	0	-2.54	1.78	-0.06

(Contd.)

(Contd.Annexure-2)

Assam State Textile Corporation Limited						
Financial Year	*Total Investment*	*Surplus Reserves*	*Accumulated losses*	*Net Worth*	*Capital Employed*	*Net Profit*
1997-98	80.88	0	-21.03	0	12.26	0
1998-99	80.88	0	-21.03	0	12.26	0
1999-00	64.03	0	-26.77	0	0.31	0
2000-01	63.3	0	-31.3	0	9.83	0
2001-02	63.3	0	-31.3	0	9.83	0
2002-03	63.3	0	-31.3	0	9.83	0
2003-04	27.57	0	0	-4.04	7.77	-5.03
2004-05	28.89	0	0	-5.36	7.77	-5.03
Assam Government Construction Corporation Limited						
1997-98	2	0	-2.87	0	-2.29	0
1998-99	2	0	-2.87	0	-2.29	0
1999-00	2	0	-2.87	0	-2.29	0
2000-01	2	0	-2.87	0	-2.29	0
2001-02	2	0	-2.87	0	-2.29	0
2002-03	0	0	0	0	0	0
2003-04	0	0	0	-2.02	-2.02	-0.45
2004-05	0	0	0	-2.02	-2.02	-0.45

(Contd.)

(Contd.Annexure-2)

Financial Year	Total Investment	Surplus Reserves	Accumulated losses	Net Worth	Capital Employed	Net Profit
Assam State Minor Irrigation Development Corporation Ltd						
1997-98	0	0	0	0	0	0
1998-99	0	0	0	0	0	0
1999-00	49.34	0	-1.92	0	32.16	0
2000-01	49.34	0	-1.92	0	32.16	0
2001-02	49.34	0	-1.92	0	32.16	0
2002-03	49.34	0	-1.92	0	32.16	0
2003-04	0	0	0	0.17	32.16	-0.67
2004-05	0	0	0	0.17	32.16	-0.67
Assam Fisheries Development Corporation Ltd						
1997-98	9.99	9.51	-3.09	-3.03	9.99	0.05
1998-99	10.56	10.07	-3.04	-3.75	10.56	0.05
1999-00	10.6	10.11	-3.28	-3.73	10.31	-0.24
2000-01	10.61	10.12	-3.55	-4.27	10.32	-0.34
2001-02	10.61	10.12	-3.72	-4.61	10.32	-0.23
2002-03	10.61	10.12	-3.69	-4.41	10.32	0.03
2003-04	0	0	0	6.66	6.66	0.007
2004-05	0	0	0	6.63	6.63	0.02

(Contd.)

(Contd.Annexure-2)

Assam Hills Small Industries Development Corporation Ltd						
Financial Year	*Total Investment*	*Surplus Reserves*	*Accumulated losses*	*Net Worth*	*Capital Employed*	*Net Profit*
1997-98	11.05	0	-1.68	0	2.77	0
1998-99	11.05	0	-1.68	0	2.77	0
1999-00	11.05	0	-1.68	0	2.77	0
2000-01	11.05	0	-1.68	0	2.77	0
2001-02	11.05	0	-1.71	0	3.13	0
2002-03	11.05	0	-1.71	0	3.13	0
2003-04	0	0	0	-8.93	3.81	-0.29
2004-05	0	0	0	-9.13	3.81	-0.29
Assam Small Industries Development Corporation Ltd						
1997-98	8.34	0	7.99	-1.47	6	0
1998-99	8.34	0	7.99	-1.47	6	0
1999-00	8.33	0	-1.97	-1.47	21.4	0
2000-01	9.27	0	-68.56	-1.47	17.44	0
2001-02	9.27	0	-3.54	-1.47	2.46	0
2002-03	9.27	0	-3.54	-1.47	2.46	0
2003-04	0	0	0	-0.5	3.22	-0.22
2004-05	0	0	0	2.18	3.22	-0.22

(Contd.)

(Contd.Annexure-2)

Financial Year	Total Investment	Surplus Reserves	Accumulated losses	Net Worth	Capital Employed	Net Profit
Assam Plantation Crop Development Corporation Ltd						
1997-98	9.29	0	0	5	9.29	0
1998-99	9.74	0	0	5	9.74	0
1999-00	10.05	0	0	5	10.05	0
2000-01	10.19	0	0	5	10.19	0
2001-02	10.34	0	0	5	10.34	0
2002-03	10.68	0	0	5	10.68	0
2003-04	0	0	0	3.43	9.21	-0.43
2004-05	0	0	0	3.43	9.21	-0.43
Assam Tourism Development Corporation Ltd						
1997-98	0.24	0	0.1	0.07	7.64	0
1998-99	0.24	0	0.05	0.07	0.98	0
1999-00	0.24	0	0.02	0.07	1.2	0
2000-01	0.24	0	-0.09	0.07	2.16	0
2001-02	0.24	0	-0.09	0.07	2.16	0
2002-03	0.24	0	-0.09	0.07	2.16	0
2003-04	0	0	0	7.07	7.1	-0.03
2004-05	0	0	0	7.1071	7.11	0.1

(Contd.)

(Contd.Annexure-2)

Financial Year	Total Investment	Surplus Reserves	Accumulated losses	Net Worth	Capital Employed	Net Profit
Assam Government Marketing Corporation Ltd						
1997-98	4.52	0	1.19	1.75	5.74	-0.49
1998-99	4.55	0	-0.53	0	2.22	-0.49
1999-00	4.55	0	-0.53	0	2.22	-0.49
2000-01	4.71	0	-0.53	0	2.22	-0.49
2001-02	4.71	0	-0.53	0	2.22	-0.49
2002-03	4.71	0	-0.53	0	2.22	-0.49
2003-04	5.07	0	0	0.8	2.38	-0.05
2004-05	5.07	0	0	0.8	2.38	-0.05
Assam State Warehousing Corporation						
1997-98	13.34	0	2.51	8.01	15.52	0.28
1998-99	11.72	0	-1.85	0	11.29	0.28
1999-00	11.77	0	-1.85	0	10.1	0.28
2000-01	12.19	0	-2.61	0	14.69	0.28
2001-02	12.19	0	-2.61	0	14.69	0.28
2002-03	12.19	0	-2.61	0	14.69	0.28
2003-04	12.7	0	0	14.94	17.2	0.1
2004-05	14.9	0	0	9.41	13.97	0.01

(Contd.)

(Contd.Annexure-2)

Assam State Electricity Board						
Financial Year	*Total Investment*	*Surplus Reserves*	*Accumulated losses*	*Net Worth*	*Capital Employed*	*Net Profit*
1997-98	2906.91	0	358.72	0	2119.61	-1.67
1998-99	2906.91	0	358.72	0	2119.61	-1.67
1999-00	2763.6	0	-1879.08	0	2013.74	-1.67
2000-01	2763.6	0	-2428.85	0	1685.2	-1.67
2001-02	2763.6	0	-2428.85	0	1685.2	-1.67
2002-03	2763.6	0	-2428.85	0	1685.2	-1.67
2003-04	1475.51	0	0	737.52	863.03	-695.51
2004-05	3403.36	0	0	-1381.5	671.86	-655.47
Assam State Transport Corporation						
1997-98	241.03	10.6	-231.98	19.65	7	-26.59
1998-99	256.62	10.68	-262.08	5.22	-7.72	-30.1
1999-00	269.74	10.68	-295.97	-15.55	-28.56	-33.89
2000-01	285.61	10.68	-336.35	-40.06	-54.06	-40.38
2001-02	328.11	10.7	-370.35	-31.54	-46.06	-34.02
2002-03	385.47	10.9	-392.17	4.2	-2.79	-21.8
2003-04	0	0	0	-130.21	19.87	-26.57
2004-05	0	0	0	-134.79	19.87	-26.57

(Contd.)

(Contd.Annexure-2)

Assam State Development Corporation for Other BC Classes Limited						
Financial Year	*Total Investment*	*Surplus Reserves*	*Accumulated losses*	*Net Worth*	*Capital Employed*	*Net Profit*
1997-98	3.05	0	0.01	0	0.44	0
1998-99	3.05	0	0.01	0	0.44	0
1999-00	4.05	0	0.01	0	0.44	0
2000-01	13.16	0	0.06	0	1.04	0
2001-02	3.05	0	0.01	0	0.44	0
2002-03	3.05	0	0.01	0	0.44	0
2003-04	6.63	0	0	-3	1.24	-0.01
2004-05	16.32	0	0	-14.35	-0.52	-0.11
Assam State Development Corporation for SC Limited						
1997-98	8.22	0	0.3	0	1.78	0
1998-99	8.22	0	0.3	0	1.78	0
1999-00	8.22	0	-0.63	0	2.3	0
2000-01	8.63	0	-0.79	0	2.98	0
2001-02	8.22	0	0.3	0	1.78	0
2002-03	8.22	0	0.3	0	1.78	0
2003-04	0	0	0	-6.55	8.45	-0.24
2004-05	0	0	0	-9.65	3.63	-0.65

Annexure-3
Common Issues in PE Reforms

Issues	*S No.*	*Recommendation of the Committee on State Public Sector Enterprises*
On Management	1	Almost all the CEOs need adequate reorientation in business activities with proper mindset to run the affairs of the public enterprises
	2	The CEOs should be appointed on contract for fixed tenure of 5 years or up-to superannuation, whichever earlier, with annual performance review as per MOU. The CEO should be changed whenever ratings are not satisfactory as per MOU targets.
	3	MOU system should be introduced with specific targets. In MOU system, administrative departments must act efficiently & promptly. Mindset of administrators should be updated. No interference of Govt. should be there and performance appraisal should be based on MOU.
	4	Management structure to switch over to CMD with a few functional Directors in the Board.
	5	The posts of CEO/CMD should be open to all without any reservation and selection should be made through PESB through open advertisement. No delay should be there in appointment of CEOs.

(Contd.)

(Contd.Annexure-3)

Issues	*S No.*	*Recommendation of the Committee on State Public Sector Enterprises*
	6	PESB should be reconstituted as independent body with experts from outside and Govt. nominees.
	7	The Boards should be revamped through adequate representation from share-holders, FIs, outside management experts, employees & Govt. representatives (not below rank of Secretary) and empowered. At least 50% Directors should be professionals and experts in the areas of operations. Govt. directors should participate in deliberations offering Govt. views.
	8	Board should meet once in 2 months with a fixed annual calendar. Chairman should have authority to hold Board meetings without interference from Govt.
	9	Independent authority like PE Deptt. Should have authority to ensure that interference of administrative deptts. in day-to-day functioning is stopped.
	10	PE Deptt. may be provided with fund to engage outside accounting firms for compilation of accounts of heavily defaulting PSUs for finalization of accounts immediately.
	11	Govt. should bring-in legislation as Transparency Act with stringent punishment to those who hide facts. Documents should be available on nominal payment and released through internet. PSUs to issue Citizen charters.
On revival	12	Govt. should constitute Empowered Committee with CS as Chairman and experts on Management & Finance as Members to decide revival of closed units either through disinvestments, joint sector, privatization, merger, restructuring and / or winding-up, in which the PE Deptt. may act as the Secretariat. The Committee should be free from political interference and may engage consultants to advise on best course.

(Contd.)

(Contd.Annexure-3)

Issues	*S No.*	*Recommendation of the Committee on State Public Sector Enterprises*
	13	GOI/ Planning Commission may be pressurized to provide special grant of Rs.200 Crore as VRS fund. Govt./PSUs should also take-up with higher authorities of banks for loans to effect VRS in potential but losing PSUs like APCL, AFDC, AFC, AIDC etc. PSUs should also increase operations for gainful employment without waiting for VRS fund.
	14	The Finance Deptt. may issue standing order to Treasuries not to entertain purchase bills of Govt. deptts., outside ASIDC & AAIDC as per APSP Act & Cabinet decision applicable. However, over-dependence on Govt. by PSUs should be avoided.
	15	Diversification is necessary for manufacturing enterprises. Preparation of Corporate Plan or vision statement is necessary for future development. ACJM, AGCL, APCL, AMDC, ARTFED, ASWC, ASC are to consider diversification.
	16	Serious views on closed PSUs – ASL, Fertichem, ASCON, ASWMC APM, APCDC need to be taken by the Govt. Privatization proposal of ASL & ASWMC should be decided immediately. Injection of fund and conversion of loan to grant are required in case of APCDC. Activities of ASHB should be reoriented on the line of DDA
	17	Govt. to provide grant of Rs.100 Lakh to AAP of ASIDC directly for renovation, expansion, plantation of herbs, in 2 installments. Bifurcation of AAP from ASIDC may be considered and CTI & MSF of ASIDC are to be wound-up.

(Contd.)

(Contd.Annexure-3)

Issues	*S No.*	*Recommendation of the Committee on State Public Sector Enterprises*
	18	Cautious steps to arrest asset stripping by lessees should be taken. Where Govt. has committed full privatization with condition of zero liability, initial lease holders should be honoured immediately and ownership transferred.
	19	It is suggested to examine that unless the future flow of institutional fund to each category of the weaker sections of the society to the merged organization is stopped, Govt. may go for merger of the welfare organizations. Similarly, some others not so doing well enterprises can be merged or leased-out.
On Financial	20	Performance of ASFC, Fertichem, ASWC, ARTFED, AHSIDC, ATDC, ASF(F&D)CL, ALPCO can be rejuvenated with injection of more fund.
	21	Govt. should pay dues to ASTPPCL, AAIDC, ASC, ASWC and Central fund lying with State Govt. in respect of ASWC & ARTFED. If payment be regular, budgetary support not required to these PSUS and AGCL, APCL, ACJM & AFDC.
	22	Vigorous steps for recovery of receivables from beneficiaries by OTS or bakijai process or by taking-over assets and auction sell are required. Govt. to enact bakijai rule allowing bakijai officer to adjust advalorem fees out of recoveries and to empower CEOs of concerned PSUs to act as bakijai officers.
	23	Govt. to stand guarantor against institutional loans, as necessary.
On Human Resource	24	There should be endeavour to pay salary regularly. Excess employees to be offloaded through VRS or redeployment with training and Govt. to manage required fund.

(Contd.)

(Contd.Annexure-3)

Issues	*S No.*	*Recommendation of the Committee on State Public Sector Enterprises*
	25	Preference to employees of closed PSUs not opting VRS should be given in recruitment / filling-up of vacant posts in Govt. on suitability & experience, by relaxing age bar. No fresh recruitment should take place in PSUs.
On Committee's Role	26	The Committee should be made responsible and have a watching brief to see that the recommendations are workable.

Annexure-4

Summary of Recommendations of the Reports on State Public Sector Enterprises

Enterprises	*Gist of discussion in the Review Meeting held on 04-09-2003.*	*Recommendations of the meetings held on 04-09 2003*
1. Assam State Electricity Board	It was exhibited that with reforms & restructuring, the turnover increased and losses decreased since 2001. The steps on reforms viz. Initiation for formation of distribution companies; doubling the transmission capacity to 1200 MW within 3-4 years and plan to create generation companies were explained. While APDP would facilitate funding improvement of distribution network, financial assistance would be available from ADB for enhancement of transmission capacity. As regards the generating sector, it was informed that Karbi-	· Continue Reform & Restructuring programme · T&D losses to reduced by arresting pilferage and system to be improved · Examine possibilities of starting production at BTPS · Expedite Karbi-Langpi Hydro Electric Project. · Examine feasibility of

(Contd.)

(Contd. Annexure-4)

Enterprises	*Gist of discussion in the Review Meeting held on 04-09-2003.*	*Recommendations of the meetings held on 04-09-2003*
	Langpi HEP was completed to the extent of 70% and PFC sanctioned Rs. 125 Crore for the same, which would be disbursed on issue of Govt. guarantee. With consultancy from National Hydro Power Corp. The project was expected to be completion in 2 yrs. Even with 20 yrs. Time overrun, the project would be economic at Rx. 5 Cr./ MW against new hydro project costing Rs. 8-9 crs./ MW. 1 unit of BTPS was been planned to be started next year and another in 2 yrs., for which life extension studies and Govt. support were essential. LTPS would also be developed with NEC fund, for which Central PIB clearance was awaited. Agreements with the parties concerned for use of natural gas through pipeline to be laid by AGCL would executed within Nov./03 and pipeline laying was expected by july/04. On T&D losses, which reduced setting up of Special Courts by the State Govt. under new Electricity Act was emphasized? District level task forces would	waste heat power project in Lakwa thermal Power Station.

(Contd.)

(Contd. Annexure-4)

Enterprises	*Gist of discussion in the Review Meeting held on 04-09-2003.*	*Recommendations of the meetings held on 04-09-2003*
	continue to check pilferage. Business turn around plan was under preparation. ASEB was supplying g full power during non-peak load hrs. And restored to scheduled load shedding in peak hrs. This would improve with improvement in transmission and distribution network. APOL would take-up the matter on revision of connected load with ASEB.	
2. Assam State Transport Corn.	It was highlighted that during finalization of recommendations on 20-08-2002, the ASTC had bus: staff ratio of 1:40 against National norm of 1:8, No. of buses on road was low at about 130 nos. fleet utilization was around 38% and load factor was 50%. It was exhibited that the earlier trend in performance of ASTC reversed i.e. turnover started increasing, annual losses started decreasing fleet utilization & bus: staff ratio improved to 75% & 1:11 respectively during last 2 years. It was explained that the turn	· Explore all possible means for generation of additional revenue. · Built-in mechanism for cross subsidization of losses incurred in uneconomic routes owing to social compulsions to be worked-out.

(Contd.)

(Contd. Annexure-4)

Enterprises	*Gist of discussion in the Review Meeting held on 04-09-2003.*	*Recommendations of the meetings held on 04-09 2003*
	around was made by (i) reduction in cost to the extent of Rs. 80 Lakh PM by reducing 1857 nos. staff through implementation of VRS for which assistance of Rs. 66 Crore was available. (ii) Increase in no. of buses to 300 including purchase of 30 new, resulting in bus: staff ratio of 1.11 & (iii) allowing around 1200 private buses to run under ASTC banner on fare share basis against utilization of ASTC's infrastructure, where by earning of Rs. 90 Lakh PM was made without investment. Introduction of courier service, incentive scheme through scratch card for prizes& concessions, facility of online ticketing, phases-wise disposal of about 140 uneconomic buses provide means of earning additional revenue. However, huge statutory liability of Rs. 65 Crore, salary dues of 11 months, dues of Rs. 10 Crore to retired employees, Operation of Own buses on uneconomic routes to the extent possible, where private operators do not prefer	

(Contd.)

(Contd. Annexure-4)

Enterprises	Gist of discussion in the Review Meeting held on 04-09-2003.	Recommendations of the meetings held on 04-09-2003
	to ply were causing concern. The pay scales of employees of ASTC were not revised. Commercial utilization of assets of ASTC was planned, with fund from NEC/HUDCO. Viability of taking-up goods carriage activity, which however would be capital incentive, was being examined.	
3. Assam Urban Water Supply and Sewerage Board	The Board reported that 24 Officers on deputation were sent back to PHE Dept. And no recruitments were made against these. With the introduction of metering system, the revenue collection in Guwahati and Jarhat improved. Seven new schemes were commissioned and two more were ready for commissioning. From the Administrative Departments end, it was indicated that earlier, schemes were taken up with out ascertaining the economic viability and such practices were stopped. It was also stressed that payment by the consumers were ensured. As regards settlement of dues to HUDCO, it was started that in	· Focus on existing schemes that are economically viable or required in quality water scarcity areas. · Take new schemes only after

(Contd.)

(Contd. Annexure-4)

Enterprises	*Gist of discussion in the Review Meeting held on 04-09-2003.*	*Recommendations of the meetings held on 04-09-2003*
	a high level meeting between the State Chief Secretary & the Chairman of HUDCO, Strategies for one time settlement were discussed. The board found another source of fund, which was non-lapsable pool fund from which Rs. 3.53 Crore was availed for Silchar water supply scheme. DRP for another four schemes for Rangiya, Sibsagar, Mangalodi and Dhekiajuli were being prepared and if these could be submitted in the current year, non-lapsable fund was likely to be available.	
4. Statfed	It was projected that as per assessment made in 2001, with the low level of margin available & huge manpower, the STATFED required business of Rs. 360 Crore PA and therefore they were required to increase business, diversify, boost-up production units and reduce manpower. Their working capital requirement was assessed at Rs. 90 Crore. It was explained that serious efforts were made to increase business and Police, Social Welfare etc.	Increase business, for which Social Welfare, Police ect. Deptts. Should procure their requirements of food stuff etc. from STATFED. Implement VRS to Shed-off surplus staff Activate production units for maximum benefits

(Contd.)

(Contd. Annexure-4)

Enterprises	*Gist of discussion in the Review Meeting held on 04-09-2003.*	*Recommendations of the meetings held on 04-09-2003*
	Depts took actions for procurements from STATFED. STATFED proposed to implement VRs to reduce its manpower by 900 nos. and the requirement of Rs. 31 Crores was projected. Against this, the provision made in the current year was Rs. 1.5 Crores and Rs. 10 Crore was assured in the next year. OTS for dues of Rs. 86 crore was made which would be paid in 1-2 years. Thereafter, banks were expected to provide working capital. The capacity of the Vanaspathi plant was decided to be enhanced to 100 MT from 50 MT and would be operated with private sector participation to generate around 30% of the salary requirement of STATFED. Other production units viz. mastered oil & Oxigen plants, Rice mills, Spice packaging of units would also be activated under joint sector. The STATFED's performance did not improve in last 2 yrswas evident from the fact that their accumulated loss rise to Rs. 70 Crore from Rs. 51 Crore and the	· Submit action plan.

(Contd.)

(Contd. Annexure-4)

Enterprises	*Gist of discussion in the Review Meeting held on 04-09-2003.*	*Recommendations of the meetings held on 04-09-2003*
	negative net-worth increased to Rs. 52 crore from Rs. 23 Crore. The Losses were explained to be primarily on account of interest liability, which would be come down to after liquidation of loans under OTS. And expenditure would also come down on implementation of VRS	
5. Assam Govt Marketing Corpn LTD.	The basic problems of AGMC were loss making emporiums, dearth of working capital & excess staff. Their turnover increased in the recent years, but the profit/loss scenario remained unchanged. It was explained that there was improvement in performance. Their 4 emporiums were identified for immediate closure and 6 more would follow. 9 emporiums were doing well but their past liabilities figured them to be losing. The liability os salaries, CPF dues were brought down and bank loans were liquidated. The Central Govt. stopped giving fund to the Corpn. Owing to past lapses and after these were cleared, the process re-started. The	Revive production centers and assist weavers and artisans directly Marketing through franchise Eight Emporiums closed but VRS to be given Working Capital Problem remains AGMC to submit copy of the details on receivables from Govt, to the PE Department

(Contd.)

(Contd. Annexure-4)

Enterprises	*Gist of discussion in the Review Meeting held on 04-09-2003.*	*Recommendations of the meetings held on 04-09-2003*
	Construction of the Urban hut project was getting started within next year and this would help AGMC to increase its business and utilize surplus staff. The restructuring proposal, one of the constituent of which was requirement of fund for VRS. A proposal for Rs. 4.51 Crore for 101 employuees was worked-out for State govt,s consideration. The receivable of AGMC constituted Rs. 4.72 Crores from State & Central Govt. and this would take care of the working capital requirement, if released. It was also clarified that AGMC was promoting cluster groups of local weavers and Artisans outside the co-operative fold.	
6. Artfed	It was reviewed that expansion of pre and post loom weaving facility to handloom weavers was very essential and technological up-gradation was called-for. ARTFED took several schemes and diversification programmes in this regard. Foreign & lead Indian designers were engaged	· Functioning Well · Central funds received to be released · State Share to be adequately provided · Expand pre and post weaving facilities to

(Contd.)

(Contd. Annexure-4)

Enterprises	*Gist of discussion in the Review Meeting held on 04-09-2003.*	*Recommendations of the meetings held on 04-09-2003*
	for improvement designs to meet global standard and their export target in the current year. was Rs. 5 Crore. They built-up their reserve of Rs. 48 Lakh ARTFED pleaded for timely release of fund against Central schemes, matching State share and other incentives to keep the. improving trend going. Limited budget provision stood on the way and the Govt liability kept on mounting. The HT and S Deptt. Was required to take-up the matter with Finance Deptt.	handloom weavers Improve traditional and ethnic design through R&D to international standards. Build Reserve Funds and declare dividends.
7. Assam State Wareho using Corpn.	It was exhibited that the ASWC, which was in profit earning status in spite of its problems of huge receivables from the State Govt. & PSUs and bankers' refusal to honour warehouse slips as security for loans to farmers started losing from 2001-02. It was explained that due to slumps in the tea industry in the last few years, the warehouse occupancy from this sector declined. Earlier, the tea sector occupied around 25-30% of the ASWC's capacity. Likewise, due to difficulties with	Arrest decline Balance funds under RPDS to be released to complete go-downs Higher level in Banks to be mover to honour Warehouse Slips as security for loans to farmers.

(Contd.)

(Contd. Annexure-4)

Enterprises	Gist of discussion in the Review Meeting held on 04-09-2003.	Recommendations of the meetings held on 04-09-2003
	the jute corporation of India, the occupancy from the jute sector also fell. The jute sector also occupied around 25-30% of the capacity of ASWC earlier. In 2001-02, the overall occupancy of ASWC's capacity was 60-65% as against 80% earlier. However, from January 2003, the position was improving gradually, because of the efforts of marketing of warehouses to other sectors like Fertilizers, Cement etc. In January 2003, the overall occupancy was around 68% and in August 2003, it increased to about 78% With occupancy rate of around 801% it was expected that the losses would be overcome and efforts to increase the occupancy rate were being made.	
8. Assam Gas Co. Ltd	AGCL, recovered its past accumulated receivables from ASEB, BVFCL, Several new projects were taken-up and modernization programme was under implementation. AGCL had already associated in a project in Tripura and was	· Functioning Well · Expand activities · Diversify · Consultancy division to be strengthens to

(Contd.)

(Contd. Annexure-4)

Enterprises	*Gist of discussion in the Review Meeting held on 04-09-2003.*	*Recommendations of the meetings held on 04-09-2003*
	planning to go outside north-east. Association with GAIL was being initiated. AGCL was a ISO 9001 company. They also rendered consultancy services on ISO 9001 system to improve the quality to LPG plant of OIL at Duliaajn.	take up turn-key jobs on all India basis.
9.Assam Plains Tribes Dev. Corpn. LTd	Because of the low margin in refinancing & absence of corporate activity, the Corporation was not likely to be viable and therefore possibility of merger was recommended, to reduce overhead costs. It was explained that merger would not be possible because of the divergent activities in different sectors. The total annual salary burden on 479 employees of the three corporations under WPT & BC department was Rs. 4.82 Crore and to earn this, the turnover required was Rs. 136 Crore. But, the turnover ranged around Rs. 5 Crore. This Corporation were in the Welfare sector and since the Corporation were not in a position to live on their own, the Govt. would be required to subsidized the	The WPT & BC Department to take a view as to whether the Corporation should continue in the Company format or it should be changed to a kind of development agency or merged with the Directorate. Continue with the activity till decided finally and intensify recovery.

(Contd.)

(Contd. Annexure-4)

Enterprises	*Gist of discussion in the Review Meeting held on 04-09-2003.*	*Recommendations of the meetings held on 04-09-2003*
	establishment costs. The APTDC was against the proposal of merger. There was a need of changing the structure of the Enterprise, as the Company structure would always keep it unviable.	
10. Assam State Dev. Corpn. For S.C Ltd	Because of low margin in refinancing & absence of corporate activity, the Corporation was not likely to be viable and therefore possibility of merger was recommended, to reduce overhead costs. It was explained that merger would not be possible because of the divergent activities in different sectors. The total annual salary burden on 479 employees of the three corporations under WPT & BC department was Rs. 4.82 Crores and to earn this, the turnover required was Rs. 136 Crore. But, the turnover ranged around Rs. 5 Crore. These Corporations were in the welfare sector and since the corporations were not in a position to live on their own, the Govt would be required to subsidize the establishment costs. The	The WPT & BC Department to take a view as to whether the Corporation should continue in the Company format or it should be changed to a kind of development agency or merged with the Directorate. Continue with the activity till decided finally and intensify recovery.

(Contd.)

(Contd. Annexure-4)

Enterprises	*Gist of discussion in the Review Meeting held on 04-09-2003.*	*Recommendations of the meetings held on 04-09-2003*
	corporation pleaded for budgetary support of 50% of the establishment cost. There was a need of changing the structure of the Enterprise, as the Company structure would always keep it unviable.	
11. Assam State Dev. Corpn for OBC Ltd.	Because of low margin in refinancing & absence of corporate activity, the Corporation was not likely to be viable and therefore possibility of merger was recommended, to reduce overhead costs. It was explained that merger would not be possible because of the divergent activities in different sectors. The total annual salary burden on 479 employees of the three corporations under WPT & BC department was Rs. 4.82 Crores and to earn this, the turnover required was Rs. 136 Crore. But, the turnover ranged around Rs. 5 Crore. These Corporations were in the welfare sector and since the corporations were not in a position to live on their own, the Govt would be required to subsidize the establishment costs. The	The WPT & BC Department to take a view as to whether the Corporation should continue in the Company format or it should be changed to a kind of development agency or merged with the Directorate. Continue with the activity till decided finally and intensify recovery.

(Contd.)

(Contd. Annexure-4)

Enterprises	*Gist of discussion in the Review Meeting held on 04-09-2003.*	*Recommendations of the meetings held on 04-09-2003*
	Corporation was in agreement with the proposal of merger with enterprises having similar activities. There was a need of changing the structure of the Enterprise, as the Company structure would always keep it unviable.	
12. Assam Minorities Dev. & Finance Corp. Ltd	The only Corporation with no employees and the activities were being carried-out through the employees of Minority Development Board. The Corporation acted as a channelising agency of National Minorities Development Corporation and Rs. 2.86 Corre of fund received was distributed to 599 beneficiaries. Non-availability of infrastructure posed problems in recovery. However, the recovery improved recently. Further fund would be available from the National Minorities Development Corporation, if State Govt. equity were available. However, the Corporation like those under the WPT & BC Department was not having corporate activity and was in the welfare sector.	A detailed study to be made and the Minority Welfare Development Department to take a view. Continue with the activity till decided finally and intensify recovery.

(Contd.)

(Contd. Annexure-4)

Enterprises	*Gist of discussion in the Review Meeting held on 04-09-2003.*	*Recommendations of the meetings held on 04-09-2003*
	They would not be making profit ever therefore in the present structure. A detailed study was required and the administrative department was required to take a view.	
13. Assam Industrial Dev. Corp. Ltd	The turnover and losses of AIDC remained almost at same level during the last few years. The AIDC was advised to restructure, intensify, recovery, settle dues to IDBI, revive viable subsidiaries and implement VRS. It was explained that the CRISIL study report on restructuring of the Corporation was being placed before the Board of Directors, indicating action points; formula for settlement of dues to IDBI was worked-out and was under negotiations; was in the process of deciding revival of viable& marginally viable subsidiaries & closure of unviable ones and that the revised guidelines on implementation of VRS was awaited from the Public Enterprise Department.	· Approach to restructuring AIDC to be informed · Recovery to be intensified-diagnostic study to help AIDC financed units back to operation to be taken-up. · Settlement of dues to IDBI to be done. · Viable Subsidiaries to be revived & unviable closed. · VRS to be implemented as per revised guidelines issued. · Govt to give annual grant to

(Contd.)

(Contd. Annexure-4)

Enterprises	*Gist of discussion in the Review Meeting held on 04-09-2003.*	*Recommendations of the meetings held on 04-09-2003*
		meet costs of promotional activities in industrial development of the State viz. for holding seminars, expo, business summit etc.
14. Assam Small Industries Dev. Corp. Ltd	The performance of ASIDC· remained almost stagnant during last few years. On the progress of actions on recommendations made earlier, it was explained that VRS proposal for 79 employees involving Rs. 7.74 Crores was submitted, but due to budgetary constraints, this could not be accommodated. This was however, being pursued. Against recovery due of Rs. 7.50 Crore from beneficiaries, 146 bakijai cases were field, which accounted for Rs. 1.58 Crore. The recovery made was however only Rs. 0.15 Crore. As regards enforcement of APSP Act, it was indicated that there was some improvement, but some departments were still flouting	Enforce APSP Act strictly and make amendments as necessary. The Govt. departments to clear dues on supplies made under provision of the Act.· Fund VRS· Possibilities of simplification of bakijai process, exemption from depositing advelorem fees, empowering field officers of the SLPEs to exercise the power of bakijai officer etc

(Contd.)

(Contd. Annexure-4)

Enterprises	*Gist of discussion in the Review Meeting held on 04-09-2003.*	*Recommendations of the meetings held on 04-09-2003*
	under some plea. The ASIDc took steps to close Cacher Textile Industries, Badarpur & Match Splint Factory, Bijni as already decided. The Public Enterprises Department had already forwarded the list of major willful defaulters of ASIDC to the Industries Department for publicizing, which might compel some defaulters to pay-up. The SLPEs were asked to adhere to the APSP Act and proposal for necessary amendment of the APSP was already sent to Industries Department. The Working capital provided to Assam Ayurvedhic Product was gainfully utilized.	to be examined by the Finance dept. Extensive promotional measures to be taken in respect of the Ayurvedhic unit.
15. Assam Financial Corporation	Huge receivable of Rs. 185 Crore crippled AFC. It was explained that with the OTS package, the recovery improved slightly, but it could not be expected to improve further, as the good loans were almost settled and the bad loans remained due. Bakijai process was intensified by personal level contacts with DCs and in some cases by joint drives with banks. On the restructuring proposal, it	Recovery efforts to be continued-diagnostic study with rehabilitation package of 1200 closed AFC financed units to be made. Restructuring proposals to be pursued

(Contd.)

(Contd. Annexure-4)

Enterprises	*Gist of discussion in the Review Meeting held on 04-09-2003.*	*Recommendations of the meetings held on 04-09-2003*
	was informed that since GOI turned down the same, some dialogue was made with ADB and massive implementation of VRS/CRS was essential to cut-down costs. Fresh restructuring proposal was submitted to the Finance Department and a synopsis would be forwarded to Public Enterprises Department	· Fund VRS
16. Assam Hills Small Industries Dev. Corp. Ltd	The AHSIDC was required to implement the recommendations made earlier but, due to fund constraints, thje production units could not be operated gainfully. The Corporation needed minimum working capital of Rs. 50 Lakhs in one installment. For the Daithor project, financial assistance under Technology Mission IV of the Central Govt was sought.	· Increase Capacity utilization of Citronella and mustered oil units& of Citronella cultivation · Improve marketing of fruit processing unit · Working capital in the shape of "revolving fund" to be provided · VRS to be affected · To diversify · Arrange fund and completed Daithor project.
17. Assam State Film	The report submitted by the Corporation did not indicate the	· Examine viable of constructing

(Contd.)

(Contd. Annexure-4)

Enterprises	*Gist of discussion in the Review Meeting held on 04-09-2003.*	*Recommendations of the meetings held on 04-09-2003*
(Fin& Dev) Corp. Ltd	profit/loss figures and the latest was shown to be declining As such, the corporation categorized earlier in the improving sector was reduced to losing sector. It was explained that as per the audited figures, their turnover was Rs. 3.98 Lakh in 2001-02 and the same increased to Rs. 4.42 Lakh in 2002-03, maintaining the accumulated loss same at Rs. 13 Lakhs. It was indicated that the reporting from the Corporation was incorrect owing to some calculation mistake tat their end and the Enterprise needed to retain in the improving category. The Corporation was asked to submit their revised report for examination by the Department.	multi-purpose mini cinema halls in small towns with private participation Examine feasibility of producing bilingual films jointly with NFDC. Take steps to seize prints of films produced by defaulting producers with right to telecast, for recovery of dues.
18.Assam Tourism Development Corporation	ATDC was in the improving category and continued to be in the same status. On the earlier recommendations it was reported that all the completed projects were handed over for management in the private sector, barring five tourist lodges which were being managed by the	Promote tourism, involving private sector· Professionalize through HRD· Prepare Project proposals on tourism related activities of

(Contd.)

(Contd. Annexure-4)

Enterprises	*Gist of discussion in the Review Meeting held on 04-09-2003.*	*Recommendations of the meetings held on 04-09-2003*
	Corporation. On HRD, it was explained that contacts with training institutes were made but they were yet to start any training programme. On association in tourism related matters in the National Games 2005, it was stated that project reports were under preparation.	National Games 2005 and get involved in implementation· Formulasse different packages e.g., eco/ pilgrimage etc. tourism· Tie-up with Assam Ayurvedic Products under ASIDC and develop tourism in herbal medicine sector· Complete all economically viable projects in pipeline viz., Cruise vessel, Craft village, Water sports, Amusement Park, Rope way etc.
19. Assam Agro Industries Dev. Corpn. Ltd	No part of the dues of Rs. 8.62· crore payable by the Agriculture Department was released for want of budget provision, though Rs. 3.64 crore was reconciled. Other than the Agriculture	Govt. due to be paid· Govt. departments to procure agricultural implements and

(Contd.)

(Contd. Annexure-4)

Enterprises	*Gist of discussion in the Review Meeting held on 04-09-2003.*	*Recommendations of the meetings held on 04-09-2003*
	Department, no other department procured agricultural inputs and implements, in terms of the Cabinet decision. Ceiling for Rs. 3 crore for implementation of VRS for 84 employees was released. Proposals of Rs. 4.15 crore for equipping bio-fertilizer production unit and central workshop for increasing manufacture of agricultural implements were submitted to the State Govt. and NEC. The requirement of working capital was minimum Rs 0.70 crore for these units.	inputs from AIDC as per the Cabinet decision· Release excess employees through implementation VRS· Increase production of bio-fertilizer and agricultural implements and pursue state Govt/ NEC for fund.
20. Assam Seeds Corpn. Ltd	The dues of Agriculture Department amounting to Rs.7.59 crore was not released; VRS proposal was submitted, but needed to be worked out afresh as per revised guidelines; feasibility of reviving sick farms was being examined by a committee and the request for exemption of tax on seeds was to be forwarded by the Agriculture Department to the Finance Department.	· Agriculture Department to release at least 25% of undisputed dues immediately to enable ASC to utilize the same as revolving working capital · VRS to be affected · Privatize farms · Make local taxes competitive

(Contd.)

(Contd. Annexure-4)

Enterprises	*Gist of discussion in the Review Meeting held on 04-09-2003.*	*Recommendations of the meetings held on 04-09-2003*
21. Assam Fisheries Dev. Corpn. Ltd	It was informed that the Corporation took-up some 'beels' for development and 12 more 'beels' were bring allotted by the Fisheries Department to the Corporation shortly. The role required to be played by the corporation in development of fishery in increasing availability of local fish in the state was emphasized.	· VRS to be continued · Allot more Govt. 'beels' to the corporation · Take-up other fisheries development schemes · Submit action plan to indicate as to how the Corporation's activities would increase fish in the State Lease rent to be paid to Govt. fo 'beels' allotted Gov tot demarcate boundary of 'beels and evict encroachers.
22. Assam State Minor Irrigation Dev.Corpn. Ltd	In the agreement was signed between the State & the Central Govt, under the Medium Term Fiscal Reforms Programme, which was approved by the Cabinet subsequently, decision of closure ASMIDC by December 2003 was taken. It was	· All required actions for closure of the corporation to be taken in compliance of the relevant provisions in the Article of

(Contd.)

(Contd. Annexure-4)

Enterprises	*Gist of discussion in the Review Meeting held on 04-09-2003.*	*Recommendations of the meetings held on 04-09-2003*
	informed that the corporation had liability of Rs.33.27 crore, which included Rs.11.78 crore on account of implementation of VRS for 203 employees, Rs.17crore for payment of arrear salary etc., Rs.2.80 crore as CPF due, Rs.0.45 crore as pension contribution & leave salary due and the rest for settlement of dues to contractors etc. since there was no budget provision to meet the liability, the Irrigation Department submitted proposal to P& D Dept., and the P&D Dept forwarded the same to finance Dept. after closure of the corpn. The recovery due to f Rs.45 crore from beneficiaries would be the liability of the Irrigation Dept.	Association and the Companies Act.
23. Assam Livestock & Poultry Dev Corpn. Ltd	It was explained that the four meat-processing plants under execution could not be commissioned, as the Central Govt. did not release the last installment of Central share, owning to non-release of state shares. Therefore, it was decided to avail FIDF loan and Rs.350 lakh was allocated for	Complete projects in hand expeditiously & manage there with private sector participation. Intensify recovery Fund for implementation of VRS be provided

(Contd.)

(Contd. Annexure-4)

Enterprises	*Gist of discussion in the Review Meeting held on 04-09-2003.*	*Recommendations of the meetings held on 04-09-2003*
	the same. The project reports etc. were prepared for the purpose. It was added that against requirement of 26 employees, the Corpn., had 11, of which the MR employees were released and the employee strength reduced to 71, for releasing the excess employees under VRS as per ASTC model, Rs.262.23 lakh was required, for which Rs.150 lakh was allocated under plan. With this, 37 employees would be released. Another Rs.112 Lakh would be required for the rest. The projects to be commissioned were being planned to be operated with private sector participation on profit sharing basis, in which the private partners would inject working capital and would provide maintenance service for the plant & machinery. The Corpn. Would also venture into marketing activity of livestock etc.	
24. Assam State	The ASTCL was glaring example where the route of lease	Should resort to disinvestments in

(Contd.)

(Contd. Annexure-4)

Enterprises	*Gist of discussion in the Review Meeting held on 04-09-2003.*	*Recommendations of the meetings held on 04-09-2003*
Textile Corpn. Ltd	failed miserably. The mill was given on management lease and transfer of share was not done in a period of around 10 years. The lesses thereby could not get working capital loan from banks and ultimately had to leave. The mill was taken-back by the Govt., and the management proposed to lease it out, to be followed by joint sector management on settlement of liabilities. It was informed that one time settlement was made in respect of dues to some financial institutions and budget provision of Rs.60.80 lakh has been made for settlement of remaining dues. The Industries Department was examining the proposal of the management and would workout a model in which, the view of the Public Enterprises Department that lease should be integrated with joint sector concept, to ensure stake of the lessee would be taken care of. This would take care of the chances of asset stripping. In order to see that the machinery do not wear-out	the ATC model. Alternatively, if leased out under compelling circumstances, it should be integrated with joint sector management concept. The mill should be made liability free.

(Contd.)

(Contd. Annexure-4)

Enterprises	Gist of discussion in the Review Meeting held on 04-09-2003.	Recommendations of the meetings held on 04-09-2003
	for want of prolonged use, the decision was needed to be taken vary fast.	
25. Assam State Weaving and Mfg. Co Ltd	The Industries Deptt. Was processing a proposal for leasing-out the mill to private sector, to be followed by disinvestments, after settlement of liabilities	Disinvestment to be preferred and if decided to be leased-out, it should be integrated with disinvestment/ joint sector participation, to ensure that the private party retain stake and chances of asset stripping is avoided.
26. Assam Tea Corpn. Ltd	The disinvestments process in ATC was initiated but nothing crystallized. Fresh advertisement indicating various incentives of offered by the State & the Central Govt was being issued. As regards settlement of the case of Bidyanagar Tea Estate, revenue dept. was being proposed for early decision	Disinvestment process to be transparent Revenue Deptt. To settle the case of Bidyanagar TE
27. Cachar Sugar Mill Ltd	The mill was decided to be closed by 31-2-2003 by the Cabinet as per Medium Term	All required actions for closure of the Corporation

(Contd.)

(Contd. Annexure-4)

Enterprises	Gist of discussion in the Review Meeting held on 04-09-2003.	Recommendations of the meetings held on 04-09-2003
	Fiscal Reform Agreement signed between the State & Central Govt. the Industries Deptt., would implement the decision.	to be taken in compliance of the relevant provisions in the Article of Association and the Companies Act.
28. Assam Spun Silk Mills Ltd	The mill was decided to be closed by 31-12-2003 by the Cabinet as per Medium Term Fiscal Reform Agreement signed between the State & Central Govt. the Industries Deptt. Would implement the decision.	All required actions for closure of the Corporation to be taken in compliance of the relevant provisions in the Article of Association and the Companies Act.
29. Ashok Paper Mills (Assam) Ltd.	The present worth of the mill was Rs. 120 Crore and the lessee was required to arrange working capital of Rs. 2 Crore. The mill being leased-out, the Govt. had no scope to provide co-lateral security and the lessee was required to arrange the same. This needed consideration on special footing and therefore a meeting was fixed on 12th September 2003 to sort-out the	Lessee to start the mill

(Contd.)

(Contd. Annexure-4)

Enterprises	*Gist of discussion in the Review Meeting held on 04-09-2003.*	*Recommendations of the meetings held on 04-09-2003*
	problems. The problem faced by APM (Assam) on the liability of 17 months' salary due to 380 employees, which was handed over to the earlier lessee was raised.	
30. Assam Petro-chemicals Ltd.	APCL was a profit making company. It was reported that in the current year, profit of Rs. 4.19 Crore was earned in the 1st quarter and in July and August 2003, it was Rs. 1.4 Crore. Had there been no shut down owning to power failure and water scarcity, the profit would have been more. The Company was going for de-bottle necking, which was considered necessary because of aging of some machinery and for raising its capacity from 80-85% to 100%. Consultant was appointed and the de-bottle necking programmes was scheduled to be completed by June, 2004. So far as diversification was concerned, the company appointed consultant for study in the feasibility of diversification into other products and after assessment, appropriate	· Consider disinvestments at appropriate time · Implement VRS · GOA to plead for reduction of gas price · Expedite Govt. approval on formation of a new company jointly by APCL and ASFC for revival of ASFC

(Contd.)

(Contd. Annexure-4)

Enterprises	Gist of discussion in the Review Meeting held on 04-09-2003.	Recommendations of the meetings held on 04-09-2003
	actions would be taken. The delay in according government approval on the proposal of floating a new company jointly by APCL and ASFC, to revive ASFC was raised.	
31. Assam State Fertilizer and Chemicals Ltd.	The revival of ASFC was delayed for want of govt. approval on floating a new company jointly by APCL and ASFC.	Expedite Govt. approval on formation of a new company jointly by APCL & ASFC for revival of ASFC Govt to expedite land settlement case Govt to release fund required for paying-up arrear dues on account of VRS and salary
32. Assam Electronics Dev. Corpn. Ltd.	It was explained that at the time of finalizing recommendations on 20-08-2002, AMTRON with capital investment of Rs. 12 Crore had accumulated loss of Rs. 4 Crore and the net-worth was going down. They had 50% excess employees and the turnover was Rs. 2 crore against BE turnover	To intensify on promotion of IT enabled and consultancy services throughout the State and the NE Region. Budgetary support for HRD to be

(Contd.)

(Contd. Annexure-4)

Enterprises	*Gist of discussion in the Review Meeting held on 04-09-2003.*	*Recommendations of the meetings held on 04-09-2003*
	of Rs. 15 Crore. Their production activities did not pay-off due to inability of facing global competition on electronic consumer goods. However, with the buy back arrangement, they improved, but being at the cost of Govt. And the same not being permanent, AMTRON was required to intensify on promoting IT services in different parts of the State. AMTRON started productions under buy back arrangements with in ONIDA, VIDOCON, BPL, AKAI, HCL F&L etc. from 14-8-2002 and earned Rs. 40 Lakh from this till date, in addition to providing employment in allied activities and additional revenue to the Govt. For budgetary support for HRD proposal was being submitted. AMTRON would continue to be the nodal agency for IT in the State, through IT deptt. is curved out as a full fledged deptt. AMTRON has been providing IT consultancy through e-governance, e-setu, CISCO curriculum, school	provided. Memorandum for tax exemption should be submitted. Electronics and IT park should be developed.

(Contd.)

(Contd. Annexure-4)

Enterprises	*Gist of discussion in the Review Meeting held on 04-09-2003.*	*Recommendations of the meetings held on 04-09-2003*
	computerization under Rajiv Gandhi Computer literacy, MLA local area dev. Programmes, DOEACC 'O' & 'A' level course etc. As regards IT services, broadband connectivity, public grievance system online, Janasanyog portal, employment news, tie-up with ISRO, Police network service etc. were taken-up. Financial assistance programme for OBC people with NBCFDC's loan for computer education, data entry, repair & maintenance etc. had been started. They also initiated action on setting-up of call centers with franchisee. Their excess employees got absorbed into the system with increased activities.	
33. Assam Powerloom Development Corporation Ltd.	The company with weaving complex needed Rs. 70 Lakh as working capital and the employees formed a society to take-over management of the mill. The Cabinet was required to consider the proposal, but the matter was pending with the Law Department.	Expedite Govt. approval

(Contd.)

(Contd. Annexure-4)

Enterprises	*Gist of discussion in the Review Meeting held on 04-09-2003.*	*Recommendations of the meetings held on 04-09-2003*
34. Assam Syntex Ltd.	ASL was given on lease and production was scheduled from September 2003	Monitor
35. Fertichem Ltd.	FERTICHEM was decided to be closed as per Cabinet approval of the MOU executed between the State & the Central Govt. on Medium Term Fiscal Reform Programme. Valuation of assets was done; actions for disposal of assets were initiated and the complex was being converted to a mini-industrial park. In this connection, the interest of AMTRON to develop a IT park in the FERTICHEM complex was raised.	Complete the process in the line of actions taken-up
36. Assam Conductors & Tubes Ltd.	ASCON's financial performance as assessed in 2001 was very bad and it became inoperative subsequently. They had no marketing problem, as ASEB used to be purchase conductors regularly. The problems faced by ASCON were dearth of working capital, which was assessed earlier at around Rs. 80 Lakh; delay in payment by ASEB and surplus manpower of 40 Nos. It was explained that proposal for fund for implementing VRS was	Workout a scheme of revival with least possible further investment, for examining the viability. A special arrangement should be made for creating a crops fund for making the same available to the

(Contd.)

(Contd. Annexure-4)

Enterprises	*Gist of discussion in the Review Meeting held on 04-09-2003.*	*Recommendations of the meetings held on 04-09-2003*
	sought from the Govt. and against working capital requirement of Rs. 150 Lakh, Rs. 34 Lakh was earmarked, after allocation of fund for compliance of court orders on various cases. In addition, arrear payment of 54 months' salary of Rs. 200 Lakh would pose a problem. The industries deptt. asked the company to prepare a scheme for revival with least financial involvement, so that the industries deptt. could find means of funding, even by exploring possibilities of barrowing working capital. As records fund for VRS however, the budget provisions could not accommodate and so some special arrangements would be required not only for ASCON, but many other enterprises, which could be revived by shadding-off excess staff. The prime land belonging to ASCON could also help it in raising fund. The need of retaining the small unit in the public sector was also raised for discussion, and it was suggested that the disposal of its prime	enterprises, which could be revived for implementation of VRS. This could even be barrowing by the Govt. from financial institutions.

(Contd.)

(Contd. Annexure-4)

Enterprises	*Gist of discussion in the Review Meeting held on 04-09-2003.*	*Recommendations of the meetings held on 04-09-2003*
	assets could generate fund to discharge all liabilities. It was explained that if it could be made viable, it would be preparable to pertain it in the public sector.	
37. Nagaon Cooperative Sugar Mills Ltd.	NCSM had the scope of revival and therefore series of recommendations were made such as, promotion of sugar cane cultivation in mill zone area, implementation of VRS and provision of working capital through "Revolving Fund". It was reported that there was no sugar cane crushing during last year and in the current year, Rs. 24 Lakh was provided by the Govt, for restarting the mill, as the Apex Bank refused to provide loan. No good efforts were made to promote sugar cane cultivatioin.	· A clear-cut Action Plan to be submitted to re-assess the scope of revival of the mill.
38. Assam Co-Op Sugar Mills Ltd.	A CBI enquiry was going on in connection with a loan provided by the Apex Bank and so disposal of assets could not be made. No employees were there and most of the records were with the CBI. However, whatever information would be gathered	· A clear-cut Action Pan to be submitted including on the process to be started for selling the assets.

(Contd.)

(Contd. Annexure-4)

Enterprises	*Gist of discussion in the Review Meeting held on 04-09-2003.*	*Recommendations of the meetings held on 04-09-2003*
	from the DC, the same would be furnished.	
39. Assam Co-Op spinning Mills Ltd.	Against the recommendations of disinvestments, in a meeting held on 28-07-03, the co-operation Department informed that fund for restarting the mill was earmarked. A court case was also pending in the Hon'ble high court with regard to private possession. The logic of recommending disinvestment was non-viability, owing to low number of spindles, huge liabilities, non-availability on fund & huge liabilities to the employees. There was however good market of cotton yarn. Unless all this were arranged in a package, the revival might not be possible.	· Co-operation Department to submit a detailed report to assess the viability of revival of the mill in the public sector.
40. Assam Co-operative Jute Mills Ltd.	ACJM was a profit-making mill in the co-operative sector. The turn over last year was Rs. 15 Crore and profit as per audited account was Rs. 0.73 Crore, against the profit of Rs. 0.43 Crore in the year before last. However, the mill was well as the jute growers in the State were under threat, as the	· Diversify · Co-operation Department to constitute a task force to going into the details of the threat owing to dilution of the Jute Packaging Material Act 1987

(Contd.)

(Contd. Annexure-4)

Enterprises	*Gist of discussion in the Review Meeting held on 04-09-2003.*	*Recommendations of the meetings held on 04-09-2003*
	Central Govt. diluted the Jute Packaging Material Act 1987, wherever by plastic packaging was likely to take-over entire jute packaging in two years. In addition, due to the price advantage, the market was also shifted to plastic packaging; through it was not environment friendly. It was informed that the matter on dilution of the Jute Packaging Material Act was challenged by the West-Bengal Govt. and Indian Jute Association in the Hon'ble Supreme Court. In consideration of the threat looming large, the public enterprises Department, in a meeting held on 17-2-2003. Recommended constitution of a task force by the Cooperation Dept. jointly with the Industries and Agriculture Departments, to go into the details of the matter and to recommend measures to overcome the crisis. In the mean time, the mill was in the process of diversifying its products like odourless cloth, fine yarn, carpet, hessian etc. and was exploring logical market of	**and recommend measures to overcome the crisis.** **· Declare dividend** **· Hold AGM**

(Contd.)

(Contd. Annexure-4)

Enterprises	*Gist of discussion in the Review Meeting held on 04-09-2003.*	*Recommendations of the meetings held on 04-09-2003*
	its products. They were supplying products to IOC for packing paraffin was and if the State govt. take-up food-grain procurement activity, the mill would survive the crisis.	
41. Assam Polyester Co-Op. Society Ltd	APOL, declared as a Relief Undertaking was faced with severe working capital crisis and their minimum need was Rs. 3 Crore. They were operating on job order basis at 20-25% capacity in 2 shifts with captive power generated at Rs.6 per unit i.e. about 1000 Kg of yam & 1200 Meters of fabric and were incurring losses. Due to arrear in payment of electricity bills, their grid power was disconnected, which had been costing them Rs.7.13 per unit. They pleaded for revision of their connected load. The effort to get working capital from UCo Bank failed as Govt guarantee was insisted and the Finance Deptt. did not accord approval to the proposal of the Co-operation Deptt. They approached NCDC and the response was favourable. NCDC identified	Co-operation Deptt. To provide working capital support. Co-operation Deptt. to nominate state representative to the Committee appointed by NCDC. APOL to take-up the matter of revision of connected load with ASEB Loan due to IDBI to be settled

(Contd.)

(Contd. Annexure-4)

Enterprises	*Gist of discussion in the Review Meeting held on 04-09-2003.*	*Recommendations of the meetings held on 04-09-2003*
	APOL to be taken-up for rehabilitation and proposed appointment of a Committee, involving the Ministry of Textiles, to prepare a restructuring proposal. Nomination of Govt. of Assam to the Committee was requested vide letter dated 31-07-2003. The mill authority was preparing a detailed rcport for the Committee. In the mean time, some restructuring viz. developing costing centers, improvement in systems & procedures etc. were taken-up. They proposed to reduce the manpower, for which Rs.1 Crare was the estimated requirement. While 50% of this could be managed by the mill, assistance from the Govt. was required for the remaining 50%. APOL availed Central Excise exemption and with the economy measures, the losses could be made-up on optimum capacity utilization. Two of their loans due to FIs were settled, but the loan due to, IDBI, the leader of the consortium (Rs.4.2 Crore	

(Contd.)

(Contd. Annexure-4)

Enterprises	*Gist of discussion in the Review Meeting held on 04-09-2003.*	*Recommendations of the meetings held on 04-09-2003*
	principal) was pending settlement. IDBI wanted settlement of entire 'loans guaranteed by the State Govt. for different SLPEs and it was necessary for taking-up APOL's case separately, for e..”Peditious disposal. Their assets were revalued and the net-worth was positive.	
42. Swahid Kushal Konwar Samabay Sutakol	About three years back, the mill was given to a private party for its running, under a provisional deed of agreement. The investment in the mill was Rs.30 Crore and the private occupier was agreeable to pay maximurri rent of Rs.3 Lakh P A. The private occupier filed a case in the Hon'ble High Court demanding finalization of the agreement, which was stuck-up on the issue of low rent. While privatization was preferred, the rent was not found reasonable and therefore it was considered to fight the case for taking back the mill. On the other hand, the society was not in a position to run the mill profitably. The private occupier was however engaging the mill's	Proper disinvestments should be done by working-out appropriate modalities.

(Contd.)

(Contd. Annexure-4)

Enterprises	*Gist of discussion in the Review Meeting held on 04-09-2003.*	*Recommendations of the meetings held on 04-09-2003*
	employees and they were getting some salary	
43. Assam Plantation Crop Dev. Corpn. Ltd	APCDC had staff strength of 202 nos. and the requirement assessed was 79 nos. Therefore, implementation of VRS was planned and in the 1" phase, applications from 77 employees were obtained. Proposal for the required fund was submitted to the Govt, which was referred to the Finance Deptt. In the 2"" phase, 46 employees would be reduced through implementation of VRS. In addition, the employees were due to be paid with salary of 56 months. Depending on the quantum of production, part salary was being paid. The liability of the Corpn. rose to Rs.7.5 Crore. The liability of CPF due of Rs.0.66 Crore was a matter of serious concern. 'The option of revival could be thought of, but in that case, apart from the liquidation of liabilities, investment in expansion of plantations would be necessary, as the existing plantation would be yielding for another 7-8 yrs only. The other	Implement VRS The question of revival or merger to be decided by the administrative department.

(Contd.)

(Contd. Annexure-4)

Enterprises	*Gist of discussion in the Review Meeting held on 04-09-2003.*	*Recommendations of the meetings held on 04-09-2003*
	option would be to merge the Corpn. with the Directorate of T e;;' as was planned earlier to bring all cash crop producing organizations under one umbrella, after reduction of staff through implementation of VRS.	
44. Assam State Textbook Production and Publication Corpn.	A Corporation with good. performance.	The Govt. to clear the dues to the Corporation.. Rationalize manpower including through implementation of VRS Utilize prime assets to generate revenue
45. Assam Mineral Development. Corpn. Ltd	It was reported that the revival. plan was prepared and the approval of the Board of. Directors was awaited. As regards implementation of. works through contractors, it was stated that the system was. in vogue and the Board of Directors was required to. consider stopping the practice. The meeting of the Board of Directors being not held since long, these matters could not be	Finalize revival plan Review system of implementation of work through contractors Settle IDBI due af Rs. 2.5 Crore Recover due from defaulting customers.

(Contd.)

(Contd. Annexure-4)

Enterprises	*Gist of discussion in the Review Meeting held on 04-09-2003.*	*Recommendations of the meetings held on 04-09-2003*
	decided. The Corpn. meanwhile took several steps viz. Steps to increase production by 10%; Utilization of in-house facilities like garnge etc. to fullest capacity to reduce cost of maintenance and putting in steessin marketing for better revenue.	
46. Assam, Govt. Construction Corpn Ltd.	The BE turnover of AGCC was assessed at Rs. 60 Crore PA but the turnover ranged between Rs. 8—10 Crore. The PWD, the administrative deptt. of AGCC committed to allot work worth minimum Rs.60 Croce annually to AGCC, but recently PWD took a stand that AGCC was required to compete for works in PWD. "The PWD even proposed for scrapping of Correction Slip No. 263- Appendix-8 of AFR Second edition 1939 which stated "All State Govt. Development Department should offer all concentrated work costing more than Rs. I0 Lakh to AGCC Ltd. and only in the event of AGCC Ltd. not being in a position to take-up the works, tenders should be floated for entrustment of execution to other	In view of the position, PWD should decide the future AGCC. Implement VRS. Explore works in Central Govt Projects Utilize own resources and infrastructure, rather than engaging contractors

(Contd.)

(Contd. Annexure-4)

Enterprises	*Gist of discussion in the Review Meeting held on 04-09-2003.*	*Recommendations of the meetings held on 04-09-2003*
	Agandas". The Finance. Deptt. sought views of the Public Enterprises Deptt. on this proposal. The AGCC pleaded that at least for another 3 - 5 yrs, the clause should not be scrapped and. PWD should honour its commitment, as otherwise the scope of survival of AGCC would be bleak. The AGCC was getting some works from other Deptts. like Transport, Agriculture, which was not sufficient and its parent department was required to provide support.	
47. Assam Police Housing Corpn.Ltd.	down to losing category, because of the decline in performance.Their accumulated loss increased from Rs.1.32 Crore in 2001 to Rs.2.95 Crore in 2003. The net-worth of (-)1.29 Crore in 2001 came down' to (-) Rs.292 Crore. It was explained that the performance of APHC was required to be looked into differently, as their Turnover depended on the amount of fund 'released for works. The Central Govt would be liberal to allocate more fund, if the fund already	A High Level Policy Decision is to be taken on direct release of Central Govt. fund to the Corporation, for construction of Police housing in the State.

(Contd.)

(Contd. Annexure-4)

Enterprises	*Gist of discussion in the Review Meeting held on 04-09-2003.*	*Recommendations of the meetings held on 04-09-2003*
	provided be utilized properly and timely. Because of the fact that in spite of recommendations for release of fund directly to the Corpn, which would enable it to complete more works, utilize its manpower and get more fund, the Finance Deptt. was not agreeable. There was inordinate delay in release of fund by the State Govt and this deprived APHC, and also the Police Deptt. in providing police housing. The Corpn. was self supporting, could deliver works cheaper & faster, but for want of procedural change, APHC might get crippled. Further, the Central Govt might assign works to CPWD. The delay in release of fund against 11'" Fin. Commission awards posed another problem that owing to cost escalation, the number of houses to be constructed would be required to be reduced. Regarding raising of own fund, it was e"'1'lained that the same would be available for personal housing only and State Govt.	

(Contd.)

(Contd. Annexure-4)

Enterprises	*Gist of discussion in the Review Meeting held on 04-09-2003.*	*Recommendations of the meetings held on 04-09-2003*
	guarantee would be required, which might be difficult to get. The EMf also worked-out to be unbearable by the employees. Further, direct housing loans became cheaper	
48. Assam State Housing Board	The turnover of ASHB improved slightly during 2000-01, but decreased. Substantially thereafter arid the losses increased. On the recommendations made earlier, it was explained that the Board was going for commercial housing schemes with private sector participation and steps for recovery were taken, including references to HODs of Govt. employees for recovery from their salaries. On rent revision, which was done last in 1998, it was stated that some Cases filed by the tenants were still pending in the Courts. However, the Board would go *for* revision of rent. The Board had 371 employees, of which 100 were identified as surplus and the Govt. would be required to fund the cost implementation of VRS, for which proposal was being	Go for commercial housing schemes involving private sector selectively Tone-up recovery-consider offering OTS package Revise rent periodically. Govt. to. release dues to the Board, including for implementation of VRS To shed-off surplus staff. Govt. to consider the proposal for selling of flats *I* residential units

(Contd.)

(Contd. Annexure-4)

Enterprises	*Gist of discussion in the Review Meeting held on 04-09-2003.*	*Recommendations of the meetings held on 04-09-2003*
	submitted. The Board also planned to sell flats / residential units, initially of the Hengrabari project and the matter was lying for decision in the Govt. The Board was due to get around Rs.9 Crore of budgetary amount, which accumulated since last 5 yrs.	

9

Heterosecdastic Frontier Model and Efficiency: A Financial Econometric Analysis of State Level Public Enterprises in India

Abstract

The purpose of this paper is to illustrate the problem of heteroscedasticity in the estimation of frontiers and thereby inefficiency measures. Because most of the measures of inefficiency are based on residuals, it is critically important to note that the residuals and consequently the inefficiency measures may be distorted by specification error of heteroscedasticity. A frontier model is estimated under the assumptions of homoscedasticity and heteroscedasticity for the one-side error term, using aggregate financial data on sate level public enterprises for fifteen selected states in India. The results show changes in the estimated frontier models and in the inefficiency measures when correction for heteroscedasticity is accounted in the estimation process. It is found that the efficiency rankings of

many states are affected markedly by the correction of heteroscedasticity.

The relatively most efficient state is frontier and its financial ratios of revenue, capital employed, net worth and total investments (with a judgemental aspect of other relevant financial information, economic and non-economic factors, and of financial ratios of some other less inefficient states) can be used as an important policy implication for financial re-engineering by other states for improving their efficiency levels in future. However, the overall performance of SLPEs in India is very poor, and requires a total business process re-engineering.

1. Introduction

A failure to produce maximum possible output (i.e. frontier output) means the technical decision is inefficient. The amount by which a firm (or, group of firms) lies below its production frontier can be regarded as a measure of technical inefficiency. After the pioneer work of Farell (1957), the serious considerations has been given to the possibility of estimating frontier in an effort to bridge the gap between theory and empirical work, especially by Richmond (1974), Schmidt (1976,1978), Greene (1980), and Forsend Lovell and Schmidt (1980). The subject inspired widespread interest with the introduction of stochastic frontier model by Aigner, Lovel and Schmidt (1977), Olsan, Schmidt and Waldman (1980), Jondraw, Lovell, Materov and Schmidt (1982), Schmidt (1985), Bauer (1980), Bera and Sharma (1999) and others. Indian econometricians (working in India) have also worked on frontier models and efficiency. Some of them are Sharma (1989-90), Remaswamy (1984), Sharma and Sinha (1995,1998,2003), Bhawani (1991), Jha, Murty and Sahni (1992), Gajanan (1995), Sharma, Verma and Sinha (2002) and Shanugam and Kulshrestha (2005).

The measures of inefficiency used in these studies are based on residuals obtained from the estimation of a frontier.

Residuals are sensitive to specification errors, particularly in frontier models, and it is likely that this sensitivity will be passed on to the inefficiency measures Heteroscedasticity is a specification error often associated with the estimation of production / cost function, and the presence of heteroscedasticity is likely to affect these inefficiency measures.

It is well known that heteroscedasticity does not have much harmful effect on estimators of average function – estimation remain unbiased but are no longer efficient. This occurs because average functions are estimated by last squares, which yields a mean regression, and means are not affected by symmetric dispersion around them. The problem of heteroscedasticity is for more serious in frontier models because, unlike the mean regression function, the frontier is changed when the dispersion increases (Caudil, Ford and Gropper; 1995).

Caudil and Ford (1993) investigated the effects of heteroscedasticity in the one-sided error on parameter estimates in a single – factor frontier production function. They found that heteroscedasticity leads to biased parameter estimates. According to Caudil, Ford and Gropper (1995) observed that inefficiency measures are also affected by the heteroscedasticity and remarked that not accounting for the heteroscedasticity in the estimation led to the overestimation of inefficiency for small firms and the underestimation of inefficiency for large firms.

Reifschneider and Stevenson (1991) were the first to incorporate heteroscedasticity into a frontier model in their investigation of firm – specific inefficiency in the electric – utility industry. They incorporated heteroscedasticity into the composed error by allowing the mean of the one-sided error to vary. This is achieved by simply adding a constant, which can very from firm to firm, to the usual one-sided error term. This flexibility permits the measurement of firm – specific inefficiency. Ynengert(1993) incerported heteroscedasticity directly into expressions for both variances and the variances are not firm-specific but group – specific. Caudel, Ford and Gropper(1995) estimated frontier cost model under assumption of homoscedasticity and heteroscedasticity for the one-sided error. When heteroscedasticity is incorporated into the estimation the inefficiency measures are changed significantly.

Heteroscedastic frontier models have further been used for refining the inefficiency measures by Hadri (1999), Giannakas, Tran and Tzouvelekas (2003), Keragiannis and Tzouvelekas (2005), Trestini (2006), Paxton (2007) and others.

In this paper homoscedastic and heteroscedastic stochastic and non-stochastic frontier models have been estimated using COLS/ moments and COLS estimation techniques on financial date of State level Public Enterprises in India, to show that inefficiency measures are sensitive to specification errors like heroscedasticity and must be viewed with caution useless the heroscedasticity is incorporated into the estimation. Section two presents a naïve modeling on homoscedastic and heteroscedastic – assumptions frontier models and efficiency / inefficiency measurements. Section three describes the area of research on state level public enterprises and the financial data for frontier model and inefficiency (inter-state). In section four, empirical results are shown and discussed. And the section five concludes and suggests policy implications for improving efficiency with special reference to financial policies in general for state level public enterprises.

2. Homoscedastic And Heteroscedastic Frontier Model And Efficiency

Production frontiers

The estimates of stochastic production frontier and the nonstochastic production frontier models are able to shed light on technical inefficiency.

Stochastic Production Frontier Model

The composed error — stochastic production frontier model is given by where y_i is observed output x_{ji} are the inputs

$$\ln Y_i = \ln \alpha_0 + \sum_{J=1}^{k} \alpha_j \ln X_{ji} + v_i - u_i, u_i \geq \qquad ....(1.1)$$

to the production process, with k inputs and a are parameters to be estimated for n observations. i=1,2 - - - n. j=1,2 - - -k..

In this case, the disturbance is assumed to be of the composite form (i.e., v_i-u_i), where v is NID (o, σ_v^2) and, a symmetric component captures the random variation in output due to factors outside the control of the firms. On the other hand, u is a one-sided error, i.e., technical inefficiency. Thus, u, assumed to be independent of v_i and X_{ji} are iid as half-normal. And $\sigma^2 = \sigma_u^2 + \sigma_v^2$, $\lambda = \frac{\sigma_u}{\sigma_v}$

In equation 1.1 the expression $\left[\ln \alpha_0 + \sum_{J=1}^{n} \alpha_j \ln X_{ji} + v\right]$ represents stochastic production frontier. Here, ln y_i is assumed to be bounded from above by the stochastic production frontier with technical efficiency in production process given by u_i per cent. Again, $u_i \geq 0$ represents the shortfall of output from the frontier.

Thus, the composite error term (v_i - u_i) has two parts, one representing randomness (or, statistical noise) and the other representing technical inefficiency. The distributional assumptions made are zero-mean normal distribution for the symmetric component and the same distribution truncated above zero for the one-sided component. This model differs from the classical regression model only in its asymmetric disturbance.

For the estimation of such a model, the COLS/ moments estimator is considered. Except for constant term the OLS is unbiased and consistent. the bias of the constant term is the mean of (v_i-u_i), i.e.,

$$E(v_i - u_i) = -E(u_i) = -\sqrt{2|\pi}\,\hat{\sigma}_u \qquad ....(1.2)$$

Variances can be estimated by

$$\hat{\sigma}_u^2 = \left(\sqrt{\pi|2}\{\pi|\pi - 4\}\hat{\mu}_3'\right)^{2/3} \qquad \text{....(1.3)}$$

$$\hat{\sigma}_v^2 = \hat{\mu}_2' - \{\pi - 2|\pi\}\hat{\sigma}_u^2$$

where $\hat{\mu}_2$ and $\hat{\mu}_3$ are the estimates of second and third order moments of the OLS residuals. The intercept, then, can be corrected by adding to the OLS estimated constant term the negative of the estimated bias, i.e. $\{2|\pi\}\hat{\sigma}_u$.á

To recapitulate, the COLS/ moments estimator of all parameters except the intercept term is the same as the OLS estimator. The element of s_u is used to convert the OLS estimate of the constant term into the COLS/Moments[1] estimate.

If the third moment of least square residual is positive, $\hat{\sigma}_u$ will be negative, and there is no need to proceed beyond the OLS.

The stochastic production frontier model estimates the shape and placement of the frontier and measures the average extent of technical inefficiency over the observations included in estimation.

Nonstochastic Production Frontier Model :

The one-sided error— NSPF model is given by

$$\ln y_i = \ln \alpha_0 + \sum_{j=1}^{k} \alpha_j \ln X_{ji} - u_i, \qquad \text{.....(1.4)}$$

$$u_i \geq 0$$

Evidently, the expression $\left[\ln \alpha_0 + \sum_{j=1}^{n} \alpha_i \ln X_{ji}\right]$

is nonstochastic. The efficiency component (u_i) is a one-sided, nonpositive error, derived from a normal (o, σ_u^2) distribution truncated from above. Technical inefficiency exists to the extent that a firm's output lies beneath the frontier. The intercept $\ln_0$ is the corrected form of the corresponding OLS estimate. $\ln_0$ has different estimates for (i) classical average function estimated by OLS (ii) nonstochastic frontier by COLS, and (iii) stochastic frontiers estimated by COLS/moments estimator.

Corrected Ordinary least squares (COLS) provides estimates for the unbiased and consistent estimate of the intercept as well. For the estimation of nonstochastic production frontier model, the COLS is used until all residuals are negative and atleast one of them is zero. This is how, the extent of relative technical efficiency of each observation can be estimated.

Test of homoscedasticity/ heteroscedasticity

Schmidt and Lin (1984) suggested a valid test on the coefficient of Skewness, i.e.,

$$\sqrt{b_1} = \left(\sum e_i^3/N\right)/\left(\sum e_i^2/N\right)^{1.5} \; or \quad b_1 = \frac{\left(\sum e_i^3/N\right)^2}{\left(\sum e_i^2/N\right)^3} = \frac{\mu_3^2}{\mu_2^3}$$

Alternatively, a test of symmetry is proposal by Pagen and Hall(1983), i.e., $h_1=[(N.\, b_1)/6]^{.5}$

There is well known Park Test available in econometric text books for detecting heteroscedasticity.

$$\ln \sigma_i^2 = \ln \sigma^2 + \beta \ln X_i + \varepsilon_i \qquad ......(1.6)$$

If β turn out to be significant it implies the presence of heteroscedasticity.

Through homoscedastic frontier model inefficiencies can be observed on an average and on individual basis. However, invalid situation of homoscedasticity (i.e, the presence of heteroscedasticity) leads to specification error.

Hence, correction for heteroscedasticity is desirable.

Under heteroscedasticity Var($U_i = \sigma_i^2$). The assumptions underlying the heteroscedasticity can be defined as

$$\sigma_i^2 = \sigma^2 (\ln X_{ki})^2$$

and transformation is given by

$$\frac{\ln Y_i}{\ln X_{ki}} = \ln b_0 \left(\frac{1}{\ln X_{ki}}\right) + \sum_{j=i}^{K} b_j \frac{\ln X_{ji}}{\ln X_{ki}} + \left(\frac{V_i - U_i}{\ln X_{ki}}\right)$$

$$Var\left(\frac{V_i - U_i}{\ln X_{ki}}\right) = E\left(\frac{V_i - U_i}{\ln X_{ki}}\right) = E\left(\frac{U_i}{\ln X_{ki}}\right)^2$$

$$= \frac{1}{(\ln X_{ki})^2} E\left(U_i^2\right) = \frac{1}{(\ln X_{ki})^2} \cdot \sigma_i^2$$

$$= \frac{1}{(\ln X_{ki})^2} \sigma^2 (\ln X_{ki})^2 = \sigma^2$$

The above transformation may remove heteroscedasticity. And the inefficiencies measured through this transformation as usual abóve are likely to be different than the inefficiency measured in the pressure of heteroscedasticity.

1. Financial Data Base Of State Level Public Enterprises in India

The Sate level Public Enterprises (SLPEs) are important component of public enterprise system India. As per the Institute of Public Enterprise (IPE) database, there were 1,129 SLPEs as on March 31, 2005 with an investment of Rs. 2,59,184 Crores. The contribution of the SLPEs to the GDP is about 5 percent as compared to 10 percent by the Central Public Enterprises (CPEs). The financial performance of the SLPEs bears the brunt of shortcomings of having greater exposure to the state political systems, characterized by weak middle management system (do not have requisite number of professionally qualified managers). The top management in these enterprises comprises mostly an IAS CEO and nominees of the state government drawn from civil services, defeated politicians and political party in power (Mishra and Kiranmai, 2006).

The aggregate financial data on Revenue, Capital Employed, Net-worth and Total Investment could be used to estimate frontier models and thereby inefficiency measures. And the number of enterprises can also be used as independent variable in the frontier models as an important reason of heteroscedasticity (Inter-State Financial Data) and thus useful for correcting the heteroscedasticity.

The data on revenue, capital employed, net-worth and total investment are considered for a cross – section (2004-05) frontier model (as per IPE-Database). The total investment comprises sum of total of the investments in the form of equity and debt capital by State Government and others which includes the Central Government, holding companies and financial institutions. The capital employed comprises the sum total of the investment in the next fixed block and working capital. The net fixed assets indicate the investments in gross fixed assets minus accumulated depreciation. The investment in working capital represents the excess of current assets over current liabilities. The capital employed is also represented by the sum total of investment arising out of equity, long-term debts and internal resources. The net worth is derived by subtracting intangible assets, accumulated losses and fictious assets from paid-up capital, and reserves and surpluses. Total revenue represents the top line of an enterprise. This provides cushion against contingencies and the cover to meet expenses. This should grow atleast at a compound growth rate of 10 percent. And should be atleast three times of the investment. The private sector multiple is five times. The foreign private sector multiple is eight times. In 2004-05 Gujarat, M.P., Maharesthra and W.B. have performed well in 2004-05. Assam, Delhi, Gujarat, Haryana, Maharesthra, U.P. and W.B. have been major net loss earners. As to the accumulated losses the loss leaders have been A.P., Arunachal Pradesh, Assam, Bihar, Delhi, Goa, Gujarat, Kerala, J.K., Karnataka, Orissa, Pondicherry, Sikkim, T.N.

Kerala, W.B., Tripura and Bihar rejected the privatization option and decided to go in for only restructuring / closure including the reference to BIFR (Board for Industrial and Financial Reconstruction). Some states such as M.P. Kernataka and Kerala have announced detailed policies regarding the SLPEs portfolio. The government of Maharastra in their Industrial Policy resolution announced the institution to privatize the SLPEs.

2. Empirical Analysis

4.1 Estimation of Technical Inefficiency under Assumption of Homoscedastic Variance

4.1.1 With reference to section 2 and its equations (1.1) to (1.3) the estimates of stochastic production frontier (SPF) models and with reference to equation (1.4) the estimates of non-stochastic production frontier (NSPF) models are given in table 1. Frontier models are also compared with traditional average production function (TAPF)

Table 1. Estimates of TAPF NSPF and SPF Models

Dependent Variable – Revenue ($\ln y_0$)
Independent Variable – Capital Employed ($\ln X_1$), Net Worth ($\ln X_2$), Total Investment ($\ln X_3$)

Model	*Estimation Method*	*Intercept*	*Estimation Details other than Technical Inefficiency*					
			$\ln x_1$	$\ln x_2$	$\ln x_3$	R^2	F	
TAPF	OLS	-4.178 (3.153)t	-.104 (.165)	.13 (.938)	1.404 (2.115)	0.904	34.497 Sig .000	
NSPF	COLS		LPR = 1.424					
SPF	COLS/ MOMENTS		$\hat{\mu}_3$	$\hat{\mu}_2$	$\hat{\sigma}_u^2$	$\hat{\sigma}_v^2$	$\hat{\lambda}$	$\hat{\sigma}_u$
			-.2486	.7333	1.0439	.3376	1.796	1.0439

TAPF = Tradition Average Production Function
NSPF = Nonstochastic Production Frontier
SPF = Stochastic Production Frontier
COLS = Corrected ordinary least squares
LPR = Largest Positive Residuals in TAPF
$\hat{\mu}_3$ = Third order Moment of Least Squares Residuals
$\hat{\mu}_2$ = Second order moment
$\hat{\sigma}_v^2$ = Variance of the symmetric error
$\hat{\sigma}_u^2$ = Variance of the One – sider error
λ = Signal to noise ratio

NSPF intercept is higher than the OLS intercept and SPF intercept is also higher than the OLS intercept. But SPF intercept is lower than the NSPF intercept, and this indicates that SPF model accommodates some statistical noise (such as some of the factors outside the control of the firms). The COLS/Moments estimator presents that theis negative and thereby is positive, and hence average technical inefficiency measure is possible.

For a single cross section of 15 states (with aggregate financial data on SLPEs), individual inefficiencies through NSPF and average inefficiency through SPF are shown in table 2.

Table 2. Estimates of Technical Inefficiencies through NSPF and SPF Models

SI.No.	*State*	*Technical Inefficiency*		*Efficiency Ranking*
		Term	*Percentage*	
1.	Andhra Pradesh	1.49	77.46	8
2.	Assam	1.713	81.97	11
3.	Goa	0.772	53.79	5
4.	Gujrat	1.75	82.62	12
5.	Haryana	2.961	94.82	14
6.	Himachal Pradesh	2.038	86.97	13
7.	Madhya Pradesh	0.52	40.55	3
8.	Maharastra	1.34	73.82	7
9.	Meghalaya	0.355	29.88	2
10.	Mizoram	3.168	95.79	15
11.	Pondichery	0	0	1
12.	Punjab	0.703	50.49	4
13.	Rajasthan	1.319	73.26	6
14.	U.P.	1.597	79.75	9
15.	W.B.	1.633	80.47	10
Average Inefficiency (NSPF)		1.42	66.77	
Average Inefficiency (SPF)		0.8331	56.53	

State number eleven turns out to be most technical efficient. Average inefficiency (SPF) is 56.53%. Minimum inefficiency is 29.88% (NSPF) and maximum is 95.79%.

4.1.2 The results in 4.1 are sensitive after inclusion of one more independent variable, i.e. number of enterprises in each state ($\ln X_4$)

Table 3: Dependent Variable – Revenue (lny) Independent Variable – Capital Employed ($\ln X_1$), Net Worth ($\ln X_2$), Total Investment ($\ln X_3$),No. of Ent ($\ln X_u$)

Model	*Estimation Method*	*Intercept*	*Estimation Details other than Technical Inefficiency*					
			ln x1	*ln x2*	*ln x3*	*ln x4*	R^2	*F*
TAPF	OLS	-4.168 (2.988)	-.091 (.133)	0.13 (.896)	1.36 (1.525)	0.71 (.078)	0.904	23.54 Sig 0.00
NSPF	COLS		LPR = 1.364					
SPF	COLS/ MOMENTS		$\hat{\mu}_3$	$\hat{\mu}_2$	$\hat{\sigma}_u^2$	$\hat{\sigma}_v^2$	$\hat{\lambda}$	$\hat{\sigma}_u$
			-0.2032	0.666	.9526	.3201	1.725	0.9760

Table 4: Estimates of Technical Inefficiencies through NSPF and SPF Models

SI.No.	*State*	*Technical Inefficiency*		*Efficiency Ranking*
		Term	*Percentage*	
1.	Andhra Pradesh	1.4017	75.38	8
2.	Assam	1.645	80.69	11
3.	Goa	0.7525	52.88	5
4.	Gujrat	1.6671	81.12	12
5.	Haryana	2.7993	93.91	14
6.	Himachal Pradesh	1.9590	85.90	13
7.	Madhya Pradesh	0.50266	39.51	3

(Contd.)

(Contd. Table 4)

Sl.No.	*State*	*Technical Inefficiency*		*Efficiency Ranking*
		Term	*Percentage*	
8.	Maharastra	1.2987	72.71	7
9.	Meghalaya	0.3294	28.07	2
10.	Mizoram	3.0335	95.19	15
11.	Pondichery	0	0	1
12.	Punjab	.6838	49.53	4
13.	Rajasthan	1.2305	70.79	6
14.	U.P.	1.57104	79.22	9
15.	W.B.	1.5923	79.65	10
Average Inefficiency (NSPF)		1.3644	65.63	
Average Inefficiency (SPF)		.7789	54.11	

State number eleven turns out to be most technical efficient. Average inefficiency (SPF) is 56.53%. Minimum inefficiency is 29.88% (NSPF) and maximum is 95.79%.

4.2 Testing for Heteroscedasticity

4.2.1 Applying the Park Test (Equation 1.6)

$$\ln \hat{U}_i^2 = 4.832 - .788\ t(3.55) \quad LnX_{1i}$$

$$\ln \hat{U}_i^2 = 1.272 -..552\ t(3.25) \quad LnX_{2i}$$

$$\ln \hat{U}_i^2 = 5.603 - .868\ t(3.712) \quad LnX_{3i}$$

The frontier models estimated in 4.1.1 are no more homoscedastic. As the coefficients of all ln X_i are significant at 1% level of significance suggest the presence of heteroscedasticity in the frontier model.

Moreover as per test (eq. 1.5)

$\sqrt{b_1} = 0.3366$, $b_1 = .1132$, h=0.5319

Three is evidence of the presence of heteroscedasticity.

4.2.2 Similarly for the frontier model in 4.1.2

$$\text{Ln } \hat{U}_i^2 = 4.855 \; -.803\,(3.369) \quad \text{LnX}_{1i}$$

$$\text{Ln } \hat{U}_i^2 = 1.26 \; -.569\,(3.164) \quad \text{LnX}_{2i}$$

$$\text{Ln } \hat{U}_i^2 = 5.723 \; -.895\,(3.592) \quad \text{LnX}_{3i}$$

$$\text{Ln } \hat{U}_i^2 = 4.772 \; -1.901\,(3.255) \quad \text{LnX}_{4i}$$

All coefficients are significant Þ presence of heteroscedasticity

$$\sqrt{b_1} = 0.3714, \; b_1 = .1379, \qquad h=0.5871$$

Also suggests the presence of heteroscedasticity.

4.3 Correction in Heteroscedasticity, Frontier Model and Inefficiency.

Following the equation 1.8 of section 2, frontier model estimates are given in table 5 and inefficiency measures in table 6.

Table 5:

Dependent Variable = $\frac{InY_i}{X_{4i}}$

Model	*Estimation Method*	*Intercept*	*Estimation Details other than Technical Inefficiency*					
			$\frac{1}{\text{lnX}_{4i}}$	$\frac{\text{lnX}_{1i}}{\text{lnX}_{4i}}$	$\frac{\text{lnX}_{2i}}{\text{lnX}_{4i}}$	$\frac{\text{lnX}_{3i}}{\text{lnX}_{4i}}$	*R^2*	*F*
TAPF	OLS	-.270 (.199)	-5.329 (4.239)	-.035 (.036)	0.97 (.577)	1.608 (1.253)	.732	6.826 Sig.006
NSPF	COLS		LPR = 1.461					
SPF	COLS/ MOMENTS		$\hat{\mu}_3$	$\hat{\mu}_2$	$\hat{\sigma}_u^2$	$\hat{\sigma}_v^2$	$\hat{\lambda}$	$\hat{\sigma}_u$
			.006	.1629	(-.000027 449	.1029		

Table 6: Estimates of Technical Inefficiencies through NSPF and SPF Models

SI.No.	*State*	*Technical Inefficiency*		*Efficiency Ranking*
		Term	*Percentage*	
1.	Andhra Pradesh	.79995	54.06	11
2.	Assam	.76003	53.23	8
3.	Goa	.37209	31.07	3
4.	Gujrat	.84804	57.17	12
5.	Haryana	1.2124	70.25	14
6.	Himachal Pradesh	.90956	59.73	13
7.	Madhya Pradesh	.46745	37.34	4
8.	Maharastra	.71807	51.23	6
9.	Meghalaya	.29846	25.8	2
10.	Mizoram	1.3043	72.85	15
11.	Pondichery	0	0	1
12.	Punjab	.58531	44.31	5
13.	Rajasthan	.76339	53.39	9
14.	U.P.	.74198	52.38	7
15.	W.B.	.77546	52.95	10
Average Inefficiency (NSPF)		.7038	47.85	
Average Inefficiency (SPF)		NA	NA	

State number 11 turns out to be most technical efficient. Minimum inefficiency is 58.8 % (NSPF) and maximum is 72.86%.

Test of Homoscedasticity

$$\ln\left(\frac{U_i}{\ln X_{4i}}\right)^2 = -7.746 + \quad 1.622\ (.683) \quad \frac{\ln X_{1i}}{\ln X_{4i}}$$

$$\ln\left(\frac{U_i}{\ln X_{4i}}\right)^2 = -2.827 - \quad .659\ (.721) \quad \frac{\ln X_{2i}}{\ln X_{4i}}$$

$$\ln\left(\frac{U_i}{\ln X_{4i}}\right)^2 = -13.535 + \quad 3.964\ (1.347) \quad \frac{\ln X_{3i}}{\ln X_{4i}}$$

$$\ln\left(\frac{U_i}{\ln X_{4i}}\right)^2 = -9.329 + \quad 17.939\ (3.869) \quad \frac{1}{\ln X_{4i}}$$

All the coefficients are not significant at 1% level of significance in first three cases, hence there is presence of homoscedasticity in the transformed model.

$b_1 = 0.000033$ $h = 0.009487$

Table 7: Inefficiency – Summary in Percentage

	Average		*Minimum*	*Maximum*
	SPF	*NSPF*		
Model 1 (With Het.)	56.53	66.77	29.88	95.79
Model 1 (With Het.)	54.11	65.63	28.07	95.19
Model 1 (With No. Het.)	NA	47.85	25.8	72.86

Table 8: Summary: Efficiency Ranking

States	*Andhra Pradesh*	*Assam*	*Goa*	*Gujrat*	*Haryana*	*Himachal Pradesh*	*Madhya Pradesh*	*Maharastra*	*Meghalaya*	*Mizoram*	*Pondichery*	*Punjab*	*Rajasthan*	*U.P.*	*W.B.*
	1	2	3	4	5	6	7	8	9	10	11	12	13	14	15
Rank-1 (Under Hetero-scedasticity)	8	11	5	12	14	13	3	7	2	15	1	4	6	9	10
Rank-2 (Under correction of Hetero-scedasticity)	11	8	3	12	14	13	4	6	2	15	1	5	9	7	10

The rank correlation coefficient is 0.93 which is significantly less than one is an evidence for changes in efficiency ranks of many states after correcting the specification error of heteroscedasticity.

3. Conclusion and Policy Implications

To estimate firm-specific inefficiency frontier model has been widely used in economics. This paper discusses the estimation of a heteroscedastic frontier model by COLS-Moments and COLS methods on financial aggregate date of state level public enterprises for a sample of fifteen states in India.

A frontier model is estimated under assumptions of homoscedasticity and heteroscedasticity for the one-sided error term. Park test and a ratio test (skewness based on third order and second order moments of the residuals) reject the null hypothesis of homoscedasticity. First the efficiencies are measured in the presence of heteroscedasticity. Then the correction of heteroscedasticity is incorporated into the estimation by dividing the model throughout including one-sided error than becomes homoscedastic. The estimated coefficients in the models are different, and the difference is found in the state – specific inefficiency measures from each model. The minimum inefficiency under the presence of heteroscedasticity is 28.07% and maximum 95.79%. However, with the correction of heteroscedasticity the minimum ineffiency is 25.8% and the maximum is 72.86%. The ranking of many states changes when the correction for heteroscedasticity is incorporated into the estimation. This is considerable evidence that inefficiency measures are sensitive to specification errors like heteroscedasticity and must be viewed with great caution unless the heteroscedasticity is corrected into the frontier estimation.

The relatively most efficient state is frontier and its existing financial ratios of revenue, capital employed, net worth and total investments (and financial ratios of some less inefficiency states with a judgemental aspect of other financial information, economic and non-economic factors) can be used as an important policy implication for financial re-engineering by other states' public enterprises for improving their efficiency levels in future. However, the overall performance of SLPEs in India is very poor, and requires a total business process re-engineering.

References

AIGNER , D. J.,C. A. K. LOVELL AND P. SCHMIDT (1977), "Formulation and Estimation of Stochastic Frontier Production Function Models", ***Journal of Econometrics***, 6, 21-37.

BAUER, P.W.(1990), Recent Development in the Econometric Estimation of Frontier, ***Journal of Econometrics***, 46, 39-56.

BERA, A.K. AND S.C. SHARMA(1999), Estimating Production Uncertainty in Stochastic Frontier Production Function Models, ***Journal of Productivity Analysis***, 12, 187-210.

BHAVANI, T. A. (1991), "Technical Efficiency In India, Modern Small Scale Sector; An Application Of Frontier Production Functions", ***The Indian Economic Review***, 26, 149-166.

CAUDIL, S.B. AND J.M. FORD (1993), "Biases in Frontier Estimation due to Heteroscedasticity", ***Econometric Letters***, 41,17-20.CAUDIL S.B., J.M. FORD AND D.M. GROPPER (1995), "Frontier Estimation and Firm-Specific Inefficiency Measures in the Presence of Heteroscedasticity", ***Journal of Business and Economic Statistics***, 13, 105-111.

FARELL, M. J. (1957), "The Measurement of Productive Efficiency", ***Journal of The Royal Statistical Society***, Series A, 120, 253-290.FORSUND F.R., C.A.K. LOVELL AND P. SCHMIDT (1980), A Survey of Frontier Production Functions and of their Relationships of Efficiency Measurement, ***Journal of Econometrics***, 13,5-25.

GAJAMAM. S.N. (1995)," Estimating Technical Inefficiency in Selected Indian Manufacturing using Frontier Production Function", ***The Indian Economic Journal***, 43, 97.

GIANNAKAS, K. ; K.C. TRAN AND V. TZOUVLEKAS (2003), Predicting Technical Efficiency in Stochastic Production Frontier Models in the Presence of Misspecification: a Monte-Carlo Analysis, ***Applied Economics***, 35,153-161.GREENE W. H. (1980), "Maximum Likelihood Estimation of Econometric Frontier Functions", ***Journal of Econometrics***, 13, 101-115.HADRI K. (1999) , "Estimation of Doubly Heteroscedastic Stochastic Frontier Cost Function", ***Journal of Economics***, 12,101-115. JONDROW J., C. A. K. LOVELL, I. S. MATEROV AND P. SCHMIDT (1982), "On the Estimation of Technical Inefficiency in the Stochastic Frontier Production Function Model", ***Journal of Econometrics***, 23, 269-274.JHA, R. M.N. Murty and B.S. Sahni (1992), Technical Efficiency in the Public Sector: An Analysis of the State Electricity Boards in India, ***Indian Economic Review***, 385-395 (special No.) KARAGIANNIS, G AND V. TZOUVELEKAS (2005), Explaining Output Growth with a Heteroscedastic Non-Neutral Production Frontier. The Case of Sheep Farms in Greece," ***European Review of Agricultural Economics***. 32-51-74MISHRA, R.K. AND KIRANMAI (2006), Restructuring of SLPEs in India – A Macro Analysis, ***The Journal of Institute of Public Enterprises***, 29,119-137.

OLSAN, J. A., P. SCHMIDT AND D.M. WALDMAN (1980), "A Monte Carlo Study of Estimators of Stochastic Frontier Production Functions", ***Journal Of Econometrics***, 13, 67-82.PAXTON, J. (2007), Technical Efficiency in a Case of Mexico;. Oxford Bulletin of Economics and Statistics, 69PAGAN, A.R. AND A.D. HALL (1983), Diagnostic Tests as Residual Analysis, ***Econometric Reviews***, 2,159-218.

RAMASWAMY, K. V. (1994), "The Efficiency In Modern Small Scale Firms In Indian Industry: Applications of Stochastic Production Frontiers", ***Journal of Quantitative Economics***, 10, 309-324.REIFSCHNEIDER, DA AND R. STEVENSON (1991), "Systematic Departures from the Frontier: A Framework for the Analysis of Firm Inefficiencies', ***International Economic Review***, 32, 75-723.

RICHMOND, J. (1974), "Estimating The Efficiency of Production", ***International Economic Review***, 15, 515-521.

SCHMIDT, P. (1976), "On The Statistical Estimation of Parametric Frontier Production Functions", ***Review of Economics and Statistics,*** 58, 238-239.SCHMIDT P. (1978), "On The Statistical Estimation Of Parametric Frontier Production Functions"; Rejoinder, ***Review Of Economics And Statistics,*** 60, 481-482.

SCHMIDT, P. (1985-86), "Frontier Production Functions", ***Econometric Reviews,*** 4, 289-328.SCHMIDT, P. AND T.F. LIN (1984)," Simple Tests of Alternative Specification in Stochastic Frontier Models", ***Journal of Econometrics***, 24,349-361SHANMUGAM, K.R. AND P. KULSHRSTHA (2005), "Efficiency Analysis of Coal Based Thermal Power Generation in India" during the post Reform Era, ***International Journal of Global Energy Issues,***. 23,15-28.

SHARMA, R. C.,(1989) "Relative Efficiency of Firms Through Estimation of Frontiers: An Econometric Approach", ***Ph.D. Thesis,*** University Of Rajasthan, Jaipur, India.SHARMA, R. C. AND NARAIN SINHA (1995), "Frontier System And Estimation of Productive Efficiency In Intra-Industrial Private and Public Enterprises" ,***The Journal of Institute of Public Enterprise***, 18, 27-35.

SHARMA, R.C., SMITA VERMA AND NARAIN SINHA(2002), "Frontier Estimation and Economic Inefficiency Measures in a Single Cross Section of Firms", paper presented at ***36th Annual Conference of the Indian Econometric Society***, Madras School of Economics, 14-16 Jan. 2002.SHARMA, R.C AND NARIAN SINHA (2003)," Data Base for Modelling Economic Efficiency through Frontier Models, VIII Annual Conference on Econometric Modelling for Africa, African Econometric Society Cont. at University of Stellenbosch, 1-4 July 2003.

SINHA, NARAIN AND R.C. SHARMA (1998), "On Efficiency Pricing through Frontier Systems for Public Enterprises under Competitive Market Environment", ***The Journal of Institute of Public Enterprises,*** 21,1-7.TREETINI, S. (2006), Technical Efficiency of Indian Beef Cattle Production Under a Heteroscedastic Non-Neutral Production Frontier Approach, 10th Joint Conference on Ford, Agriculture and Environment, 26-30 Aug. 2006YUENGERT, A.W. (1983)," The Measurement of Efficiency in Life Insurance: Estimates of a Mixed Normal-Gamma Error Models', ***Journal of Banking and Finance*** 17, 483-496.

10

Public Enterprise Management: Extending Theory to Practice

The concept of *laissez-faire* was considered to have outlived its utility during the early parts of the 20th century as every government in both the eastern and western hemispheres was involved in some economic and entrepreneurial activities. Such state interference in economic activities not only laid the foundation for an industrial society but also accomplished the objective of ameliorating the living conditions of the people. However, the interference of the state in the economic and entrepreneurial activities, hitherto considered to be sanctum sanctorum, began to be considered as an anathema in the changed new economic order. The state is gradually retreating, limiting itself to a mere regulatory role by divesting itself from business activities, both in developed and developing countries. The race towards diminution of the role of the state in economic activities has begun. India joined the race as well by gradually divesting itself from its stake in those enterprises which were hitherto considered as the *economic arm* of the state and have played an important role in the economic development of the country.

The role of public sector enterprises is coming under scanner from all directions which are expected to increase their performance from time to time in the competitive environment. The role of the government as the owner of these enterprises has changed as it is just one of the stakeholders. Such a concept has gained ground in the recent past and the government is expected to be more conscious of its role by acting as a mere facilitator rather than the owner. Such a shift of paradigm has necessitated the induction of *corporate culture* in the functioning of the public sector enterprises, where performance is emphasized more than anything else.

The property rights school contends that agency problems are more acute under public ownership. Managers will perform only if they are monitored and incentivized. From the standpoint of the property rights school, managers in the public sector lack monitoring and incentives. These, in turn, stem from the fact that ownership is dispersed and hence property rights in the shape of rights to profit ill-defined. Very often, the firms are not publicly traded and hence not vulnerable to the threat of takeover and this reinforces the poor level of monitoring.

Thus, from the perspective of the property rights school, inefficiency in public sector undertakings arises from the failure to clearly assign property rights.

Multiplicity of objectives arises from the fact that public sector managers are answerable to different constituents, such as legislators, civil servants and ministers, each with its own objective. In particular, politicians, who are answerable to constituents such as labour, would tend to push public sector managers to pursue objectives, such as an increase in employment, that militate against profit maximisation. Broadly speaking, both the approaches suggest that behaviour and hence performance of managers will differ in the public and private sectors because the objective functions are different and also the constraints are different. Neither is good performance incentivised in the public sector nor is bad performance penalised through takeover or bankruptcy.

Agency theory proposes that a utility-maximising economic agent may take actions that are consistent with the interest of the principal. In some situations, managers may prefer to undertake actions that run counter to the preferences of shareholders. Examples of such actions include the payment of excessive salaries to managers, resistance to value-increasing take-over bids, and outright shirking. This is because the agent is not perfectly monitored, either because the actions are not observable or because the principal does not have the incentive to monitor. The separation between ownership and control and ensuring conflicts results in agency costs that reduce the value of the firm.

A second approach to agency problem, presented by Holmstrom and others is to focus on unobservable managerial efforts and the moral hazard problems arising from it. When shareholders do not know how hard managers work, managers may slack off. Moral hazard exists due to a lack of efforts (shirking) on the part of the agent. Stated differently, the principal cannot adequately verify the agent's effort. Adverse selection exists when the agent misrepresents his or her ability or, more generally does not behave in the manner as assumed and preferred by the principal. Agency costs are incurred in order to reduce or eliminate the effects of moral hazard and adverse selection.

Mostly debated among the think tanks, had been the role of government in the economy. The economists furthered the scope of this issue to the spheres of welfare economics, public choice, public finance, industrial organization, law and economics, corporate finance, and macroeconomics. The economic theory of privatisation is a subset of the large literature on the economics of ownership and the role for government ownership (or regulation) of productive resources.

With the increasing competition from companies in the private sector, the public sector enterprises are also compelled to make introspection of their activities and reorient themselves to suit the changing conditions. Such reorientation has been to a large extent successful for the simple reason that the number of central public sector enterprises which have been making profits were 126 during the year 1998-99 increased to 157 during the year 2005-06 and the number is expected to increase further as more and more central public sector enterprises are signing Memorandum of Understanding with the Government.

Issues in Marketing Management

Traditionally, marketing function is neglected in the public sector. Firstly, public sector enterprises enjoyed the patronage of the government and functioned in a well protected market. As government departments and other government agencies purchased goods and services in large quantities, the issue of marketing always remained a neglected area and the public sector enterprises made little or no efforts to strengthen the marketing domain. The problem of monopoly has further complicated the entire issue of marketing as no public sector exhibited the zeal and enthusiasm to market their products and services. The continual reliance of these enterprises on assured market of the government departments and agencies debilitated their marketing capacities and poor attraction of talented marketing strategists. Besides, these enterprises could not think for out of box marketing strategies for marketing their products and services as they did not feel it necessary to do so.

The excessive dependence on government and its agencies for selling their products and services led to the gradual neglect of marketing function in the public enterprises finally leading to the retarding growth and development of these enterprises. Of course, marketing as an important area of growth and development was recognized by the private sector well in advance than its counterparts in the government, which created a wide gulf between the performance of public sector enterprises and private sector companies.

With the advent of liberalization, privatization and globalization and the same play ground for the public sector enterprises and private sector companies, things have changed drastically and the public sector giants have woken up from hibernation. As happens with the woken up giants from a deep and long sleep, the public sector enterprises are hungry for markets and sources of raw materials. It is in this direction, the three public sector enterprises Steel Authority of India Ltd, National Mineral Development Corporation and Rashtriya Ispat Nigam Ltd have decided to pool their strengths and resources for setting up an integrated iron and steel plant at Bailadila in Chhattisgarh State. It is in this direction, the public sector giant ONGC has formed a joint venture with Mittal, although, the shareholding pattern of ONGC is well below the 50% mark i.e., 49.90%.

Hence, it can be expected that the public sector enterprises are on the growth trajectory and can be expected to attain mammoths in the near future and compete wide and far in the global competition.

Issues in Financial Management

Public sector enterprises were designed and established with a view to build industrial base for the country and thereby funded from public exchequer; hence, it is but natural that they are accountable for their acts of omission and commission to the popular will i.e., the Parliament. Parliamentary control over the public sector enterprises was very much emphasized for ensuring effective and efficient utilization of public money invested in the development of various public sector enterprises. Such a pursuit led the government to devise the administrative procedures and fiscal policies, to ensure their proper accountability to the Parliament leading to lack in actual day to day freedom and autonomy for them to act wisely during the hours of crises. Lack of proper financial planning, jumbling of directives, modifications of financial plans, poor maintenance of records led to financial mismanagement which led to financial crises like conditions for these enterprises necessitating a new approach for managing them.

The Department of Public Enterprises in its various directives made attempts to set the things right by issuing directives from time to time. In one of its directive (DPE O.M. No.4/6/94-Fin. dated 14th December, 1994), the Department of Public Enterprises has issued guidelines with regard to investment of surplus funds and placed onus on the respective public sector enterprise board. Similarly, the Department, in another directive (DPE O.M. No. DPE/16/22/90-Fin.G-I dated 8th October, 1998) delegated powers to the Board of Directors of PSEs to incur capital expenditure, provided such expenditure is met from the internal resources of the company. In another directive, (DPE O.M. No. 18(24)/2003-GM- GL.66 dated, 5th August, 2005), the Department has enhanced the financial powers of the profit making public sector enterprises keeping in view the pledge made in the National Common Minimum Programme (NCMP) i.e., to devolve managerial and commercial autonomy to profit making companies operating in a competitive environment. As per the directive, the board of directors of the profit making public sector enterprises can incur capital expenditure without government approval up to Rs. 150 crore or equal to 50% of the net worth and the Chief Executive of the public sector enterprise is entitled to approve business tours abroad of functional directors up to 5 days' duration.

Issues in Production Management

One of the main objectives of the establishment and enlargement of the public sector enterprises was to accelerate the rate of economic development through speedy industrial growth. The public sector enterprises were entrusted with the task of supplying basic and strategic gods, machinery and equipment, etc. essential for economic development. The ultimate aim of production programmes of the public sector enterprises to become self reliant so as to promote the principles and programmes of social justice as envisaged by the Constitution. The production programmes of the public sector enterprises are designed to produce modern equipment, machinery, and other end products of quality. However, production in most of the public sector enterprises lagged behind the scheduled time limit due to various reasons like under utilization of production capacities, locking up of scarce resources, inflating costs, strikes, industrial disputes, delay in procurement of the raw materials, etc.

However, changes are bound to come and after the process of liberalization has set in, the change is conspicuous in the public sector enterprises. The public sector enterprises are entering into Memorandum of Understanding, which is nothing but the contract for better and higher performance. The number of central public sector enterprises which entered into Memorandum of Understanding was just 4 during the year 1987-88 which increased to 149 in the year 2007-08, which is an indication of production consciousness on the part of public sector enterprises.

Issues in Sickness and turnaround

The National Common Minimum Programme (NCMP) states that the government is committed for a strong and efficient public sector whose social objectives are met by its commercial functioning. While every effort will be made to modernize and restructure sick public sector companies and revive sick industry, chronically loss-making companies will either be sold-off, or closed, after all workers have got their legitimate dues and compensation. One of the methods of addressing the issue of sickness of public sector enterprise is to induct private industry in those enterprises which have the potential for revival.

There are manifold reasons for sickness of public sector enterprises and differ from sector to sector and from unit to unit. Some of the causes could be attributed to old and obsolete plant and machinery, outdated technology, resource crunch, low capacity utilization, excess manpower, heavy interest burden, weak marketing strategies, stiff competition, reluctance of financial institutions to provide funds for revival/ rehabilitation, high input cost, erosion of net worth due to continuous losses and inherent problems of sick taken over enterprises, etc.

Government has come out with different strategies for restructuring/revival of public sector enterprises which include financial restructuring, business restructuring, etc. According to financial restructuring, investment is made in the form of equity participation, write-off of past losses and infuse fresh capital, waiver of loan/interest/penal interest, conversion of interest including penal interest, etc. Under business restructuring, it is envisaged to restructure the organization, hiving off viable units from and form them as separate entities, formation of joint ventures, etc.

The Finance Minister during his budget speech (2004-2005) announced that the government would constitute a Board for Reconstruction of Public Sector Enterprises (BRPSE) to address the problems relating to strengthening, modernization, reviving and restructuring of public sector enterprises. The functions of the Board include, to advise the Government on ways and means for strengthening public sector enterprises in general and making them more autonomous and professional; to consider restructuring - financial, organizational and business of public sector enterprises and suggest ways and means for funding such schemes, to examine the proposals of the administrative Ministries for revival/ restructuring of sick/loss making public sector enterprises for their turnaround; to advise the Government on disinvestments/ closure/sale in full or part, in respect of chronically sick/loss making companies, which cannot be revived. In respect of such unviable companies, to monitor incipient sickness in public sector enterprises, etc.

Besides, in the pursuit of the goals of the National Common Minimum Programme (NCMP), with regard to the public sector enterprises, the government felt the need to attract Board level executives capable for turning around sick public sector enterprises by giving them continuity of tenure by extending up to 65 years.

The management theory identifies the following as the symptoms of sickness : (i) continuous shortage of cash, (ii) deteriorating financial ratio, (iii) wide spread usage of creative accounting, (iv) continuous decrease in prices of shares, (v) frequent request to banks and financial institutions, (vi) delay in audit of annual reports, (vii) degradation in the employees morale and (viii) disparities among the top and middle level management.

The causes of sickness as identified by management theory could be internal and external. *Internal Causes* are those which affects the industry and are related to the organization structure, production channel, distribution channel, technical know how etc. Following are internal enterprise problems which influence industrial sickness.

(i) choice of wrong and defective idea of industry
(ii) poor management prevailing in the industry
(iii) poor production capacity
(iv) poor quality maintenance
(v) poor marketing ability of the industry
(vi) poor utilization of capacity
(vii) lack of horizontal and vertical integration
(viii) lack of managing strategies
(ix) poor project implementation and
(x) poor handling of labor and so on.

External Causes include (i) Infrastructural problems such as location problems scarcity of power and water, communication problem etc; (ii) financial problems with reference to working capital management, railing of long term funds, recovery and (iii) marketing lacks standardization, poor designing. Ignorance of potential market.

PE management has to draw upon the management theory and weave the focal points for formulating a canvas for strategic action. We present management matrix for Public Enterprises showing the focal points and the action agenda which can act as a catalyst for the sustenance of PEs in the years to come.

Management Matrix for Public Enterprises

Area	*Focal point*	*Strategic action*
Finance	Working capital management	• Policy on working capital management • Policy on inventory management • Policy on receivables management • Policy on cash management • Policy on current liabilities management • Policy on working capital financing •
	Capital Expenditure management	• Formulation of project cycle management • Project appraisal techniques • Incorporation of uncertainty and risk • Project financing
	Financing	• Optimal finance mix • Cost of capital • New financing instruments • Listing on capital markets
	Dividends	• Rate of dividends • Internal accruals • Bonus shares
	Accounting Systems	• Disclosures • GAAP • Activity based and Life cycle costing

(Contd.)

(Contd.)

Area	*Focal point*	*Strategic action*
Marketing	Product marketing	• Direct marketing • Distribution management • Brand management • Launch advertising • Market share
	Pricing	• Cost based pricing • Import parity pricing • Administrative prices • ROI pricing
	Channel Management	
Production / operations	Design	• Indigenous vs. exogenous
	Production	• Batch manufacturing • Flexible • World class manufacturing • R & D • Technology • Supply Chain Management
	Quality	• Six sigma • TQM
Personnel / HRD	Recruitment and selection	• Campus • Advertisement • Assessment centres
	Training and management development	• On the job • Continuous training • In house • Unit based • Selection of appropriate pedagogical tool
	Performance appraisal, motivation and wages	• Performance linked salaries • Structure of salaries • Productivity linked bonus • ESOPs

(Contd.)

(Contd.)

Area	*Focal point*	*Strategic action*
		• Management by objectives • Labour adjustments and VRS
Strategic Management	Organisational structure	• Line and staff • Divisionalised • Function based • Matrix based • Flexible • Restructuring of technology, capital base, market mix
	Boards	• Professional boards • Independent director • Corporate Governance
	Form	• Company • Holding company • Corporation • Joint ventures • Mergers and acquisitions
	Controls	• Management by exception • Transfer pricing • Computer based management information systems • Economic Value Added (EVA) • Balance Score Card (BSC) • Divestment • Internal audit
	Financing	• Debt equity mix • Leveraged buy outs • Synthetic instruments

Conclusion

PEs have to be reckoned as the core of the Indian economy as recognized by the 13th Plan Document. These enterprises have to draw a lot from the management theory to keep their relevance intact during the years to come. A study of the management matrix as related to PEs points out very clearly that in each area of management there is a considerable scope to initiate further action and thereby pep-up their performance.

11

Performance of Public Enterprises in Jammu and Kashmir

Abstract

The present paper makes an attempt to provide an overview of the State Level Public Enterprises (SLPEs) in J&K, depict their financial performance, present a comparative scenario of the financial performance of the SLPEs in J&K vis-à-vis other states, point out reasons responsible for their negative financial performance and offer suggestions to improve in their financial functioning and contribute thereby to the development of the economy of J&K.

Jammu and Kashmir (J&K) is the northern most State of Republic of India. The development of the State is crucial for the competitiveness of the Indian economy on account of its strategic importance and combating poverty and exclusion. The resource crunch is one of the vital factors impeding the turnaround of the economy of the State. The total impact on state finances as a percentage of the State's own tax revenue shows that the losses incurred by the SLPEs measured to 40 per cent of the State's own tax revenue[1]. The performance of the State Level Public Enterprises (SLPEs) has been found wanting in this respect as the SLPEs have not functioned well in the past and contributed to the worsening financial position of J&K[2].

Overview of SLPEs in J&K

The growing realization on the part of the Indian Government for expanding the public sector as the medium of industrialization and removing regional imbalances motivated the State of J&K to set up the SLPEs[3]. The State had 5 enterprises by way of inheritance. These enterprises were mostly manufacturing silk and related products. By the end of the Ninth Five Year Plan the number of SLPEs increased to 23.

Table 1
Plan-wise Enterprises

Sectors	*Five Year Plans*										
	I	*II*	*III*	*IV*	*V*	*VI*	*VII*	*VIII*	*IX*	*Total*	*Present Status as on 31st March 2006.*
Manufacturing	1	1	-	1	4	-	4	3	-	13^	11
Trading and Services	-	1	-	1	-	-	-	-	-	2	2
Financial	1	-	-	1	-	-	-	1	-	3	3
Promotional	-	1	3	1	-	1	1	1	-	8#	3
Welfare	-	-	-	-	-	-	1	1	-	2	2
Utilities	-	-	-	-	-	-	1	1	-	2	2
Total	**2**	**3**	**3**	**4**	**4**	**1**	**7**	**6**	**-**	**30@**	**23**

S*ource*: IPE Database on SLPEs in India.

^ 2 enterprise in Manufacturing sector is not in operation

Out of 8 promotional enterprises five are not in operation and three are working

@ Out of 30 SLPEs, 7 SLPEs were wound up. As on 31st March 2006, there are 23 SLPEs out of which 20 are working and three are non-working

These comprised 11 manufacturing, 2 Trading & Services 3 financial, 3 promotional, 2 welfare and 2 utilities enterprises. Table 1 shows the growth of SLPEs during the Five-Year Plans. The Table 1 reveals that the maximum numbers of SLPEs were set up during the Fifth Five Year Plan.

Profile of SLPEs in J&K

Table 2 presents the profile of SLPEs in J&K as related to working and non-working SLPEs, total equity, total debt, total investment, profit making and loss making enterprises, net profit / loss secured and accumulated losses / profit.

Table 2
Profile of SLPEs in Jammu & Kashmir

(Rs. in crore)

Items	*2002-03*	*2003-04*	*2004-05*	*2005-06*
1. Total No. of SLPEs	22	23	23	23
2. No. of Working SLPEs	19	20	20	20
3. No. of Non-Working SLPEs (i) Under liquidation (ii) Under Closure (iii) Under Merger (iv) Others	3	3	3	3
4. Total Equity	421.88	395.79	390.42	398.80
5. Total Debt	2467.66	1968.09	2603.55	2806.26
6. Total Investment	2889.54	2363.88	2993.97	3205.06
7. No. of Profit making enterprises	6	6	8	8
8. No. of Loss making enterprises	13	14	12	12
9. Net Profit/Loss	249.25	304.91	-4.74	68.89
10. Accumulated Loss(-) / Profit	-782.92	-917.18	- 1056.25	- 1172.45

Source: Comptroller and Auditor General of India, Srinagar Civil Reports, 2002-03 to 2005-06.

Table 3

Budgetary Support to SLPEs in J&K

Particulars	2003-04				2004-05				2005-06			
	Companies		Corporation		Companies		Corporations		Companies		Corporations	
	No	Amount	No	Amount	No	Amount	No	Amount	No	Amount	No	Amount
Equity Capital from Budget	4	2.8	-	-	5	3.23	1	0.8	4	7.55		
Loans Given from Budget	6	10.04	1	25.43	6	8.51	2	68.42	5	13.08	1	21.84
Grants towards Projects, Programmes/Schemes	8	25.84	-	-	3	1.89	-	-	7	312.76	-	-
Subsidy	3	1.45	-	-	4	11.6	-	-	3	6.8	-	-
Total outgo	12	40.13	1	25.43	10	25.23	2	69.22	12	340.19	1	21.84

Source: Comptroller and Auditor General of India, Srinagar Civil Reports, 2002-03 to 2005-06.

Table 2 makes some interesting revelations. The number of non-working enterprises is on increase. The continuation of non-functioning enterprises adds to the financial woes of the State and undermines the profitability of the SLPEs as a whole. The total equity is on decline showing disenchantment of the State. A similar tendency is seen with regard to total investment which is also on decline due to the presence of heavy accumulated losses as much as half of the total investment and more than five times that of the equity.

Budgetary Support to SLPEs in J&K

Table 3 reveals that the budgetary support to the SLPEs in J&K is on increase. During the period 2003-04 to 2005-06, the budgetary support increased five fold. To add to the woes, guarantees outstanding during 2005-06 stood at Rs.1624 crores. The State Government became the guarantor for the J&K State Power Development Corporation Limited to the tune of Rs.2362.69 crores.

Sectoral Analysis of SLPEs in J&K

The sectoral analysis of SLPEs in J&K has been undertaken by classifying the SLPEs into 6 cognizant groups viz., Manufacturing, Trading & Services, Financial, Promotional, Welfare and Utilities[A]. The Planning Commission and 8th, 9th, 10th and 11th Finance Commissions have formulated optimal rates of return that the SLPEs should yield in each group of these enterprises on the basis of the framework developed by the Institute of Public Enterprise (IPE) in its studies[4]. As per the yardstick rates of return, the Manufacturing Enterprises, Trading & Services, Financial, Promotional, Welfare and Utilities should earn rates of return of the order of 12 per cent, 10 per cent, 8 per cent, 5 per cent, 4 per cent and 12 per cent, respectively. The sectoral position of the SLPEs shows that on the whole their profitability was dismal. Broadly the classification suggests that the enterprises involved in manufacture of products come under manufacturing sector. The enterprises such as the Handlooms and Handicrafts Development Corporations and the State Trading Corporation can be classified under trading and marketing enterprises. The enterprises such as the Industrial Development Corporations and the State Finance Corporations can be classified as financing institutions whereas enterprises like Small Scale Industrial Development Corporations, Mineral Development Corporations and Fisheries Development Corporations can be classified as promotional enterprises. The welfare enterprises are those which have as their mission the task of improving the welfare of some targeted group of people or area. The Backward Classes Corporations and the Scheduled Castes Corporations and the enterprises to promote welfare of women come under this category.

Table 4

Financial Performance of Manufacturing Sector SLPEs in J&K*

(Rs. In Crores)

Year	*Total Investment*	*Net profit / Net loss (-)*	*Reserves and Surplus*	*Net Worth*	*Capital Employed*
1997-98	424.93	-37.75	6.08	178.56	114.58
1998-99	481.97	-46.16	6.09	198.98	115.64
1999-00	545.93	-47.7	6.53	224.51	132.8
2000-01	561.08	-46.15	20.16	210.29	129.29
2001-02	625.24	-48.78	23.99	215.05	146.58
2002-03	683.79	-46.81	25.16	245.35	136.17
2003-04	554.87	-34.29	0	-415.77	46.19
2004-05	554.87	-34.29	0	-421.25	40.71

Source: IPE Database on SLPEs in India.

**Data for 3 non-working SLPEs and J&K Police Housing Corporation are not included due to non-availability.*

Manufacturing Sector SLPEs in J&K

The manufacturing and promotional enterprises dominated the SLPEs scenario in J&K. The manufacturing enterprises were set up to use the local resources whereas the promotional enterprises were set up to use the local resources and promote private sector development and also the informal sector.

This sectoral group has the highest number of the SLPEs. The total investment in manufacturing SLPEs increased from Rs.424.93 crores during 1997-98 to Rs. 554.87 crores during 2004-05. The net loss of the SLPEs in this sector declined from Rs. 37.75 crores in 1997-98 to Rs. 34.29 crores during 2004-05. The performance of the manufacturing SLPEs left much to be desired.

J&K Cements Limited held an olive branch in profit making by earning a profit of Rs. 0.72 crore. The financial performance of Manufacturing sector SLPEs is depicted in Table 4.

Trading and Service Sector SLPEs in J&K

Table 5
Financial Performance of Trading and Service Sector SLPEs in J&K*

(Rs. In Crores)

Year	*Total Investment*	*Net profit / Net loss (-)*	*Surplus Reserves*	*Net Worth*	*Capital Employed*
1997-98	23.12	-0.08	2.47	12.86	17.28
1998-99	23.9	-0.1	3.24	14.17	18.95
1999-00	24.89	-0.11	3.99	16.32	21.79
2000-01	24.86	-0.11	4.69	17.62	22.96
2001-02	25.24	-0.11	5.88	19.1	24.07
2002-03	28.38	-0.16	6.77	22.12	27.3
2003-04	27.82	-0.88	0	1.42	5.74
2004-05	27.82	-0.88	0	1.94	6.26

Source: IPE Database on SLPEs in India.

J&K Tourism Development Corporation Limited was the only working enterprise in this category of SLPEs. The financial performance of this enterprise was not encouraging as the total investment was static and the net worth underwent significant erosion due to consistent loss making. The capital employed faced depletion which was a cause of great concern and indicative of the fact that the corporation was folding up.

Promotional Sector SLPEs in J&K

The enterprises in this category were involved in promotional as well as manufacturing activities. The financial performance of these enterprises is depicted in Table 6. The total investment in promotional sector SLPEs increased from Rs. 58.47 crores during 1997-98 and increased to Rs.153.64 crores during 2004-05. In other words, the investment trebled during

Table 6
Financial Performance of Promotional Sector SLPEs

(Rs. In Crores)

Year	*Total Investment*	*Net profit / Net loss*	*Surplus Reserves*	*Net Worth*	*Capital Employed*
1997-98	58.47	-29.84	-4.49	-40.7	31.32
1998-99	63.68	-28.54	-4.75	2.05	28.67
1999-00	67.6	-36.64	-4.8	3.35	21.93
2000-01	72.55	-11.62	-5.3	6.97	22.13
2001-02	76.34	-11.49	-5.65	10.22	23.62
2002-03	81.68	-10.13	-5.83	14.44	23.59
2003-04	153.64	-2.2	0	0	1.31
2004-05	153.64	-2.2	0	0	10.5

Source: IPE Database on SLPEs in India.

the eight year period under reference. The investment in J&K State Forest Corporation shot-up from Rs. 18.05 crores in 1997-98 to Rs. 83.16 crores in 2004-05. The significance attached to the development of forest sector during the IX and X five year plans was responsible for this upsurge in investment. The net loss declined from Rs. 29.84 crores in 1997-98 to Rs. 2.2 crores during 2004-05. The performance in the promotional sector showed an uptrend but the capital employed decreased from 31.32 crores during 1997-98 to 10.5 crores during 2004-05.

Financial Sector SLPEs in J&K

The financial enterprises form an important component of the SLPE system. The financial enterprises included J&K State Industrial Development Corporation, J&K Bank Limited

Table-7
Financial Performance of Financial Sector SLPEs #

(Rs. In Crores)

Financial Year	*Total Investment*	*Net profit / Net loss (-)*	*Surplus Reserves*	*Net Worth*	*Capital Employed*
1997-98	243.61	0	6.07	-18.85	126.9
1998-99	233.15	0	6.07	-34.76	128.64
1999-00	232.79	0	6.07	-46	129.72
2000-01	232	0	6.07	-54.66	132.5
2001-02	244.71	0	6.07	-52.13	133.48
2002-03	256.43	0	8.07	-43.37	143
2003-04	181.36	-16.89	0	173.42	273.35
2004-05	181.36	-16.89	0	173.07	273

Source: IPE Database on SLPEs in India.
Does not include data for J&K Bank.

and J&K State Financial Corporation. J&K Bank was doing extremely well and earned a profit of Rs. 196.84 crores in 2005-06 and declared dividends of amounting Rs. 38.78 crores which turned out to be 25 per cent of the profits earned. The bank had a capital employed of Rs. 7607.23 crores in 2005-06. The bank has national designs to expand. These corporations are involved in accelerating the rate of industrialization in the state, removing regional imbalances and promoting growth of tiny, medium and small scale industries. According to table this sector's total investment was Rs. 263.97 crores in 1997-98 and it has decreased to Rs. 204.32 crores during the period 2004-05. The J&K State Industrial Development Corporation registered a decline in its operations and financial performance, whereas J&K State Financial Corporation showed statisism.

Table 8
Financial Performance of Welfare Sector SLPEs

(Rs. In Crores)

Year	*Total Investment*	*Net profit / Net loss (-)*	*Reserves and Surplus*	*Net Worth*	*Capital Employed*
1997-98	3.05	-0.49	0	1.03	1.75
1998-99	6.13	-0.78	0	1.18	1.4
1999-00	3.24	-0.7	0	1.19	0.91
2000-01	5.76	-1.83	0	1.18	0.96
2001-02	9.75	0.9	0	1.16	0.99
2002-03	7.25	0.99	0	1.33	1.15
2003-04	27.16	0.06	0	0	6.57
2004-05	27.16	0.06	0	0	6.57

Source: IPE Database on SLPEs in India.

Welfare Sector SLPEs in J&K

The performance of the welfare sector SLPEs was under cloud as seen in Table 8. Although the total investment increased 9 times over the period 1997-98 to 2004-05. The net worth remained static and profitability was negative.

Utility Sector SLPEs in J&K

The utility SLPEs comprise the J&K State Road Transport Corporation and J&K State Power Development Corporation. In both the cases the total investment is predominated by debt which resulted in a sub-optimal debt-equity ratio leading to incurrence of heavy losses by these enterprises. Table 9 depicts the financial performance of these enterprises.

Table 9
Financial Performance of Utility Sector SLPEs

(Rs. In Crores)

Years	*Total Investment*	*Net profit / Loss*	*Reserves and Surplus*	*Net Worth*	*Capital Employed*
1997-98	254.37	-38.22	907.84	736.64	460.29
1998-99	378.34	-43.04	958.23	750.23	1030.08
1999-00	628.3	-42.96	1117.01	931.05	1497.17
2000-01	1121.5	-45.25	1177.01	890.16	2001.07
2001-02	1572.31	-44.91	1177.81	851.01	1977.14
2002-03	2468.77	-45.65	908.39	544.19	2534.25
2003-04	1265.2	-45.65	0	0	-1.62
2004-05	1265.2	-45.65	0	0	160.19

Source: IPE Database on SLPEs in India.

Comparative Performance of SLPEs

The composition of the SLPEs in J&K went along with the national average as 50 per cent of its enterprises turned out to be manufacturing enterprises. In regard to the parameter of net worth, they have trodden the path of erosion as against the path of accumulation opted by Andhra Pradesh and Karnataka and Rajasthan. The total management performance in terms of sales to investment ratio is far below the national level. It is 0.20 in the case of J&K enterprises as compared to 0.80:1 in the case of the national average for all the SLPEs taken together for the year 2002-03.

SLPEs Reforms in J& K

In line with the national[5] approach, the State Government has initiated reforms in SLPEs in J&K. The reforms could be classified in two categories: (i) generic reforms, and (ii) enterprise specific reforms. These reforms are discussed hereunder.

Generic Reforms

The generic reforms relate to the introduction of the golden handshake through voluntary retirement scheme. Although the government of J&K has created a Public Enterprises (PEs) Restructuring Fund in the Finance Department, the state has closed down two SLPEs viz., Himalayan Wool Combers Ltd and Handloom, Handicrafts Raw Material Supply Organisation. The employees of these two enterprises were given Golden Handshake. The main features of the Golden Handshake Scheme adopted for the Himalayan Wool Combers Ltd. and Handloom, Handicrafts Raw Material Supply Organisation are as follows:

(a) Terminal Benefits: These include the balance in provident fund account, cash equivalent to accumulated earned leave and Gratuity as per Gratuity Act;

(b) Ex-gratia benefits of 35 days salary for every completed year of service and 25 days salary for balance of service left which ever is lower;

(c) Income Tax exemption will be applicable to employees who have completed at least ten years of service or 40 years of age;

(d) The State Government in the Finance Department provides budgetary support for implementation of the Golden Handshake Scheme;

(e) There will be more recruitment against the vacancies arising out of the scheme.

Insofar as the enterprise specific reforms are concerned, J&K State Tourism Development Corporation has decided for privatization / sale of its loss making units. In pursuance of the decision, the Company leased out (between December 2003 and June 2006) five of its units and earned revenue of Rs. 2.31 crore on account of rent. No further action was taken by the Company to lease out its remaining loss making units. It may be noted that the Godbole Committee recommended restructuring/ reengineering of some of these enterprises.

Problems and Issues

The SLPEs in J&K had operational problems in all the areas of management[6]. They suffered from very low capacity utilization. The shortage of raw materials, delay in receiving orders, shortage of labour and dearth of technical personnel obstructed a higher capacity utilization. The marketing problems included slump in the demand and price fluctuations. Managerial problems included lack of availability of suitable personnel and delay in decision-making. Financial management was in a total disarray. The project appraisal skills were non-existent. The utilities suffered due to operational inefficiencies and lack of insights into management of assets and liabilities. The promotional enterprises did not innovate new schemes and got involved into the development of private sector. The welfare enterprises drew a big blank owing to their lack of understanding of the working of such enterprises. Out of 20 working SLPEs, accounts of 11 SLPEs were in arrears for 10 years or more, and in case of 5 SLPEs, the accounts were in arrears for periods between 6 and 10 years. Moreover 4 working companies had finalized only four year accounts during the five year period ended 2005-06, while one statutory corporation (J&K State Forest Corporation) had not finalized its accounts since 1996-97.

Suggestions

The SLPEs in J&K could do better with generic and enterprise-specific frameworks. The generic framework requires them to tone up their internal management capabilities and ability to interface better with the state government, and social and economic environment. This would require these enterprises to internalize the principles of corporate governance and set up effective internal control systems relating to pricing, material control, budgeting, auditing, management control systems, project appraisal, recruitment of personnel and their performance appraisal, motivation and incentives to work force and stability of tenures of chief executives. The enterprises should also develop benchmarks based on their own performance levels and also inter-firm comparisons. The culture of training and management development, innovation, mergers and acquisitions and research and development is sure to lift the performance of these enterprises from woods. The State Government could help by extending an appropriate debt-equity ratio and appointing competent professionals on the boards of these enterprises. The State Government may initiate the system of Memorandum of Understanding on the patter of the Central Public Enterprises.

The enterprise specific suggestions relate to J&K Handloom and Handicrafts Development Corporation, J&K Tourism Development Corporation, J&K Small Industries Development Corporation, J&K Bank Limited, J&K Power Development Corporation, J&K Horticultural Produce Marketing and Processing Corporation, J&K Industrial Development Corporation and J&K State Financial Corporation. All these enterprises need to have a vision and mission document and corporate plans based on their vision and mission.

J&K Handloom and Handicrafts Development Corporation needs to take up certain measures to improve its performance comprising improvement in the productivity of the weavers, introduction of more efficient looms and other related equipment, widening market access of the handloom products, focusing on product diversification and new designs, development of cluster approach for design development and brand promotion of Kashmir handicrafts through exhibitions in Indian and international market.

J&K Horticultural Produce Marketing and Processing Corporation could provide better marketing facilities to cultivators, set export promotion zones and improve the income of the cultivators by better gradation. It may take initiatives for development of new variety of fruits like kiwi fruit, wild apricot, black cherry, broccoli and mushroom and agreement with airlines to transport cargo from Lah, Srinagar and Jammu to centres of consumption like Delhi, Chandigarh and Mumbai. The corporation could contribute to the export economy through promotion of exports of processed food, fruit juice concentrate, herbs and herbal products, flowers, pesticides, leather products, silk and silk products.

J&K Tourism Development Corporation could further strengthen preligrim tourism and promote adventure tourism, ski tourism, golf tourism and eco tourism. Some of the explored tourist destinations like Wardwan Valley, Zanskar Valley, Pangong/ Tsomoriri Lakes, Nubra Valley, Gurez, Telel. The corporation should develop Patnitop complex needs to attract large tourist inflows from the neighboring states.

J&K Small Industries Development Corporation, could encourage local youth to setup their own units by the provision of the soft loans by J&K Bank. It may undertake intensive entrepreneurship development programmes. J&K Bank could reach new heights by improving its asset-liability management, prudential ratio and introduction of new schemes for mopping up deposits from India and abroad. It may attract potential investors like the NRIs through attractive websites.

J&K State Road Transport Corporation needs to improve its occupancy ratio, fuel consumption, tariffs and economize on stores and spares, and wage costs. It may promote public-private-partnership to cover more routes at economic prices with higher operational efficiency. J&K Power Corporation has unlimited potential to grow by promoting new projects, public-private-partnership for future growth, economizing on output costs and diversifying areas of operations in line with the power sector reforms introduced by the Government of India.

Conclusion

The SLPEs in J&K play a very vital role in the State economy. There is a need to tone up their performance through restructuring, reforms, privatisation and public-private-partnership whereas the State Government has to take some police initiatives for their turnaround and future continuation in its portfolio, the SLPEs have to strengthen their internal controls and operational efficiency. This will result in improving their financial performance which will cut into the fiscal deficits of the State and thereby strengthening the fiscal discipline.

References

1. http//:www.jakfinance.nic.in, dated 10-10-2007.
2. R K Mishra and J Kiranmai, Restructuring of SLPEs in India: A Macroanalysis, Economic and Political Weekly, Mumbai, September 30, 2006, pp. 4172.
3. Planning Commission (Government of India, New Delhi), Study Group on Reforms in State Public Sector Undertaking, Final Report: Vol I 2002, pp. 130.
   + Annexure incorporates the sector-wise list of SLPEs in J&K
   Å Annexure II incorporates enterprise-wise financial data.
4. Reports by VIII, IX X and XI Finance Commissions (Government of India, New Delhi).
5. R K Mishra, Privatisation Challenges for Good Governance: A Case of India, in Jabes, Jak (Ed), The Role of Public Administration in Alleviating Poverty and Improving Governance, ADB-NAPSIPAG & INTAN, Manila, 2005, pp. 443-445.
6. T L Sankar, R Nandgopal and R K Mishra, Management of State Level Public Enterprises in India, Printwell, Jaipur, 1992, pp. 113.

Annexure-I

SECTOR-WISE CLASSIFICATION OF SLPES IN J&K

Manufacturing Sector SLPEs

1. J&K Police Housing Corporation Limited
2. J&K Agro Industries Development Corporation Limited
3. J&K Horticultural Produce Marketing and Processing Corporation
4. J&K Industries Limited
5. J&K State Handloom Development Corporation
6. J&K Minerals Limited
7. J&K Projects Construction Corporation Limited
8. J&K Cements Limited
9. J&K Cable Car Corporation Limited
10. Tawi Scooters Limited
11. Himalayan Wool Coombers Limited

Trade and Service Sector SLPEs

1. J&K State Tourism Development Corporation
2. J&K State Handloom Handicrafts Raw Materials Supplies Organization Limited.

Promotional enterprises included:

1. J&K Small Scale Industrial Development Corporation

2. J&K Handicrafts Development Corporation Limited
3. J&K State Forest Corporation

Financial Sector SLPEs

1. J&K State Industrial Development Corporation,
2. J&K Bank Limited,
3. J&K State Financial Corporation

Welfare Sector SLPEs

1. J&K SC/ST/OBC Development Corporation
2. J&K State Women's Development Corporation.

Utility Sector SLPEs

1. J&K State Power Development Corporation
2. J&K Road Transport Corporation.

Annexure-II

Jammu & Kashmir Agro Industries Development Corporation

Financial Year	*Total Investment*	*Surplus Reserves*	*Net Worth*	*Capital Employed*	*Net profit / Net loss (-)*
1997-98	13.8	0.16	6.6	13.95	1.33
1998-99	14.69	Nil	2.89	14.69	-1.65
1999-00	15.5	Nil	2.31	15.5	-1.39
2000-01	16.21	Nil	1.82	16.21	-1.18
2001-02	16.85	Nil	-0.03	16.85	-2.5
2002-03	18.02	Nil	-1.39	18.02	-2.53
2003-04	13.77	Nil	-12.8	-2.56	-1.95
2004-05	13.77	Nil	-11.87	-1.63	-1.95

Jammu and Kashmir Small Scale Industries Development Corporation

Financial Year	*Total Investment*	*Surplus Reserves*	*Net Worth*	*Capital Employed*	*Net profit / Net loss (-)*
1997-98	6.56	-5.72	-2.6	0.84	-0.69
1998-99	7	-5.98	-3.7	2.95	-1.43
1999-00	6.49	-6.03	-3.9	4.33	-2.52
2000-01	6.43	-6.53	-4.02	3.08	-2.15
2001-02	5.43	-6.88	-4.68	2.37	-1.78
2002-03	6.06	-7.06	-4.96	2.45	-0.7
2003-04	9.19	Nil	-3.14	2.94	0.09
2004-05	9.19	Nil	-2.85	3.23	0.09

Jammu and Kashmir Industrial Development Corporation Ltd.

Financial Year	*Total Investment*	*Surplus Reserves*	*Net Worth*	*Capital Employed*	*Net profit / Net loss (-)*
1997-98	87.34	0.48	34	57.52	Nil
1998-99	91.6	0.48	33.06	59.26	Nil
1999-00	98.78	0.48	34.27	60.34	Nil
2000-01	104.31	0.48	36.07	63.12	Nil
2001-02	110.85	0.48	36.07	64.1	Nil
2002-03	123.48	0.48	45.07	71.62	Nil
2003-04	48.53	Nil	20.73	51.62	-5.43
2004-05	48.53	Nil	20.38	51.27	-5.43

Jammu and Kashmir State Financial Corporation

Financial Year	*Total Investment*	*Surplus Reserves*	*Net Worth*	*Capital Employed*	*Net profit / Net loss (-)*
1997-98	156.27	5.59	-52.85	69.38	Nil
1998-99	141.55	5.59	-67.82	69.38	Nil
1999-00	134.01	5.59	-80.27	69.38	Nil
2000-01	127.69	5.59	-90.73	69.38	Nil
2001-02	133.86	5.59	-88.2	69.38	Nil
2002-03	132.95	7.59	-88.44	71.38	Nil
2003-04	132.83	Nil	152.69	221.73	-11.46
2004-05	132.83	Nil	152.69	221.73	-11.46

Jammu and Kashmir Horticultural Produce Marketing and Processing Corporation

Financial Year	*Total Investment*	*Surplus Reserves*	*Net Worth*	*Capital Employed*	*Net profit / Net loss (-)*
1997-98	104.19	0.01	79.4	15.58	Nil
1998-99	119.94	0.01	95.66	15.08	Nil
1999-00	139	0.01	114.45	15.33	Nil
2000-01	124.14	0.01	101.39	13.53	Nil
2001-02	135.73	0.01	113.34	13.18	Nil
2002-03	135.73	0.01	113.34	13.18	Nil
2003-04	104.76	Nil	-84.67	10.89	-6.07
2004-05	104.76	Nil	-84.77	10.79	-6.07

Jammu and Kashmir Industries Ltd.

Financial Year	*Total Investment*	*Surplus Reserves*	*Net Worth*	*Capital Employed*	*Net profit / Net loss (-)*
1997-98	180.48	1.32	117.33	15.47	-22.88
1998-99	205.01	1.32	143.04	19.04	-26.17
1999-00	230.1	1.32	169.59	25.93	-26.45
2000-01	245.46	14.58	185.56	23.64	-25.57
2001-02	281.54	17.6	209.72	24.9	-26.84
2002-03	309.41	17.52	242.22	32.89	-27.3
2003-04	150.12	Nil	-148.41	-16.12	-22.05
2004-05	150.12	Nil	-159.64	-27.35	-22.05

Jammu and Kashmir Handloom Development Corporation

Financial Year	*Total Investment*	*Surplus Reserves*	*Net Worth*	*Capital Employed*	*Net profit / Net loss (-)*
1997-98	13.24	3.93	-2.04	8.13	-2.08
1998-99	16.17	3.93	-4.85	8.15	-2.91
1999-00	17.99	3.93	-8.79	13.15	-4.13
2000-01	19.7	3.93	-12.64	13.04	-3.88
2001-02	21.78	3.93	-19.08	11.49	-6.54
2002-03	23.52	3.93	-23.44	0	-4.45
2003-04	39.9	Nil	-27.57	9.09	-0.18
2004-05	39.9	Nil	-27.1	9.56	-0.18

Jammu and Kashmir Handicrafts (S & E) Corporation

Financial Year	*Total Investment*	*Surplus Reserves*	*Net Worth*	*Capital Employed*	*Net profit / Net loss (-)*
1997-98	24.83	Nil	-21.03	0.18	-5.08
1998-99	29.6	Nil	24.99	-1.28	-5.37
1999-00	34.03	Nil	29.37	-2.08	-5.35
2000-01	39.04	Nil	33.63	-1.42	-4.25
2001-02	43.83	Nil	38.09	-1.98	-5.09
2002-03	48.54	Nil	42.59	-2.09	-4.81
2003-04	52.26	Nil	-46.75	-1.63	-2.29
2004-05	52.26	Nil	-37.85	7.27	-2.29

Jammu and Kashmir Cements Ltd.

Financial Year	*Total Investment*	*Surplus Reserves*	*Net Worth*	*Capital Employed*	*Net profit / Net loss (-)*
1997-98	37.37	0.15	7.6	27.2	1.71
1998-99	33.61	0.15	10.23	27.95	2.51
1999-00	33.28	0.15	11.08	28.3	0.6
2000-01	26.82	0.15	15.15	28.8	1.51
2001-02	22.68	0.15	15.15	35.84	1.24
2002-03	22.81	0.15	15.15	29.5	2.1
2003-04	18.67	Nil	10.58	14.26	-1.53
2004-05	18.67	Nil	20.2	23.88	-1.53

Jammu and Kashmir State Cable Car Corporation Ltd.

Financial Year	*Total Investment*	*Surplus Reserves*	*Net Worth*	*Capital Employed*	*Net profit / Net loss (-)*
1997-98	24.03	Nil	23.93	23.93	Nil
1998-99	24.4	Nil	24.21	21.78	loss
1999-00	24.56	Nil	24.4	22.17	loss
2000-01	24.71	Nil	24.69	22.51	0.13
2001-02	24.85	Nil	24.85	22.45	0.08
2002-03	34	Nil	34	26.22	(-) 0.23
2003-04	34.6	Nil	23.12	23.12	Nil
2004-05	34.6	Nil	23.12	23.12	Nil

Jammu and Kashmir Projects Construction Corporation Limited

Financial Year	*Total Investment*	*Surplus Reserves*	*Net Worth*	*Capital Employed*	*Net profit / Net loss (-)*
1997-98	1.82	0.51	2.04	2.32	0.42
1998-99	1.82	0.68	2.21	2.49	0.17
1999-00	1.82	1.12	2.64	2.93	0.43
2000-01	1.82	1.49	3.02	3.3	0.37
2001-02	1.82	2.3	3.82	4.14	0.8
2002-03	1.82	3.55	4.97	5.26	1.15
2003-04	2.93	Nil	-0.16	1.25	-0.36
2004-05	2.93	Nil	-0.31	1.1	-0.36

Jammu and Kashmir Minerals Limited

Financial Year	*Total Investment*	*Surplus Reserves*	*Net Worth*	*Capital Employed*	*Net profit / Net loss (-)*
1997-98	50	Nil	-56.3	8	-16.25
1998-99	66.33	Nil	-74.41	6.46	-18.11
1999-00	83.68	Nil	-91.17	9.49	-16.76
2000-01	102.22	Nil	-108.7	8.26	-17.53
2001-02	119.99	Nil	-132.72	17.73	-15.02
2002-03	138.48	Nil	-139.5	11.1	-15.78
2003-04	190.12	Nil	-175.86	6.26	-2.15
2004-05	190.12	Nil	-180.88	1.24	-2.15

Jammu and Kashmir Tourism Development Corporation

Financial Year	*Total Investment*	*Surplus Reserves*	*Net Worth*	*Capital Employed*	*Net profit / Net loss (-)*
1997-98	23.12	2.47	12.86	17.28	-0.08
1998-99	23.9	3.24	14.17	18.95	-0.1
1999-00	24.89	3.99	16.32	21.79	-0.11
2000-01	24.86	4.69	17.62	22.96	-0.11
2001-02	25.24	5.88	19.1	24.07	-0.11
2002-03	28.38	6.77	22.12	27.3	-0.16
2003-04	27.82	Nil	1.42	5.74	-0.88
2004-05	27.82	Nil	1.94	6.26	-0.88

Jammu and Kashmir State Forest Corporation

Financial Year	*Total Investment*	*Surplus Reserves*	*Net Worth*	*Capital Employed*	*Net profit / Net loss (-)*
1997-98	27.08	1.23	-17.07	30.3	-24.07
1998-99	27.08	1.23	-19.24	27	-21.74
1999-00	27.08	1.23	-22.12	19.68	-28.77
2000-01	27.08	1.23	-22.64	20.47	-5.22
2001-02	27.08	1.23	-23.19	23.23	-4.62
2002-03	27.08	1.23	-23.19	23.23	-4,62
2003-04	92.19	Nil	-83.16	Nil	Nil
2004-05	92.19	Nil	-83.16	Nil	Nil

Jammu and Kashmir Road Transport Corporation

Financial Year	*Total Investment*	*Surplus Reserves*	*Net Worth*	*Capital Employed*	*Net profit / Net loss (-)*
1997-98	223.22	Nil	-176.2	43.74	-38.22
1998-99	244.58	Nil	-213	63	-43.04
1999-00	274.33	Nil	-250.96	74.95	-42.96
2000-01	313.71	Nil	-291.85	88.1	-45.25
2001-02	329.07	Nil	-331.8	94.7	-44.91
2002-03	353.53	Nil	-369.2	99.8	-45.65
2003-04	375.82	Nil	-402.75	-132.76	-47.22
2004-05	375.82	Nil	-402.75	-132.76	-47.22

Jammu and Kashmir State Power Development Corporation

Financial Year	*Total Investment*	*Surplus Reserves*	*Net Worth*	*Capital Employed*	*Net profit / Net loss (-)*
1997-98	31.15	907.84	912.84	416.55	-0.72
1998-99	133.76	958.23	963.23	967.08	-10.64
1999-00	353.97	1117.01	1182.01	1422.22	-1.72
2000-01	807.79	1177.01	1182.01	1912.97	-20.57
2001-02	1243.24	1177.81	1182.81	1882.44	-34.83
2002-03	2115.24	908.39	913.39	2434.45	-18.95
2003-04	889.38	Nil	-753.24	131.14	Nil
2004-05	889.38	Nil	-591.43	292.95	Nil

Jammu and Kashmir State Women's Development Corporation

Financial Year	*Total Investment*	*Surplus Reserves*	*Net Worth*	*Capital Employed*	*Net profit / Net loss (-)*
1997-98	2.03	Nil	1.03	1.75	Nil
1998-99	2.29	Nil	1.18	1.4	Nil
1999-00	2.97	Nil	1.19	0.91	Nil
2000-01	3.77	Nil	1.18	0.96	Nil
2001-02	5.35	Nil	1.16	0.99	Nil
2002-03	6.9	Nil	1.33	1.15	Nil
2003-04	7.72	Nil	-5.03	0.26	Nil
2004-05	7.72	Nil	-5.03	0.26	Nil

Jammu and Kashmir SC/ ST / OBC Development Corporation

Financial Year	*Total Investment*	*Surplus Reserves*	*Net Worth*	*Capital Employed*	*Net profit / Net loss (-)*
1997-98	1.02	Nil	Nil	Nil	-0.49
1998-99	3.84	Nil	Nil	Nil	-0.78
1999-00	0.27	Nil	Nil	Nil	-0.7
2000-01	1.99	Nil	Nil	Nil	-1.83
2001-02	4.4	Nil	Nil	Nil	0.9
2002-03	0.35	Nil	Nil	Nil	0.99
2003-04	19.44	Nil	-0.65	6.31	0.06
2004-05	19.44	Nil	-0.65	6.31	0.06

12

Post Privatization Efficiency of Select Central Public Sector Enterprises in India

Background

The Indian Economy entered the decade of the 1990s with large imbalances on internal and external accounts, which made the economy highly vulnerable to exogenous and external shocks. Those imbalances were exacerbated by the gulf crisis and the distributed and uncertain situation in the domestic policy during 1990-91. Taken together, these developments led to a severe external liquidity crunch and a crisis of unprecedented dimensions during 1991-92. Our foreign exchange reserves began to decline to a level of Rs. 5480 crore ($3.11 billion) at the end of August 1990 to Rs.1666 crore ($ 896 million) on 16th January 1991, prompting the government to borrow from the IMF. (Economic Survey, 1991-92).

The immediate cause of the loss of reserves beginning in September 1990 was a sharp rise in the imports of oil and refined products with corresponding sharp rise in world oil prices on the annexation of Kuwait. The spot purchases made to prevent the avergence of shortage in the domestic market were very costly. The rise in the cost of imports more than accounted for the rise in trade deficit from an average of Rs. 619 crore ($356 million) per month in June-August 1990 to Rs.1229 crore ($677 million) per month in the following six months. The effect of the rise in oil prices was aggravated by the evens that followed.

The payment crisis of 1990-91 was accompanied by other adverse developments on the capital account reflecting the loss of confidence in the government's ability to manage the situation. External commercial borrowing came down drastically from Rs. 5479 crore in 1989-90 to Rs.1559 crore in the first half of 1991-92. The drying up of commercial loans in 1990-91 was accompanied by a net outflow of NRI deposits.

The state of our public finances had also reached crisis proportions by the end of the 1980s. The public debt to Gross Domestic Product (GDP) ratio increased through the 1980, going up to almost 60 per cent at the end of the decade, implying a doubling of the ratio as compared to the ratio at the end of the previous decade. As is now well known, the proximate reasons for this situation were the failure of the public sector to generate investible resources and the explosive growth of government current spending that saw the budget deficit as a proportion of GDP rise from 6.4 to 9 percent during the 1980s. (Economic Survey, 1991-92)

At the end of 1990-91, the total internal debt amounted to Rs. 2,60,100 crore, which constituted 50.2 per cent of the GDP. External debt at the end of 1990-91 amounted to Rs.66,020 crore, which was 12.7 per cent of the GDP. Thus, the total public debt formed 62.9 per cent of the GDP.

With the launching of stabilization and structural adjustment programme under the new economic policy, the government of India has initiated privatization programme. Various measures are being taken to improve the performance of the existing PEs. Under the leadership of the new government at the center, many roll back operations are taking place. The Governments decision to disinvest 31 of the central PEs, in five rounds to reduce its holdings to 49% was seen as the first step to privatize in the country supported by the existing policy, economic paradigms are taking a new shape.

The fiscal crunch has rung its bell in the case of the states of the Indian Union. Hence, the state governments have started to take a second look at the huge amount that has been locked up in the SLPEs. The bulging deficit budget is compelling them to rewind the activities of the various SLPEs that had not been performing upto the mark. Therefore privatization programme should be able to generate more revenue on one hand and improve efficiency on the other. A trade-off has to be achieved between these two. Generating revenue is a short term goal where as enhancement of efficiency is a long term one. Depending upon the position of particular PE in economy, the concept of privatization should be thought off.

Privatization has attracted much attention in recent years, and reflects a world-wide interest in reducing the role of the state in national economies, while enhancing the scope of private ownership and the private sector. The growing appeal of privatization embraces both the ideological desire for smaller government and a belief in the superior economic performance of the private sector.

Privatisation Theory and Concept

The concept of privatization was better explained by Mishra et.al., (2004). According to them Privatisation can be defined as the transfer of ownership of State Owned Enterprises to private sector by the sale – full or partial of on going concerns or by the sale of assets following liquidation. Any rolling back of the government's involvement in the economy can be called privatization. The most common connotation is selling public assets like the sale of British Telecom in the UK. But as privatization is a process that aims at reducing the involvement of the state or the public sector in the nation's economic activities, this involves not only divestiture of public enterprises or their leasing or franchise financing, but also the transfer of management control to private enterprise is a part of privatization.

Privatization has been used to describe a range of different policy initiatives in different countries. In developed countries it is change of ownership of an enterprise or a part of enterprise from the public to the private sector whereas in developing countries where till recently government policy was based on socialist views or externally influenced by theory of communism, liberalisation, or deregulation or entry of private enterprises into activities previously restricted to public enterprises.

The word privatization also encompasses where the provision of goods or services is transferred from public to private sector, while government retains ultimate responsibility for supplying the service. Franchising or contracting out of the public services and the leasing of public assets to the private sector are examples of this form of privatization.

Privatization in India

Privatization in India generally goes by the name of 'disinvestment' or divestment' of equity. This is because privatization has thus far not meant transfer of ownership or even of controlling interest from government to anybody else. The government has sold stakes ranging from one per cent to 40% in 40 PEs, but in no company has its stake fallen below the magic figure of 51% which is seen as conferring controlling interest.

The privatization programme is itself relatively new to the country. It is part of economic reforms covering industry, trade, the financial sector and agriculture and also involving a program of macro-economic stabilization focused on the federal budget, which commenced in 1991. privatization is seen as a necessary concomitant of deregulation of industry, necessary in order to enable firms in the public sector to compete and survive in the new environment.

The major element in industrial deregulation has been the Industrial policy Statement of June 1991 which, among other things, drastically reduced the number of sectors of industry reserved from the public sector from 17 to eight. The list has since been reduced to four: defence, atomic energy, specified minerals and railway transport. Moreover, all the areas earlier reserved for the public sector have also been exempted from the system of industrial licensing under which the private sector was required to obtain a license from the government in order to start a business.

Disinvestment of equity in 40 PEs has raised about Rs. 12 billion ($2.8) so far. Only profit-making enterprises have been offered for sale. In the first round of disinvestment, the government offered "bundles" of shares of various PSUs (each bundle carrying a notional reserve price) to local institutions. Later, the bidding process was opened to foreign institutional investors and the public at large.

After the initial round of disinvestment in 1991-92, the process was guided by recommendations made by a Committee on Disinvestment set up in 1993. Later, realizing the sensitivity in political terms of the whole process, the government constituted in 1996 an independent body, the Disinvestment Commission to draw up a comprehensive programme of disinvestment over a 5-10 year period of public enerprises (PEs) referred to the Commission by a Core Group of government secretaries. The Commission was asked to advise on such matters as the extent of disinvestment, the mode of disinvestment, selection of financial advisors to facilitate the process etc.

The 1st Disinvestment Commission has formulated a broad approach to disinvestment and also made specific recommendations in respect of 19 out of 50 PEs referred to it by the Core Group. The Commission has broadly distinguished between a "core" group and "non-core" group of industries. In the "core" group are industries such as telecommunications, power, petroleum etc that are capital-intensive and where the market structure could be on oligopoly. The "core" group also includes basic industries in which PEs have a considerable market presence and in which private sector presence is still limited. For the "core" group, the Commission advocates selling government equity upto 49% that is, the government would retain 15% of equity. In the "non-core" group, the Commission advocates sale of upto 74% of government equity. As for the 19 PEs for which the Commission has made specific recommendations, these include strategic sale of a large chunk of equity to a private party (domestic or foreign), offer of shares to the public, outright sale and deferment of disinvestment.

An attempt is made inorder to analyse the post-privatisation performance of Public Enterprises (PEs). The major objectives are:

1. To do a comparative study on financial/physical performance in PEs pre and post privatization and
2. Evaluate the lessons that can be learnt regarding privatisation/disinvestment
3. Examine the best practices with regard to valuation in privatization/disinvestment in these PEs.

Hypothesis and Methodology

Almost all governments expect that disinvestment will lead to increase in profitability of public enterprises and their in operating efficiency. It is tested whether the envisaged goal of improvement in performance was in fact achieved. It is examined the impact of disinvestment on profitability and operating efficiency in terms of sales efficiency, employment levels.

Based on the empirical results available on divestiture, it is expected that

- The switch from public to private ownership will cause profitability and operating efficiency to improve;
- There will be a decrease in the proportion of debt in the capital structure both because of the state's withdrawal of

debt guarantees and increase in enterprises' cost of borrowing;

- Dividend payouts will increase on disinvestment as private investors would demand dividends; and
- There would be a relative change in the level of employment.

A null hypotheses is assumed for the computed ratios like Return on Sales (ROS), Return on Assets (ROA) $ROS_A = ROS_B$, where A and B stands for after privatisaiton and B for before privatization as given in the table 1. This hypotheses focuses on the financial characteristics, which will examine changes resulting from divestiture. Then for each divested PE, paired sample t-test is applied ('pre' and 'post') for the identified parameters. This method is selected as the number of observations is less than 10. It is a procedure by which sample

Table 1

No	*Performance Variable*	*Ratios / Parameters*	*Null Hypothesis*
1.	Profitability Return on Sales (ROS)[1]	(i) Profit Before Depreciation, Interest and Taxes (PBDIT)/Sales (ii) Profit After Tax (PAT)/Sales	$ROS_A = ROS_B$
2.	Return on Assets (ROA)[2]	(i) PBDIT/Assets (ii) PAT/Assets	$ROA_A = ROA_B$
3.	Return on Equity (ROE)[3]	(i) PBDIT/Equity (ii) PAT/Equity	$ROE_A = ROE_B$
4.	Asset Turnover ratio[4]	(i) Total sales/Assets	
5.	Debt-Equity ratio[5]	Total debt/Total Equity	

results are used to verify the truth of falsity of a null hypothesis. The decision to accept or reject Ho is made on the basis of the value of the test statistics obtained from the data.

Procedure applied in Paired Samples T-Test

1. Eight[6] public enterprises were identified that were privatized/disinvested during the period 1997-98 to 2004-05.
2. Data on selected parameters (Profit Before Depreciation, Interest and Taxes (PBDIT), Profit After Tax (PAT), Sales, Total Assets, Total Equity, Current Assets and Current Liabilities) were collected.
3. Ratios on Return on Sales, Return on Assets, Return on Equity, Asset Turnover Ratio and Debt-Equity Ratio were calculated for each enterprise before privatisation and after privatisation. Four years before privatisation period is taken i.e., 1997-98 to 2000-2001 in case of BALCO, CMC, HTPL and from 1998-99 to 2001-02 in case of VSNL, IBP,

Table 2
Enterprise-wise Privatisation

BALCO	*March 2001*	*Sterlite Industries*
CMC	Sep 2001	Tata Sons Ltd
Hindustan Teleprinters Ltd	Oct 2001	Himachal Futuristic
VSNL	Feb 2002	Tata Group
IBP	Feb 2002	Indian Oil Corporation Ltd
Hindustan Zinc Ltd	Feb 2002	Sterlite Industries
Indian Petrochemical Corp.Ltd	May 2002	Reliance Industries
Maruti Udyog	May 2002	Suzuki Motor Corp

HZL, MUL and IPCL. Four years after privatisation period is taken i.e., from 2001-02 to 2004-05 in case of BALCO, CMC,HTPL and from 2002-03 to 2005-06 in case of VSNL, IBP, HZL, MUL and IPCL. The privatisation details are given in the table 2 below:

4. Paired Samples T-statistics is used in order to compare the financial performance of the enterprises before and after privatisation.

Outline of the Research

The findings and conclusions of the study have been organized as follows:

1. Objectives of the study
2. Hypothesis of the study
3. Findings and Analysis of the study
4. Conclusions of the study

1. Objectives: Objective I has been addressed with the following methodology

Ist Objective: *Conduct a comparative study on financial / physical performance in PEs before and after privatization and*

2. Hypothesis:

$H_0: á_1 = á_2$

(where $á_1$ symbolises financial variables of pre privatisation period and $á_2$ symbolises financial variables of post privatisation period)

3. Findings and Analysis of the study

Return on Sales (ROS) Ratio

This ratio is widely used to evaluate an enterprise operational efficiency. ROS is also known as a firm's "operating profit margin". It is calculated using the formula (Profit Before Depreciation Interest and Taxes/Sales). This will provide insight to how much profit is being produced per rupee of sales. As with

Table 3
Paired Samples T-Test

Balco		*Mean Difference*	*Std.Deviation*	*Std.Error Mean*	*t*	*df*	*Sig (2-tailed)*
			1. BALCO				
Pair 1	PBDIT/Sales	1.39	12.61	6.30	.220	3	.840
Pair 2	PAT/Sales	-1.63	9.38	4.69	-.349	3	.750
			2. CMC				
Pair 1	PBDIT/Sales	48.05	17.12	8.56	5.61	3	.011*
Pair 2	PAT/Sales	17.10	5.94	2.97	5.75	3	.010*
			3. HTPL				
Pair 1	PBDIT/Sales	22.32	13.56	7.83	2.85	2	.104
Pair 2	PAT/Sales	29.99	18.95	1.94	2.74	2	.111
			4. VSNL				
Pair 1	PBDIT/Sales	-12.41	13.08	6.54	-1.898	3	.154
Pair 2	PAT/Sales	1.7	10.022	5.011	.339	3	.757

(Contd.)

(Contd.Table 3)

Balco		*Mean Difference*	*Std.Deviation*	*Std.Error Mean*	*t*	*df*	*Sig (2-tailed)*
			5. MUL				
Pair 1	PBDIT/Sales	-3.487	6.988	3.494	-.998	3	.03*
Pair 2	PAT/Sales	-1.985	4.003	2.001	-.992	3	.04*
			6. IPCL				
Pair 1	PBDIT/Sales	8.35	7.04	3.52	2.37	3	.09
Pair 2	PAT/Sales	-1.61	4.41	2.20	-.73	3	.51
			7. IBP				
Pair 1	PBDIT/Sales	-.122	.245	.122	-.99	3	.3
Pair 2	PAT/Sales	-.015	.031	.015	-.96	3	.4
			8. HZL				
Pair 1	PBDIT/Sales	-16.49	14.91	7.45	-2.21	3	.11
Pair 2	PAT/Sales	-13.54	9.43	4.71	-2.87	3	.06

* Indicates at 5% level of significance.

many ratios, it is best to compare a Enterprise's ROS over time to look for trends, and compare it to other companies in the industry. An increasing ROS indicates the Enterprise is growing more efficient, while a decreasing ROS could signal looming financial troubles.

Table 3 gives paired samples t-test for the selected enterprises in the study. Out of eight enterprises CMC (Computer Maintenance Centre), Maruti Udyog Limited, IPCL (Indian Petroleum Corporation Limited), HZL (Hindustan Zinc Limited), has shown significant difference in the post privatisation period compared to pre privatisation period. Hence we reject the null hypothesis.

Return on Assets (ROA) Ratio

Return on Assets is an indicator of how profitable an enterprise is relative to its total assets. ROA gives an idea as to how efficient management is at using its assets to generate earnings. Calculated by dividing a Enterprise's annual earnings by its total assets, ROA is displayed as a percentage. Sometimes this is referred to as "return on investment". ROA explains the earnings that were generated from invested capital (assets). ROA for public companies can vary substantially and will be highly dependent on the industry. This is why when using ROA as a comparative measure, it is best to compare it against an enterprise's previous ROA numbers or the ROA of a similar Enterprise. The assets of the Enterprise are comprised of both debt and equity. Both of these types of financing are used to fund the operations of the Enterprise. The ROA figure gives investors an idea of how effectively the Enterprise is converting the money it has to invest into net income. The higher the ROA number, the better, because the Enterprise is earning more money on less investment.

Table 4 shows that IPCL and HZL showed significant difference in the post privatisation period. This means that these enterprises are generating more returns out of the assets.

Table 4

		Mean Difference	*Std.Deviation*	*Std.Error Mean*	*t*	*df*	*Sig (2-tailed)*
			BALCO				
Pair 1	PBDIT/Assets	2.81	5.54	2.77	1.01	3	0.386
Pair 2	PAT/Assets	-.492	5.25	2.62	-.188	3	0.863
			CMC				
Pair 1	PBDIT/Assets	.095	2.16	1.08	.088	2	0.936
Pair 2	PAT/Assets	-1.95	1.71	0.856	-2.27	2	0.107
			HTPL				
Pair 1	PBDIT/Assets	22.92	9.90	5.74	4.00	2	0.05
Pair 2	PAT/Assets	27.98	13.51	7.80	3.58	2	0.07
			VSNL				
Pair 1	PBDIT/Assets	2.96	7.04	3.52	.841	3	.46
Pair 2	PAT/Assets	6.55	5.07	2.53	2.58	3	.08

(Contd.)

(Contd.Table 4)

		Mean Difference	*Std.Deviation*	*Std.Error Mean*	*t*	*df*	*Sig (2-tailed)*
MUL							
Pair 1	PBDIT/Assets	-6.74	13.54	6.77	-.99	3	.39
Pair 2	PAT/Assets	-3.83	7.75	3.87	-.99	3	.40
6. IPCL							
Pair 1	PBDIT/Assets	-7.2	3.44	1.72	-4.2	3	.02*
Pair 2	PAT/Assets	-4.8	4.01	2.00	-2.4	3	.09
7. IBP							
Pair 1	PBDIT/Assets	-.77	1.56	.78	-.99	3	.39
Pair 2	PAT/Assets	-.13	.215	.107	-1.20	3	.31
8. HZL							
Pair 1	PBDIT/Assets	-13.54	9.43	4.71	-2.85	3	.06
Pair 2	PAT/Assets	-11.61	6.50	3.25	-3.57	3	.03*

*** Indicates at 5% level of significance.**

Table 5

		Mean Difference	*Std.Deviation*	*Std.Error Mean*	*t*	*df*	*Sig (2-tailed)*
			1. BALCO				
Pair 1	PBDIT/Equity	-29.09	47.27	23.63	-1.23	3	.306
Pair 2	PAT/Equity	-22.69	37.49	18.74	-1.21	3	.313
			2.CMC				
Pair 1	PBDIT/Equity	-396.79	99.9	49.96	-7.94	3	.004*
Pair 2	PAT/Equity	-213.89	70.52	35.26	-6.06	3	.009*
			3. HTL				
Pair 1	PBDIT/Equity	427.02	149.82	86.5	4.93	2	.03*
Pair 2	PAT/Equity	441.22	279.89	161.59	2.73	2	.11
			4. VSNL				
Pair 1	PBDIT/Equity	1036.5	480.45	240.22	4.31	3	.023*
Pair 2	PAT/Equity	770.59	348.44	174.22	4.42	3	.021*

(Contd.)

(Contd.Table 5)

		Mean Difference	*Std.Deviation*	*Std.Error Mean*	*t*	*df*	*Sig (2-tailed)*
			5. MUL				
Pair 1	PBDIT/Equity	-362.10	721.26	360.63	-1.004	3	.38
Pair 2	PAT/Equity	-206.05	412.59	206.299	-.99	3	.4
			6. IPCL				
Pair 1	PBDIT/Equity	-203.50	124.75	62.3	-3.26	3	.04*
Pair 2	PAT/Equity	-156.58	143.68	71.84	-2.18	3	.11
			7. IBP				
Pair 1	PBDIT/Equity	-93.27	177.73	88.86	-1.05	3	.37
Pair 2	PAT/Equity	-16.28	25.14	12.57	-1.29	3	.28
			8. HZL				
Pair 1	PBDIT/Equity	-201.54	201.92	100.96	-1.99	3	.01*
Pair 2	PAT/Equity	-134.00	125.80	62.90	-2.13	3	.01*

***Indicates at 5% level of significance.**

Return on Equity (ROE) Ratio

Return on Equity is a measure of an enterprise profitability that reveals how much profit an enterprise generates with the money that shareholders have invested. ROE is useful for comparing the profitability of an enterprise to that of other firms in the same industry.

Table 5 shows that CMC, HTPL, VSNL, IPCL and HZL showed significant difference in the post privatisation period. This shows that there is significant difference in Return on Equity (PBDIT/Equity and PAT/Equity) in the pre-privatisation period and post-privatisation period. Hence the null hypothesis (Return on Equity in Per-privatisation period is equal to Return on Equity in the post-privatisation period) is rejected.

Asset Turn Over Ratio

This ratio is useful to determine the amount of sales that are generated from each rupee of assets. Enterprises with low profit margins tend to have high asset turnover, those with high profit margins have low asset turnover.

Table 6

		Mean Difference	*Std. Deviation*	*Std.Error Mean*	*t*	*df*	*Sig (2-tailed)*
			1.BALCO				
Pair 1	Sales/Total Assets	13.13	32.28	16.14	.813	3	.475
			2. CMC				
Pair 1	Sales/Total Assets	-112.73	13.69	6.84	-16.46	3	.000*
			3. HTPL				
Pair 1	Sales/Total Assets	33.89	26.76	15.45	2.19	2	0.16
			4. VSNL				
Pair 1	Sales/Total Assets	33.51	7.43	3.71	9.0	3	.003*

(Contd.)

(Contd.Table 6)

		Mean Difference	*Std. Deviation*	*Std.Error Mean*	*t*	*df*	*Sig (2-tailed)*
5. MUL							
Pair 1	Sales/Total Assets	-47.84	95.95	.47	-1.02	3	.3
6. IPCL							
Pair 1	Sales/Total Assets	-84.64	41.16	20.58	-4.12	3	.02*
7. IBP							
Pair 1	Sales/Total Assets	-154.70	308.99	154.49	-1.001	3	.39
8. HZL							
Pair 1	Sales/Total Assets	1.28	25.16	12.58	.10	3	.92

* Indicates at 5% level of significance.

Table 6 shows that CMC, VSNL, IPCL showed significant difference in the post privatisation period. This signifies that there is a significant difference in Asset Turn Over in the pre-privatisation period and post-privatisation period. Hence the null hypothesis (Asset Turnover ratio in Per-privatisation period is equal to Asset Turnover ratio in the post-privatisation period) is rejected.

Debt Equity Ratio

Total liabilities divided by total assets. The debt/asset ratio shows the proportion of a enterprise assets which are financed through debt. If the ratio is less than one, most of the enterprise assets are financed through equity. If the ratio is greater than one, most of the enterprise assets are financed through debt. Enterprises with high debt/asset ratios are said to be "highly leveraged," and could be in danger if creditors start to demand repayment of debt.

Table 7 shows that CMC, HTPL showed significant difference in the post privatisation period. This signifies that there is significant difference in Debt-Equity ratio in the pre-

Table 7

		Mean Difference	*Std. Deviation*	*Std. Error Mean*	*t*	*df*	*Sig (2-tailed)*
BALCO							
Pair 1	Total Debt/Total Assets	-22.54	20.98	10.49	-2.14	3	0.12
CMC							
Pair 1	Total Debt/Total Assets	-7.87	3.86	1.93	-4.07	3	0.02*
HTPL							
Pair 1	Total Debt/Total Assets	-26.54	7.35	4.24	-6.25	2	0.02*
VSNL							
Pair 1	Total Debt/Total Assets	-1.61	1.14	.574	-2.08	3	0.06**

(Contd.)

(Contd.Table 7)

		Mean Difference	*Std.Deviation*	*Std.Error Mean*	*t*	*df*	*Sig (2-tailed)*
MUL							
Pair 1	Total Debt/Total Assets	-.49	.95	.47	-1.02	3	.38
IPCL							
Pair 1	Total Debt/Total Assets	22.62	18.29	9.14	2.47	3	.09**
IBP							
Pair 1	Total Debt/Total Assets	-2.8	6.6	3.3	-.86	3	.45
HZL							
Pair 1	Total Debt/Total Assets	-9.2	10.62	5.31	-1.74	3	.18

* Indicates at 5% level of significance.

** Indicates at 10% level of significance.

privatisation period and post-privatisation period. Hence the null hypothesis (Debt-Equity ratio in Per-privatisation period is equal to Debt-Equity ratio in the post-privatisation period) is rejected.

Out of the sample size of 8 units mixed results has been evidenced. Out of eight five units (CMC, IPCL, VSNL, HZL, HTP) registered improvement all through the study period. The remaining four units (BALCO, MUL, IBP) has not shown any performance improvement. These observations are supported by the tests of significance at 0.05% level.

Conclusions

It is clear from the results that BALCO, MUL, IBP have not shown a significant difference in their performance improvement in the post privatisation period compared to pre privatisation period.

CMC has experienced a tremendous improvement in the post privatisation period with 95% level of confidence it can be accepted that there is a significant improvement in the post privatisation period. HTP has shown improvement in case of heir assets, equity and debt-equity ratios at 95% confidence interval.

The financial performance of VSNL, HZL has shown significant improvement in case of sales, Assets, Equity and debt-equity ratio. IPCL has shown a good performance improvement in the post-privatisation period compared to pre privatisation period. The above conclusions were drawn basing on the t-test computation.

The review of empirical findings of the various studies conducted within and outside the country had shown varied results.

- Privatisation strategies should be specific and focused according to the characteristics of the country concerned[7].
- In the process of privatisation government commitment should be there. Moreover the value of the enterprise

should be assessed approximately prior to sale and the stock market need to be democratized before privatization[8].

- The major objective of privatisation should be proper allocation and efficient utilization of resources rather than broad policy objectives[9].
- Privatisation is to be understood, not merely in the structural sense of who owns an enterprise, but in the substantive sense of how far the operations of an enterprise are brought within the discipline of market force.[10]

Privatisation was expected to improve the public enterprises' efficiency in various ways. It would give the owners the right to appropriate their returns for assets, and to introduce incentives. Further, privatisation was believed to encourage measures of innovation and stimulate the productivity of the enterprises. In addition, the public finance difficulties were expected to be resolved by the market mechanism. Studies claim that privtisation has resulted in higher outputs, an increase in investments, the production of quality goods and services at low prices, the introduction of modern technology and know-how, and efficiency improvements in enterprises corporate governance. It was expected that post-privatisation would be advantageous in the following ways:

- The new management policies would be less bureaucratic and more profit-oriented, thereby contributing to the economic welfare of the enterprises.
- They would be closely associated with economic rewards and a more efficient allocation of resources, combined with new initiatives, such as total quality management and improved employee benefits.
- They would focus on market information
- Politics and bureaucracy played no role in post-privatisation. They were incentive-based and supported through market-driven budgets.

- They would require the participation of both managers and employees, thereby ensuring a thorough and reliable control process.

The detailed case studies of each of the selected CPSEs have been taken up in the ensuing chapters.

Case 1
Bharat Aluminium Company Limited (BALCO)

Background

Bharat Aluminium Company Limited (BALCO) was established in 1965 as the primary aluminium industry in India. BALCO is a dividend paying, profit-making enterprise in the aluminium sector. BALCO has two working units, an integrated aluminium complex situated at Korba in Chhattisgarh and a plant in West Bengal at Bidhanbag. BALCO is vertically integrated from sourcing of bauxite from its captive mines, refining and smelting to produceing aluminium and a variety of semi finished products.

BALCO is the third largest producer of Aluminium in the country. It has a turnover exceeding Rs. 900 crores and has huge real estate, including the BALCO township. The replacement cost of its 270 MW power plant itself is more than Rs. 1,500 crore, and the replacement cost of its fixed assets is valued at over Rs. 5000 crore. Ironically for only Rs. 552 crore, Sterlite Industry purchased a 51 per cent stake in the company and tookover control of BALCO. In handing over BALCO to Sterlite group, the Central Government showed undue haste. It ignored the Supreme Court order prohibiting the transfer of tribal lands to non-tribals. Land for BALCO was acquired for public purpose and cannot be transferred to private hands as per section 44(A) of the Land Acquisition Act. It has claimed that the valuation of BALCO is just and fair that it was done by experts and it could not be challenged in the court. However, these experts took only 11 days to complete the valuation. The replacement cost of both units, the power plant and township was calculated in three days flat, which includes travel time.

The government had 100 percent stake in BALCO prior to disinvestment. In 1997, the Disinvestment Commission classified BALCO as non-core for the purpose of disinvestment and recommended immediate disinvestment of 40 percent of the government stake to a Strategic Partner (SP), and further reduction to 26 per cent within two years of the strategic sale, through a domestic public offering. It further recommended divestment of the entire remaining stake at an appropriate time thereafter. The Cabinet accepted the recommendation of the Disinvestment Commission for divestment of 40 percent stake through strategic sale and further divestment through the capital market. Later, in 1998, the Disinvestment Commission revised its recommendation and advised the government to consider 51 percent divestment in favour of a strategic buyer Sterlite Industries along with transfer of management which was accepted by the Cabinet. The government thereupon appointed M/s Jardine Fleming as advisor to assist in the sale of its 51 per cent stake in BALCO to a strategic buyer.

As BALCO had a bloated equity of Rs. 489 crore (Rs. 4.89 billion) and large unutilized free reserves of Rs. 424 crore (Rs. 4.24 billion) it was suggested by the Ministry of Mines that BALCO's equity be reduced by 50 per cent prior to disinvestment, using its substantial cash surplus. This proposal was accepted. As a result, the government received Rs. 244 crore (Rs. 2.44 billion) from the capital restructuring of BALCO, and another Rs. 31 crore (Rs. 310 million) as tax on this amount, in March 2000 prior to disinvestment.

Disinvestment

The Government has classified PEs into those functioning in strategic and non-strategic areas for the purpose of disinvestment. All PEs, except those in the three areas of arms and ammunition and allied items of defence equipment, defence air-craft and warships, atomic energy and railway transport, were to be considered non-strategic. The Government has disinvested its stake in nine PEs namely, Modern Food Industries Limited (MFIL), Bharat Aluminium Company Limited (BALCO), Hindustan Teleprinters Limited (HTL), Computer Maintenance Corporation Limited (CMC), Hindustan Zinc Limited (HZL), Videsh Sanchar Nigam Limited (VSNL), Indo Burma Petroleum Limited (IBP), Indian Petro Chemicals Corporation Limited and Paradeep Phosphates Limited (PPL) between 1999-2000 and 2002-2003 through the strategic sale route.

Valuation

The Disinvestment Commission had emphasized that valuation of the PEs proposed for disinvestment should be independent, transparent and free from bias and had suggested that three methods of valuation, namely the 'Discount cash flow' (DCF), 'Relative valuation' and 'Net asset value' could be adopted. The Ministry of Disinvestment issued guidelines in May 2001, according to which four methodologies, namely Discounted Cash

Table 1
Valuation under Different Methods

Valuation Method	*Value*
Discounted cash flow (DCF) (computes likely earnings in coming years)	651.2 to 994.7
Comparables (looks at peer group companies)	587.0 to 909.0
Balance sheet method (looks at net worth from balance sheet)	597.2 to 681.9
Asset valuation (replacement cost/sale value of assets)	1054.9 to 1072.2

(Source: Ministry of Disinvestment, Government of India).

Flow (DCF) Method, Transaction Multiple Method, Balance Sheet Method and Asset Valuation Method were to be used for valuation of the PEs to be disinvested.

The valuation of BALCO for 100 per cent equity done by various methods is given in Table 1.

Industry Overview

The use of aluminium in India remains moderate compared to the rest of the world, but with significant growth potential, increased global demand of aluminium has again positively raised the prices. Aluminium prices have been on the upsurge both in the domestic and international markets during the year. The upsurge has been primarily due to all round improvement in aluminium consuming industries such as electrical, construction, packaging, transport and other consumer durable segments. With the progressive reduction in import duty structure the domestic prices would follow the international trends more closely. It is therefore essential that the Indian aluminium industry also become more competitive to match the international markets. This essentially requires improvement in quality and cost efficiency for which mining plays a major role. The nature of the bauxite reserves in India, which has low overburden, and is available in continuous large blocks, reduces the cost of production significantly. Therefore planned mining of the vast untapped high quality bauxite reserves in the country should be undertaken. Besides, the Indian aluminium industry has an inherent advantage of having integrated set ups for mining of bauxite, production of alumina and aluminium and captive power plants, which increases their competitiveness.

Internal Controls

The enterprise has an adequate system of internal controls to ensure that transactions are properly recorded, authorised and reported apart from safeguarding its assets. The internal control systems are supplemented by established policies, procedures and reviews carried out by the enterprise's internal audit function, which submits reports periodically to the Management and the Audit Committee of the Board. The Audit Committee of the Board of Directors presently comprises the Chairman and members. The Audit Committee besides reviewing the internal audit, control and procedures, reviews the unaudited and audited accounts of the enterprise before submission to the Board for approval.

Human Resources

The employment status during the disinvestment period is given in Table 2.

Table 2

Employment Status During Disinvestment Period (2001-02 to 2003-04)

Category	VRS March-01	Registration Retirement etc March 31, 2004
Executive / Officers Workmen Trainees	1055 5381 31	714 3432 165
Total	6467	4311

Source: Sterlite Annual Reports.

Sterlite has started construction of a new power plant and smelter. The workers are recruited from various states like TamilNadu, West Bengal, Orissa, Bihar, and Rajasthan. These workers are not allowed to go anywhere except to their place of work, and are almost like bonded labour. Local workers are not recruited due to fear of workers movements. The minimum wage is not paid to the workers. The management is violating the labour laws. Sterlite has violated the shareholders agreement concerning workers conditions.

BALCO is a profit making enterprise. The workers had played a major role in running the plant on profit. Now their condition is worsening. The management wants to remove all permanent workers and recruit new workers as trainees.

BALCO was the foremost profit making public enterprise producing aluminum in the country prior to the selling of 51 percent of its shares and transfer of its management to a strategic partner, Sterlite Industry in 2001 during the NDA regime. This strategic sale was opposed tooth and nail by the BALCO trade unions and the Left parties. There were serious charges of gross undervaluation of assets, collusive bidding leading to the sale of prime public assets at a throwaway price to Sterlite, which became a subsidiary of Vedanta Resources, a London stock exchange listed company. The 7,000 strong workforce put up a stiff resistance through a continuous strike for 67 days after the sale of BALCO, which, apart from highlighting the shady deal, symbolised their genuine apprehensions about their job security, sustenance of existing terms and conditions of work as well as the future of local development in the backward area of Korba in Chhattisgarh where BALCO is located. The report on "Impact of Privatisation on Labour: A Study of BALCO Disinvestment" done by V.V.Giri National Labour Institute says that, "From detailed interviews with the VRS optees, it was evident that various modes of coercion were engaged in implementing the VRS agenda by the new management. Many of the respondents felt that they were forcefully dragged into the scheme, though there was no open or direct threat from the management to accept the VRS. A commonly used methodology was to prepare the workers to accept the VRS by creating ambiguities and uncertainties. According to some of the respondents, prior to the introduction of each VRS offer, the management was resorting to many indirect pressurisation tactics at the workplace, which forced the workers to seriously think of leaving their job, whenever a suitable situation comes".

An important strategy adopted by management was to humiliate the workers by directly attacking their self-esteem and questioning their loyalty to the firm. Many of the respondents suggested that one of the major considerations while contemplating VRS was the demoralisation and trauma that they had experienced at the workplace during the post-disinvestment period. It was widely reported that Sterlite appointed some youngsters, who were given 'huge' salaries and positions, bypassing all the existing norms in recruitment. The major qualification for these managerial staff was their proximity to Sterlite authorities".

Environment Safety

As part of the operational process, the enterprise takes measures to control and monitor emission quality. The enterprise has obtained ISO-14001 certification relating to environment and OHSAS (Occupational Health & Safety Management Systems) 18001 certification. The enterprise continues to pay priority to safety measures and improvements have been made in housekeeping, road conditions and safety measures in the plant and township. This has contributed to significant reduction in the total number of accidents. The enterprise is also initiating steps for productive utilization of wastes to minimize the impact on the environment due to such wastes. Besides ensuring that the prescribed procedure for disposal of wastes is followed, the enterprise is also working on the possibility of utilization of red mud and spent pot lining.

Corporate Social Responsibiltiy

Working with the communities in which the enterprise operates is critical to the ongoing success of its operations. The enterprise has not only provided direct employment opportunities but also indirect employment opportunities by way of support services provided to the enterprise by local and regional economies. The enterprise continues to be actively involved in community development programmes involving provision of drinking water, education, health, sports and games infrastructure development etc. medical facilities, organising medical camps, immunisation programmes, adoption of villages where water, education, health, sports, games and electricity related facilities are provided. The enterprise has also been making significant contribution in the construction / maintenance of roads in State of Chattisgarh. Besides the enterprise is also involved in promotion of various cultural and literary activities. The enterprise is committed to enlarging the scope of corporate social responsibilities in order to extend the benefits to a larger section of the population.

Financial Performance

Sales and Services

Net sales and service revenue increased by Rs.11,269 crore to Rs.24,387 crore in 2006-07, a growth of 86 percent over the year 2005-06. The enterprise was able to achieve this substantial increase on account of better prices and improved efficiency. Total exports revenues increased by Rs.7,293 crore to Rs.12,536 crore in 2006-07, a growth of 139 percent over the year 2005-06. Other income aggregated Rs.682 crore representing interest earned, dividend income, profit from the sale of fixed assets and profit from the sale of current investments.

Capital Employed

The total capital employed by the enterprise increased by 40 percent from Rs.13,676 crore to Rs19,135 crore in 2006-07. The ratio of sales-to-capital employed increased significantly from 0.96 in the year 2005-06 to 1.27 times on account of higher realizations and better terms of trade.

Capital structure

Total shareholders' funds as at March 31st, 2007 aggregated Rs.9,982 crore of which equity was Rs. 112 crore comprising

55,84,94,411 shares of Rs.2 each. Of the above, 16,76,07,704 shares were converted into equity shares on account of a sub-division of shares from a face value of Rs. 5 to Rs.2 each; 27,91,48,238 equity shares of Rs.2 each were allotted as fully paid-up bonus shares by way of capitalisaiton of general reserve and share premium reserves.

Dividend

The enterprise paid an interim dividend of Rs. 4 per share on face value of Rs. 2 each (200%) aggregating Rs.254.73 crore (including dividend distribution tax).

Reserves and Surplus

Reserves and Surplus aggregated Rs.9,870 crore in the year 2006-07. retained earnings accounted fro 73 percent of the reserves and security premium the balance. During this period reserves and surplus increased 65 per cent.

To analyse the performance of selected companies certain key ratios are taken into account. In the case of BALCO there is an improvement in such ratios in the post-privatisation period. Profit Before Depreciation, Interest and Taxes (PBDIT)/Sales moved from 17.56 as an average to 14.67 in the post-privatisation period. On the other hand Profit After Tax (PAT)/Sales moved from 5.56 to 5.24, PBDIT/Assets moved from 12.02 to 6.47, PAT/Assets from 3.59 to 2.84, PBDIT/Equity from 39.03 to 54.96, PAT/Equity from 9.59 to 25.21. Sales/Total assets from 71.29 to 46.74. Total Debt/Assets from 7.33 to 24.44 and Current Ratio from 222.36 to 112.91. The ratios explained that after privatization organization has given more importance to profitability as certain ratios indicate the same. Profit After Tax to Sales was remain constant but Profit After Tax to Assets declined significantly.

Further, the return to equity shareholders was very attractive after the privatization. Similarly, Total Debt Ratio has also shown a significant change from pre-privatisation period to post-privatisation period, which means that the organization started using debt capital for leveraging its profitabilities. Hence, the current ratio of the organization which is condensed to 112.91 is also a significant change or indication in its liquidity and profitability and its approach towards management of working capital also. Further, it indicates that the organization has switched over itself from conservative approach to moderate approach in managing its finances. On the whole based on the ratios it can be asserted that the financial performance of BALCO has improved in the post-privatisation period which is proved by all the selected ratios. A graphical representation is also made to give a clear picture of the pre and post privatisation performance of BALCO.

Table 3 A
Financial Ratio Analysis

	Pre-Privatisation				
	1997	1998	1999	2000	2001
PBDIT/Sales	23.56	21.46	20.90	18.01	3.88
PAT/Sales	8.11	9.31	8.70	6.18	-4.53
PBDIT/Assets	16.53	15.17	13.74	11.29	3.38
PAT/Assets	5.69	6.58	5.72	3.88	-3.94
PBDIT/Equity	36.72	37.63	37.50	66.58	16.71
PAT/Equity	12.64	16.33	15.61	22.86	-19.51
Sales/Total Assets	70.19	70.68	65.72	62.70	87.15
Total debt/Total Assets	4.65	3.62	2.75	17.76	7.88
CA/CL	287.82	267.2	239.55	183.84	133.40
No. of employees	7454	7317	7294	6321	6231

Source: Compiled from Appendix 1A.

Graph 1

Pre and Post Privatisation Performance of BALCO

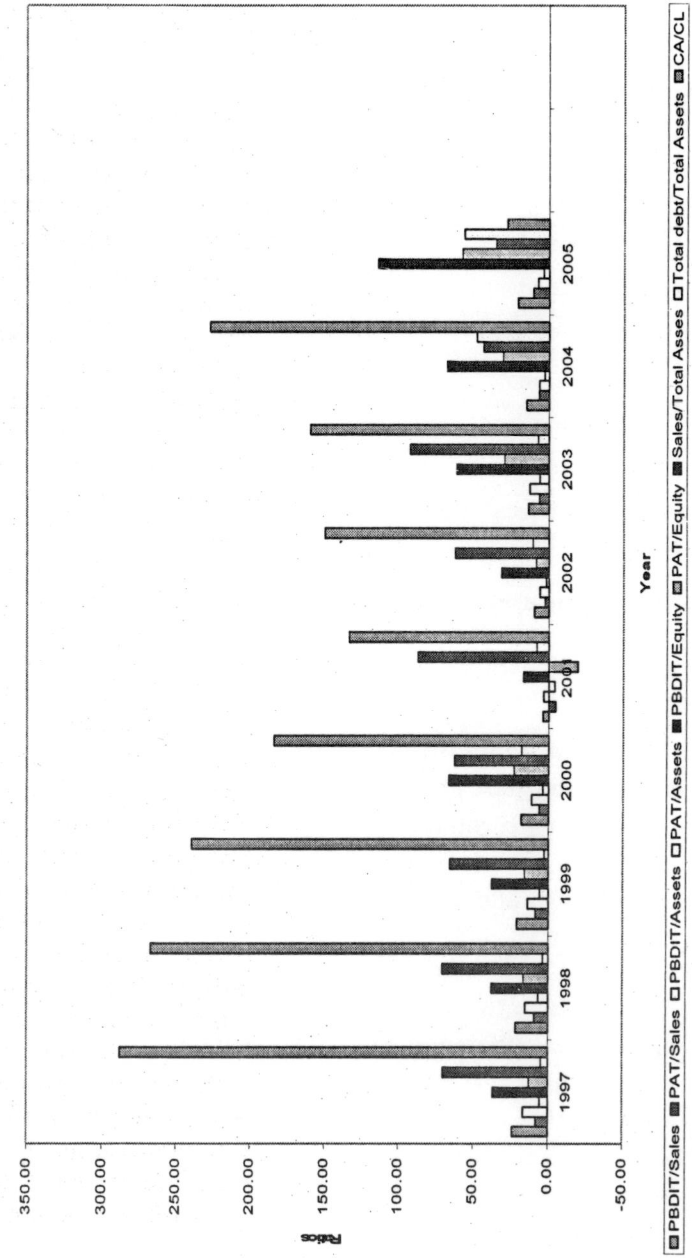

Table 3 B
Financial Ratio Analysis

	Post-Privatisation			
	2002	2003	2004	2005
PBDIT/Sales	9.60	13.63	14.81	20.65
PAT/Sales	2.60	6.48	6.67	10.46
PBDIT/Assets	6.00	12.57	6.48	7.29
PAT/Assets	1.63	5.97	2.92	3.69
PBDIT/Equity	31.36	61.48	67.91	114.04
PAT/Equity	8.50	29.23	30.58	57.76
Sales/Total Assets	62.52	92.18	43.74	35.29
Total debt/Total Assets	10.41	7.11	48.17	56.50
CA/CL	149.89	159.46	227.34	27.87
No. of employees	6102	5984	5963	5963

Source: Compiled from Appendix 1B.

An attempt is made to test the performance of BALCO in the pre and post privatisation periods using paired samples t-statistics with reference to Return on Sales, Return on Equity and Return on Assets and Current Assets/Current Liabilities. The performance in case of each ratio is explained separately.

Return on Sales (ROS) Ratio

This ratio is widely used to evaluate an enterprises operational efficiency. ROS is also known as a firm's "operating profit margin". It is calculated using the formula Profit Before Depreciation Interest and Taxes/Sales. This measure is helpful to management and provides an insight into how much profit is being produced per rupee of sales. As with many ratios, it is best to compare the enterprise's ROS over time to look for trends, and also compare it with similar PEs. An increasing

ROS indicates the Enterprise is growing more efficient, while a decreasing ROS could signal looming financial troubles.

Table 4 shows the paired samples t-test for PBDIT/Sales and PAT/Sales in the pre-privatisation. From the table it is observed that for pair 1&2 (Return on Sales (ROS)) the mean difference is 1.39 and -1.63 and standard deviation is 12.61 and 9.38. Standard error is 6.30 and 4.69 and t-values are 0.22 and -0.34 respectively and the corresponding significance values are 0.84 and 0.75 which are greater than 0.05 per cent significance level. This signifies that the difference in Return on Sales (PBDIT/Sales and PAT/Sales) in the post-privatisation period. Hence the null hypothesis (Return on Sales in Per-privatisation period is équal to Return on Sales in the post-privatisation period) is accepted.

Table 4
Paired Samples Test for Return on Sales

		Mean Difference	*Std.Deviation*	*Std.Error Mean*	*t*	*df*	*Sig (2-tailed)*
Pair 1	PBDIT/Sales pre PBDIT/Sales post	1.39	12.61	6.30	.220	3	.840
Pair 2	PAT/Sales pre PAT/Sales post	-1.63	9.38	4.69	-.349	3	.750

The graph on Return on Sales shows a positive trend in the post-privatisation period. There is an improvement in post-privatisation period but not significant when compared to pre-privatisation period.

Return on Assets (ROA) Ratio

Return on Assets is an indicator of how profitable an enterprise is relative to its total assets. ROA gives an idea as to

Graph 2
Return on Sales

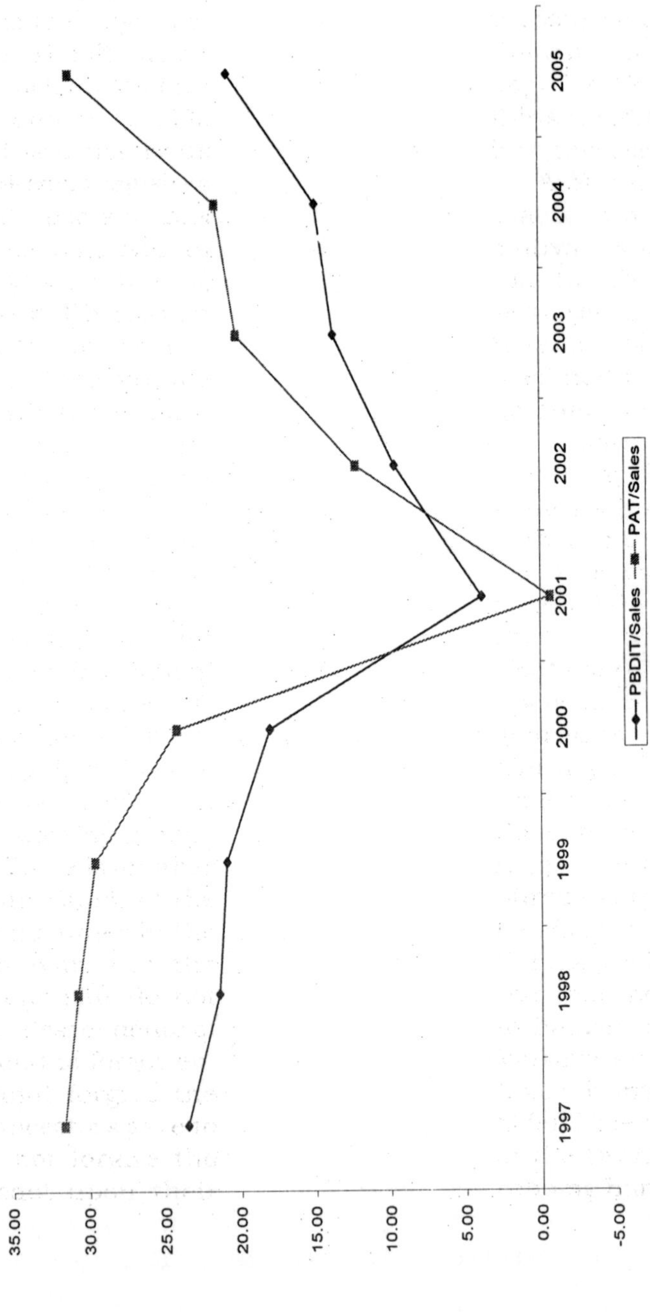

how efficient management is at using its assets to generate earnings. Calculated by dividing an enterprise's annual earnings by its total assets, ROA is displayed as a percentage. Sometimes this is referred to as "return on investment". ROA explains the earnings that were generated from invested capital (assets). ROA for public companies can vary substantially and will be highly dependent on the industry. This is why when using ROA as a comparative measure, it is best to compare it against the enterprise's previous ROA numbers or the ROA of a similar enterprise. The assets of the enterprise are comprised of both debt and equity. Both of these types of financing are used to fund the operations of the enterprise. The ROA figure gives investors an idea of how effectively the Enterprise is converting the money it has to invest into net income. The higher the ROA number the better, because the Enterprise is earning more money on less investment.

Table 5 shows the paired samples t-test for PBDIT/Assets, PAT/Assets in pre-privatisation period and PBDIT/Assets, PAT/Assets in the post-privatisation period. From the table it is observed that for pair 1&2 (Return on Assets (ROA) the mean difference is 2.81 and -.492 and standard deviation is 5.54 and 5.25. Standard error is 2.77 and 2.62 and t-values are 1.01 and

Table 5
Paired Samples Test for Return on Assets

		Mean Difference	*Std. Deviation*	*Std.Error Mean*	*t*	*df*	*Sig (2-tailed)*
Pair 1	PBDIT/Assets pre PBDIT/Assets post	2.81	5.54	2.77	1.01	3	0.386
Pair 2	PAT/Assets Pre PAT/Assets Post	-.492	5.25	2.62	-.188	3	0.863

-0.188 respectively and the corresponding significance values are 0.386 and 0.863 which is greater than 0.05 per cent significance level. This signifies that there is no significant difference in Return on Assets (PBDIT/Assets and PAT/Assets) in the post-privatisation period. Hence the null hypothesis (Return on Assets in Per-privatisation period is equal to Return on Assets in the post-privatisation period) is accepted.

The graph on Return on Assets in the pre and post privatisation period shows a positive trend in the post-privatisation period. There is an improvement in this period but not significant when compared to pre-privatisation period.

Graph 3
Return on Assets

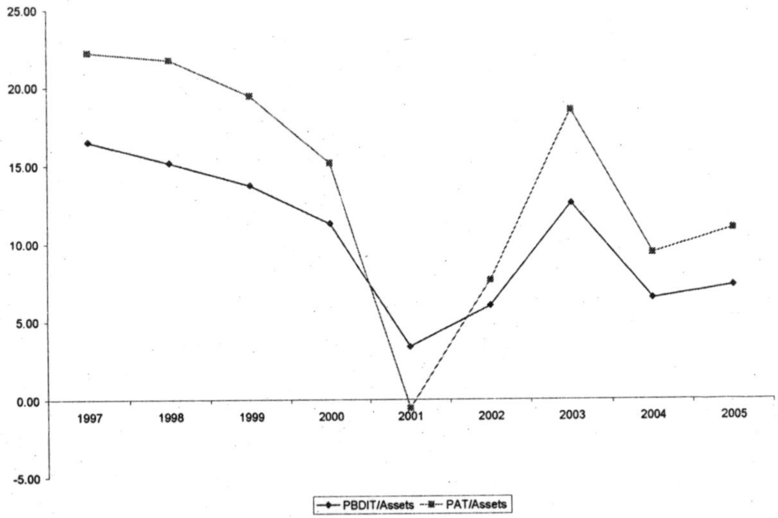

Return on Equity (ROE) Ratio

Return on Equity is a measure of the profitability that reveals how much profit the enterprise is generating with the money that shareholders have invested. ROE is useful for comparing the profitability of an enterprise with that of other firms in the same industry.

Graph 4
Return on Equity

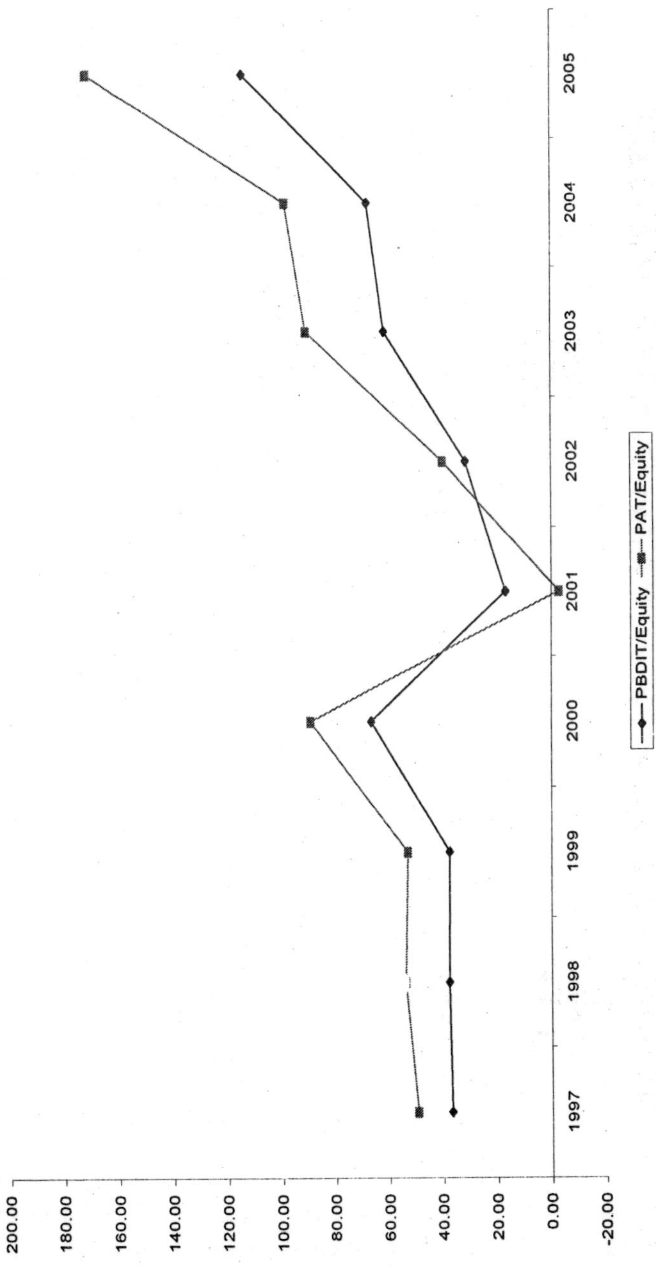

Table 6 shows the paired samples t-test for PBDIT/Equity, PAT/Equity in pre-privatisation period and PBDIT/Equity, PAT/ Equity in the post-privatisation period. From the table it is observed that for pair 1&2 (Return on Equity (ROE)) the mean difference is -29.09 and -22.69 and standard deviation is 47.27 and 37.49. Standard error is 23.63 and 18.74 and t-values are -1.23 and -1.211 respectively and the corresponding significance values are .306 and 0.313 which are greater than 0.05 per cent significance level. This signifies that there is no significant difference in Return on Equity (PBDIT/Equity and PAT/Equity) in the post-privatisation period. Hence the null hypothesis (Return on Equity in Per-privatisation period is equal to Return on Equity in the post-privatisation period is) accepted.

Table 6
Paired Samples T-Test

		Mean	*Std. Deviation*	*Std. Error Mean*	*t*	*df*	*Sig (2-tailed)*
Pair 1	PBDIT/Equity pre PBDIT/Equity post	-29.09	47.27	23.63	-1.23	3	.306
Pair 2	PAT/Equity Pre PAT/Equity Post	-22.69	37.49	18.74	-1.21	3	.313

The graph on Return on Equity in the pre and post privatisation period shows a positive trend. There is an improvement in this period but not significant when compared to pre-privatisation period.

Asset Turn Over Ratio

This ratio is useful to determine the amount of sales that are generated from each rupee of assets. Enterprises with low profit margins tend to have high asset turnover, those with high profit margins have low asset turnover.

Graph 5
Asset Turnover Ratio

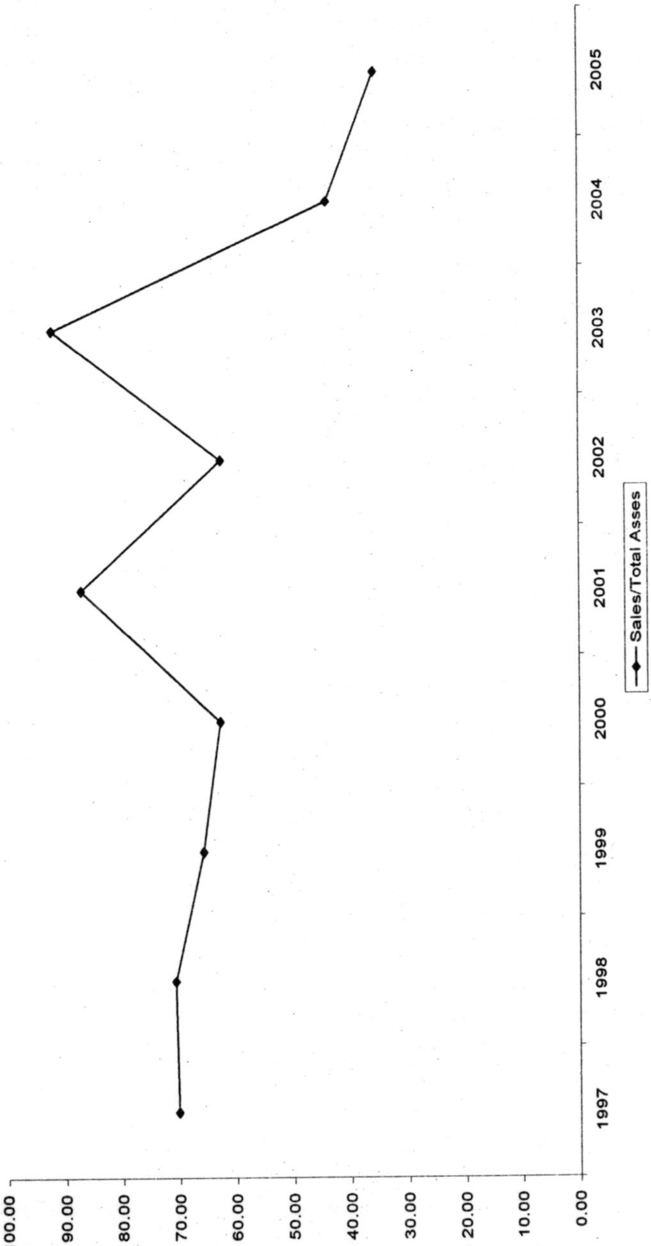

Table 7 shows the paired samples t- test for Sales/Total Assets in pre-privatisation period and in the post-privatisation period. From the table it is observed that for pair 1 (Asset Turn Over) the mean difference is 13.13 and standard deviation is 32.28. Standard error is 16.14 and t-value is .813 and the corresponding significance value is .475 which are greater than 0.05 per cent significance level. This signifies that there is no significant difference in Asset Turn Over in the post-privatisation period. Hence the null hypothesis (Asset Turnover ratio in Per-privatisation period is equal to Asset Turnover ratio in the post-privatisation period) is accepted.

Table 7
Paired Samples Test for Asset Turn Over Ratio

		Mean Difference	*Std. Deviation*	*Std.Error Mean*	*t*	*df*	*Sig (2-tailed)*
Pair 1	Sales/Total Assets Pre Sales/Total Assets Post	13.13	32.28	16.14	.813	3	.475

The graph on Asset Turn Over in the pre and post privatisation period shows a negative trend.

Debt Equity Ratio

The debt/asset ratio (Total liabilities divided by total assets) shows the proportion of enterprise assets which are financed through debt. If the ratio is less than one, most of the enterprise assets are financed through equity. If the ratio is greater than one, most of the enterprise assets are financed through debt. Enterprises with high debt/asset ratios are said to be "highly leveraged," and could be in danger if creditors start to demand repayment of debt.

Graph 6
Debt Equity Ratio

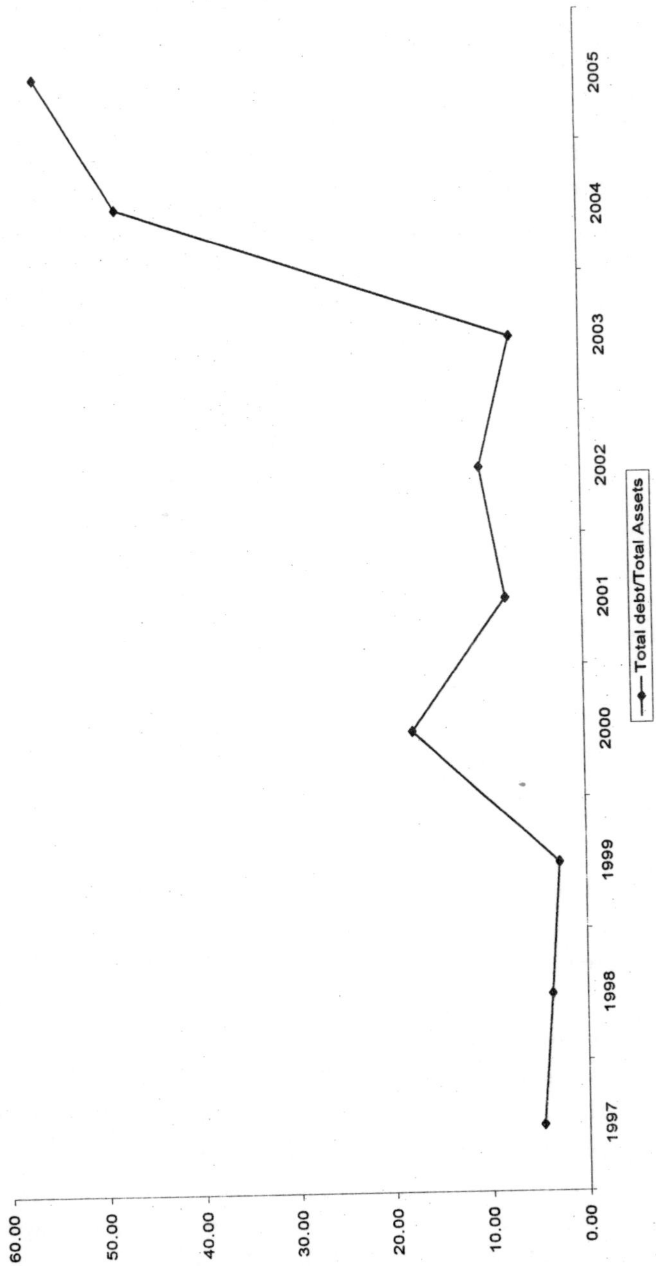

Table 8 shows the paired samples t-test for Total Debt/ Total Assets in pre-privatisation period and in the post-privatisation period. From the table it is observed that for pair 1 (Debt Equity Ratio) the mean difference is -22.54 and standard deviation is 20.98. Standard error is 10.49 and t-value is -2.14 and the corresponding significance value is .12 which is greater than 0.05 per cent significance level. This signifies that there is no significant difference in Debt-Equity ratio in the post-privatisation period. Hence the null hypothesis (Debt-Equity ratio in Per-privatisation period is equal to Debt-Equity ratio in the post-privatisation period) is accepted.

Table 8
Paired Samples T-Test

		Mean Difference	*Std.Deviation*	*Std.Error Mean*	*t*	*df*	*Sig (2-tailed)*
Pair 1	Total Debt/Total Assets Pre Total Debt/Total Assets Post	-22.54	20.98	10.49	-2.14	3	.12

The graph on Debt-Equity in the pre and post privatisation period shows an increasing trend. This means that most of the enterprise assets are financed through debt.

Conclusion

It is from the analysis that, a significant improvement has not taken place in the financial performance of the enterprise. But the year 2001 experienced a lower performance and in the same year the government has marched towards disinvestment. In the successive years there is an improvement with respect to Return on Sales, Return on Equity, Return on

Assets, Asset Turnover and Debt-Equity ratios. A detailed financial overview (given in appendix 1) makes it clear. However, the growth rate is very low. That is why, the statistical results have not shown an significant improvement and the hypothesis of the study (Financial performance in the pre-privatisation period is equal to financial performance in the post privatisation period) was accepted.

Appendix 1 A
Financial Performance of BALCO During Pre Privatisation

(Rs. In Crore)

	1997	*1998*	*1999*	*2000*	*2001*
PBDIT	179.52	183.96	183.34	162.73	36.87
Sales	762.1	857.19	877.21	903.44	950.94
PAT	61.79	79.84	76.32	55.87	-43.04
Assets	1085.83	1212.72	1334.68	1440.78	1091.21
Equity	488.85	488.85	488.85	244.42	220.62
No.of Employees	7454	7317	7294	NA	NA
Total Debt	50.44	43.92	36.68	255.95	85.94
Dividend	15.4	22	25.3	20.09	0
Current Assets	666.07	822.83	925.54	913.55	621.47
Current Liabilities	231.42	307.95	386.36	496.94	465.88
Debt-Equity Ratio	0.06	0.05	0.04	0.38	0.14

Source: Annual Report of BALCOs, CMIE Prowess Data Base.

Appendix 1 B
Financial Performance of BALCO During Post Privatisation

(Rs. In Crore)

	2002	*2003*	*2004*	*2005*
PBDIT	69.2	135.65	149.82	251.61
Sales	720.91	994.92	1011.57	1218.48
PAT	18.75	64.48	67.47	127.44
Assets	1153.17	1079.29	2312.85	3453.08
Equity	220.63	220.63	220.63	220.63
No.of Employees	NA	NA	NA	NA
Total Debt	120.09	76.78	1113.99	1951.11
Dividend	0	0	12.44	0
Current Assets	661.42	552.76	1098.93	360.52
Current Liabilities	441.28	346.64	483.38	1293.68
Debt-Equity Ratio	0.2	0.13	1.64	2.39

Source: Annual Report of BALCOs, CMIE Prowess Data Base.

Case 2
COMPUTER MAINTENANCE CENTRE
Background

CMC was established in 1975, and is one of the premier information technology solution providers in India, with a consolidated turnover of Rs. 814 crore for 2004-05. Operating out of 18 offices and 180 service locations in the country, CMC employs over 3000 people and has a wholly owned subsidiary in the USA called CMC Americas, Inc.

CMC's vision is to operate globally and use the benefit of information technology to improve the productivity of its customers and the quality of its customer's products and services. It combines horizontal expertise in information technology with its vertical experience developed by working in a wide range of Industries. After the successful disinvestment of CMC by the

Government of India, CMC has become a part of the TATA Group and closely working with TCS Asia's largest software company.

Disinvestment

In August 1990, the Government approved an increase in its authorized capital to Rs.35 crore with the additional equity capital being raised in the market the Government's stake should not however be less than 60%. In 1992 the Government disinvested 16.69% equity. In April 1999, CMC was referred to the Disinvestment Commission but was latter withdrawn as the Government decided to raise of additional equity either by private placement or by directly going for public issue. The company could not raise the funds till November 2000, either by way of private placement of shares or through public issue. On 1st February 2001, the Government decided to bring down its equity to 26% by way of induction of a Strategic Partner and other means.

Valuation

The valuation of the 100% equity shares of CMC Ltd. by different methods is as under:

Table 1
CMC: Valuation under Different Methods

S. No.	*Method of Valuation*	*Rs. / Crore*
1.	Discounted Cash Flow	213.49
2.	Asset Valuation	37.58
3.	Balance Sheet	72.74
4.	Comparable Companies	102.53

Source: Ministry of Disinvestment, Government of India.

Industry Overview

The Indian economy has accelerated the growth rate from 7.5 percent in 2004-05 to 8.1% in 2005-06. Other economic indicators like foreign exchange reserves, inward FDI remittances and exports are also showing a healthy growth. The Indian IT industry is set to cross $36 billion in annual revenues as per Nasscom estimates for 2005-06. The domestic market contributes just over $6 billion and this is expected to double in the next few years. The domestic market is transforming from being predominantly hardware-driven to a solution-oriented approach. This is driving demand for a host of solution and services like customized application development, system integration and network integration. The domestic spending on outsourced IT services is expected to reach Rs. 23,800 crore by 2009 up from Rs.10,300 crore in 2004. Large e-Governance initiatives launched by the Government under the National e-Governance Plan (NeGP) are expected to provide sustained growth in domestic demand for IT services over the next few years. Apart from the government sector, civil aviation, insurance, telecom and banking sectors would drive growth in the domestic services market in the coming years.

Internal Controls

The enterprise has an adequate system of internal controls implemented by the management towards achieving efficiency in operations, optimum utilisation of resources and effective monitoring thereof and compliance with applicable laws. The system is continuously reinforced with analysis of data to strengthen it to meet the changing requirements. The system comprises a well defined organisation structure, pre-identified authority levels and documented policy guidelines and manuals for delegation of authority. A qualified and independent Audit Committee of the Board of Directors reviews the internal audit reports and the adequacy of internal controls.

Human Resources

CMC recognizes human resources as the backbone for its long-term success and has tried continuously to provide a challenging work environment, thereby adding value to their professional growth.

CMC's key focus has been to change the mindset from 'human resource utilization' to 'nurturing and leveraging talent'. Towards this, the enterprise has initiated the C-change initiative. C-change is the new internal change for betterment initiative meant to empower every employee to actively participate in the making of a better enterprise.

In support of its business objectives, the enterprise has added significantly to its talent pool in high technology and niche areas like embedded systems, real time systems etc, thereby building capacity to deliver solutions/services in the medium and longterm. The compensation structure has also been further modified to include premium for niche technical skills and domain expertise so as to attract and retain the required talent.

The total manpower strength has increased to 3509 as on 31st March 2007 compared to 3431 at the beginning of the year. The manpower cost as a percentage of operating revenue has declined from 19.2% to 17.7%. Other operating expenses increased by 32.3% mainly on account of increased outsourced services from Rs. 61.60 crores to Rs. 77.53 crores (an increase of 25.9%) due to increased business, Rs. 23.47 crores provisioning on account of possible losses that may arise from a contract under dispute.

Corporate Social Responsibility

CMC is committed to improve the quality of life of the underprivileged community. As a part of fulfilling its social obligations, the enterprise generates active participation among the staff members so that emphasis shifts from donation to volunteering on the part of its staff members. As part of this, staff members keenly participate in different ways such as blood donation, educating the underprivileged children, conducting Quiz programmes on Science in schools, imparting skills in tailoring, stitching, etc. to the underprivileged women, arranging exhibition-cum-sale stall for selling products manufactured by the National Blind Association, etc.

CMC staff members made generous financial contributions to the Tata Relief Fund to help the victims of the recent national tragedy resulting from the Tsunami. CMC volunteers also visited the Tsunami affected areas and rendered physical help, distributed materials like clothes etc.

Financial Performance

Sales and Services

The income from Sales and Services stood at Rs. 988.91 crore registered a growth of 19% compared with Rs. 828.79 crores earned in the last year, mainly on account of 126% growth in ITES, 28% growth in SI, 11% growth in E&T and 10% growth in CS business.

Capital Employed

The total capital employed by the enterprise in the year 2006-07 is Rs.5,585,611 crore against Rs.5,597,835 crore during the year 2005-06.

Dividend

The enterprise paid a dividend at 80% of paid-up equity share capital for the year ended March 31, 2007.

Reserves and Surplus

Reserves and surplus aggregated Rs. 2,322,359 crore during the year 2006-07. The reserves and surplus during the year 2005-06 stood at Rs. 2,107,167 crore.

To analyse the performance of selected companies certain key ratios are taken into account. In the case of CMC there is a significant change in the financial performance in the post-privatisation period when compared to pre-privatisation period. PBDIT/Sales changed from 47.89 to 10.12 in the post-privatisation period. PAT/Sales moved from 16.35 to 5.31, PBDIT/Assets increased from 12.02 to 14.09, PAT/Assets moved from 3.59 to 7.42, PBDIT/Equity moved from 39.03 to 441.40, PAT/Equity also moved from 9.59 to 230.76, Sales/Total Equity moved from 30.42 to 138.28, Total Debt/Total Assets from 2.86 to 10.65 and Current Ratio from 105.45 to 126.71. The ratios explained that after privatization there is a significant improvement in the profitability. Except return on sales the other two viz., Return on Assets and Return on Equity showed a positive sign of improvement after privatization. This means that in the post privatization period the returns to equity shareholders has increased. On the whole based on the ratios it can be stated that the financial performance of CMC has

Table 2 A
Financial Ratio Analysis

	Pre-Privatisation				
	1997	1998	1999	2000	2001
PBDIT/Sales	80.05	63.82	53.74	35.09	6.77
PAT/Sales	27.55	27.70	22.37	12.05	-7.90
PBDIT/Assets	16.53	15.17	13.74	11.29	3.38
PAT/Assets	5.69	6.58	5.72	3.88	-3.94
PBDIT/Equity	36.72	37.63	37.50	66.58	16.71
PAT/Equity	12.64	16.33	15.61	22.86	-19.51
Sales/ Assets	20.65	23.77	25.56	32.19	49.92
Debt/ Assets	3.44	2.99	2.19	2.50	3.17
CA/CL	103.60	107.98	102.58	105.09	108.03
No.of emp	2564	2645	2763	2847	2852

Source: Compiled from table given in appendix 1A.

Graph 1

Pre and Post Privatisation Performance of CMC

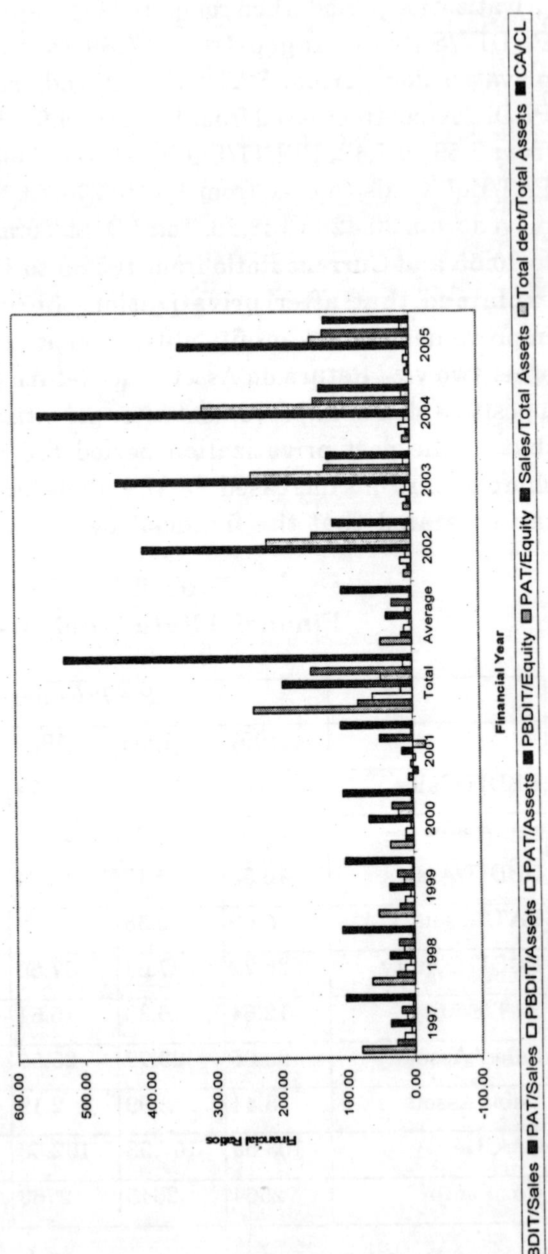

improved considerably in the post-privatisation period. This was further proved by calculating the t-value for each profitable ratio. Except for PBDIT/Assets, for all the other ratios the null-hypothesis was rejected at 90% confidence level and proved that profitability has increased in the post-privatisation period. The organization's financial performance is certainly better in the post-privatisation period.

Table 2 B
Financial Ratio Analysis

	Post-Privatisation			
	2002	*2003*	*2004*	*2005*
PBDIT/Sales	11.17	11.09	11.38	6.84
PAT/Sales	5.98	5.99	6.36	2.92
PBDIT/Assets	16.63	14.31	16.51	8.90
PAT/Assets	8.91	7.73	9.23	3.80
PBDIT/Equity	407.06	445.87	562.24	350.43
PAT/Equity	218.15	240.79	314.26	149.83
Sales/ Assets	148.93	129.04	145.05	130.10
Debt/ Assets	6.03	10.44	12.43	13.70
CA/CL	117.13	125.23	136.15	128.32
No.of emp	3121	3368	2985	3162

Source: Compiled from table given in appendix 1B.

An attempt is being made to test the performance of CMC in pre and post privatisation periods using paired sample t-test with reference to Return on Sales, Return on Equity and Return on Assets and Current Assets/Current Liabilities. The performance in case of each ratio is explained separately.

Return on Sales (ROS) Ratio

This ratio is widely used to evaluate an enterprise's operational efficiency. ROS is also known as a firm's "operating profit margin". It is calculated using this formula Profit Before Depreciation Interest and Taxes/Sales. This measure is helpful to management, providing insight into how much profit is being produced per rupee of sales. As with many ratios, it is best to compare an enterprise's ROS over time to look for trends, and compare it to other companies in the industry. An increasing ROS indicates that the enterprise is growing more efficient, while a decreasing ROS could signal looming financial troubles.

Table 3 shows paired samples t-test for PBDIT/Sales and PAT/Sales in the pre-privatisation period and the post-privatisation period From the table it is observed that for pair 1&2 (Return on Sales (ROS)) the mean difference is 48.05 and 17.10 and standard deviation is 17.12 and 5.94. Standard error is 8.56 and 2.97 and t-values are 5.6 and 5.7 respectively and the corresponding significance values are .011 and 0.010 which is less than 0.05 per cent significance level. This signifies that there is significant difference in Return on Sales (PBDIT/Sales and PAT/Sales) in the pre-privatisation period and in the post-privatisation period. Hence the null hypothesis (Return on Sales

Table 3

Paired Samples T-Test

		Mean Difference	*Std. Deviation*	*Std.Error Mean*	*t*	*df*	*Sig (2-tailed)*
Pair 1	PBDIT/Sales pre PBDIT/Sales post	48.05	17.12	8.56	5.61	3	.011
Pair 2	PAT/Sales Pre PAT/Sales Post	17.10	5.94	2.97	5.75	3	.010

Table 3
Paired Samples T-Test

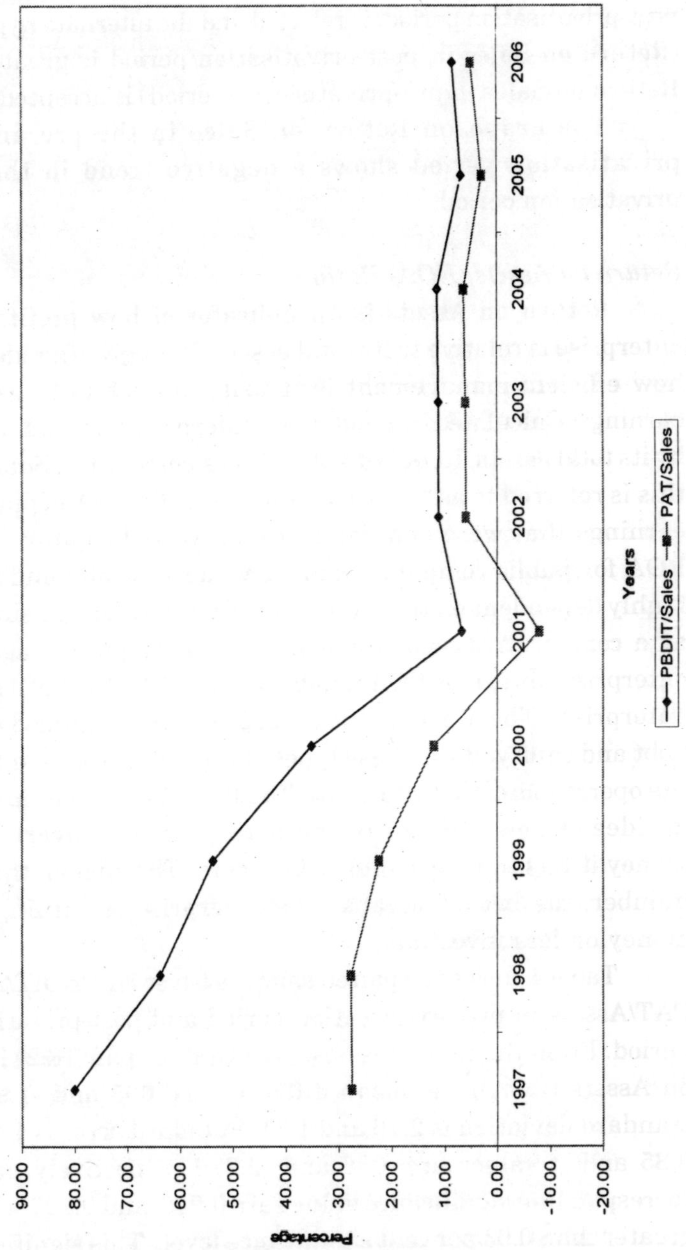

in per-privatisation period is equal to Return on Sales in the post-privatisation period) is rejected and the alternate hypothesis (Return on Sales in post-privatisation period is greater than Return on Sales in pre-privatisation period) is accepted.

The graph on Return on Sales in the pre and post privatisation period shows a negative trend in the post-privatisation period.

Return on Assets (ROA) Ratio

Return on Assets is an indicator of how profitable an enterprise is relative to its total assets. ROA gives an idea as to how efficient management is at using its assets to generate earnings. Calculated by dividing an enterprise's annual earnings by its total assets, ROA is displayed as a percentage. Sometimes this is referred to as "return on investment". ROA explains the earnings that were generated from invested capital (assets). ROA for public companies can vary substantially and will be highly dependent on the industry. This is why when using ROA as a comparative measure, it is best to compare it against a enterprise's previous ROA numbers or with the ROA of a similar enterprise. The assets of the enterprise are comprised of both debt and equity. Both these types of financing are used to fund the operations of the enterprise. The ROA figure gives investors an idea of how effectively the enterprise is converting the money it has to invest into net income. The higher the ROA number, the better, because the enterprise is earning more money on less investment.

Table 4 shows the paired samples t-test for PBDIT/Assets, PAT/Assets in pre-privatisation period and post-privatisation period. From the table it is observed that for pair 1&2 (Return on Assets (ROA)) the mean difference is .095 and -1.95 and standard deviation is 2.16 and 1.71. Standard error is 1.08 and 0.85 and t-values are .088 and -2.276 respectively and the corresponding significance values are 0.936 and 0.107 which is greater than 0.05 per cent significance level. This signifies that

Graph 3

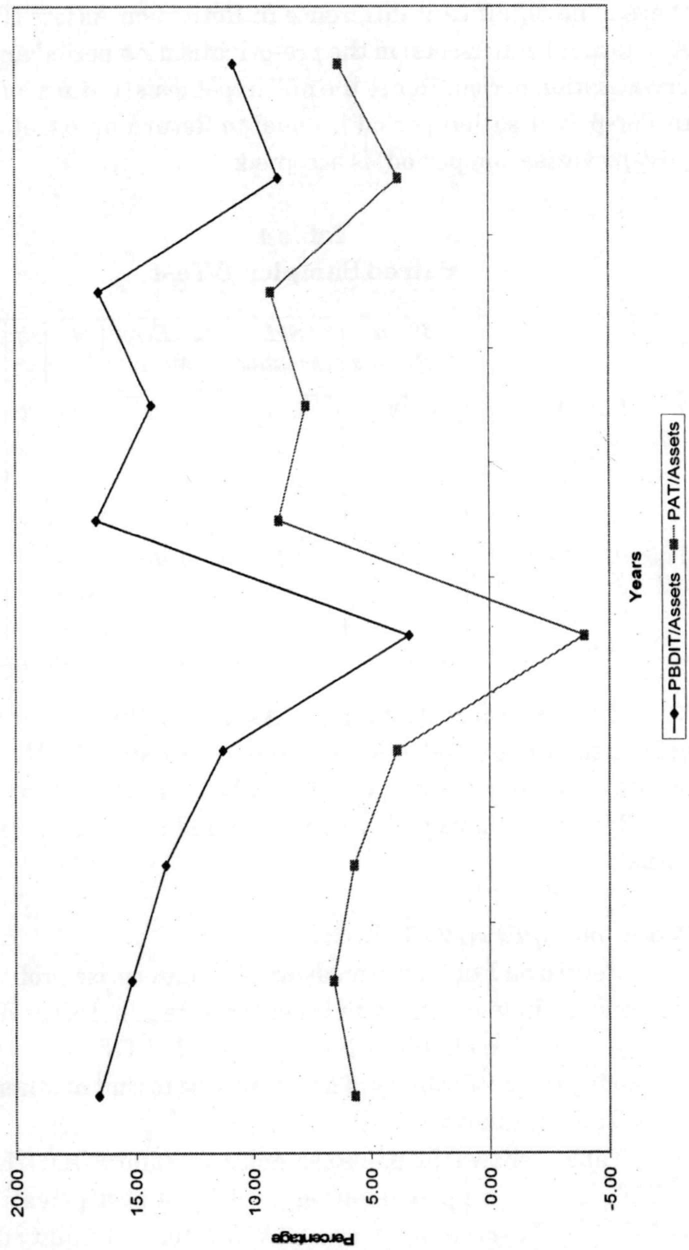
20.00
15.00
10.00
5.00
0.00
-5.00
Percentage
Years
PBDIT/Assets
PAT/Assets

there is no significant difference in Return on Assets (PBDIT/ Assets and PAT/Assets) in the pre-privatisation period and post-privatisation period. Hence the null hypothesis (Return on Assets in Per-privatisation period is equal to Return on Assets in the post-privatisation period) is accepted.

Table 4
Paired Samples T-Test

		Mean Difference	*Std. Deviation*	*Std.Error Mean*	*t*	*df*	*Sig (2-tailed)*
Pair 1	PBDIT/Assets pre PBDIT/Assets post	.095	2.16	1.08	.088	3	.936
Pair 2	PAT/Assets Pre PAT/Assets Post	-1.95	1.71	0.856	- 2.27	3	.107

The graph on Return on Assets in the pre and post privatisation period shows a positive trend in the post-privatisation period. There is certainly an improvement in this period but not significant when compared to pre-privatisation period.

Return on Equity (ROE) Ratio

Return on Equity is a measure of an enterprise profitability that reveals how much profit an enterprise generates with the money that shareholders have invested. ROE is useful for comparing the profitability of an enterprise to that of other firms in the same industry.

Table 5 shows the paired samples t-test for PBDIT/Equity, PAT/Equity in pre-privatisation period the post-privatisation period. It is observed that for pair 1&2 (Return on Equity (ROE)) the mean difference is -396.79 and -213.89 and standard deviation

Graph 4
Return on Equity

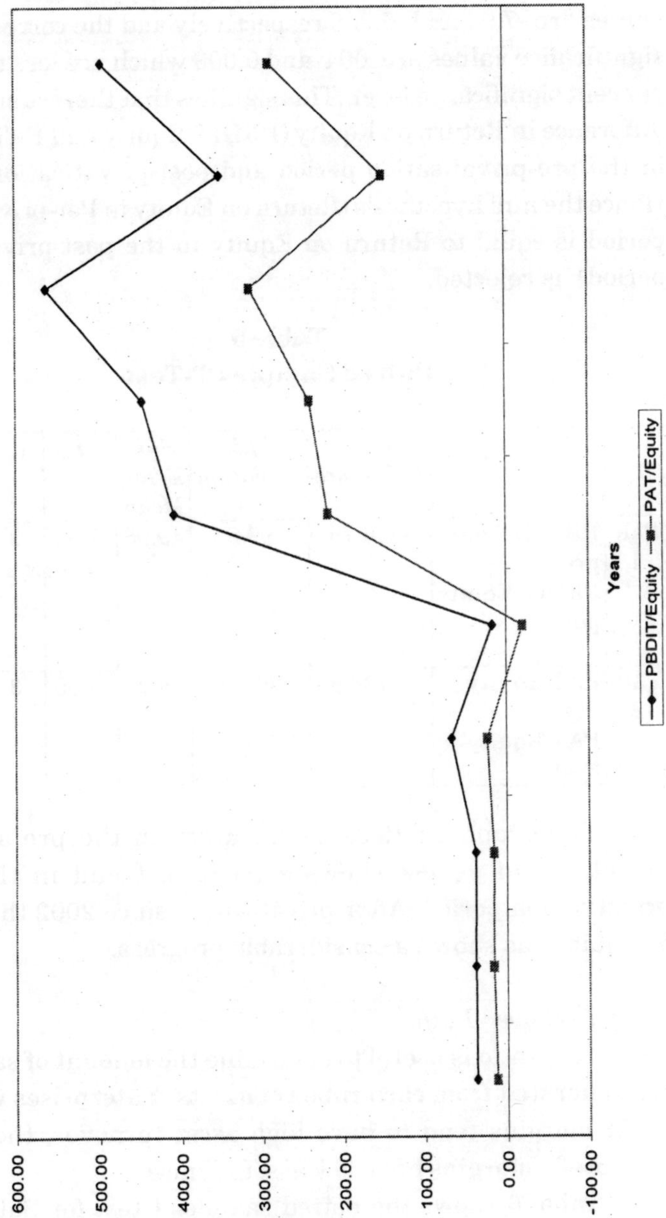

is 99.92 and 70.52 and standard error is 49.96 and 35.26 and t-values are -7.94 and -6.066 respectively and the corresponding significance values are .004 and 0.009 which are less than 0.05 per cent significance level. This signifies that there is significant difference in Return on Equity (PBDIT/Equity and PAT/Equity) in the pre-privatisation period and post-privatisation period. Hence the null hypothesis (Return on Equity in Per-privatisation period is equal to Return on Equity in the post-privatisation period) is rejected.

Table 5
Paired Samples T-Test

		Mean Difference	*Std. Deviation*	*Std. Error Mean*	*t*	*df*	*Sig (2-tailed)*
Pair 1	PBDIT/Equity pre PBDIT/Equity post	-396.79	99.9	49.96	-7.94	3	.004
Pair 2	PAT/Equity Pre PAT/Equity Post	-213.89	70.52	35.26	-6.06	3	.009

The graph on Return on Equity in the pre and post privatisation period shows a positive trend in the post-privatisation period. After privatisation since 2002 the return on equity has shown a considerable progress.

Asset Turnover Ratio

This ratio is useful to determine the amount of sales that are generated from each rupee of assets. Enterprises with low profit margins tend to have high asset turnover, those with high profit margins have low asset turnover.

Table 6 shows the paired samples t-test for Sales/Total Assets in pre-privatisation period and in the post-privatisation

Graph 5
Asset Turnover

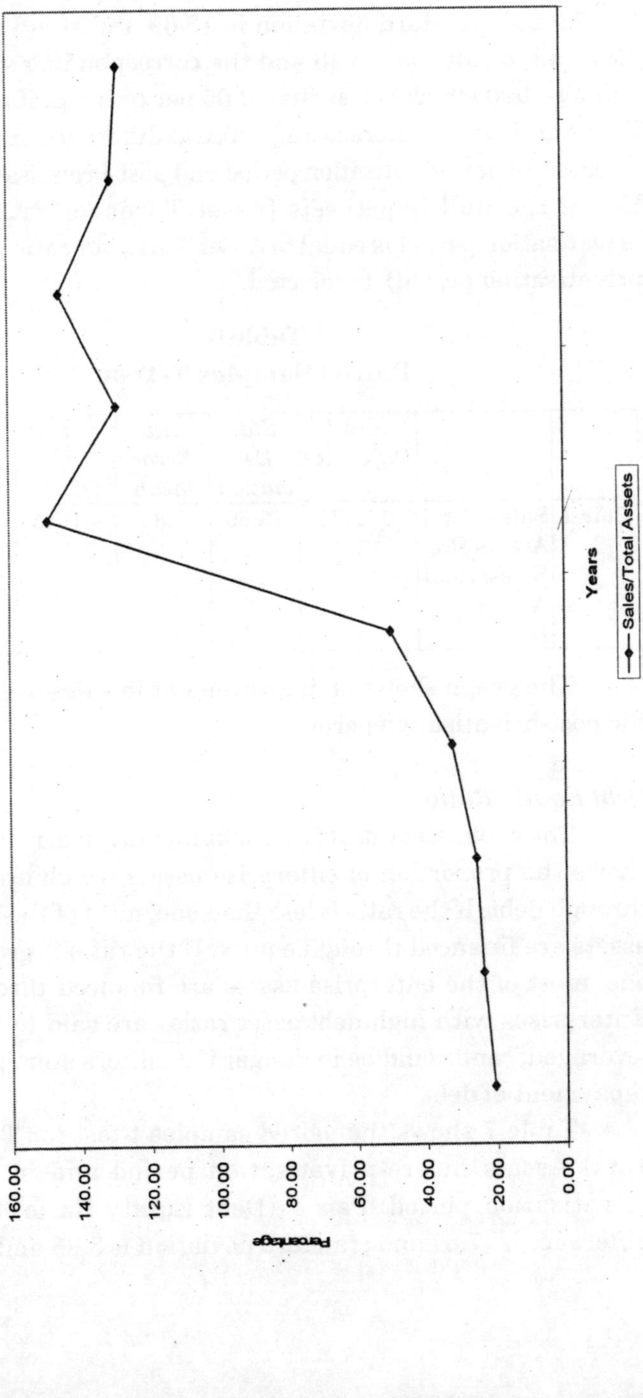

period. For pair 1 (Asset Turn Over) the mean difference is -112.73 and standard deviation is 13.69 and standard error is 6.84 and t-value is -16.46 and the corresponding significance value is .000 which is less than 0.05 per cent significance level. This signifies that there is a significant difference in Asset Turn Over in the pre-privatisation period and post-privatisation period. Hence the null hypothesis (Asset Turnover ratio in Per-privatisation period is equal to Asset Turnover ratio in the post-privatisation period) is rejected.

Table 6
Paired Samples T-Test

		Mean Difference	*Std. De-viation*	*Std. Error mean*	*t*	*df*	*Sig (2-tailed)*
Pair 1	Sales/Total Assets Pre Sales/Total Assets Post	-112.73	13.69	6.84	-16.46	3	.000

The graph shows an improvement in sales over assets in the post-privatisation period.

Debt Equity Ratio

The debt/asset ratio (Total liabilities divided by total assets) shows the proportion of enterprise assets which are financed through debt. If the ratio is less than one, most of the enterprise assets are financed through equity. If the ratio is greater than one, most of the enterprise assets are financed through debt. Enterprises with high debt/asset ratios are said to be "highly leveraged," and could be in danger if creditors start to demand repayment of debt.

Table 7 shows the paired samples t-test for Total Debt/ Total Assets in pre-privatisation period and in the post-privatisation period. Pair 1 (Debt Equity Ratio) the mean difference is -7.87 and standard deviation is 3.86 and standard

Graph 6
Debt Equity Ratio

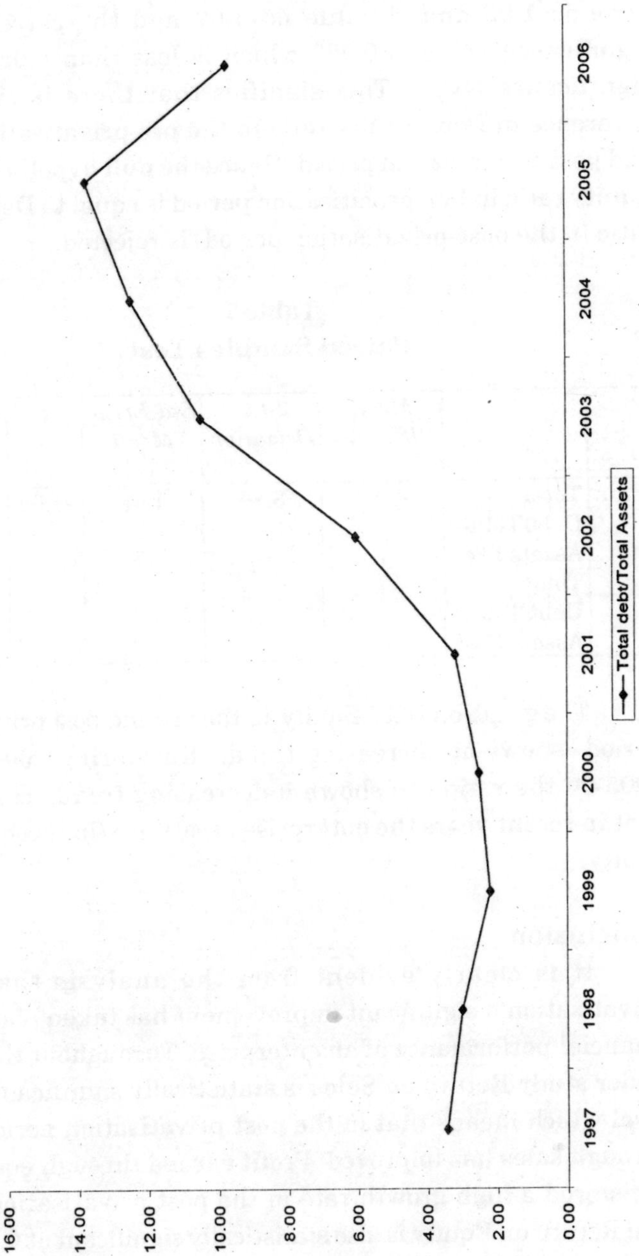

error is 1.93 and t-value is -4.07 and the corresponding significance value is 0.027 which is less than 0.05 per cent significance level. This signifies that there is significant difference in Debt-Equity ratio in the pre-privatisation period and post-privatisation period. Hence the null hypothesis (Debt-Equity ratio in Per-privatisation period is equal to Debt-Equity ratio in the post-privatisation period) is rejected.

Table 7

Paired Samples Test

		Mean Difference	*Std. Deviation*	*Std.Error Mean*	*t*	*df*	*Sig (2-tailed)*
Pair 1	Total Debt/Total Assets Pre Total Debt/Total Assets Post	-7.87	3.86	1.93	-4.07	3	.027

The graph on Debt-Equity in the pre and post privatisation period shows an increasing trend. But during 2004-05 and 2005-06 the ratio has shown a decreasing trend. This means that in recent years the enterprise assets are financed through equity.

Conclusion

It is clearly evident from the analysis that, after privatisation a significant improvement has taken place in the financial performance of an enterprise. Throughout the period under study Return on Sales is statistically significant at 0.05 level which means that in the post privatisation period profit through sales has improved. Profit earned through equity also registered a high growth rate in the post privatisation period and Return on Equity is also statistically significant at 0.05 level. In the post privatisation period sales also showed a significant improvement, Asset Turnover ratio and debt-equity ratio are statistically significant at 0.05 level. Finally, it can be concluded that the enterprise financial performance has improved in the post privatisation period. Hence, null hypothesis is rejected.

Appendix-1 A
Financial Performance of CMC during the Pre-Privatisation Period

	1997	*1998*	*1999*	*2000*	*2001*
PBDIT	179.52	183.96	183.34	162.73	36.87
Sales	224.27	288.26	341.13	463.72	544.77
PAT	61.79	79.84	76.32	55.87	-43.04
Assets	1085.83	1212.72	1334.68	1440.78	1091.21
Equity	488.85	488.85	488.85	244.42	220.62
No.of Employees	7454	7317	7294	7294	7294
Total Debt	37.3	36.26	29.21	36.06	34.63
Dividend	1.21	1.67	1.67	3.7	5.84
Current Assets	127.82	149.44	170.06	239.47	286.29
Current Liabilities	123.38	138.4	165.78	227.88	265.01
Debt-Equity Ratio	0.06	0.05	0.04	0.38	0.14

(Source: Annual Report of CMCs, CMIE Prowess Data Base)

Appendix-1 B

Financial Performance of CMC during the Post-

	2002	*2003*	*2004*	*2005*
PBDIT	61.67	67.55	85.18	53.09
Sales	552.35	609.29	748.46	776.24
PAT	33.05	36.48	47.61	22.7
Assets	370.88	472.16	515.99	596.65
Equity	15.15	15.15	15.15	15.15
No.of Employees	3121	3368	2985	3162
Total Debt	22.36	49.31	64.16	81.72
Dividend	6.06	6.84	9.4	7.78
Current Assets	298.42	402.78	446.68	527.73
Current Liabilities	254.78	321.64	328.09	411.26
Debt-Equity Ratio	0.24	0.4	0.4	0.47

Source: Annual Report of CMCs, CMIE Prowess Data Base.

Case 3
Hindustan Teleprinters Limited (HTL)

Background

Hindustan Teleprinters Limited (HTL) was wholly owned by the Government of India, and was incorporated in 1960 primarily for manufacture of electromechanical teleprinters, to cater to the needs of the erstwhile Post and Telegraph Department. Since the early 1990s HTL diversified its product portfolio from manufacture of electromechanical teleprinters to digital telephone exchange products, transmission products, access products and data and terminal products. Main manufacturing facility at Guindy Industrial Estate in Chennai and there is a supplementary facility at the Hosur Industrial Estate near Bangalore city on Tamil Nadu- Karnataka border.

It operates through a sales and distribution network of six regional offices and sub-offices. HTL employs approximately 1100 people.

Disinvestment

The Disinvestment Commission in its 2nd report of April 1997 had classified HTL in the non-core category and inter alia recommended for strategic sale of either 100% or 50% of the shares of HTL through competitive bidding. The Cabinet on 16.12.1998 decided to disinvest 50% of the equity in HTL to a strategic partner. Subsequently, on 26.5.2000 Government decided to disinvest 74% of the equity in HTL as there was lukewarm response from the bidders for the earlier proposal of 50% disinvestment. The Global Advisor is KPMG India Private Limited. The Legal Advisors and Asset Valuers are Amarchand & Mangaldas & Suresh A Shroff & Co and M/s P.T. Shanamugam

The GoI selected the Global Advisor for the disinvestment process on 13 September 1999. An Inter Ministerial Group ("IMG") meeting was constituted. GoI initially planned to divest 51% of its share holding to a long-term strategic investor. However, this mandate was then changed to a sale of 74% disinvestment of as the GoI found it to be more investor friendly.

The Global Advisor received the Expressions of Interest (EoIs) from the interested parties, which included Motorola India Limited, Wipro Peripherals Limited along with Huawei Technologies of China, Tamil Nadu News Prints and Papers Limited (TNPL), Alcatel Trade International AG, Himachal Futuristic Communications Limited (HFCL) and Gokina Infotech (Pvt) Limited. TNPL later tied up with United Telecom. Of the above, Motorola and Alcatel dropped out due to their perception of the telecom equipment market. Wipro, HFCL and TNPL and United Telecom consortium were invited to visit the data room in Chennai. Wipro dropped out after the data room citing lack of R&D facilities in HTL. Draft shareholders agreement and share purchase agreements were issued to TNPL & UTL and

HFCL, and binding bids were invited. The GoI received bids from these prospective candidates on September 27, 2001.

Valuation

KPMG presented the valuation report to GoI on September 27, 2001. Based on the various pricing methodologies, the indicative pricing range for 100% equity stake in HTL is summarised in Table 1.

Table 1
Valuation under Different Methods

(Rs. Million)

Pricing methodology	*Basis*	*Value*
Discounted cash flow	Going concern pricing as on 31 March 2001 based on the management's Strategic Business Plan and value of surplus assets as assigned by the Government approved valuer	524.36
Asset valuation	Liquidation as on 31 March 2001	527.92
Balance sheet	Net worth as on 31 March 2001	574.73
Comparable companies	Market comparable stock of telecom equipment companies in India	403.17

It was considered that the value as per the DCF Methodology would be the most appropriate indicator of the value that a potential strategic acquirer may be willing to pay, given that the transaction is being pursued as a strategic sale. The Evaluation Committee therefore recommended that the reserve price should be Rs. 388.02 million for 74% equity value of HTL.

Himachal Futuristic Communications Limited, a leading Indian telecom equipment manufacturer won the transaction at Rs 550 million for 74% of the equity. This corresponds to Rs. 743 million for 100% of the equity.

Industry Overview

In the era of liberalization and globalization marked by intense competition and changing customer preferences, HTL has surmounted enormous challenges in terms of broadbasing its product profile and enhancing the skills of its manpower. With the electro-mechanical technology becoming obsolete and Teleprinters (both Mechanical and Electronics) branded as vintage products of 1980s, the Company embarked on a diversification plan and entered into fields forming the telecom spectrum.

With changes in technology, sea change in market and customer preferences, the company embarked on an aggressive diversification plan to become a multi-product company. Through a saga of perseverance and persuasion, diligence and dedication to survive, it has become a leader in the field of telecom equipments.

The Company has very old outstanding dues both from BSNL/MTNL which have not been settled inspite of vigorous follow up and taking up the matter with their senior authorities as well with DoT. If these issues are resolved, the Company will have a substantial inflow of funds which can take care of immediate need of working capital requirement for execution of the orders. In addition, BSNL has also not resolved the issue of differential sales-tax payment to the Company which it has committed on its formation from DTS. The amount of differential sales-tax is very high and if not paid immediately, may create a lot of problems from the Sales-tax department. The Company's application to BIFR, although registered, has not progressed further and hence a scheme for revival through BIFR process could not be made so far.

Human Resources

Regarding employee protection adequate provisions have been made in the Shareholders agreement that both parties envision that all employees of the enterprise will continue in the employment of the enterprise and recognises principles for the benefit of the members of the Scheduled Caste/Scheduled Tribes, physically handicapped persons and other socially disadvantaged categories of the society. The shareholders agreement provides that the strategic partner shall not retrench any employees of the enterprise for a period of one year other than any dismissal or termination of employees of the enterprise from their employment in accordance with the applicable staff regulations and standing orders of the enterprise or applicable laws. Any restructuring of the labor force of the enterprise shall be implemented in the manner recommended by the Board and in accordance with all applicable laws; and in the event of any reduction in the strength of the enterprise's employees the SP shall ensure that the enterprise offers its employees, an option to voluntarily retire on terms that are not, in any manner, less favorable than the voluntary retirement scheme applicable to the enterprise at the time of closing. In the handing over ceremony held at Sanchar Bhawan, New Delhi on 16 October 2001, the new management of HTL announced that there were no plans to retrench the workforce. In fact, the new management took this opportunity to announce the grant of two increments that were earlier assured prior to disinvestment to all employees of HTL, but had not yet been implemented

Financial Performance

Table 2 explains about the financial performance in the pre and post privatization period of Hindustan Tele Printers Limited. PBDIT/Sales changed from 6.34 to -14.23 in the post-privatisation period. PAT/Sales moved from -0.03 to -28.29, PBDIT/Assets changed from 8.06 to -12.03, PAT/Assets moved from 0.88 to -25.64, PBDIT/Equity moved from 160.68 to -197.51,

PAT/Equity also moved from 25.11 to -393.89, Sales/Total Equity moved from 117.88 to 101.38, Total Debt/Total Assets from 13.41 to 38.68 and Current Ratio from 118.01 to 69.41. The profitability ratios shows a negative performance after privatization except debt equity ratio and current ratio. This is because of the fact that in the year 2001 the last year before privatization the Profit after tax to sales and profit after tax to assets is nearing to zero. Therefore after privatization it takes long time for the organization to improve its performance. This can be stated from the fact that the t-value rejected the null-hypothesis and accepted the alternate hypotheses. This shows that after privatisation the organization will perform well in the long run. Moreover, a decrease in the current ratio after privatization is a good sign. It indicates more liquidation which in turn increases the working capital of an organization. On the whole based on the ratios it can be stated that the financial performance of HTL will takes long time to improve its efficiency.

Table 2 A

Financial Performance of HTL

	Pre-Privatisation				
	1997	*1998*	*1999*	*2000*	*2001*
PBDIT/Sales	1.89	5.51	4.87	10.59	8.84
PAT/Sales	-7.34	2.06	1.89	2.76	0.47
PBDIT/Assets	1.29	6.36	6.85	14.50	11.32
PAT/Assets	-5.01	2.38	2.66	3.77	0.60
PBDIT/Equity	13.93	100.93	117.67	318.80	252.07
PAT/Equity	-54.20	37.73	45.60	83.00	13.40
Sales/Total Assets	68.20	115.40	140.85	136.85	128.09
Total debt/Total Assets	20.71	9.91	9.17	10.00	17.24
CA/CL	129.95	113.98	114.79	115.13	116.22
No.of Emp	1487	1314	1123	1057	0

Source: Compiled from table given in Appendix 1A.

Graph 1
Pre and Post Privatisation Performance

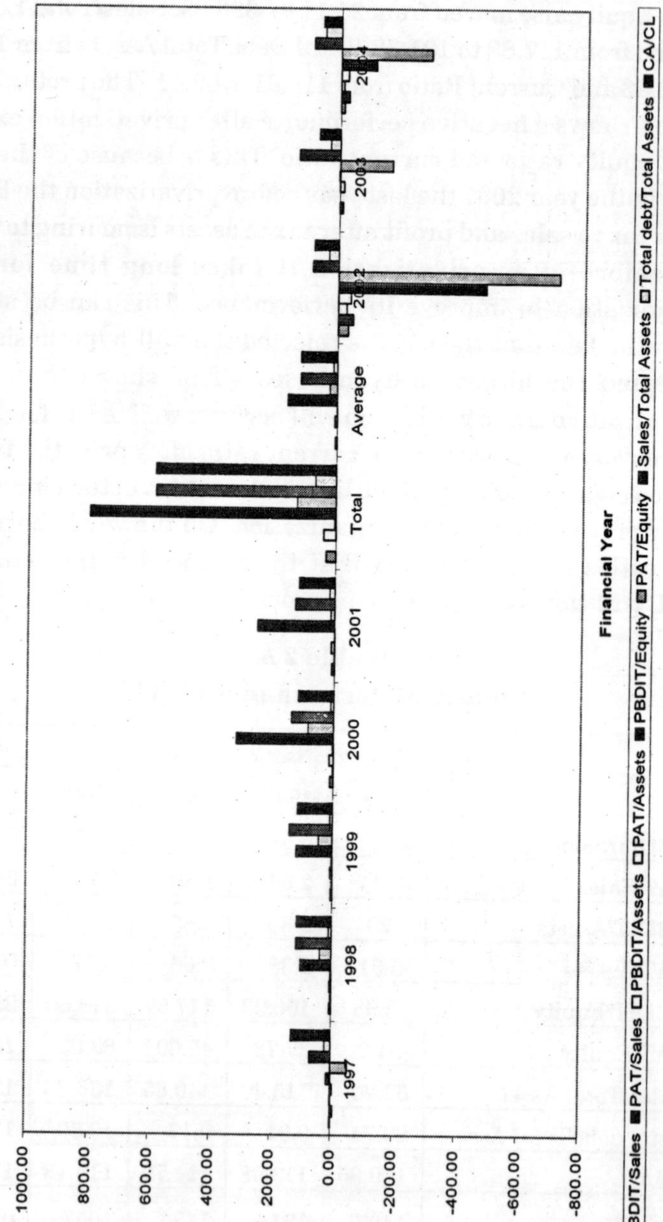

Table 2 B
Financial Performance of HTL

	Post-Privatisation		
	2002	*2003*	*2004*
PBDIT/Sales	-32.25	0.12	-10.55
PAT/Sales	-48.21	-9.69	-26.96
PBDIT/Assets	-26.92	0.15	-9.34
PAT/Assets	-40.24	-12.80	-23.87
PBDIT/Equity	-479.93	2.07	-114.67
PAT/Equity	-717.40	-171.13	-293.13
Sales/Total Assets	83.46	132.10	88.56
Total debt/Total Assets	32.06	31.74	52.25
CA/CL	80.24	68.91	59.09

Source: Compiled from table given in Appendix 1B.

An attempt is being made to test the performance of HTL in pre and post privatisation periods using paired samples t-test with reference to Return on Sales, Return on Equity and Return on Assets an Current Assets/Current Liabilities. The performance in case of each ratio is explained separately.

Return on Sales (ROS) Ratio

This ratio is widely used to evaluate an enterprise's operational efficiency. ROS is also known as a firm's "operating profit margin". It is calculated using the formula Profit Before Depreciation Interest and Taxes/Sales. This measure is helpful to management, as it provides insight into how much profit is being produced per rupee of sales. As with many ratios, it is best to compare a Enterprise's ROS over time to look for trends, and compare it to other companies in the industry. An increasing ROS indicates the Enterprise is growing more efficient, while a decreasing ROS could signal looming financial troubles.

Table 3 shows the paired samples t-test for PBDIT/Sales, Pat/Sales in pre-privatisation period and post-privatisation

Graph 2
Return on Sales

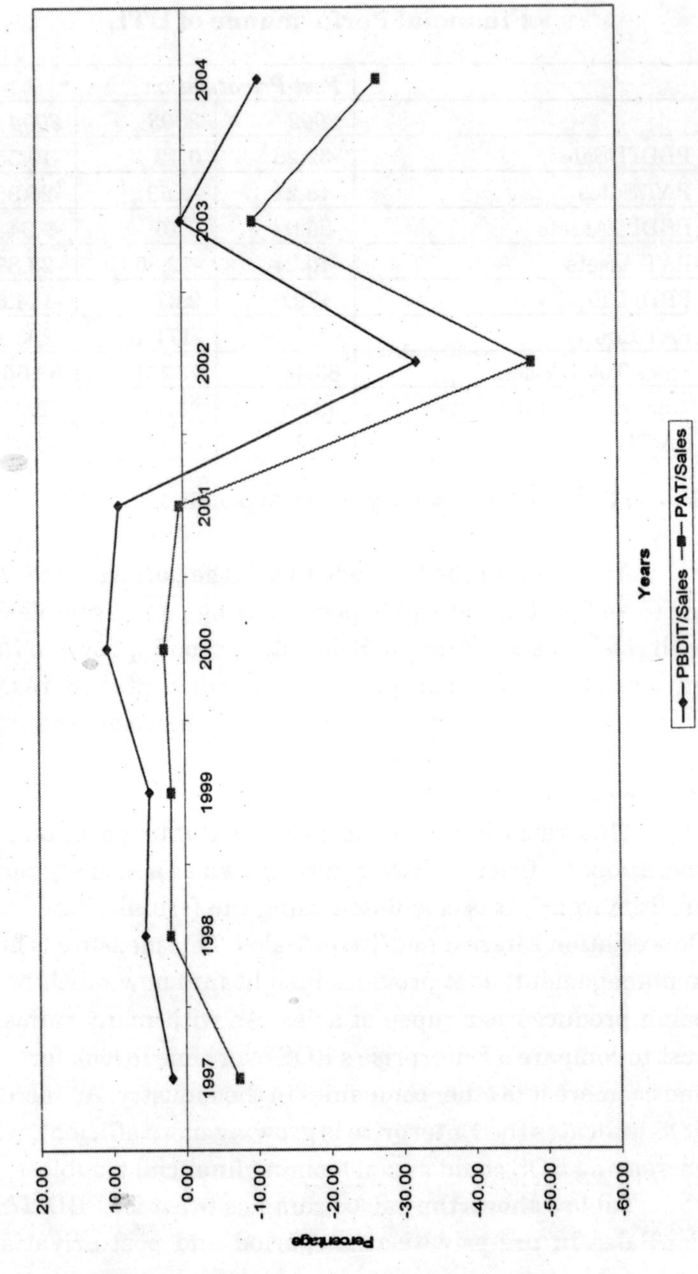

period. It is observed that for pair 1&2 (Return on Sales (ROS)) the mean difference is 22.32 and 29.99 and standard deviation is 13.56 and 18.95 and standard error is 7.83 and 10.94 and t-values are 2.85 and 2.74 respectively and the corresponding significance value is 0.104 and 0.111 which is greater than 0.05 per cent significance level. This signifies that there is no significant difference in Return on Sales (PBDIT/Sales and PAT/Sales) in the post-privatisation period compared to pre-privatisation period. Hence the null hypothesis (Return on Sales in Per-privatisation period is equal to Return on Sales in the post-privatisation period) is accepted.

Table 3
Paired Samples T-Test

		Mean Difference	*Std. Deviation*	*Std. Error Mean*	*t*	*df*	*Sig (2-tailed)*
Pair 1	PBDIT/Sales pre PBDIT/Sales post	22.32	13.56	7.83	2.85	2	.104
Pair 2	PAT/Sales Pre PAT/Sales Post	29.99	18.95	10.94	2.74	2	.111

The graph on Return on Sales in the pre and post privatisation period shows a positive trend. In the post privatisation enterprise sales has come down, because in the years 1999-00 and 2000-01, the sales are very low it is touching x-axis in the year 2000-01. The enterprise sales position will recover after three to four years.

Return on Assets (ROA) Ratio

Return on Assets is an indicator of how profitable an enterprise is relative to its total assets. ROA gives an idea as to how efficient management is at using its assets to generate earnings. Calculated by dividing an enterprise's annual earnings by its total assets, ROA is displayed as a percentage. Sometimes this is referred to as "return on investment". ROA explains the earnings that were generated from invested capital (assets). ROA for public companies can vary substantially and will be highly dependent on the industry. This is why when using ROA as a comparative measure, it is best to compare it against a enterprise's previous ROA numbers or the ROA of a similar enterprise. The assets of the enterprise are comprised of both debt and equity. Both of these types of financing are used to fund the operations of the enterprise. The ROA figure gives investors an idea of how effectively the enterprise is converting the money it has to invest into net income. The higher the ROA number, the better, because the enterprise is earning more money on less investment.

Table 4 shows that paired samples t-test for PBDIT/Assets, PAT/Assets in pre-privatisation period and post-privatisation period. Pair 1&2 (Return on Assets (ROA)) the mean difference is 22.92 and 27.98 and standard deviation is 9.90 and 13.511 and standard error is 5.71 and 7.80 and t-values are 4.00 and 3.58 respectively and the corresponding significance values are .05

Table 4
Paired Samples T-Test

		Mean Difference	*Std. Deviation*	*Std. Error Mean*	*t*	*df*	*Sig (2-tailed)*
Pair 1	PBDIT/Assets pre PBDIT/Assets post	22.92	9.90	5.71	4.00	2	.05
Pair 2	PAT/Assets Pre PAT/Assets Post	27.98	13.511	7.80	3.58	2	.07

Graph 3
Return on Assets Ratio

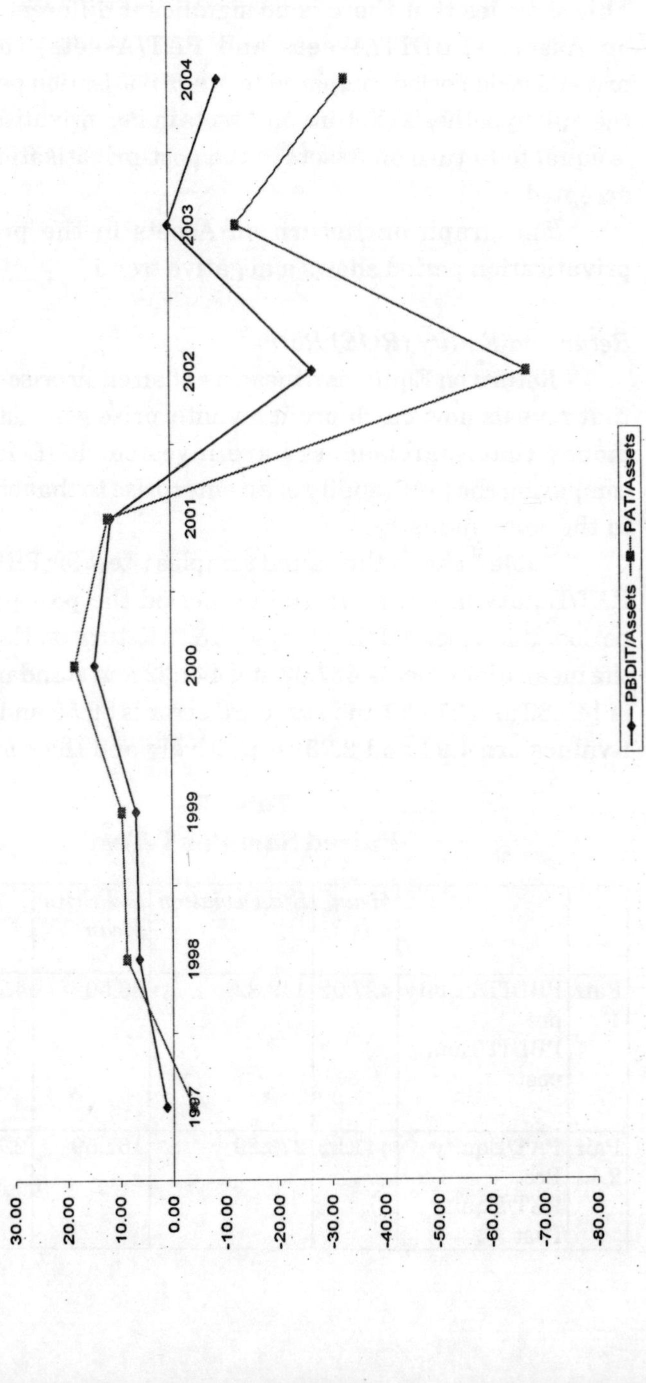

and 0.07 which is greater than 0.05 per cent significance level. This signifies that there is no significant difference in Return on Assets (PBDIT/Assets and PAT/Assets) in the post-privatisation period compared to pre-privatisation period. Hence the null hypothesis (Return on Assets in Per-privatisation period is equal to Return on Assets in the post-privatisation period) is accepted.

The graph on Return on Assets in the pre and post privatisation period shows a negative trend.

Return on Equity (ROE) Ratio

Return on Equity is a measure of an enterprise profitability that reveals how much profit an enterprise generates with the money that shareholders have invested. ROE is useful for comparing the profitability of an enterprise to that of other firms in the same industry.

Table 5 shows the paired samples t-test for PBDIT/Equity, PAT/Equity in pre-privatisation period the post-privatisation period. It is observed that for pair 1&2 (Return on Equity (ROE)) the mean difference is 427.02 and 441.22 and standard deviation is 149.82 and 279.89 and standard error is 86.50 and 161.59 and t-values are 4.93 and 2.73 respectively and the corresponding

Table 5
Paired Samples T-Test

		Mean	*Std.Deviation*	*Std.Error Mean*	*t*	*df*	*Sig (2-tailed)*
Pair 1	PBDIT/Equity pre PBDIT/Equity post	427.02	149.82	86.50	4.93	2	.03
Pair 2	PAT/Equity Pre PAT/Equity Post	441.22	279.89	161.59	2.73	2	.11

Graph 4
Return on Equity Ratio

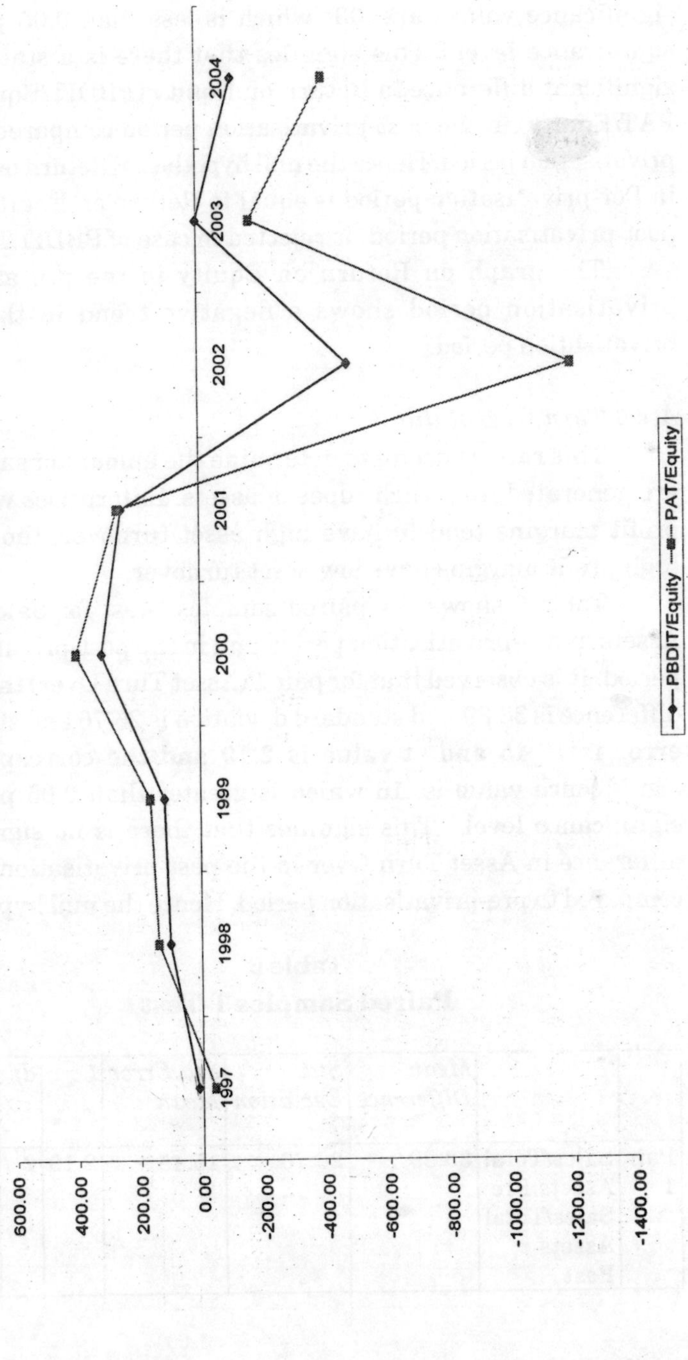

significance values are .03 which is less than 0.05 per cent significance level. This signifies that there is a statistically significant difference in Return on Equity (PBDIT/Equity and PAT/Equity) in the post-privatisation period compared to pre-privatisation period. Hence the null hypothesis (Return on Equity in Per-privatisation period is equal to Return on Equity in the post-privatisation period) is rejected in case of PBDIT/Equity.

The graph on Return on Equity in the pre and post privatisation period shows a negative trend in the post-privatisation period.

Asset Turn Over Ratio

This ratio is useful to determine the amount of sales that are generated from each rupee of assets. Enterprises with low profit margins tend to have high asset turnover, those with high profit margins have low asset turnover.

Table 6 shows the paired samples t-test for Sales/Total Assets in pre-privatisation period and in the post-privatisation period. It is observed that for pair 1 (Asset Turn Over) the mean difference is 33.89 and standard deviation is 26.76 and standard error is 15.45 and t-value is 2.19 and the corresponding significance value is .16 which is greater than 0.05 per cent significance level. This signifies that there is no significant difference in Asset Turn Over in the post-privatisation period compared to pre-privatisation period. Hence the null hypothesis

Table 6
Paired Samples T-Test

		Mean Difference	*Std. Deviation*	*Std.Error Mean*	*t*	*df*	*Sig (2-tailed)*
Pair 1	Sales/Total Assets Pre Sales/Total Assets Post	33.89	26.76	15.45	2.19	2	.16

Graph 5
Asset Turnover Ratio

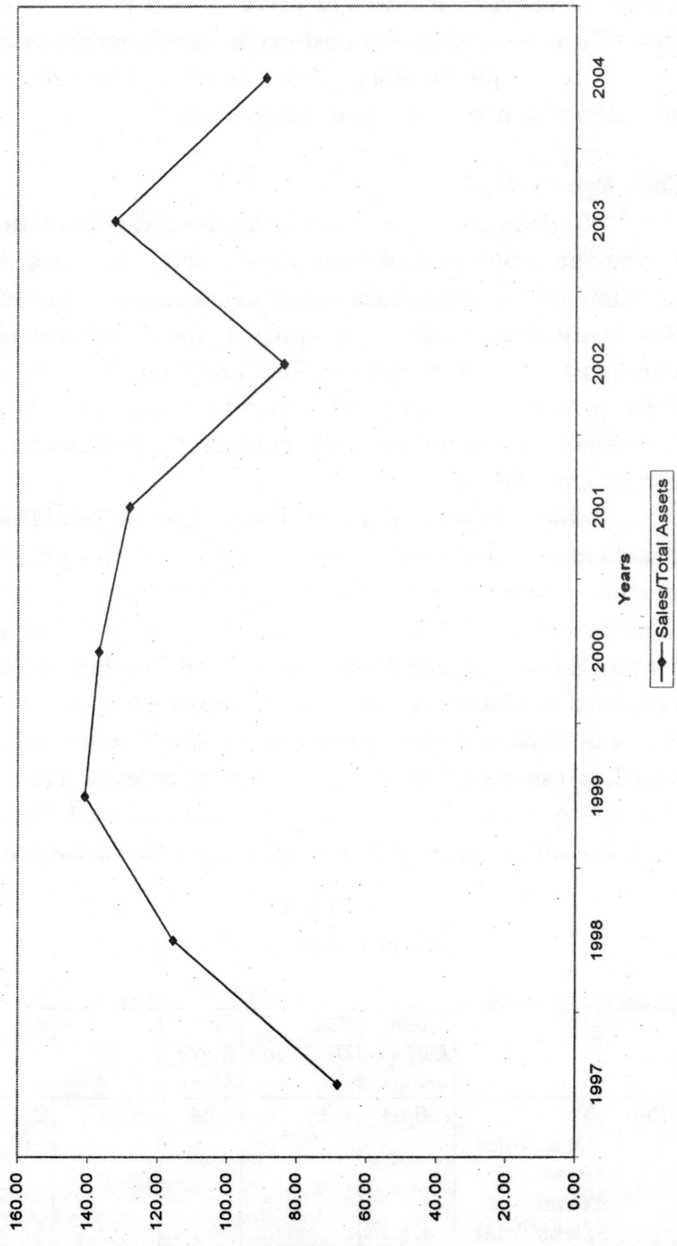

(Asset Turnover ratio in Per-privatisation period is equal to Asset Turnover ratio in the post-privatisation period) is accepted.

The graph on Asset Turn Over in the pre and post privatisation period shows a positive trend

Debt Equity Ratio

The debt/asset ratio (Total liabilities divided by total assets) shows the proportion of enterprise assets which are financed through debt. If the ratio is less than one, most of the enterprise assets are financed through equity. If the ratio is greater than one, most of the enterprise assets are financed through debt. Enterprises with high debt/asset ratios are said to be "highly leveraged," and could be in danger if creditors start to demand repayment of debt.

Table 7 shows that paired sample test for Total Debt/Total Assets in pre-privatisation period and in the post-privatisation period is showed where in paired differences, t-test and significance are represented. From the table it is observed that for pair 1 (Debt Equity Ratio) the mean difference is -26.54 and standard deviation is 7.35 and standard error is 4.24 and t-value is -6.25 and the corresponding significance value is .02 which is less than 0.05 per cent significance level. This signifies that there is a significant difference in Debt-Equity ratio in the post-privatisation period compared to pre-privatisation period.

Table 7
Paired Samples T-Test

		Mean Differe-nce	*Std. Deviation*	*Std. Error Mean*	*t*	*df*	*Sig (2-tailed)*
Pair 1	Total Debt/Total Assets Pre Total Debt/Total Assets Post	-26.54	7.35	4.24	-6.25	2	.02

Graph 6
Debt-Equity Ratio

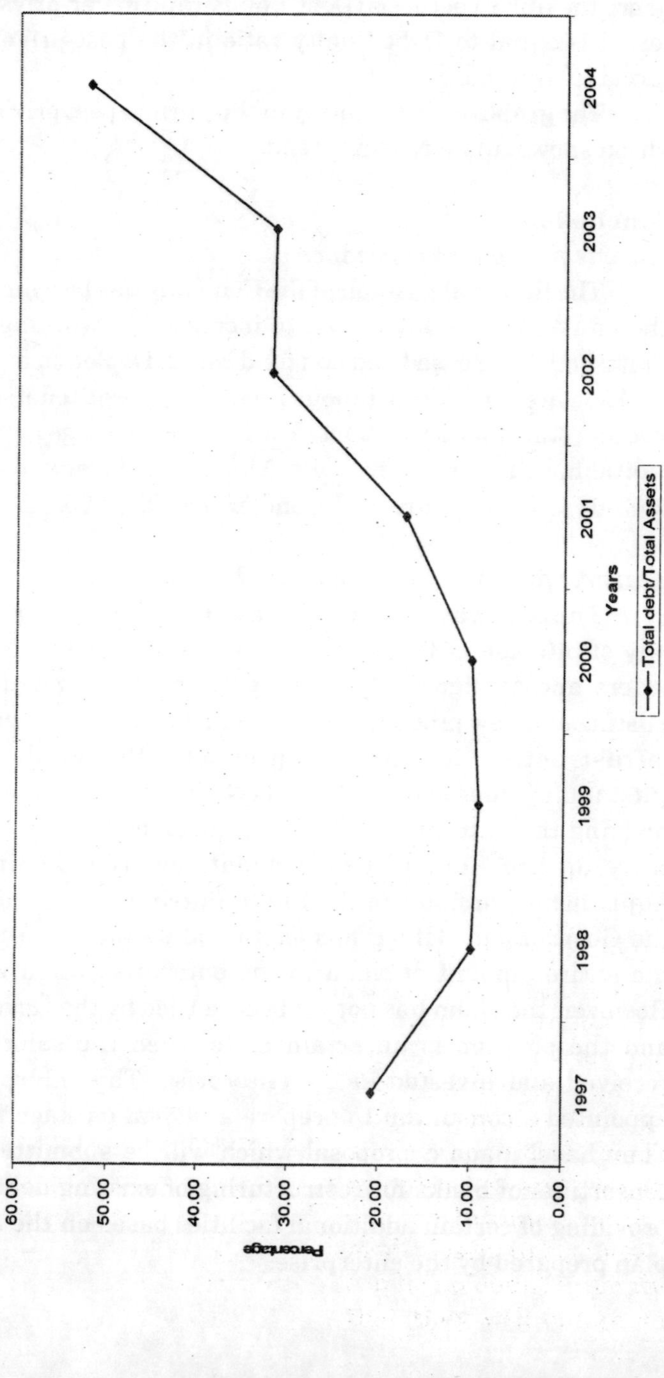

Hence the null hypothesis (Debt-Equity ratio in Per-privatisation period is equal to Debt-Equity ratio in the post-privatisation period) is rejected.

The graph on Debt-Equity in the pre and post privatisation period shows an increasing trend.

Conclusion

Reasons for Poor Performance

The financial position of the Company has become critical. The bankers have not agreed to increase the working capital limits; both fund based and non fund based. Depletion of working funds on account of continuous losses have resulted in delay in meeting statutory obligations, The bank borrowings for working capital have increased from Rs. 57 crore at the end of the year 2003-04 to Rs. 93 crore at the end of year 2004-05.

Measures for Improving Financial Position

The only way by which an enterprise can be revived is by way of infusion of funds to execute the present and expected orders and to vigorously participate in the new tenders for existing and new products. In addition, it has to create necessary infrastructure for the new products. Realisation of old outstanding dues from BSNL / MTNL can also go a long way in reviving the enterprise. HFCL has made a claim of Rs. 56.49 crore on the Central Government towards Closing Date Adjustment pursuant to the Share Purchase Agreement with the Government. HFCL has expressed its intention to invest the entire amount of claim in the enterprise when received. However, the claim has not yet been settled by the Government and the position is uncertain as to when the same will be received and invested in the enterprise. The enterprise has appointed a consultant to prepare a revival package for HTL. They have' made a proposal which will be submitted to the consortium of banks for restructuring of existing debt and for providing of certain additional facilities based on the business plan prepared by the enterprise.

It can be concluded from the study that the financial performance in the post-privatisation period is not showing an significant improvement when compared with pre-privatisation period. all the four ratios i.e., return on sales, return on assets, return on equity, asset turn over, debt-equity ratio showed a negative trend in the post-privatisation period.

Appendix 1 A
Financial Performance of HTL During Pre-Privatisation Period

(Rs. In crore)

	1997	*1998*	*1999*	*2000*	*2001*
PBDIT	2.09	15.14	17.65	47.82	37.81
Sales	110.69	274.58	362.75	451.42	427.78
PAT	-8.13	5.66	6.84	12.45	2.01
Assets	162.31	237.94	257.54	329.87	333.97
Equity	15	15	15	15	15
No.of Employees	1487	1314	0	0	0
Total Debt	33.61	23.59	23.61	33	57.57
Dividend	0	0.17	0.5	1.1	0.99
Current Assets	146.53	220.26	237.82	306.74	313.93
Current Liabilities	112.76	193.24	207.18	266.43	270.11

Source: Annual Report of HTLs, CMIE Prowess Data Base.

Appendix 1 B
Financial Performance of HTL During Post-Privatisation Period

(Rs. In crore)

	2002	*2003*	*2004*
PBDIT	-71.99	0.31	-17.2
Sales	223.21	264.89	163.11
PAT	-107.61	-25.67	-43.97
Assets	267.43	200.52	184.18
Equity	15	15	15
No.of Employees		0	0
Total Debt	85.74	63.64	96.23
Dividend	0	0	0
Current Assets	249.71	185.98	169.23
Current Liabilities	311.19	269.89	286.41

Source: Annual Report of HTLs, CMIE Prowess Data Base.

Case 4
Videsh Sanchar Nigam Limited (VSNL)

Background

Until the mid-1980s, India's telecommunications services segment was a public sector monopoly controlled by the Government of India (GoI) through the Department of Posts and Telegraphs of the Ministry of Communications. In the mid-1980s, the Government of India began reorganising the sector to bring in new technology and stimulate growth. Accordingly, the Department of Posts and Telegraphs was divided into the Department of Telecommunications (DoT) and the Department of Posts.

As part of the reorganisation, VSNL was incorporated on March 19,1986 as a wholly owned GoI Company. On April 1, 1986 VSNL took over the responsibility and management of all international telecommunication services from the Overseas Communications Service, a department of the Ministry of Communications. The DoT assumed regulatory authority over VSNL and other public sector enterprises and acted on the Government of India's behalf as the sole shareholder in such entities.

The Telecom Commission was established in 1986 as an executive body under the Ministry of Communications to make and implement policy decisions. In 1997, the Telecom Regulatory Authority of India (TRAI) was established to provide policy inputs and to ensure fair competition and protection of consumer interests. As part of the latest National Telecommunication Policy (NTP) 1999, the Government of India separated and corporatised the services function of the DoT leaving DoT with its regulatory role. Through various policy initiatives and successive NTPs in 1994 and 1999, the Government of India reaffirmed its commitment to take India to international standards in telecommunications by 2010.

Disinvestment

VSNL ceased to be a government enterprise on February 13, 2002 when the Government of India, which owned 52.97% of VSNL's equity, divested 25% stake to the Tata Group as a strategic partner along with the right to manage the enterprise. Following its subsequent open offer for a further 20% of VSNL's equity, the Tata Group is the enterprise biggest shareholder with a holding of over 46%, while the GoI is VSNL's second-largest shareholder with a 26.12% stake.

Valuation

The Disinvestment Commission had emphasized that valuation of the PEs proposed for disinvestment should be independent, transparent and free from bias and had suggested that three methods of valuation, namely the 'Discounted cash flow' (DCF), 'Relative valuation' approach and 'Net asset value' approach could be adopted. The Ministry of Disinvestment issued the guidelines in May 2001 according to which four methodologies, namely Discounted Cash Flow (DCF) Method, Transaction Multiple Method, Balance Sheet Method and Asset Valuation Method were to be used for valuation of the PEs to be disinvested.

Table 1
Valuation under Different Methods

(Rs. In crore)

Valuation Method	*Value*
Discounted Cash flow (DCF)	4560 to 5757
Balance Sheet	4018.5
Asset Valuation	5301
Comparable Company	5500.5-6241.5

Source: Department of Disinvestment, Government of India.

Industry Overview

The Indian telecom industry has changed significantly over the last decade with all its segments opening to competition. This market is now highly competitive, complex and evolving rapidly, with numerous service offerings of different kinds, including fixed-line, mobile, Internet, long distance and various data services. India's telecom market is growing rapidly and by 2010, telecom is expected to be a Rs.1380 billion sector, contributing 5.4% to India's gross domestic product (GDP).

Videsh Sanchar Nigam Limited (VSNL), a member of the US$ 27 billion TataGroup, is a leading global communications solutions company offering next-generation voice, data and value-added services to enterprises, carriers and retail consumers. Voted the Best Wholesale Service Provider at the World Communications Awards, 2006, VSNL is one of the world's largest providers of wholesale international voice services and operates one of the largest global submarine cable networks. VSNL's customer base includes 1500 Global Carriers, 450 Mobile Operators, 10,000 Enterprises, 500,000 Broadband and Internet subscribers and 300 Wi-Fi public hotspots.

Rated amongst the Top 100 Emerging Global Challengers by the Boston Consulting Group,VSNL has of. ces in over 35 countries including the United States of America, Canada, the United Kingdom, South Africa,Singapore, Hong Kong, Sri Lanka and India. VSNL's global transmission network of over 200,000 route kilometers and its IP range of services that include voice, private leased circuits, IP VPN, Internet access, global Ethernet, hosting, mobile signaling and other IP services. Our philosophy of BusinessnRich drives us to empower our

customers to achieve enhanced value in their global businesses. VSNL (www.vsnl.in) is listed on the Bombay Stock Exchange and the National Stock Exchange in India, and its American Depositary Receipts (ADRs) are listed on the New York Stock Exchange in US.

Internal Controls

VSNL has a well-developed internal control system and has also implemented the SAP system for accounting. The financial powers of various executives are clearly defined in the delegation of powers. Technical and financial operations are controlled by state-of-the-art technology. The accounts of the Company are subjected to statutory audit.

Human Resources

VSNL employed 2,479 people as on March 31, 2005 as against 1,736 on March 31, 2004. Of these, 1,786 are executives and 693 are non-executives. The increase in manpower was mainly due to the acquisition of the broadband business of Dishnet and the merger of the Tata Indicom Enterprise Business Unit with VSNL. During the year, VSNL inducted fresh resources to strengthen the areas of customer service, sales, networks and finance.

The enterprise enlisted the Gallup Organization to conduct an Employee Satisfaction survey. The results indicated that a significant percentage of the employees are satisfied with the enterprise policies and practices. The enterprise subsequently constituted cross-functional teams for specific action plans on various issues, which are currently being implemented. The enterprise conducts in-house training programmes with the help of external faculty, covering functional, behavioral and technical areas. To facilitate communication among employees, members of the senior management team periodically interact with employees through videoconferencing.

Environment Safety

As a Tata Company, VSNL is also proactive in addressing environmental, ecological and biodiversity concerns arising out of its operations, integrated with its social responsibility approach. Towards that end, VSNL has also become the first telecom service providing company in India to obtain ISO 14001 Certification.

Corporate Social Responsibility

As a member of the Tata family, VSNL is committed to the Group's philosophy of improving the quality of life in the communities they serve. To institutionalise corporate sustainability initiatives at VSNL and to synchronise them with those of the Tata Group, VSNL declared its Corporate Social Responsibility (CSR) Policy on November 18, 2003. VSNL joined the Tata Council for Community Initiatives (TCCI) in 2003-04. Since then the enterprise has been taking steps to foster an internal culture of volunteerism. The CSR establishment is driving the managerial and technical competency of employees, for the socio-economic development of the communities the Company operates in.

VSNL sponsors street children for computer education, gives financial assistance to physically handicapped persons and to non-governmental organisations (NGOs) working for leprosy eradication, rehabilitation and treatment. It is engaged in creating health awareness against cancer in partnership with NGOs like the Cancer Patients Aid Association (CCPA).VSNL has promoted the cause of reputed NGOs like Child Relief and You (CRY) by buying their products and by encouraging employees to participate in their ventures. VSNL employees are always encouraged to participate in blood donations. VSNL has given generous financial grants to employees residents associations for celebrating national festivals like Independence Day and Republic Day and has been maintaining public gardens and bus-stop shades across India. As a part of quality month celebrations, CSR Day, christened as Corporate Citizenship Day, was celebrated all over VSNL on November 22, 2004. To address CSR as a sustainable business activity, VSNL has formalised an annual CSR action plan for 2005-06.

Financial Performance

Sales and Services

Net sales and service revenue increased from Rs. 4,797.37 crore during 2005-06 to Rs. 8,856.60 crore during 2006-07, a growth of more than 50 per cent over the year 2005-06

Capital Employed

The total capital employed by the enterprise increased from Rs.8,057.97 crore during 2005-06 to Rs. 8,171.86 crore during 2006-07. A significant growth has not taken place in case of capital employed.

Capital Structure

During the year 2006-07, the total investment in the enterprise is Rs.285 crore.

Dividend

A dividend of Rs.4.50 per share (Rs.4.50 per share for the previous year) for the financial year 2006-07 is declared. The amount available for appropriation is Rs.19.40 billion, out of which the enterprise proposes to transfer Rs.468.60 million to general reserves, leaving Rs.17.43 billion to the balance sheet.

Reserves and Surplus

The reserves and surplus aggregated to Rs. 5,115.19 crore in the year 2006-07, where as in 2005-06 it was Rs.4,967.41 crore showing a 2 per cent growth rate over the year 2005-06.

Table 2 explains about the financial performance of Videsh Sanchar Nigam Limited (VSNL). PBDIT/Sales changed from 27.31 to 43.46 in the post-privatisation period. PAT/Sales moved from 17.13 to 17.34, PBDIT/Assets changed from 22.85 to 21.42, PAT/Assets moved from 14.27 to 8.48, PBDIT/Equity moved from 1333.13 to 560.66, PAT/Equity also moved from 827.26 to 223.87, Sales/Total Equity moved from 85.60 to 49.34, Total Debt/Total Assets remained same at 2.46 and Current Ratio from 217.61 to 235.99. The profitability ratios explained that even after privatization there is less significant improvement

Table 2 A
Financial Performance of VSNL

	Pre-Privatisation					
Ratios	1997	1998	1999	2000	2001	2002
PBDIT/Sales	17.06	23.86	29.09	22.55	36.91	34.38
PAT/Sales	9.69	15.76	19.32	12.00	24.38	21.62
PBDIT/Assets	17.11	21.83	22.59	19.52	26.75	29.29
PAT/Assets	9.72	14.42	15.01	10.39	17.67	18.42
PBDIT/Equity	964.41	1542.7	2099.24	1662.1	944.98	785.19
PAT/Equity	547.68	1018.86	1394.68	884.49	624.15	493.70
Sales/ Assets	100.26	91.48	77.66	86.57	72.47	85.18
Debt/ Assets	4.82	2.33	0.03	0.06	0.00	7.53
CA/CL	169.15	193.16	190.09	313.01	216.80	223.42
Employees	2873	2861	2975	2928	2991	-

Source: Compiled from Appendix 1A..

Graph 1

Pre and Post Privatisation Performance of VSNL

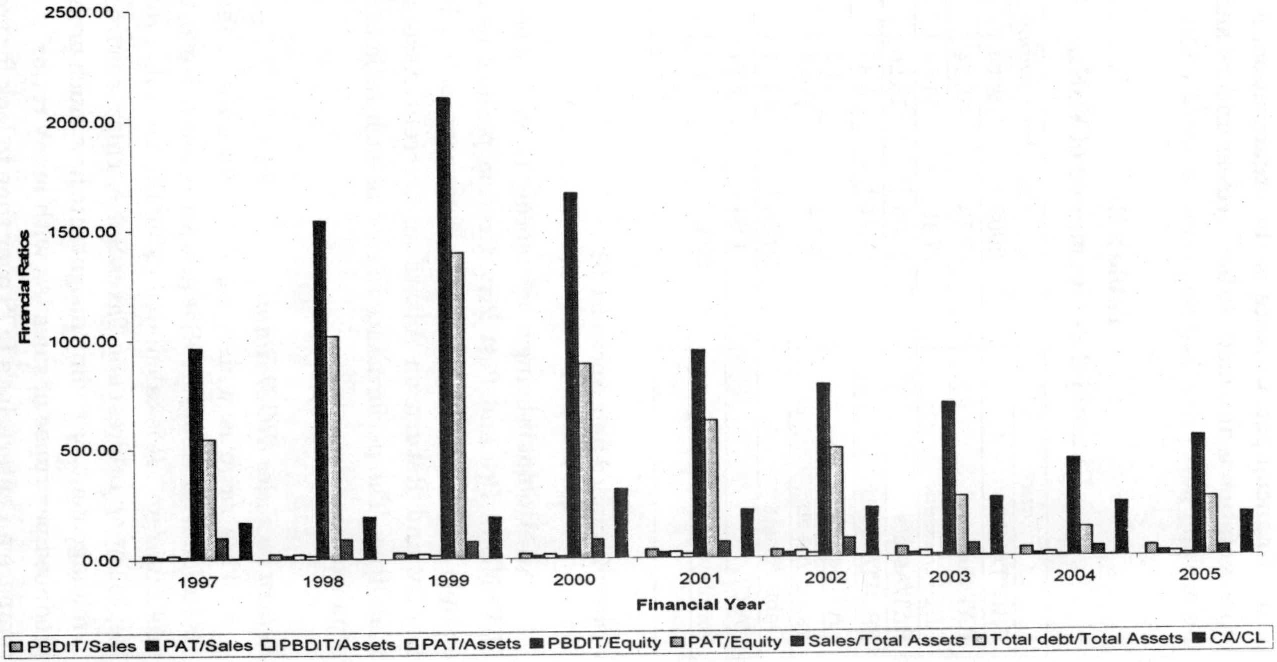

in the financial performance of the organization. A graphical representation is also made to have a clear understanding about the pre and post privatisation performance of VSNL.

Table 2 B
Financial Performance of VSNL

Ratios	*Post-Privatisation*		
PBDIT/Sales	2003	2004	2005
PAT/Sales	43.79	39.74	46.87
PBDIT/Assets	17.19	11.94	22.89
PAT/Assets	26.00	18.28	19.97
PBDIT/Equity	10.21	5.49	9.75
PAT/Equity	697.3	441.1	543.4
Sales/ Assets	273.7	132.5	265.3
Debt/ Assets	59.38	46.01	42.62
CA/CL	4.63	2.64	0.10
Employees	266.7	244.6	196.5
	2752	1736	2479

Source: Compiled from Appendix 1B.

An attempt is being made inorder to test the performance of VSNL in Pre and Post Privatisation periods using paired sample t-test[1] with reference to Return on Sales, Return on Equity and Return on Assets an Current Assets/Current Liabilities. The performance in case of each ratio is explained separately.

Return on Sales (ROS) Ratio

This ratio is widely used to evaluate an enterprise operational efficiency. ROS is also known as a firm's "operating profit margin". It is calculated using the formula Profit Before Depreciation Interest and Taxes/Sales. This measure is helpful to management, providing insight into how much profit is being produced per rupee of sales. As with many ratios, it is best to compare an enterprise's ROS over time to look for trends, and compare it to other companies in the industry. An increasing ROS indicates the enterprise is growing more efficient, while a decreasing ROS could signal looming financial troubles.

Table 3 shows the paired samples t-test for PBDIT/Sales, Pat/Sales in pre-privatisation period and in the post-privatisation period. It is observed that for pair 1&2 (Return on Sales (ROS)) the mean difference is -12.41 and 1.700 and standard deviation is 13.08 and 10.02 and standard error is 6.54 and 5.01 and t-values are -1.89 and 0.33 respectively and the corresponding significance value is 0.15 and 0.75 which is greater than 0.05 per cent significance level. This signifies that there is no significant difference in Return on Sales (PBDIT/Sales and PAT/ Sales) in the pre-privatisation period and post-privatisation period. Hence the null hypothesis (Return on Sales in Per-privatisation period is equal to Return on Sales in the post-privatisation period) is accepted.

Table 3
Paired Samples T- Test

		Mean Difference	*Std. Deviation*	*Std.Error Mean*	*t*	*df*	*Sig (2-tailed)*
Pair 1	PBDIT/Sales pre PBDIT/Sales post	-12.41	13.08	6.54	-1.898	3	.154
Pair 2	PAT/Sales Pre PAT/Sales Post	1.7	10.022	5.011	.339	3	.757

The graph on Return on Sales shows a positive trend in the post- privatisation period. There is certainly an improvement in this period but not significant. It shows that return on sales showed a steep fall in 2004 and again gained momentum in 2005 and showed a declining trend in 2006

Graph 2
Return on Sales

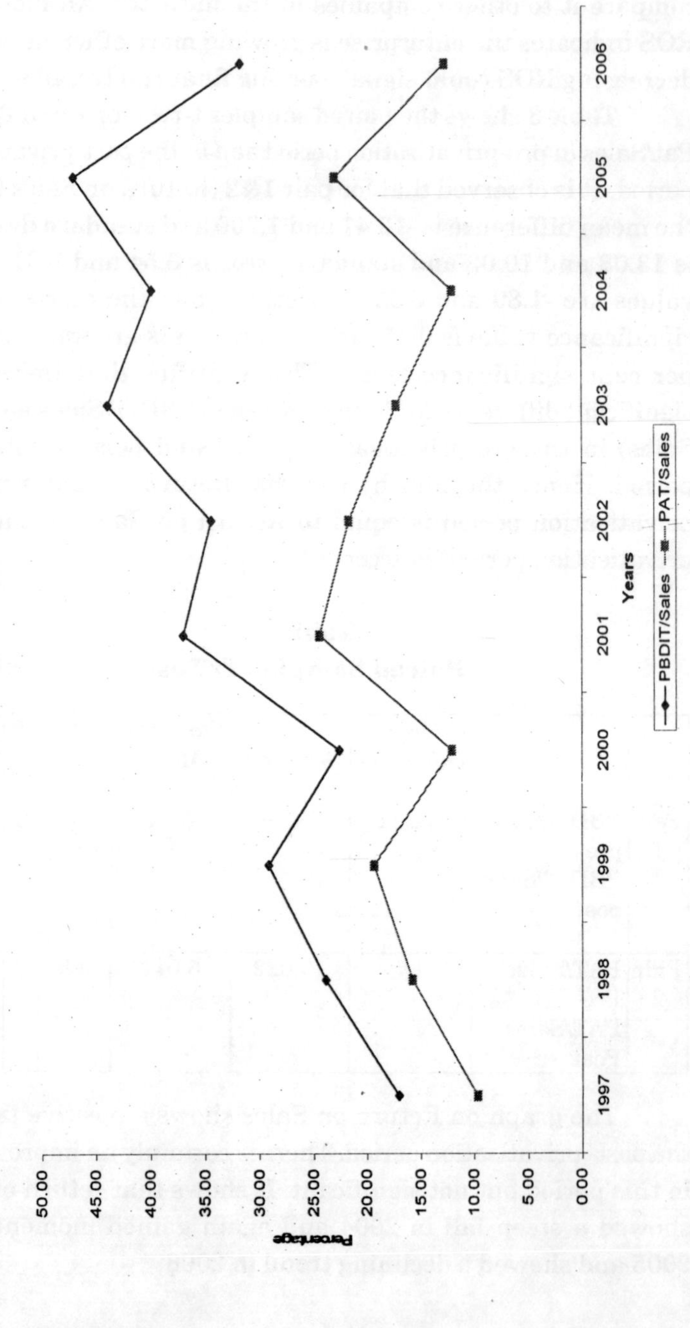

Return on Assets (ROA) Ratio

Return on Assets is an indicator of how profitable an enterprise is relative to its total assets. ROA gives an idea as to how efficient management is at using its assets to generate earnings. Calculated by dividing an enterprise's annual earnings by its total assets, ROA is displayed as a percentage. Sometimes this is referred to as "return on investment". ROA explains the earnings that were generated from invested capital (assets). ROA for public companies can vary substantially and will be highly dependent on the industry. This is why when using ROA as a comparative measure, it is best to compare it against an enterprise's previous ROA numbers or the ROA of a similar enterprise. The assets of the enterprise are comprised of both debt and equity. Both of these types of financing are used to fund the operations of the enterprise. The ROA figure gives investors an idea of how effectively the enterprise is converting the money it has to invest into net income. The higher the ROA number, the better, because the enterprise is earning more money on less investment.

Table 4 shows the paired samples t-test for PBDIT/Assets, PAT/Assets in pre-privatisation period and the post-privatisation period. It is observed that for pair 1&2 (Return on Assets (ROA))

Table 4
Paired Samples T-Test

		Mean Difference	*Std. Devia-tion*	*Std. Error Mean*	*t*	*df*	*Sig (2-tailed)*
Pair 1	PBDIT/Sales pre PBDIT/Sales post	1.39	12.61	6.30	.220	3	.840
Pair 2	PAT/Sales pre PAT/Sales post	-1.63	9.38	4.69	-.349	3	.750

Graph 3
Return on Assets

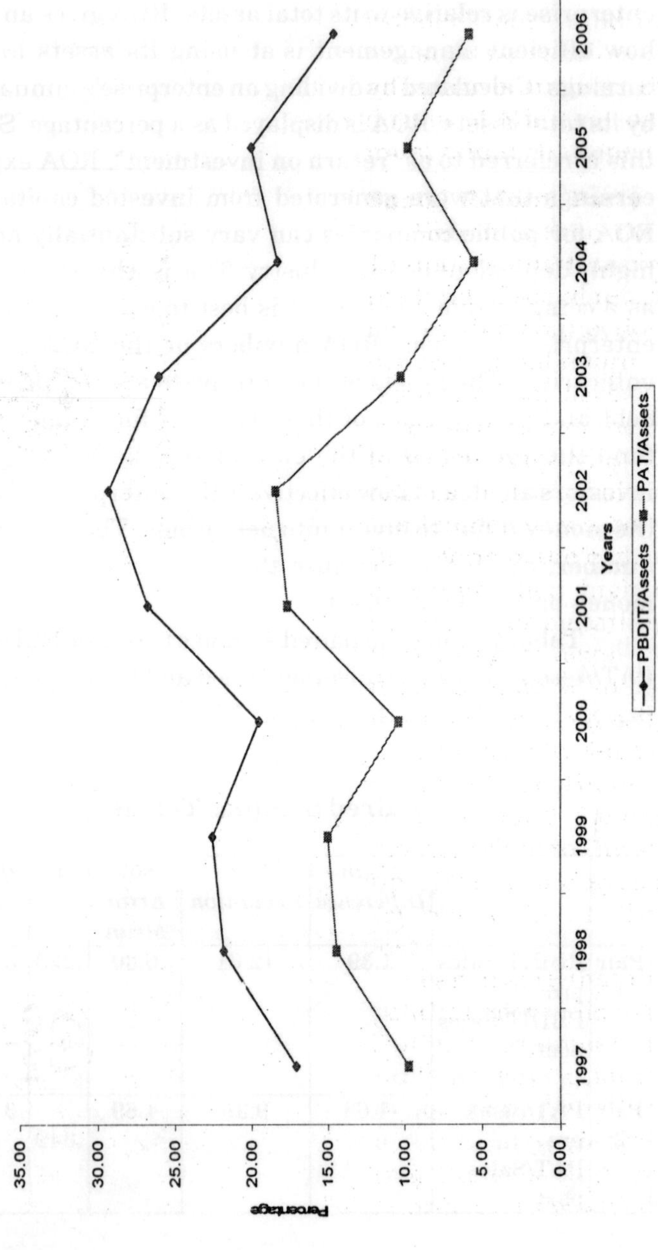

the mean difference is 2.96 and 6.55 and standard deviation is 7.04 and 5.07 and standard error is 3.52 and 2.53 and t-values are .84 and 2.58 respectively and the corresponding significance values are 0.46 and 0.08 which is greater than 0.05 per cent significance level. This signifies that there is no significant difference in Return on Assets (PBDIT/Assets and PAT/Assets) in the pre-privatisation period and post-privatisation period. Hence the null hypothesis (Return on Assets in Per-privatisation period is equal to Return on Assets in the post-privatisation period) is accepted.

The graph on Return on Assets in the pre and post privatisation period shows mixed performance.

Return on Equity (ROE) Ratio

Return on Equity is a measure of an enterprise profitability that reveals how much profit an enterprise generates with the money that shareholders have invested. ROE is useful for comparing the profitability of an enterprise to that of other firms in the same industry.

Table 5 shows the paired samples t-test for PBDIT/Equity, PAT/Equity in pre-privatisation period and post-privatisation period. It is observed that for pair 1&2 (Return on Equity (ROE)

Table 5
Paired Samples T-Test

		Mean Difference	*Std. Deviation*	*Std.Error Mean*	*t*	*df*	*Sig (2-tailed)*
Pair 1	PBDIT/Assets pre PBDIT/Assets post	2.81	5.54	2.77	1.01	3	0.386
Pair 2	PAT/Assets Pre PAT/Assets Post	-.492	5.25	2.62	-.188	3	0.863

Graph 4
Return on Equity

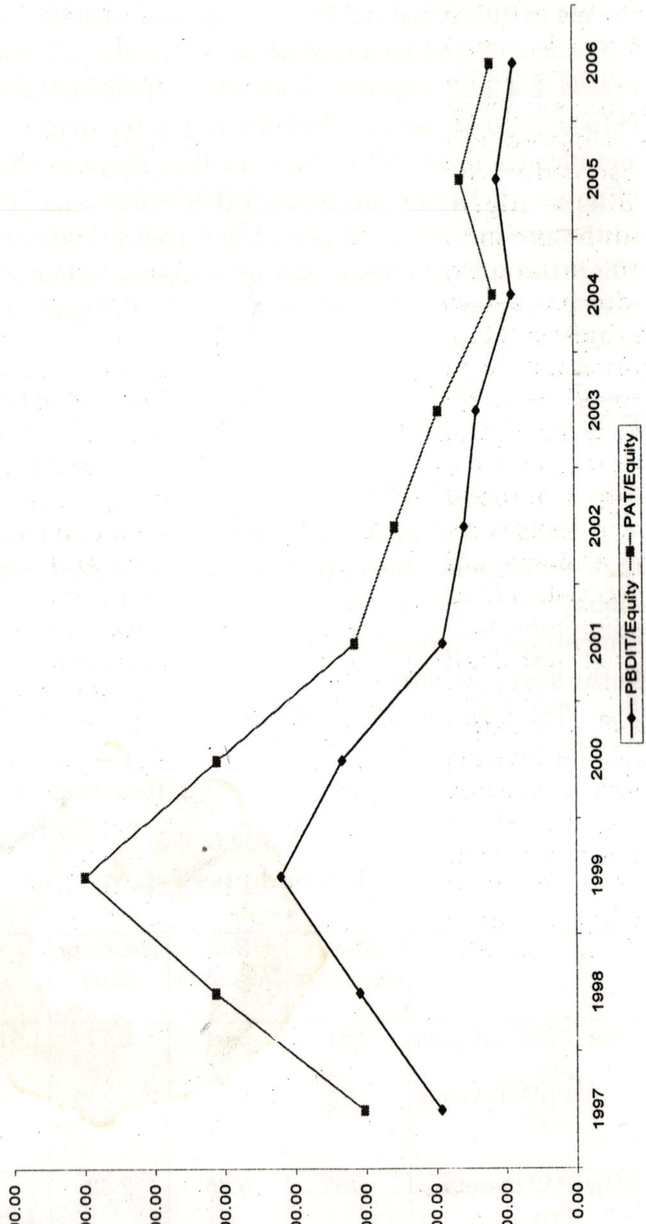

the mean difference is 1036.5 and 770.59 and standard deviation is 480.45 and 348.44 and standard error is 240.22 and 174.22 and t-values are 4.3 and 4.4 respectively and the corresponding significance values are .02 and 0.02 which are greater than 0.05 per cent significance level. This signifies that there is no significant difference in Return on Equity (PBDIT/Equity and PAT/Equity) in the pre-privatisation period and post-privatisation period. Hence the null hypothesis (Return on Equity in Per-privatisation period is equal to Return on Equity in the post-privatisation period) is accepted.

The graph on Return on Equity in the pre and post privatisation period shows a negative trend.

Asset Turn Over Ratio

This ratio is useful to determine the amount of sales that are generated from each rupee of assets. Enterprises with low profit margins tend to have high asset turnover, those with high profit margins have low asset turnover.

Table 6 shows the paired samples t- test for Sales/Total Assets in pre-privatisation period and in the post-privatisation period. From the table it is observed that for pair 1 (Asset Turn Over) the mean difference is 33.51 and standard deviation is 7.43 and standard error is 3.71 and t-value is 9.01 and the corresponding significance value is .003 which is less than 0.05

Table 6
Paired Samples T-Test

		Mean Diffe-rence	*Std. Deviation*	*Std.Error Mean*	*t*	*df*	*Sig (2-tailed)*
Pair 1	Sales/Total Assets Pre Sales/Total Assets Post	33.51	7.43	3.71	9.0	3	.003

Graph 5
Asset Turn Over

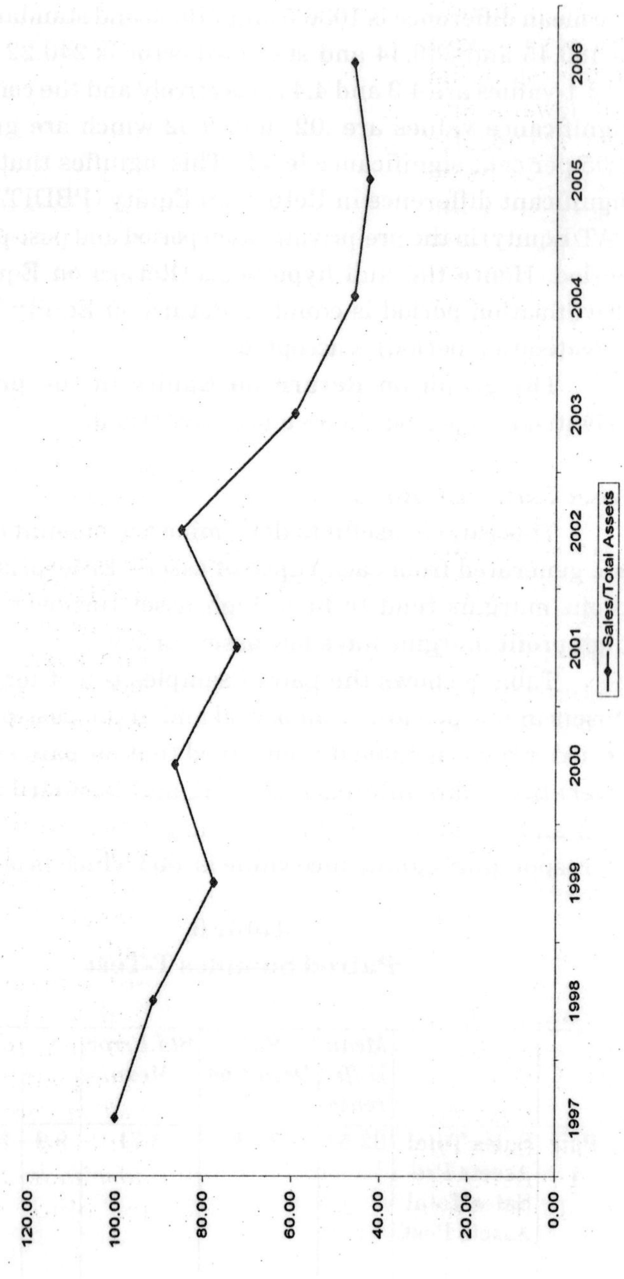

per cent significance level. This signifies that there is a significant difference in Asset Turn Over in the pre-privatisation period and post-privatisation period. Hence the null hypothesis (Asset Turnover ratio in Per-privatisation period is equal to Asset Turnover ratio in the post-privatisation period) is rejected and can say that the amount of sales that are generated from each rupee of assets in the post privatisation period shows an increasing trend.

The graph on Asset Turn Over in the pre and post privatisation period shows a steep decline over the period and the year 2006-07 shows a slight improvement.

Debt Equity Ratio

The debt/asset ratio (Total liabilities divided by total assets) shows the proportion of enterprise assets which are financed through debt. If the ratio is less than one, most of the enterprise assets are financed through equity. If the ratio is greater than one, most of the enterprise assets are financed through debt. Enterprises with high debt/asset ratios are said to be "highly leveraged," and could be in danger if creditors start to demand repayment of debt.

Table 7
Paired Samples T-Test

		Mean Difference	*Std. Deviation*	*Std.Error Mean*	*t*	*df*	*Sig (2-tailed)*
Pair 1	Total Debt/Total Assets Pre Total Debt/Total Assets Post	-1.61	1.14	.574	-2.08	3	.068

Graph 6
Debt-Equity Ratio

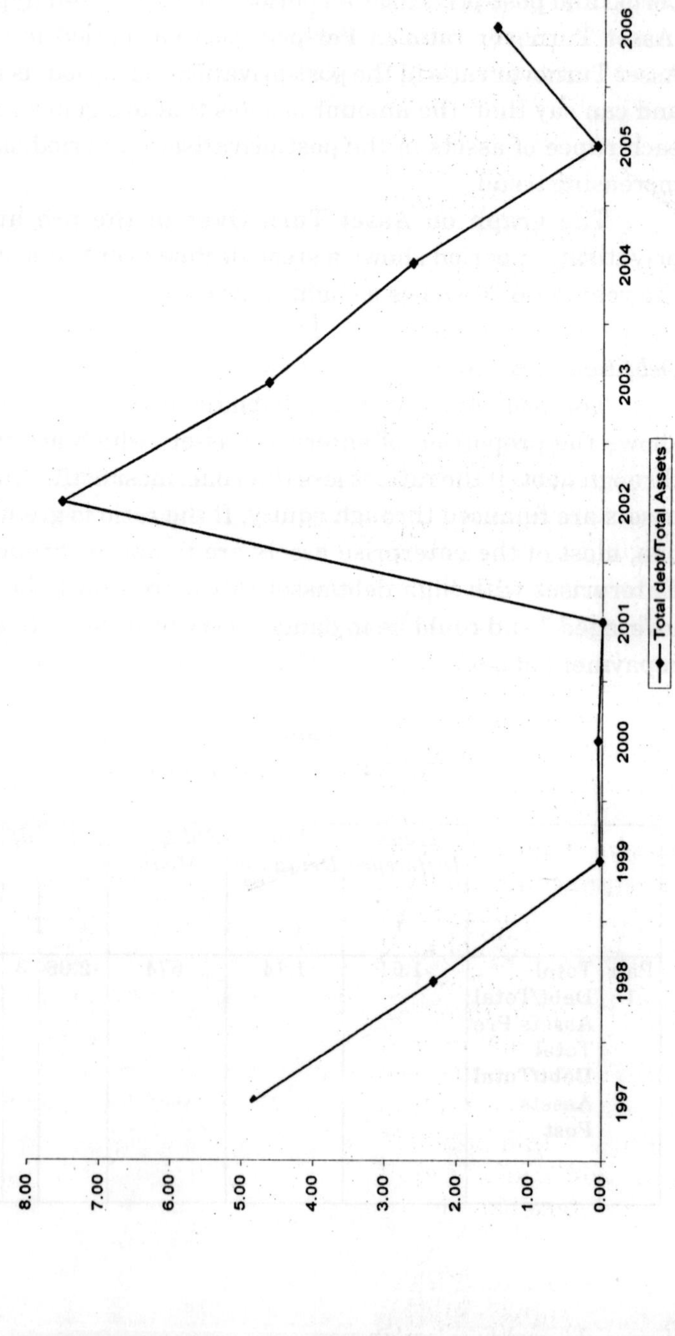

Table 7 shows the paired samples t-test for Total Debt/ Total Assets in pre-privatisation period and in the post-privatisation period is showed where in paired differences, t-test and significance are represented. From the table it is observed that for pair 1 (Debt Equity Ratio) the mean difference is -1.61 and standard deviation is 1.14 and standard error is 0.574 and t-value is -2.8 and the corresponding significance value is .06 which is greater than 0.05 per cent significance level. This signifies that there is no significant difference in Debt-Equity ratio in the pre-privatisation period and post-privatisation period. Hence the null hypothesis (Debt-Equity ratio in Per-privatisation period is equal to Debt-Equity ratio in the post-privatisation period) is accepted.

The graph on Debt-Equity in the pre and post privatisation period it shows an increasing trend in the post- privatisation period. This means that most of the enterprise assets are financed through debt.

Conclusion

It is clearly evident from the analysis that, a significant improvement has not taken place in the financial performance of the enterprise in the post privatisation period. Infact the year 2001 has saw a lower performance and in the same year the government has marched towards disinvestment. In the successive years there is an improvement with respect to Return on Sales, Return on Equity, Return on Assets, and Debt-Equity ratios, but the growth rate is very low. The Asset Turnover ratio is statistically significant and is considered as an important tool in assessing the performance of an enterprise viz., the amount of sales generated from each rupee of assets in the post privatisation period shows an increasing trend. That is why, the statistical results has not shown an significant improvement and the hypothesis of the study (Financial performance in the pre-privatisation period is equal to financial performance in the post privatisation period) was accepted.

Appendix 1 A
Financial Performance of VSNL During Pre-Privatisation Period

(Rs. In crore)

	1997	*1998*	*1999*	*2000*	*2001*
PBDIT	888.8	1465.64	1994.28	1579.06	2693.2
Sales	5208.86	6141.57	6856.17	7001.74	7297.51
PAT	504.74	967.92	1324.95	840.27	1778.83
Assets	5195.32	6713.89	8828.43	8087.55	10069.27
Equity	92.16	95	95	95	285
No.of Employees	2873	2861	2975	0	2991
Total Debt	250.28	156.23	2.55	4.57	0
Dividend	30.8	41.8	84.36	86.45	1570.35
Current Assets	3750.83	4893.96	6478.09	5974.6	7545.63
Current Liabilities	2217.44	2533.58	3407.87	1908.77	3480.52
Debt-Equity Ratio		0.04	0	0	0

Source: Annual Report of VSNL, CMIE Prowess Data Base.

Appendix 1 B
Financial Performance of VSNL During Post-Privatisation Period

(Rs. In crore)

	2003	*2004*	*2005*
PBDIT	1987.46	1257.32	1548.83
Sales	4538.55	3164.2	3304.86
PAT	780.07	377.66	756.37
Assets	7643.82	6876.68	7754.22
Equity	285	285	285
No.of Employees	2752	1736	2479
Total Debt	354	181.43	7.46
Dividend	273.29	144.68	195.31

(Contd.)

(Contd.Appendix -1B)

	2003	*2004*	*2005*
Current Assets	4520.27	3765.24	3617.44
Current Liabilities	1694.73	1538.86	1840.39
Debt-Equity Ratio	0.06	0.04	0

Source: Annual Report of VSNL, CMIE Prowess Data Base.

Case 5
Maruti Udyog Limited (MUL)

Background

Maruti Udyog Limited (MUL) was established in February 1981 through an Act of Parliament, to meet the growing demand for a personal mode of transport arising from the lack of an efficient public transport system. Suzuki Motor Company was chosen from seven prospective partners worldwide. This was due not only to their undisputed leadership in small cars but also to their commitment to actively bring to MUL contemporary technology and Japanese management practices (which had catapulted Japan over USA to the status of the top auto manufacturing country in the world).

A licence and a Joint Venture agreement was signed between Govt of India and Suzuki Motor Company (now Suzuki Motor Corporation of Japan in October 1982

Objectives of MUL

§ Modernization of the Indian Automobile Industry.

§ Production of fuel-efficient vehicles to conserve scarce resources.

§ Production of a large number of motor vehicles which was necessary for economic growth.

Disinvestment

On 14-05-2002 Government approved disinvestment in Maruti Udyog Limited (MUL) through a two-stages:

§ A rights issue by MUL in the first phase of Rs.400 crores with Government renouncing its rights share to Suzuki. Suzuki would gain majority control and pay Rs 1000 crore to Government as control premium.

§ Sale of its existing shares through a public issue in the second phase; the issue to be underwritten by Suzuki.

Valuation

Table 1
MUL: Valuation under Different Methods

Valuation Method	*Value*
Discounted cash flow (DCF) (computes likely earnings in coming years) Comparables (looks at peer group companies) Balance sheet method (looks at net worth from balance sheet Asset valuation) (replacement cost/sale value of assets)	

Source: Ministry of Disinvestment, Government of India.

Industry Overview

MUL in collaboration with Suzuki Motor Corporation (SMC) has established a new Company, viz. Maruti Suzuki Automobiles India Limited for setting up a new manufacturing plant. The total investment would be Rs. 15,242 million. While the Company will hold 70% equity in the the new company the balance will be held by SMC. The capacity of the plant will initially be 1,00,000 cars per annum with scope to scale it up to 2,50,000 cars per annum. The new car manufacturing plant will begin commercial production by the end of 2006.

The Company has embarked upon this new project in collaboration with SMC for the manufacture of diesel engines, petrol engines and transmission assemblies for four wheeled vehicles. The project is being implemented in the existing Joint Venture Company viz. Suzuki Metal India Limited (renamed Suzuki Power train India Limited). The total plant capacity is 300,000 diesel engines per annum to be developed in phases. The initial annual capacity of this facility is 100,000 diesel engines, 20,000 petrol engines and 140,000 transmission assemblies. The total investment in this facility is Rs. 17,477 million and began its commercial production in the year 2006.

Internal Controls

Maruti Udyog has a proper and adequate system of internal controls to ensure that all assets are safeguarded and protected against loss from unauthorized use or disposition, and that transactions are authorized, recorded and reported correctly. The internal control system is designed to ensure that financial and other records are reliable for preparing financial information and other data, and for maintaining accountability of assets. The internal control system is supplemented by an extensive program of internal audits, reviews by management, and documented policies, guidelines and procedures. In 2004-05, during the process of internal audits and reviews, one case of misappropriation of funds amounting to Rs. 20.62 million by a company official was detected.

The enterprise has taken adequate and appropriate steps to Strengthen general information, systems controls and automated application controls over the payable processes as soon as the need for such action came to light.

Human Resources

To stay ahead in a competitive market and leverage growing opportunities, the enterprise is working in a focused manner to develop capabilities of its people. Training was stepped up through customized programmes for employees at each level. For instance, for the first time, an advanced leadership programme was conducted for senior management to lead and manage talent in the organization.

Representatives of the employees Union were sent to Suzuki Motor Corporation to familiarize themselves with the parent organization and acquire knowledge of good practices. A programme for workmen, "Sankalp", started in the year 2004-05 to expose employees to changes in the car market and the global economic environment, was extended to more workers during the year.

In order to improve corporate competitiveness and rationalize salary structure in line with competitors, the salary structure is now redesigned and made simple, transparent, principle driven and more people-friendly. Importantly, based on the overall HR Best Practices, the enterprise was given an award for the "Organization with Innovative HR Practices" by HT-Power Jobs.

As on March 31, 2005, MUL has 3453 employees. Industrial Relations remained cordial and not a single day's work was lost due to strikes or disputes during the year.

Corporate Social Responsibility

During the Tsunami tragedy, your company was among the first corporates to commit a contribution to the Prime Minister's Relief Fund. MUL's employees, dealers and suppliers, in addition to their individual contributions, also pooled resources under the Maruti umbrella. In all, the contribution to the Prime Minister's Relief Fund was Rs. 21.6 million. In addition to the three Maruti Driving Schools set up so far, the Institute of Driving Training and Research managed by MUL continued to do excellent work in the areas of driver training and research.

The enterprise began work on a similar institute in South Delhi to further efforts to improve road safety. The Children's Park at India Gate in New Delhi, managed by your company, is now a popular destination for families. The Delhi Public School in Maruti Kunj, Gurgaon, supported by your company, has improved prospects of employees' children by giving them quality education. The school is also working actively in the local community, providing education to underprivileged children and mothers with support provided by your company.

Financial Performance

Sales and Services

Net sales and service revenue increased to Rs.1459.22 crore in the year 2006-07 and the net sales and service revenue in the year 2005-06 was Rs.1200.34 crore. The enterprise is able to achieve a growth rate of 21 per cent.

Capital Employed

The total capital employed by the enterprise increased by 22 per cent from Rs.55,281 crore in the year 2005-06 to Rs.67,445 crore in the year 2006-07.

Dividends

The enterprise paid a dividend of Rs.1,300 crore during the year 2006-07 and Rs.1,001 crore.

Reserves and Surplus

Reserves and Surplus aggregated Rs.70,065 crore in the year 2006-07. the year 2005-06 registered Rs.55,730 crore, showing an average growth rate of 25 per cent.

To analyse the performance of selected companies certain key ratios are taken into account. In the case of Maruti Udyog Limited, there is an improvement in such ratios from the pre-privatisation to the post-privatisation period. Profit Before Depreciation, Interest and Taxes (PBDIT)/Sales experienced a declining trend during the period of privatisation i.e, for the years 2000 -2001 to 2002-2003, but immediately after privatisation PBIT/Sales improved from 0.06 to 0.14. and Profit

After Tax (PAT)/Sales also increased in the post-privatisation period. PBDIT/Assets moved from 0.11 to 0.29, PAT/Assets from 0.02 to 0.13, PBDIT/Equity from 3.98 to 12.91, PAT/Equity from

Table 2 A
Financial Ratio Analysis of Maruti Udyog Limited

	Pre-Privatisation					
	1997	*1998*	*1999*	*2000*	*2001*	*2002*
PBDIT/Sales	0.14	0.15	0.13	0.07	0.01	0.06
PAT/Sales	0.07	0.08	0.07	0.03	-0.03	0.01
PBDIT/Assets	0.36	0.34	0.24	0.15	0.02	0.11
PAT/Assets	0.17	0.18	0.12	0.07	-0.05	0.02
PBDIT/Equity	8.03	9.19	7.60	5.35	0.94	3.98
PAT/Equity	3.86	4.93	3.95	2.50	-2.04	0.79
Sales/Total Assets	2.64	2.31	1.86	1.93	1.81	1.92
Total debt/Total Assets	0.07	0.05	0.04	0.12	0.23	0.16
CA/CL	1.19	0.95	1.45	1.03	1.08	1.17
employees	5324	5642	5719	4825	4765	4627

Source: Compiled from Appendix 1A.

Table 2 B
Financial Ratio Analysis of Maruti Udyog Limited

	Post-Privatisation		
Paramers	*2003*	*2004*	*2005*
PBDIT/Sales	0.07	0.12	0.14
PAT/Sales	0.02	0.05	0.06
PBDIT/Assets	0.12	0.23	0.29
PAT/Assets	0.03	0.09	0.13
PBDIT/Equity	4.46	9.22	12.91
PAT/Equity	1.01	3.75	5.91
Sales/Total Assets	1.69	1.94	2.06
Total debt/Total Assets	0.12	0.07	0.06
CA/CL	1.68	2.28	2.67
employees	4590	3334	3453

Source: Compiled from Appendix 1B.

Graph 1

Pre and Post Privatisation Performance

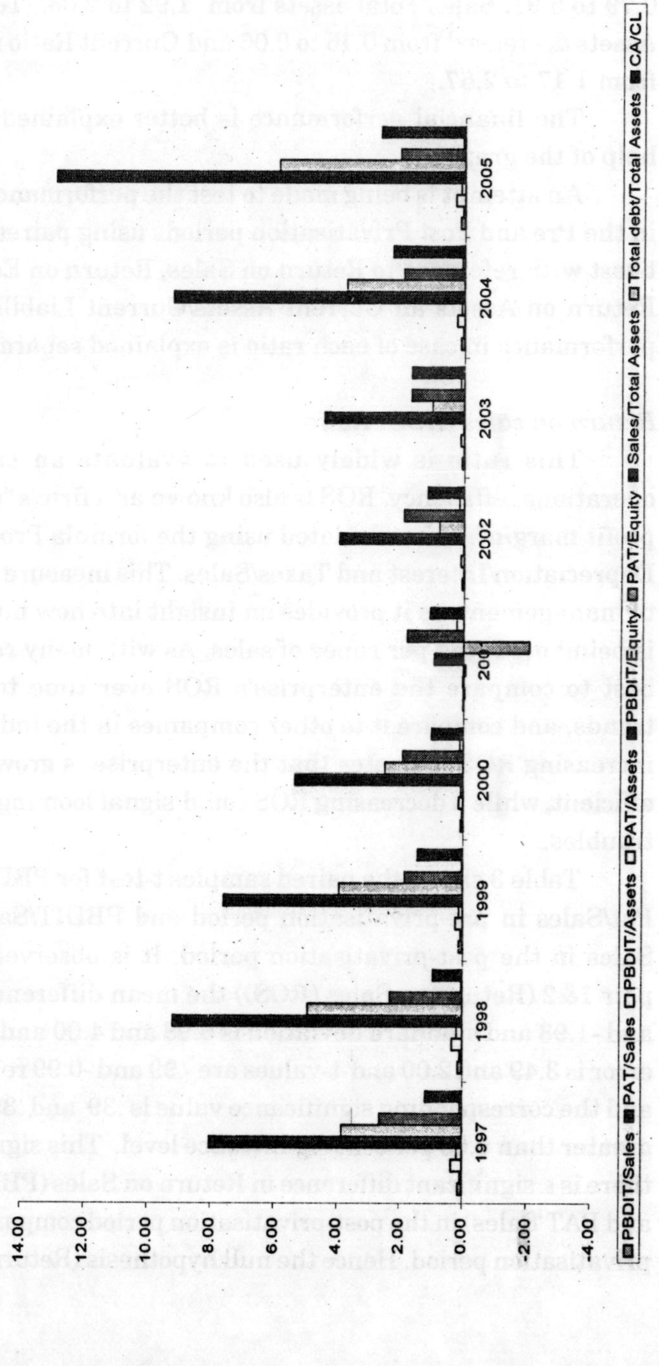

0.79 to 5.91. Sales/Total assets from 1.92 to 2.06. Total Debt/ Assets decreased from 0.16 to 0.06 and Current Ratio increased from 1.17 to 2.67.

The financial performance is better explained with the help of the graph.

An attempt is being made to test the performance of MUL in the Pre and Post Privatisation periods using paired samples t-test with reference to Return on Sales, Return on Equity and Return on Assets an Current Assets/Current Liabilities. The performance in case of each ratio is explained separately.

Return on sales (ROS) Ratio

This ratio is widely used to evaluate an enterprise operational efficiency. ROS is also known as a firm's "operating profit margin". It is calculated using the formula Profit Before Depreciation Interest and Taxes/Sales. This measure is helpful to management, as it provides an insight into how much profit is being produced per rupee of sales. As with many ratios, it is best to compare the enterprise's ROS over time to look for trends, and compare it to other companies in the industry. An increasing ROS indicates that the enterprise is growing more efficient, while a decreasing ROS could signal looming financial troubles.

Table 3 shows the paired samples t-test for PBDIT/Sales, Pat/Sales in pre-privatisation period and PBDIT/Sales, PAT/ Sales in the post-privatisation period. It is observed that for pair 1&2 (Return on Sales (ROS)) the mean difference is -3.48 and -1.98 and standard deviation is 6.98 and 4.00 and standard error is 3.49 and 2.00 and t-values are -.99 and -0.99 respectively and the corresponding significance value is .39 and .39 which is greater than 0.05 per cent significance level. This signifies that there is a significant difference in Return on Sales (PBDIT/Sales and PAT/Sales) in the post-privatisation period compared to pre-privatisation period. Hence the null hypothesis (Return on Sales

Graph 2
Return on Sales

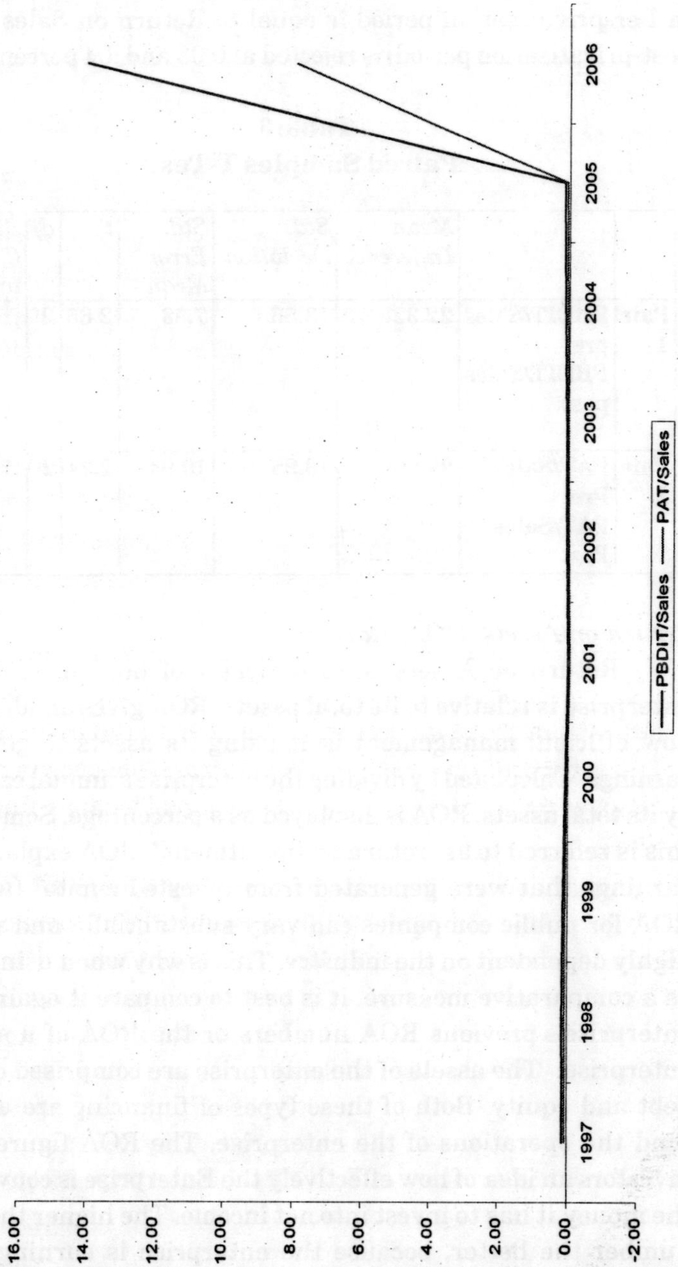

in Per-privatisation period is equal to Return on Sales in the post-privatisation period) is rejected at 0.03 and .04 percent level.

Table 3
Paired Samples T-Test

		Mean Difference	*Std. Deviation*	*Std. Error Mean*	*t*	*df*	*Sig (2-tailed)*
Pair 1	PBDIT/Sales pre / PBDIT/Sales post	22.32	13.56	7.83	2.85	2	.104
Pair 2	PAT/Sales Pre PAT/Sales Post	29.99	18.95	10.94	2.74	2	.111

Return on Assets (ROA) Ratio

Return on Assets is an indicator of how profitable an enterprise is relative to its total assets. ROA gives an idea as to how efficient management is at using its assets to generate earnings. Calculated by dividing the enterprise's annual earnings by its total assets, ROA is displayed as a percentage. Sometimes this is referred to as "return on investment". ROA explains the earnings that were generated from invested capital (assets). ROA for public companies can vary substantially and will be highly dependent on the industry. This is why when using ROA as a comparative measure, it is best to compare it against the enterprise's previous ROA numbers or the ROA of a similar enterprise. The assets of the enterprise are comprised of both debt and equity. Both of these types of financing are used to fund the operations of the enterprise. The ROA figure gives investors an idea of how effectively the Enterprise is converting the money it has to invest into net income. The higher the ROA number the better, because the enterprise is earning more money on less investment.

Graph 3
Return on Assets

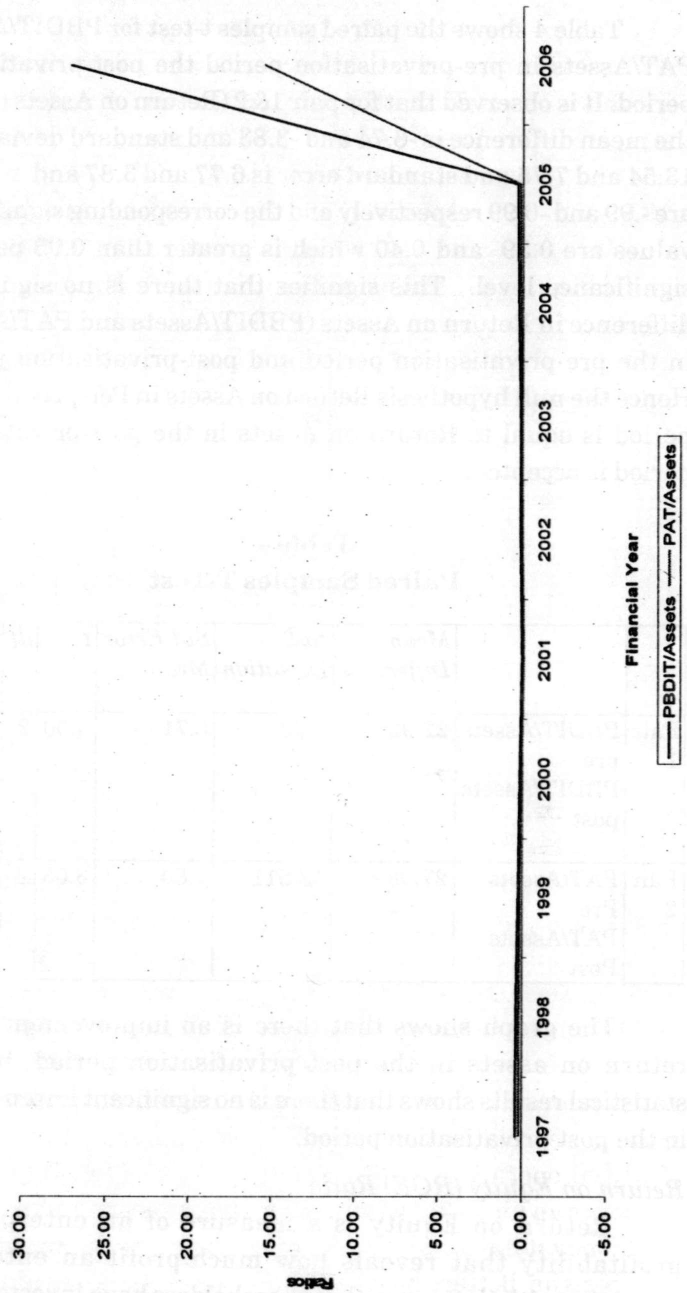

Table 4 shows the paired samples t-test for PBDIT/Assets, PAT/Assets in pre-privatisation period the post-privatisation period. It is observed that for pair 1&2 (Return on Assets (ROA)) the mean difference is -6.74 and -3.83 and standard deviation is 13.54 and 7.75 and standard error is 6.77 and 3.87 and t-values are -.99 and -0.99 respectively and the corresponding significance values are 0.39 and 0.40 which is greater than 0.05 per cent significance level. This signifies that there is no significant difference in Return on Assets (PBDIT/Assets and PAT/Assets) in the pre-privatisation period and post-privatisation period. Hence the null hypothesis Return on Assets in Per-privatisation period is equal to Return on Assets in thc post-privatisation period is accepted.

Table 4
Paired Samples T-Test

		Mean Difference	*Std. Deviation*	*Std.Error Mean*	*t*	*df*	*Sig (2-tailed)*
Pair 1	PBDIT/Assets pre PBDIT/Assets post	22.92	9.90	5.71	4.00	2	.05
Pair 2	PAT/Assets Pre PAT/Assets Post	27.98	13.511	7.80	3.58	2	.07

The graph shows that there is an improvement in the return on assets in the post privatisation period, but the statistical results shows that there is no significant improvement in the post privatisation period.

Return on Equity (ROE) Ratio

Return on Equity is a measure of an enterprise in profitability that reveals how much profit an enterprise generates with the money that shareholders have invested. ROE is useful for comparing the profitability of an enterprise with that of other firms in the same industry.

Table 5 shows the paired samples t-test for PBDIT/Equity, PAT/Equity in pre-privatisation period and in the post-privatisation period. From the table it is observed that for pair 1&2 (Return on Equity (ROE)) the mean difference is -362.10 and -206.05 and standard deviation is 721.26 and 412.59 and standard error is 360.63 and 206.299 and t-values are -1.004 and -.99 respectively and the corresponding significance values are .38 and 0.39 which are greater than 0.05 per cent significance level. This signifies that there is no significant difference in Return on Equity (PBDIT/Equity and PAT/Equity) in the pre-privatisation period and post-privatisation period. Hence the null hypothesis (Return on Equity in Per-privatisation period is equal to Return on Equity in the post-privatisation period) is accepted.

Table 5
Paired Samples T-Test

		Mean	*Std. Deviation*	*Std.Error Mean*	*t*	*df*	*Sig (2-tailed)*
Pair 1	PBDIT/Equity pre PBDIT/Equity post	427.02	149.82	86.50	4.93	2	.03
Pair 2	PAT/Equity Pre PAT/Equity Post	441.22	279.89	161.59	2.73	2	.11

The graph shows that there is an improvement in the return on assets in the post privatisation period, but the statistical results shows that there is no significant improvement in the post privatisation period.

Graph 4
Return on Equity

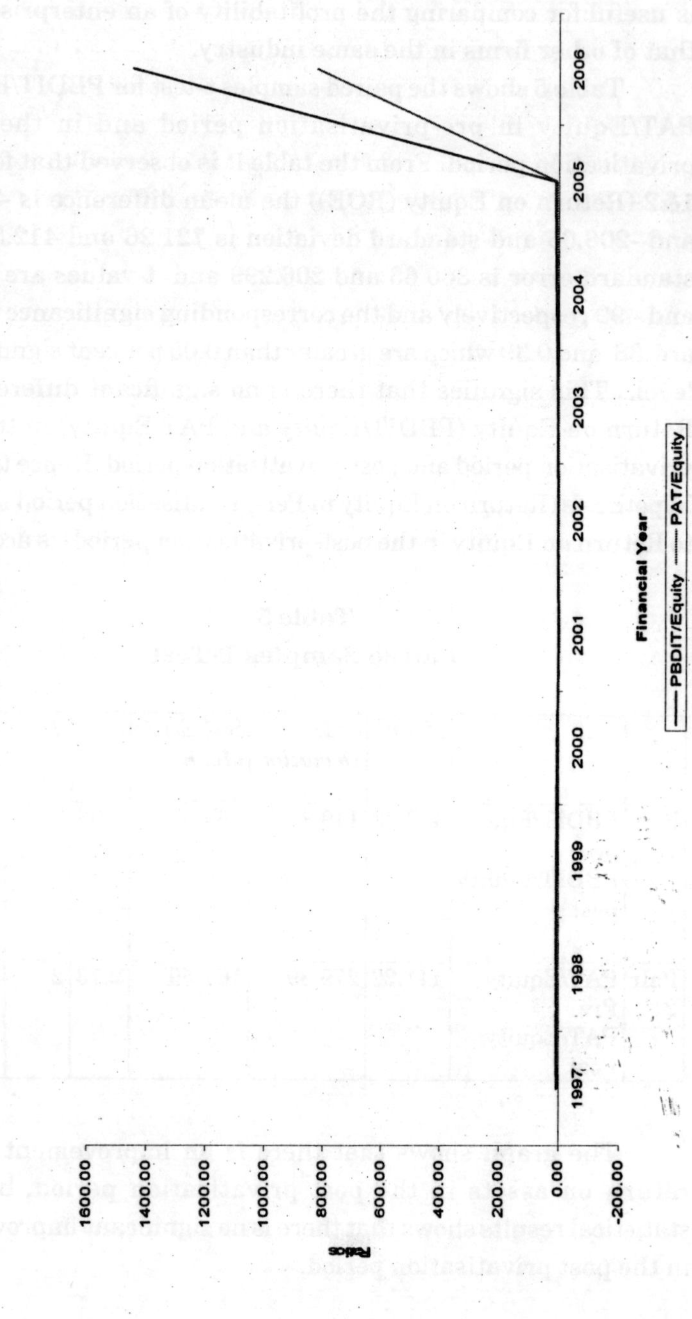

Graph 5
Asset Turnover Ratio

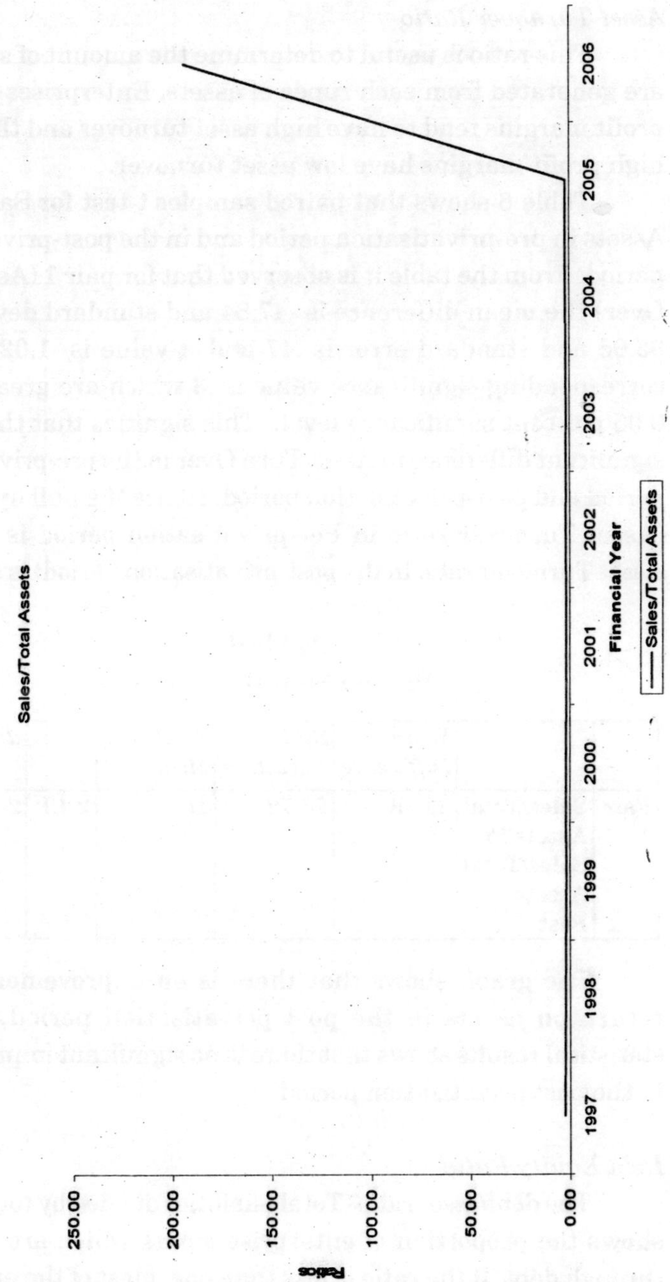

Asset Turnover Ratio

This ratio is useful to determine the amount of sales that are generated from each rupee of assets. Enterprises with low profit margins tend to have high asset turnover and those with high profit margins have low asset turnover.

Table 6 shows that paired samples t-test for Sales/Total Assets in pre-privatisation period and in the post-privatisation period. From the table it is observed that for pair 1 (Asset Turn Over) the mean difference is -47.84 and standard deviation is 95.95 and standard error is .47 and t-value is -1.02 and the corresponding significance value is .3 which are greater than 0.05 per cent significance level. This signifies that there is no significant difference in Asset Turn Over in the pre-privatisation period and post-privatisation period. Hence the null hypothesis (Asset Turnover ratio in Per-privatisation period is equal to Asset Turnover ratio in the post-privatisation period) is accepted.

Table 6
Paired Samples T-Test

		Mean Difference	*Std. Deviation*	*Std.Error Mean*	*t*	*df*	*Sig (2-tailed)*
Pair 1	Sales/Total Assets Pre Sales/Total Assets Post	33.89	26.76	15.45	2.19	2	.16

The graph shows that there is an improvement in the return on assets in the post privatisation period, but the statistical results shows that there is no significant improvement in the post privatisation period.

Debt Equity Ratio

The debt/asset ratio (Total liabilities divided by total assets) shows the proportion of enterprise assets which are financed through debt. If the ratio is less than one, most of the enterprise assets are financed through equity. If the ratio is greater than one, most of the enterprise assets are financed through debt. Enterprises with high debt/asset ratios are said to be "highly leveraged," and could be in danger if creditors start to demand repayment of debt.

Table 7 shows that paired sample test for Total Debt/Total Assets in pre-privatisation period and in the post-privatisation period is showed where in paired differences, t-test and significance are represented. From the table it is observed that for pair 1 (Debt Equity Ratio) the mean difference is -.49 and standard deviation is .95 and standard error is .47 and t-value is -1.02 and the corresponding significance value is .38 which is greater than 0.05 per cent significance level. This signifies that there is no significant difference in Debt-Equity ratio in the pre-privatisation period and post-privatisation period. Hence the null hypothesis (Debt-Equity ratio in Per-privatisation period is equal to Debt-Equity ratio in the post-privatisation period) is accepted.

Table 7
Paired Samples T-Test

		Mean Differe-nce	*Std. Deviation*	*Std.Error Mean*	*t*	*df*	*Sig (2-tailed)*
Pair 1	Total Debt/Total Assets Pre Total Debt/Total Assets Post	-26.54	7.35	4.24	-6.25	2	.02

The graph on Debt-Equity in the pre and post privatisation period it shows an increasing trend in the post- privatisation period. This means that most of the enterprise assets are financed through debt.

Graph 6
Debt Equity Ratio

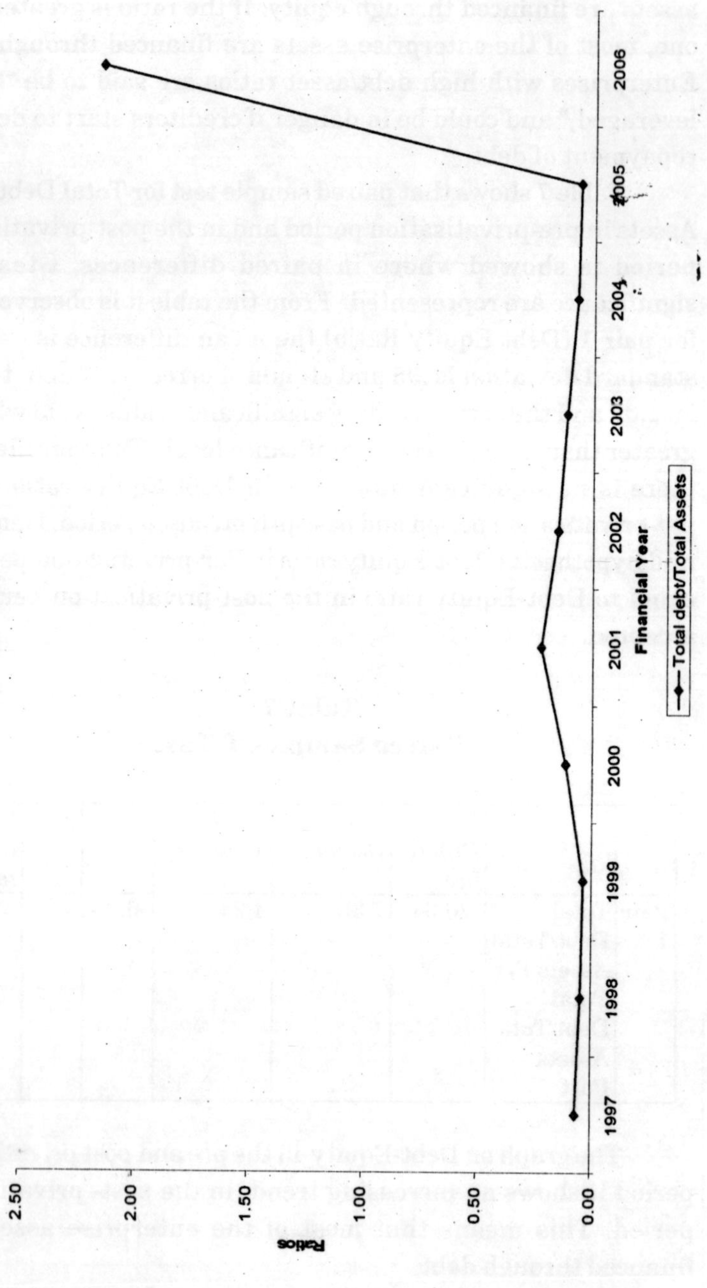

Conclusion

Maruti Udyog Limited has improved its performance in the Post-Privatisation period. But the growth rate is not significant. Therefore the statistical results could not identified

Appendix 1 A
Financial Performance of Maruti Udyog Limited in the Pre Privatisation Periods

(Rs. In crore)

	1997	*1998*	*1999*	*2000*	*2001*
PBDIT	2.09	15.14	17.65	47.82	37.81
Sales	110.69	274.58	362.75	451.42	427.78
PAT	-8.13	5.66	6.84	12.45	2.01
Assets	162.31	237.94	257.54	329.87	333.97
Equity	15	15	15	15	15
No.of Employees	1487	1314	0	0	0
Total Debt	33.61	23.59	23.61	33	57.57
Dividend	0	0.17	0.5	1.1	0.99
Current Assets	146.53	220.26	237.82	306.74	313.93
Current Liabilities	112.76	193.24	207.18	266.43	270.11

Source: Annual Reports of Maruti Udyog Limited, various issues.

Appendix 1 B
Financial Performance of Maruti Udyog Limited in the Post Privatisation Periods

(Rs. In crore)

	2002	*2003*	*2004*
PBDIT	-71.99	0.31	-17.2
Sales	223.21	264.89	163.11
PAT	-107.61	-25.67	-43.97
Assets	267.43	200.52	184.18
Equity	15	15	15
No.of Employees		0	0

(Contd.)

(Contd.Appendix-1B)

	2002	*2003*	*2004*
Total Debt	85.74	63.64	96.23
Dividend	0	0	0
Current Assets	249.71	185.98	169.23
Current Liabilities	311.19	269.89	286.41

Source: Annual Reports of Maruti Udyog Limited, various issues.

these changes. Graphical representation of the data shows performance improvement in the post privatisation period over the years.

Case 6
Indian Petroleum Corporation Limited (IPCL)

Background

IPCL was incorporated on 22nd March 1969, in the public sector as a consequence of the failure of several rounds of negotiations with prospective transnational companies.

Disinvestment

The disinvestment by the Government of India in IPCL was one of the most watched events of its time. On 4th June 2002, Reliance Petroinvestments Limited (RPIL) paid Rs.14.91 billion (US$338.86 million) to the Government of India towards 26% equity of IPCL. At this stage the Government held nearly 34% of the company's paid up equity. Later, RPIL under the guidelines of the SEBI for acquisition made on open offer to other IPCL shareholders. Through this route RPIL acquired another 20% of IPCL's paid up capital at Rs.231 (US $ 5.25) per equity share. Earlier IPCL had expanded its equity by making an initial public offer in October/November 1992. Today RPIL is the single largest shareholder in IPCL with 46% holding. The government of India divested its entire equity in favour of the public in February/March 2004.

Industry Overview

IPCL, one of the India's leading petrochemical products company has been classified as operating in 'non-core' sector. The total paid up equity of the company is Rs. 248.22 crore, out of which Government holds shares of Rs.148.80 crore. The equity sold to the strategic partner would be of face value Rs.64.54 crore (26.6%). The Government on 16.12.1998 had decided 'in principle' to the disinvestment in IPCL through strategic sale. IPCL's first petrochemical complex at Vadodara commenced production of aromatics in 1973 and a Naphtha cracker plant with a wide range of petrochemicals. The demand for petrochemicals in India has grown from half a million tones in the mid-seventies to nearly six million tones during the year 2007. IPCL'S production needs more than 25% of this demand. This erstwhile government owned and operated company is now a leading integrated manufacturer of petrochemical products. IPCL is the second largest petrochemical company in India, next to reliance industries till the year 2002.

Internal Controls

The Company has a proper and adequate system of internal controls to ensure that all assets are safeguarded and protected against loss from un authorised use or disposition and that transactions are authorised, recorded and reported correctly. The internal control systems are supplemented by an extensive programme of internal audits, review by management, guidelines and procedures. The internal control systems are designed to ensure that the financial and other records are reliable for preparing the financial statements and other data and for maintaining the accountability of assets. The use of SAP financial and business management systems, which provide a high level of system based checks and controls, have helped in improving efficiency and effectiveness of the Company's internal control systems.

Human Resources

The Company regards its human resources as one of its prime resources. A continuous effort for improving contribution of its human resources towards attainment of organizational goals has been the area of focus. Fiscal 2004-05 was a year for stabilization and consolidation in the process of change management, growth and development. The human resource processes and systems are being geared for business focussed and competency driven performance.

IPCL's employee strength as on March 31, 2005 was 11,088 as compared to the strength of 11,294 as on March 31, 2004.

Number of employees with professional qualification:

Qualification	*No. of Employees*
Ph.D	48
Engineers	1,064
MBAs	143
CA/ACWA/CS/IAAS/MFM/SAS/LLB	70

Environment Safety

The enterprise has made successive efforts in identifying energy conservation projects that qualify for registration as CDM (Clean Development Mechanism) projects with United Nations Framework Conservation on Climate Change under the Kyoto Protocol. Two projects "Conversion of totally condensing STG into extraction type" and "Heat integration through Pinch Technology in (1) LAB Plant, (2) PX Plant", have been identified as potential CDM projects from the site leading to Certified Emission Reductions (CER) by 52,000 units/year *High because of Flood. At the Hazira plant, over 40 energy The Hazira unit has implemented an innovative energy conservation project at its aromatics plant. The innovation is in terms of process modification by changing the sequence of operation in the BTX separation train without compromising the quality of final products. The Jamnagar unit has identified seven projects as potential CDM projects and one of the projects has been submitted for Host country approval. The potential CER credit will be 36,600 units/year from the above two projects and is expected to bring in a revenue of around 300,000 US$/annum to the company. Composites development and its applications in furniture sectors in addition to the transparent PVC grades development.

Corporate Social Responsibility

Towards community assistance and social development, RIL has provided financial as well as administrative support for supplying drinking water to villages in the vicinity of its manufacturing site and also established a primary health center. RIL also helps the local school children through distribution of books annually. Financial assistance is offered to the cultural functions of the villagers and for conducting medical camps and sports events annually.

Financial Performance

Sales and Services

The sales and services increased by 22 per cent from Rs 73,164 crore in the year 204-05 to Rs 89,124 crore (US$ 19,976 million). In the year 2005-06. The enterprise scaled the unique milestone of becoming the first Indian private sector company to record a net profit of over US$ 2 billion thereby doubling its profit in a span of just 24 months.

Capital Employed

The total capital employed by the enterprise increased by 52.61 percent from Rs.47,290.13 crore in 2005-06 to Rs.72,171.41 crore in the year 2006-07.

Dividends

The enterprise has recommended a dividend of Rs. 10.00 per Equity Share (last year Rs. 7.50 per Equity Share) on

139,35,08,041 Equity Shares of Rs 10/- each for the financial year 2005-06, the enterprise has consistently increased dividend paid out for the past 14 years. In the past 5 years, the dividend paid out has increased at the rate of 25.5% on an annual basis.

Reserves and Surplus

Reserves and Surplus aggregated Rs.49, 804.26 crore during 2006-07 as against Rs. 40,403.32 crore during 2005-06.

To analyse the performance of selected companies certain key ratios are taken into account. In the case of IPCL there is an improvement in such ratios from pre-privatisation period to post-privatisation. Profit Before Depreciation, Interest and Taxes (PBDIT)/Sales moved from 32.42 to 18.83 in the post-privatisation period. On the other hand Profit After Tax (PAT)/Sales moved from 14.86 to 8.34, PBDIT/Assets moved from 15.08 to 23.10 PAT/Assets from 6.91 to 10.23, PBDIT/Equity from 448.51 to 716.04, PAT/Equity from 205.58 to 317.26. Sales/Total assets

Table 1 A
Financial Ratio Analysis

	Pre-Privatisation					
	1997	*1998*	*1999*	*2000*	*2001*	*2002*
PBDIT/Sales	32.42	26.62	22.86	21.27	21.56	10.05
PAT/Sales	14.86	6.54	0.76	3.78	4.22	-0.46
PBDIT/Assets	15.08	11.15	9.81	11.41	15.14	10.27
PAT/Assets	6.91	2.74	0.33	2.03	2.97	-0.47
PBDIT/Equity	448.51	399.61	356.24	425.71	510.45	344.79
PAT/Equity	205.58	98.18	11.83	75.73	99.94	-15.86
Sales/Total Assets	46.52	41.88	42.90	53.64	70.22	102.27
Total debt/Total Assets	44.53	48.59	51.44	50.95	51.66	50.27
CA/CL	184.46	192.42	105.48	55.62	98.79	70.28
employees	14520	14120	13904	13756	13802	13840

Source: Compiled from Appendix 1A..

Graph 1
Pre and Post Privatisation Performance

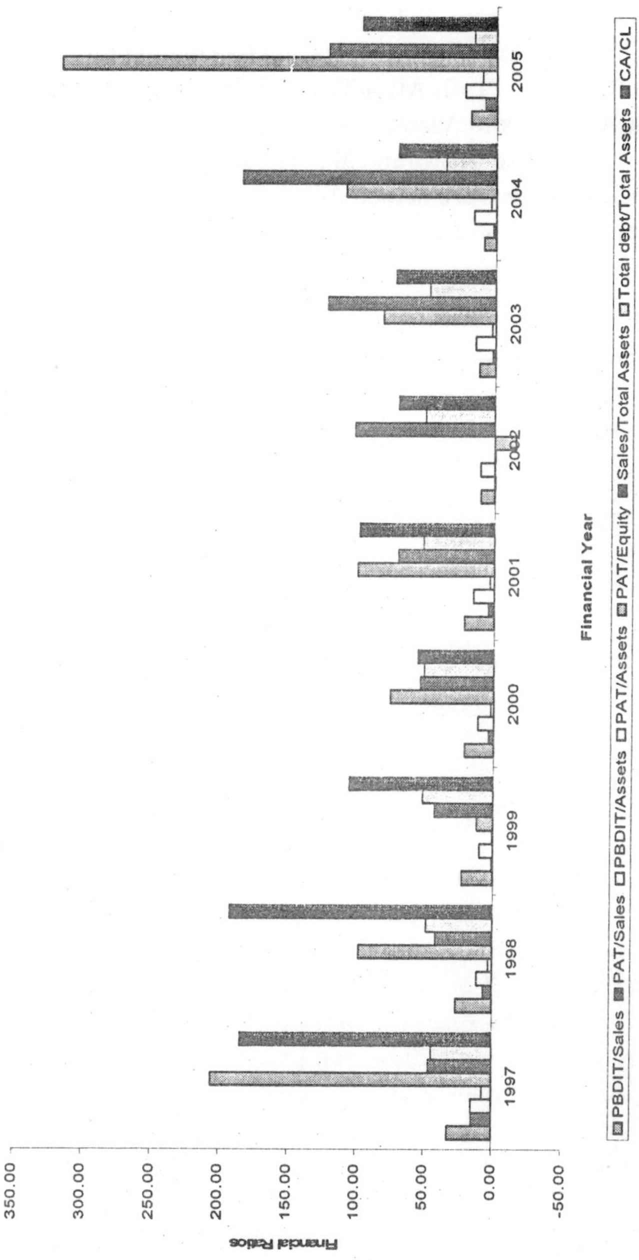

from 46.52 to 122.66 Total Debt/Assets from 44.53 to 16.24 and Current Ratio from 184.46 to 98.29.The ratios indicates that after privatization the organization has given more importance to profitability. Profit After Tax to Sales remained constant but Profit After Tax to Assets declined significantly.

To analyse the financial performance of IPCL, certain key financial ratios were selected like Return on Sales, Return on Equity, Return on Assets.

Table 1 B
Financial Ratio Analysis

	Post-Privatisation		
	2003	*2004*	*2005*
PBDIT/Sales	11.83	8.75	18.83
PAT/Sales	2.05	2.01	8.34
PBDIT/Assets	14.52	16.22	23.10
PAT/Assets	2.52	3.73	10.23
PBDIT/Equity	473.30	477.84	716.04
PAT/Equity	81.98	109.84	317.26
Sales/Total Assets	122.80	185.37	122.66
Total debt/Total Assets	47.90	36.71	16.24
CA/CL	72.97	71.63	98.29
employees	13306	11294	11088

Source: Compiled from Appendix 1B.

Return on Sales (ROS) Ratio

This ratio is widely used to evaluate an enterprise operational efficiency. ROS is also known as a firm's "operating profit margin". It is calculated using the formula Profit Before Depreciation Interest and Taxes/Sales. This measure is helpful to management, providing insight into how much profit is being produced per rupee of sales. As with many ratios, it is best to compare the enterprise's ROS over time to look for trends, and compare it to other companies in the industry. An increasing ROS indicates the enterprise is growing more efficient, while a decreasing ROS could signal looming financial troubles.

Graph 2
Return on Sales

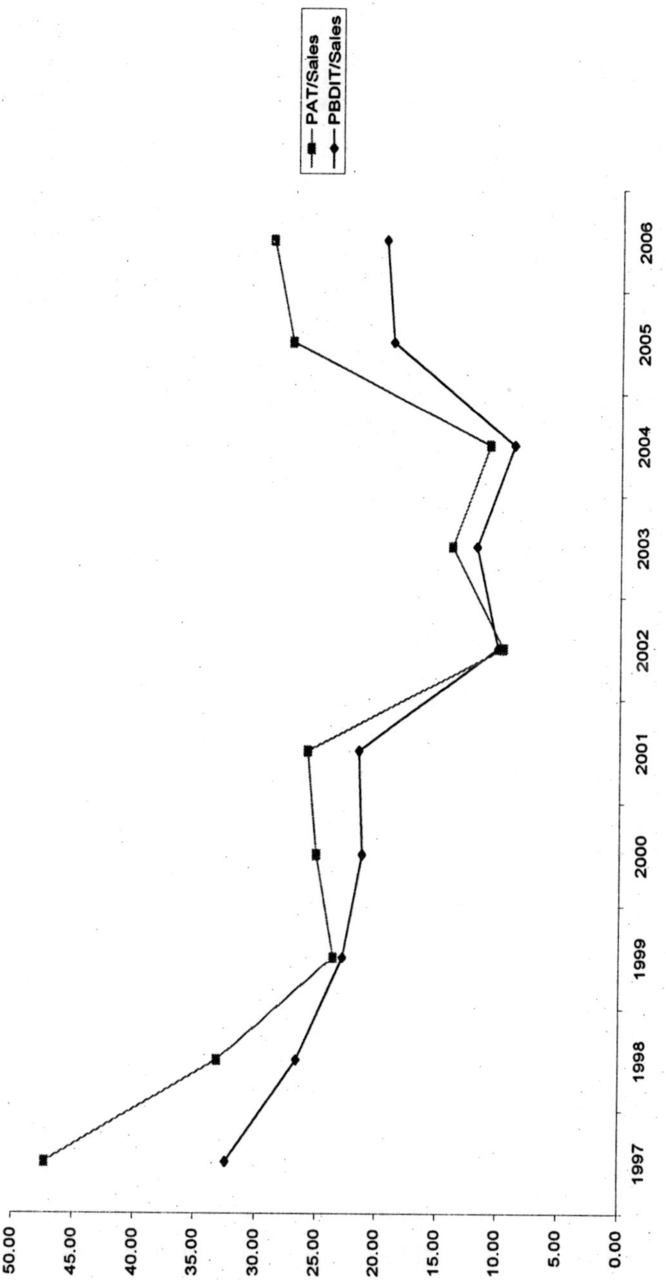

Table 2 shows the paired samples t-test for PBDIT/Sales, Pat/Sales in pre-privatisation period and in the post-privatisation period. It is observed that for pair 1&2 (Return on Sales (ROS)) the mean difference is 8.35 and -1.61 and standard deviation is 7.04 and 4.41 and standard error is 3.52 and 2.2 and t-values are 2.37 and -.73 respectively and the corresponding significance value is .09 and .51 which is greater than 0.05 per cent significance level. This signifies that there is no significant difference in Return on Sales (PBDIT/Sales and PAT/Sales) in the pre-privatisation period and post-privatisation period. Hence the null hypothesis Return on Sales in Per-privatisation period is equal to Return on Sales in the post-privatisation period is accepted.

Table 2
Paired Samples T-Test

		Mean Difference	*Std. Deviation*	*Std.Error Mean*	*t*	*df*	*Sig (2-tailed)*
Pair 1	PBDIT/Sales pre PBDIT/Sales post	8.35	7.04	3.52	2.37	3	.09
Pair 2	PAT/Sales Pre PAT/Sales Post	-1.61	4.41	2.20	-.73	3	.51

The graph shows a increasing trend in case of return on sales in the post privatisation period.

Return on Assets (ROA) Ratio:

Return on Assets is an indicator of how profitable an enterprise is relative to its total assets. ROA gives an idea as to how efficient management is at using its assets to generate earnings. Calculated by dividing a Enterprise's annual earnings by its total assets, ROA is displayed as a percentage. Sometimes this is referred to as "return on investment". ROA explains the earnings that were generated from invested capital (assets). ROA for public companies can vary substantially and will be highly dependent on the industry. This is why when using ROA as a comparative measure, it is best to compare it against a Enterprise's previous ROA numbers or the ROA of a similar Enterprise. The assets of the Enterprise are comprised of both debt and equity. Both of these types of financing are used to fund the operations of the Enterprise. The ROA figure gives investors an idea of how effectively the Enterprise is converting the money it has to invest into net income. The higher the ROA number, the better, because the Enterprise is earning more money on less investment.

Table 3 shows the paired samples t-test for PBDIT/Assets, PAT/Assets in pre-privatisation period and the post-privatisation period. From the table it is observed that for pair 1&2 (Return on Assets (ROA)) the mean difference is -7.2 and -4.8 and standard deviation is 3.4 and 4.01 and standard error is 1.72 and 2.00 and t-values are -4.2 and -2.4 respectively and the corresponding significance values are 0.02 and 0.09. Here PBDIT/Assets ratio is less than 0.05 per cent significance level. This signifies that

Table 3
Paired Samples T-Test

		Mean Difference	*Std. Deviation*	*Std. Error Mean*	*t*	*df*	*Sig (2-tailed)*
Pair 1	PBDIT/Assets pre PBDIT/Assets post	-7.2	3.44	1.72	-4.2	3	.02
Pair 2	PAT/Assets Pre PAT/Assets Post	-4.8	4.01	2.00	-2.4	3	.09

Graph 3
Return on Assets

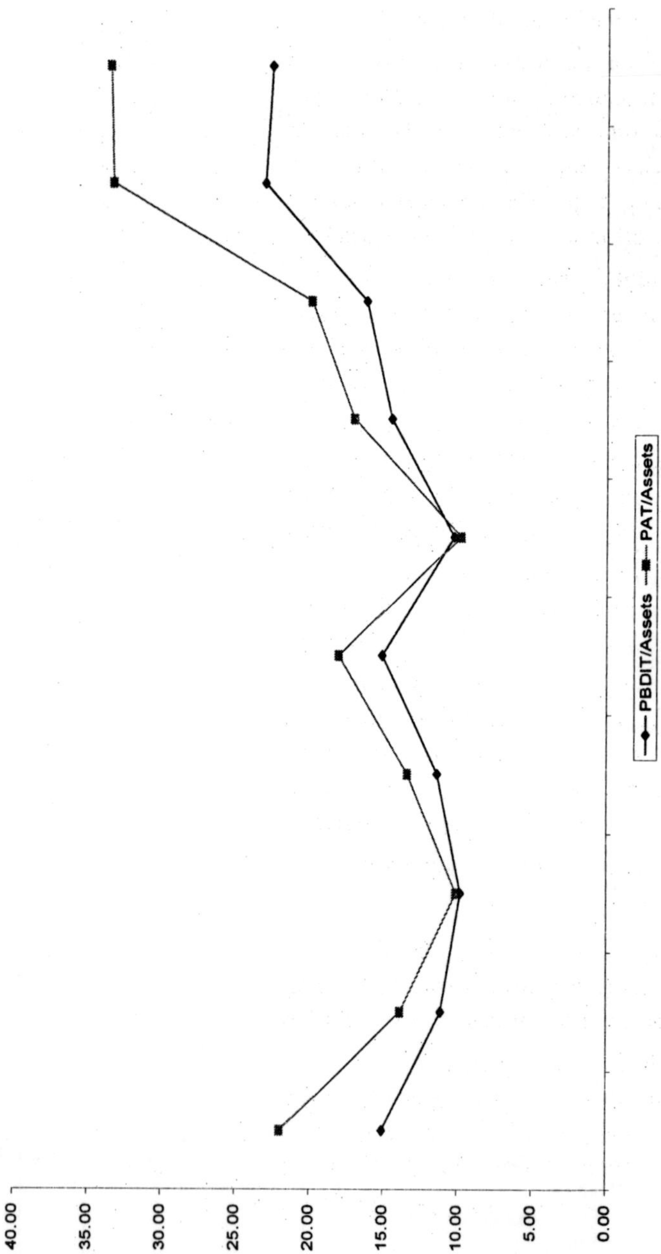

there is a significant difference in Return on Assets (PBDIT/ Assets) in the pre-privatisation period and post-privatisation period. Hence the null hypothesis Return on Assets in Per-privatisation period is equal to Return on Assets in the post-privatisation period is rejected. Graph 3 also clearly shows that after privatisation there is an improvement in the performance.

Return on Equity (ROE) Ratio

Return on Equity is a measure of an enterprise profitability that reveals how much profit an enterprise generates with the money that shareholders have invested. ROE is useful for comparing the profitability of an enterprise to that of other firms in the same industry.

Table 4 shows that paired samples t-test for PBDIT/Equity, PAT/Equity in pre-privatisation period and in the post-privatisation period. From the table it is observed that for pair 1&2 (Return on Equity (ROE)) the mean difference is-203.50 and -156.58 and standard deviation is 124.75 and 143.68 and standard error is 62.37 and 71.84 and t-values are -3.2 and -2.18 respectively and the corresponding significance values are 0.04 and 0.11. Here PBDIT/Equity ratio is less than 0.05 per cent significance level. This signifies that there is a significant

Table 4
Paired Samples T-Test

		Mean Differe-nce	*Std. De-viation*	*Std. Er-or Mean*	*t*	*df*	*Sig (2-tailed)*
Pair 1	PBDIT/Equity pre PBDIT/Equity post	-203.50	124.75	62.3	-3.26	3	.04
Pair 2	PAT/Equity Pre PAT/Equity Post	-156.58	143.68	71.84	-2.18	3	.11

Graph 4
Return on Equity

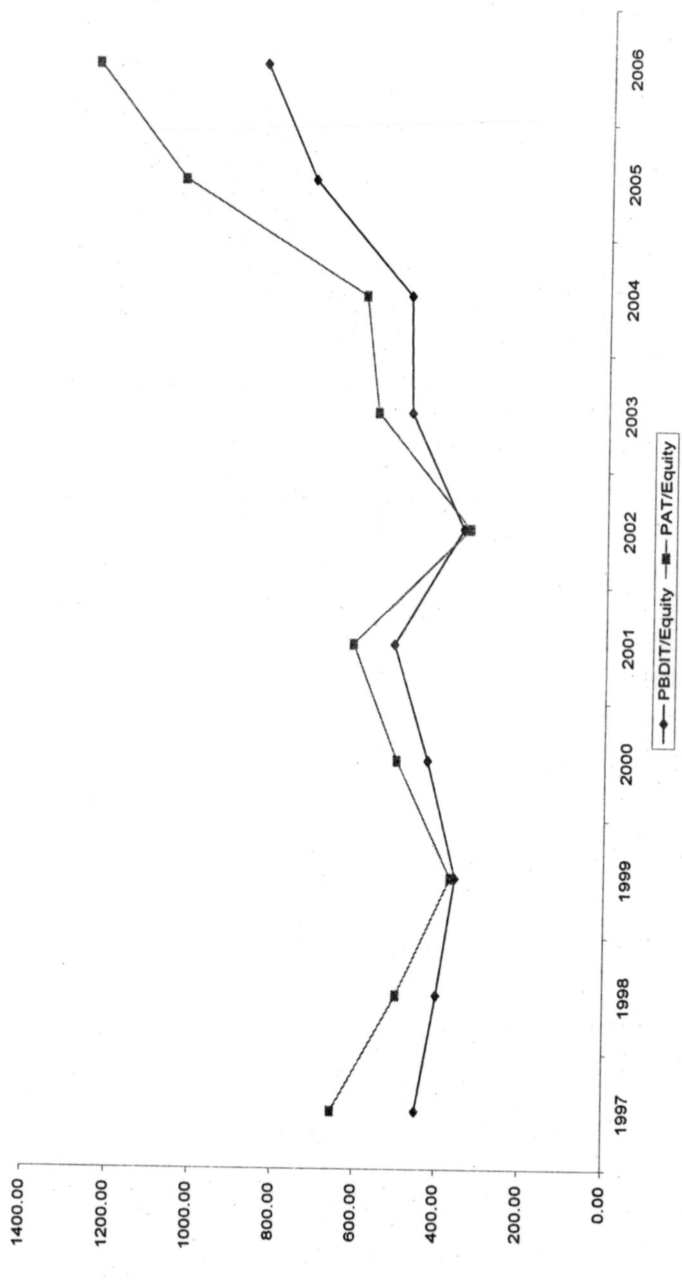

difference in Return on Assets (PBDIT/Assets) in the pre-privatisation period and post-privatisation period. Hence the null hypothesis Return on Assets in Per-privatisation period is equal to Return on Assets in the post-privatisation period is rejected. Graph 6.6.4 also clearly shows that after privatisation there is an improvement in the performance.

Asset Turnover Ratio

This ratio is useful to determine the amount of sales that are generated from each rupee of assets. Enterprises with low profit margins tend to have high asset turnover, those with high profit margins have low asset turnover.

Table 5 shows the paired samples t-test for Sales/Total Assets in pre-privatisation period and post-privatisation period. From the table it is observed that for pair 1 (Asset Turn Over) the mean difference is -84.64 and standard deviation is 41.16 and standard error is 20.58 and t-value is -4.12 and the corresponding significance value is .02 which is less than 0.05 per cent significance level. This signifies that there is a significant difference (i.e., improvement in financial performance) in Asset Turn Over in the pre-privatisation period and post-privatisation period. Hence the null hypothesis (Asset Turnover ratio in Per-privatisation period is equal to Asset Turnover ratio in the post-privatisation period) is rejected. The improvement in the financial performance after privatisation is clearly seen from Graph 5.

Table 5
Paired Samples T-Test

		Mean Difference	*Std. Deviation*	*Std. Error Mean*	*t*	*df*	*Sig (2-tailed)*
Pair 1	Sales/Total Assets Pre Sales/Total Assets Post	-84.64	41.16	20.58	-4.12	3	.02

Graph 5
Asset Turnover Ratio

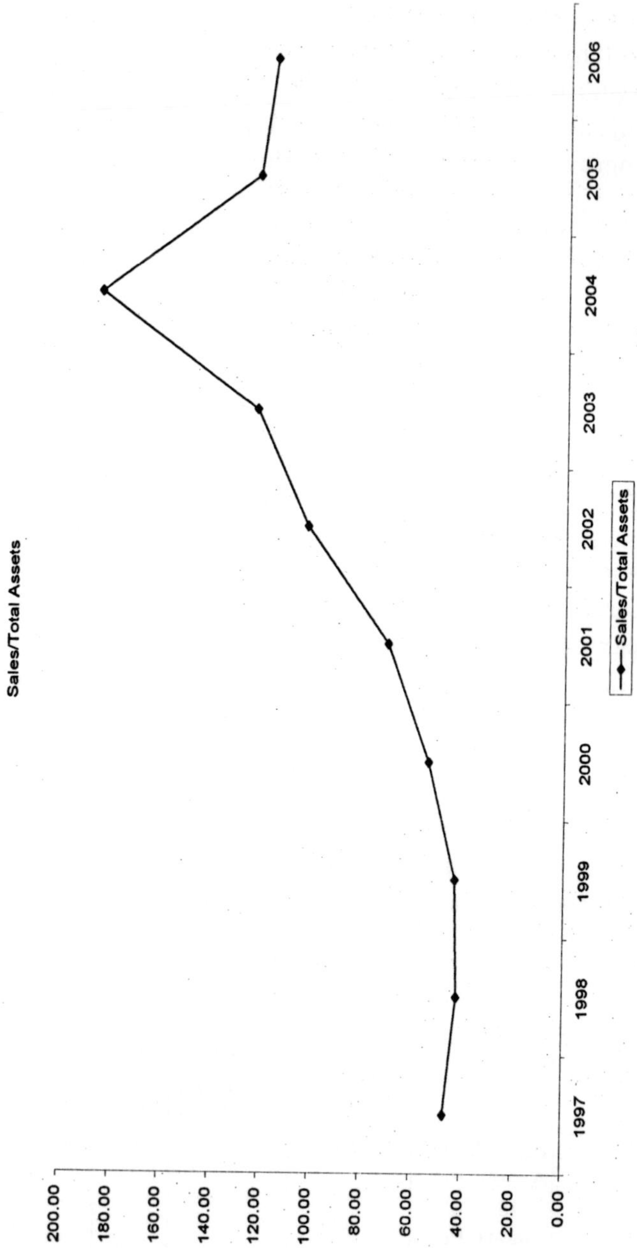

Debt Equity Ratio

The debt/asset ratio (Total liabilities divided by total assets) shows the proportion of enterprise assets which are financed through debt. If the ratio is less than one, most of the enterprise assets are financed through equity. If the ratio is greater than one, most of the enterprise assets are financed through debt. Enterprises with high debt/asset ratios are said to be "highly leveraged," and could be in danger if creditors start to demand repayment of debt.

Table 6 shows that paired sample test for Total Debt/Total Assets in pre-privatisation period and in the post-privatisation period is showed where in paired differences, t-test and significance are represented. From the table it is observed that for pair 1 (Debt Equity Ratio) the mean difference is -22.67 and standard deviation is 18.29 and standard error is 9.14 and t-value is -2.47 and the corresponding significance value is .09 which is slightly greater than 0.05 per cent significance level. This signifies that there is no significant difference in Debt-Equity ratio in the pre-privatisation period and post-privatisation period. Hence the null hypothesis (Debt-Equity ratio in Per-privatisation period is equal to Debt-Equity ratio in the post-privatisation period) is accepted.

Table 6
Paired Samples T-Test

		Mean Difference	*Std. Deviation*	*Std. Error Mean*	*t*	*df*	*Sig (2-tailed)*
Pair 1	Total Debt/Total Assets Pre Total Debt/Total Assets Post	22.62	18.29	9.14	2.47	3	.09

Graph 6
Debt Equity Ratio

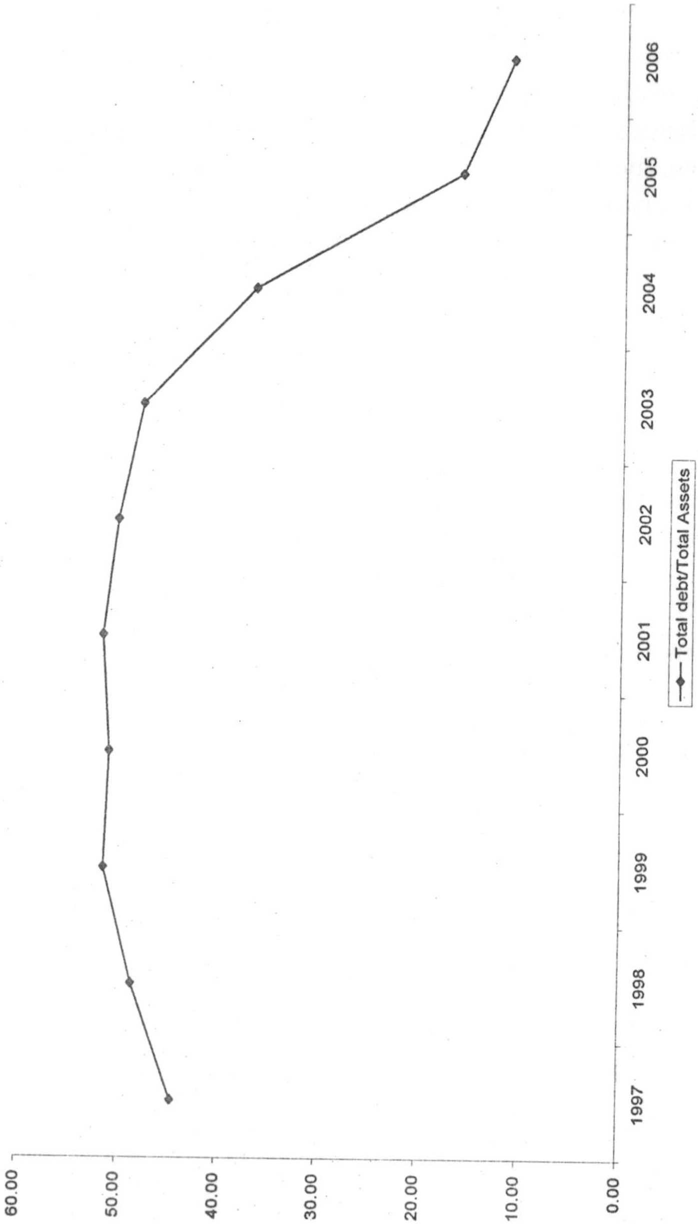

The graph on Debt-Equity in the pre and post privatisation period shows an decreasing trend. This means that most of the enterprise assets are financed through equity and the enterprise is risk free.

Conclusion

The econometric analysis proves that there is a significant improvement in the financial performance of the enterprise after privatisation. Indian Petrochemicals Corporation Limited (IPCL) completing three years under the management of the Reliance Group, in highlighting the fact that net profits have multiplied more than seven-fold; from Rs. 107 crore (US$ 22 million) in the year 2001-02 to Rs. 786 crore (US$ 180 million) in the year 2004-05. The last year alone saw an increase in net profits by 188% on revenues of Rs.9,386 crore (US$ 2,146 million). This seven-fold increase in net profit and associated shareholder returns, was possible by an accent on significant improvements in operational and labour productivity, synergistic integration with Reliance operations and prudent financial management. An early phase of a cyclical upswing in petrochemical markets in the last year also contributed to IPCL's stellar profit performance. As a result, the Board of Directors of IPCL have recommended to raise the dividend rate to 45% from 25% paid last year. This is the highest dividend ever in IPCL.

Appendix 1 A
Financial Performance of IPCL During Pre-Privatisation Period

(Rs. In crore)

IPCL						
	1997	*1998*	*1999*	*2000*	*2001*	*2002*
PBDIT	1113.11	991.9	884.27	1060.22	1271.28	858.7
Sales	3433.82	3726.76	3868.79	4985.23	5895.18	8548.26
PAT	510.2	243.69	29.36	188.6	248.91	-39.51

(Contd.)

(Contd.Appendix-1A)

IPCL						
	1997	*1998*	*1999*	*2000*	*2001*	*2002*
Assets	7381.16	8898.52	9018.52	9293.67	8394.82	8358.3
Equity	248.18	248.22	248.22	249.05	249.05	249.05
No.of Employees	0	0	13904	0	0	13840
Total Debt	3286.73	4323.7	4639.14	4734.77	4336.89	4201.58
Dividend	109.2	109.22	27.3	60.57	82.07	49.65
Current Assets	2934.45	3447.4	2348.58	2528.58	2083	1738.93
Current Liabilities	1590.84	1791.57	2226.57	4545.95	2108.52	2474.24
Debt-Equity Ratio	1.16	1.46	1.57	1.6	1.38	1.5

Source: Annual Report of IPCL, CMIE Prowess Data Base.

Appendix 1 B
Financial Performance of IPCL During Post-Privatisation Period

(Rs. In crore)

	2003	*2004*	*2005*
PBDIT	1178.76	1190.05	1783.29
Sales	9967.34	13602.49	9470.4
PAT	204.17	273.56	790.14
Assets	8116.69	7337.98	7720.8
Equity	249.05	249.05	249.05
No.of Employees	13306	11294	11088
Total Debt	3888.19	2693.96	1253.64
Dividend	63	70	127.53
Current Assets	1841.69	1600.89	2432.17
Current Liabilities	2524.06	2234.84	2474.58
Debt-Equity Ratio	1.72	1.19	0.43

Source: Annual Report of IPCL, CMIE Prowess Data Base.

Case 7
Indo Burma Petroleum Limited (IBP)

Back ground

Indo Burma Petroleum Limited (IBP) which was established in the year 1909 is the only Petroleum Company in India having diversified activities viz. Petroleum, Explosives and cryogenics, contributing to the national growth in the core and high technology sector of the economy related to Petroleum/ energy, Explosives and cryogenics. The business group is entrusted with the duty of manufacturing and marketing world-class cryo-vessels for industrial and biological applications. This Group has maintained its past leadership position in the manufacturing and marketing of small cryogenics containers. By applying the high vacuum technology, this Group has successfully developed larger capacity super insulated cryogenics containers having capacity as large as 12,000 liters, which are utilized for transport and storage of liquid Nitrogen, Oxygen and Argon. IBP has been merged with Indian Oil Corporation with effect from 2.5.2007.

Disinvestment

Government of India (GOI) finalized strategic sale of 33.58% of the IBP's equity out of Government holding of 59.58% on 5.02.2002. The total paid up equity of the company is Rs. 22.15 crore, out of which Government holds shares of Rs. 13.20 crore. The equity sold to strategic partners would be of face value Rs. 7.44 crore. The company is engaged in the retail marketing of petroleum products, manufacture and marketing of industrial explosives and Cryo-Vessels for industrial and biological applications. Unlike other oil companies in the public sector it does not own any refining capacity and markets products of other refineries. Based on competitive bidding, M/s. HSBC Securities and Capital Markets (India) Ltd. (HSBC) were appointed as Advisor for the transaction in December 2000 on a fee of 0.65% of the transaction value. The legal advisors were Amarchand Mangaldas A. Suresh Shroff and Co. and the Asset Valuers were M/s S.K.Godbole & Associates, Mr. A.P. Saxena, M/s Meticulous Consultants Pvt. Ltd., Mr. N.K. Chakravarty and M/s M.M. Kulkarni. Interested investors submitted expression of interest (EoI) in February 2001. The short listed parties completed the due diligence exercise and the transaction documents were agreed upon, after a number of rounds of discussions with bidders. Thereafter, based on these documents, Govt. invited financial bids from the bidders on 31.1.2002. Seven bidders, including PEs, national and international bidders, submitted the bids. The CCD, in its meeting on 5.2.2002 considered the recommendations of the Evaluation Committee, the IMG and CGD and approved the bids of Indian Oil Corporation for a price of Rs. 1153.68 crore i.e. Rs. 1551/- per share at a P.E. ratio of 63.

Industry Overview

The importance of petroleum sector is evident from the fact that petroleum products refining in the country has increased to 120.47 million metric tonnes (MMT) during 2004-05 compared to 115.78 MMT in 2003-04, which represents a growth of about 4%.

With progressive industrialization of the country and growth in Gross Domestic Product, the consumption of petroleum products has shown steady increase aggregating 111.70 MMT during 2004-05 as against 107.75 MMT in the year 2003-04, reflecting a growth of 3.7%.

The demand for petroleum products is linked to the socio-economic development of the country. The Indian economy has been on a long-term growth trend since the 1980s, with the GDP growth rate moving since then beyond 3.5% a year to an average rate of 6% per year in the 1990s. Over the past five years, the GDP has grown at an average of 5.6% per year. While the International Monetary Fund has projected a growth rate of 6% to 6.5%, as per the National Common Minimum Programme of the Government of India, the GDP growth is expected to be anywhere between 7- 8%.

India is presently undergoing major economic and industrial reforms for integrating its economy with the global economy. With the continuing reforms and expected high growth in almost all the economic sectors, the demand for petroleum products is expected to show a compounded growth of about 3.5 - 4% in the immediate future. Policy changes are also envisioned for making the petroleum sector globally competitive.

Petroleum marketing activities, which forms the core business of your Company, consists of four major activities viz., Retail, Consumer, Lubes and LPG. At present, marketing of petroleum products in India is dominated by the four public sector companies viz., Indian Oil, Hindustan Petroleum, Bharat Petroleum and IBP. The vast expanse of the country and its large populace is served through an extensive retail network of these companies, comprising of about 26,540 Retail Outlets, 6,588 SKO agencies and 9,001 LPG distributorships. Ambitious programmes for modernizing the Retail Outlets and bringing them at par with international standards, have been initiated by all the petroleum marketing companies. Besides catering to the requirements of the country's retail customers, the petroleum marketing companies in the public sector also cater to bulk of the requirements of the industrial units in the country, by way of direct supplies. These industries operate in important areas like shipping, transport, aviation, power, petrochemicals, fertilizers, steel, mining, etc. With the liberalization and opening up of the economy, industrial activity is bound to accelerate, thereby generating additional demand for petroleum products in the industrial and infrastructure segments.

In the liberalized scenario, the Government had opened the refining sector to the joint sector as well as to the private sector, for achieving rapid growth. Currently, the country has 18 refineries, with total installed capacity of 127.4 MMT, which are owned and operated by both the public and private sector companies.

On the supply front, near stagnant domestic crude oil production is an area of concern, considering the increasing demand for petroleum products. To meet this supply-demand gap arising out of growing demand for petroleum products and resultant increase in requirement of crude oil for the refineries, substantial tonnage of crude oil is being imported by India. The New Exploration Licensing Programme has already been implemented by Government of India, which would help in adding to the oil and gas reserves of the country. In addition, the Government is also encouraging the domestic petroleum companies to acquire oil and gas assets overseas.

The amalgamation scheme for the proposed merger of IBP with Indian Oil has been approved by Board of Directors and a fair exchange ratio of 125 shares of Indian Oil for every 100 shares of IBP was recommended, subject to approval of the Government of India and other regulatory authorities. The swap ratio was recommended by the Board based on due diligence and relative valuation of the equity shares of Indian Oil and your Company carried out by the reputed accounting firm, Deloitte, Haskins and Sells & Co.

Internal Controls

The enterprise has in place a robust system of internal controls with the objectives of effective and efficient operation, correct and accurate reporting of financial transactions, compliance of the various applicable statutes and compliance of internal policies and procedures to protect the Company's interest. Towards this end, a well-defined organization structure, authority levels and internal policies / guidelines / rules for conducting business transactions are in place. In particular, the Company has in place a streamlined Delegation of Authority-cum-Purchase Procedure regulation to enable it to function systematically and in a transparent manner with due checks and balances. The internal control systems of the Company operate within the mechanism of preventive and corrective controls.

It is worth noting that the internal control systems are supplemented by Internal Audit Department, which reviews on a continuous basis, the adequacy of internal controls, adherence to management policies and compliance with laws and regulations of the country.

Human Resource Management

The enterprise has always emphasized on development and management of human resource, since it is a key driver for creating sustainable competitive advantage. The human resource philosophy of the enterprise is basically aimed at nurturing an organizational culture. that respects people and enables them to deliver high quality performance.

With the competitive environment requiring highly responsive mindsets, the enterprise aims at developing its human resource not only in terms of high quality performance and improved productivity but also in terms of achieving excellence on individual basis with emphasis on understanding the power of mind and its capability to innovate and respond proactively, thus translating into organizational excellence.

During the year 2004-05, the enterprise organized a number of training programmes and workshops in functional as well as developmental areas for, various sections of employees to hone their skills and capabilities and to enhance motivational levels. The training programmes included in-house conferences as well as seminars conducted by reputed external agencies. Training programmes were also organized based on Presidential Directives / Government Orders on reservation and concessions to SC, ST, OBC and physically challenged employees and maintenance of Reservation Rosters.

As part of the synergy between the enterprise and Indian Oil, training calendars and faculty assistance for conducting in-house training programmes were exchanged between the two companies. IBP employees were nominated for attending training programmes conducted by Indian Oil, and Indian Oil employees were nominated for training programmes organized by IBP. Infrastructural facilities at the training centers were also shared with each other.

IBP continued to maintain its tradition of healthy and harmonious industrial relations. The Company maintained a conducive and congenial work atmosphere with the support' and co-operation of the Trade Unions and the Officers' Association.

Corporate Social Responsibility

Towards corporate social responsibility the enterprise has organized a number of welfare activities under the Special Component Plan and Tribal Sub-Plans. In West Bengal financial assistance was extended for installation of tube-well, construction of primary school building, low-cost houses and sanitary facilities in villages and in drought-prone tribal areas of Jharkhand. Furniture and other accessories were provided to Neuropsychiatry Institute at Kolkata. Financial assistance was given for expansion of non- formal education centres run by Ramakrishna Mission in the 24 Parganas (North) of West Bengal. Donation was given for creation of 'IBP Endowment Scholarship' and 'IBP Endowment Documentation' at the University of Madras for awarding annual scholarships to two research students belonging to SC / ST category, and for subscribing to periodicals / journals for benefit of SC / ST research students.

Financial Performance

To analyse the financial performance of IBP in the pre and post-privatisation periods certain key ratios have taken. Table 6.7.1 explains that all the ratios that are selected for the study did not showed any significant improvement in the post-privatisation period. Multiple variations were observed among all the ratios in the pre as well as in the post privatisation period.

Table 1 A
Financial Ratio Analysis

Ratios	*Pre-Privatisation*					
	1997	*1998*	*1999*	*2000*	*2001*	*2002*
PBDIT/Sales	0.02	0.03	0.02	0.02	0.02	0.04
PAT/Sales	0.01	0.01	0.01	0.01	0.01	0.02
PBDIT/Assets	0.11	0.12	0.10	0.10	0.12	0.25
PAT/Assets	0.03	0.03	0.03	0.03	0.04	0.14
PBDIT/Equity	4.37	5.49	5.87	7.37	8.26	16.25
PAT/Equity	1.15	1.43	1.59	1.88	2.45	8.84
Sales/Total Assets	4.24	4.56	4.56	4.38	5.71	5.88
Total debt/Total Assets	0.48	0.48	0.45	0.40	0.29	0.00
CA/CL	2.13	1.88	1.48	1.21	1.05	0.85

Source: Compiled from Appendix 1A..

Table 6.7.1 B
Financial Ratio Analysis

	Post-Privatisation			
Ratios	*2003*	*2004*	*2005*	*2006*
PBDIT/Sales	0.02	0.04	0.01	0.51
PAT/Sales	0.01	0.02	0.00	0.07
PBDIT/Assets	0.10	0.16	0.05	3.24
PAT/Assets	0.05	0.09	0.02	0.49
PBDIT/Equity	8.56	17.07	6.44	7.03
PAT/Equity	3.96	9.69	2.66	6.16
Sales/Total Assets	4.62	4.39	5.11	6.9
Total debt/Total Assets	0.00	0.00	0.00	13.1
CA/CL	0.90	0.89	0.82	0.55

Source: Compiled from Appendix 1B.

Graph 1

Pre and Post Privatisation Performance

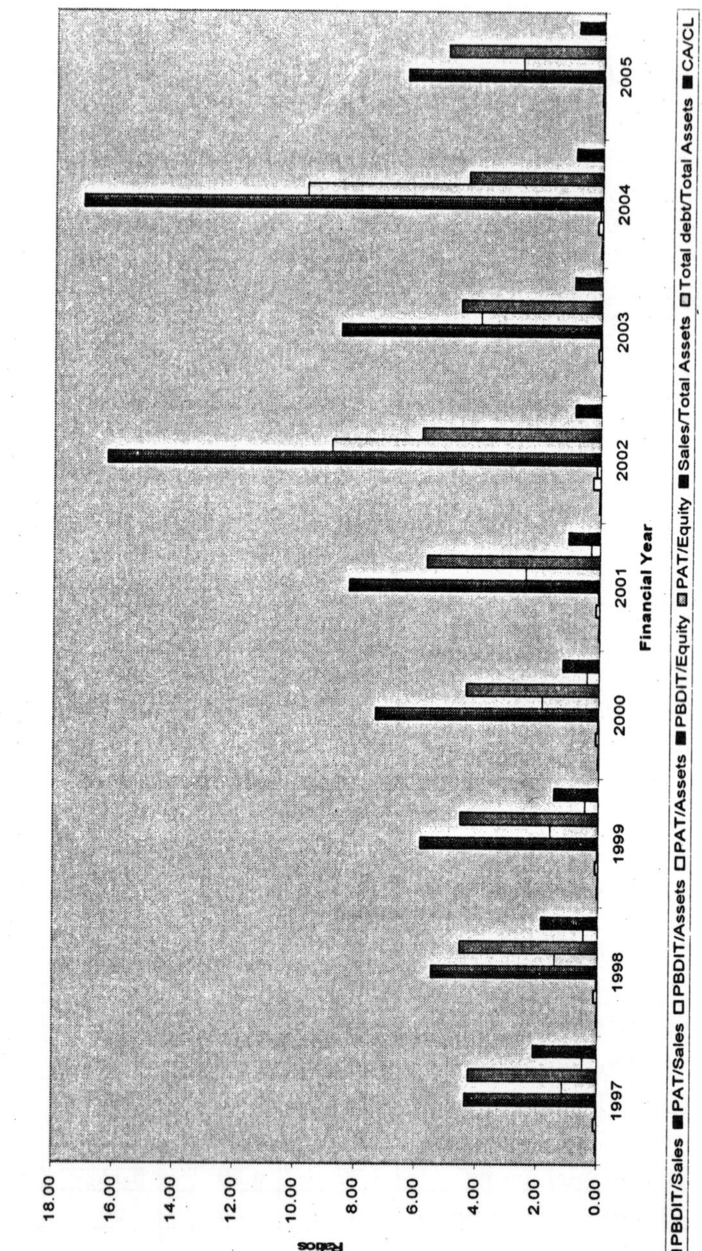

This scenario was proved using paired sample t-statistics with reference to Return on Sales, Return on Equity and Return on Assets an Current Assets/Current Liabilities.

Graph 1 shows that PBIT/Equity has improved in the post-privatisation period. This is a clear indication that the shareholders money which was invested in the post-privatisation period yield good profits.

Return on Sales (ROS) Ration

This ratio is widely used to evaluate an enterprise operational efficiency. ROS is also known as a firm's "operating profit margin". It is calculated using the formula Profit Before Depreciation Interest and Taxes/Sales. This measure is helpful to management, providing insight into how much profit is being produced per rupee of sales. As with many ratios, it is best to compare an enterprise's ROS over time to look for trends, and compare it to other companies in the industry. An increasing ROS indicates the enterprise is growing more efficient, while a decreasing ROS could signal looming financial troubles.

Table 2 shows the paired samples t-test for PBDIT/Sales, Pat/Sales in pre-privatisation and post-privatisation period. From the table it is observed that for pair 1&2 (Return on Sales (ROS))

Table 2
Paired Samples T-Test

		Mean Difference	*Std. Deviation*	*Std. Error Mean*	*t*	*df*	*Sig (2-tailed)*
Pair 1	PBDIT/Sales pre PBDIT/Sales post	-0.122	0.245	0.122	-0.99	3	0.3
Pair 2	PAT/Sales Pre PAT/Sales Post	-0.015	0.031	0.015	-0.96	3	0.4

Graph 2
Return on Sales

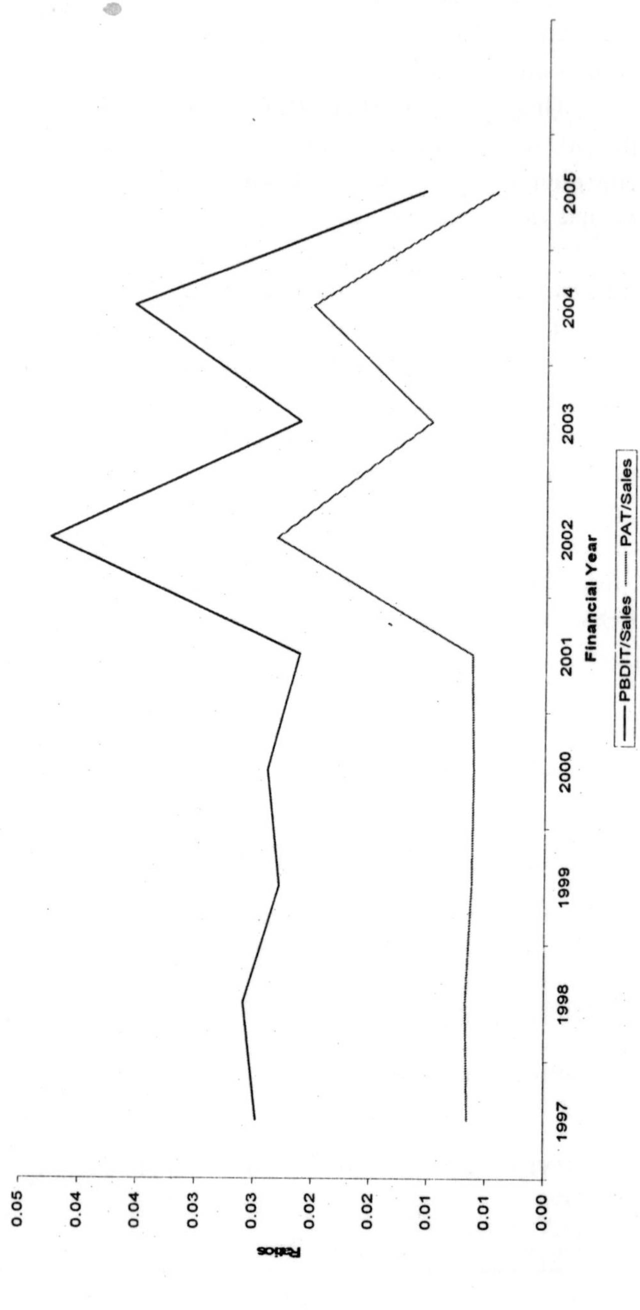

the mean difference is -0.122 and -0.015 and standard deviation is 0.245 and 0.031 and standard error is 0.122 and 0.015 and t-values are -0.99 and -0.96 respectively and the corresponding significance value is 0.39 and 0.40 which is greater than 0.05 per cent significance level. This signifies that there is no significant difference in Return on Sales (PBDIT/Sales and PAT/Sales) in the pre-privatisation period and post-privatisation period. Hence the null hypothesis Return on Sales in Per-privatisation period is equal to Return on Sales in the post-privatisation period is accepted.

Graph 2 shows that PBDIT to Sales and PAT to Sales have shown slight improvement in the post-privatisation period. during 2005-06 the profits have imprcved drastically. As the performance has not improved through out the years continuously the statistical results have not shown an significant change in the post privatisation period.

Return on Assets (ROA) Ratio

Return on Assets is an indicator of how profitable an enterprise is relative to its total assets. ROA gives an idea as to how efficient management is at using its assets to generate earnings. Calculated by dividing an enterprise's annual earnings by its total assets, ROA is displayed as a percentage. Sometimes this is referred to as "return on investment". ROA explains the earnings that were generated from invested capital (assets). ROA for public companies can vary substantially and will be highly dependent on the industry. This is why when using ROA as a comparative measure, it is best to compare it against an enterprise's previous ROA numbers or the ROA of a similar enterprise. The assets of the enterprise are comprised of both debt and equity. Both of these types of financing are used to fund the operations of the enterprise. The ROA figure gives investors an idea of how effectively the enterprise is converting the money it has to invest into net income. The higher the ROA number, the better, because the enterprise is earning more money on less investment.

Table 3 shows the paired samples t-test for PBDIT/Assets, PAT/Assets in pre-privatisation period and in post-privatisation period. From the table it is observed that for pair 1&2 (Return on Assets (ROA)) the mean difference is -0.77 and -0.13 and standard deviation is 1.56 and 0.215 and standard error is 0.78 and 0.107 and t-values are -0.99 and -1.2 respectively and the corresponding significance values are 0.39 and 0.314 which is greater than 0.05 per cent significance level. This signifies that there is no significant difference in Return on Assets (PBDIT/ Assets and PAT/Assets) in the pre-privatisation period and post-privatisation period. Hence the null hypothesis (Return on Assets in Per-privatisation period is equal to Return on Assets in the post-privatisation period) is accepted.

Table 3
Paired Samples T-Test

		Mean Difference	*Std. Deviation*	*Std. Error Mean*	*t*	*df*	*Sig (2-tailed)*
Pair 1	PBDIT/Sales pre PBDIT/Sales post	1.39	12.61	6.30	.220	3	.840
Pair 2	PAT/Sales pre PAT/Sales post	-1.63	9.38	4.69	-.349	3	.750

Graph 3 also shows that after privatisation the performance has showed wide flucations. As the period of study is very short i.e., three years, it is difficult to assess the performance improvement. It can be expected that over a period of ten year the performance will improve certainly as the IBP is merged with Indian Oil Corporation which is a profit making enterprise.

Graph 3
Return on Assets

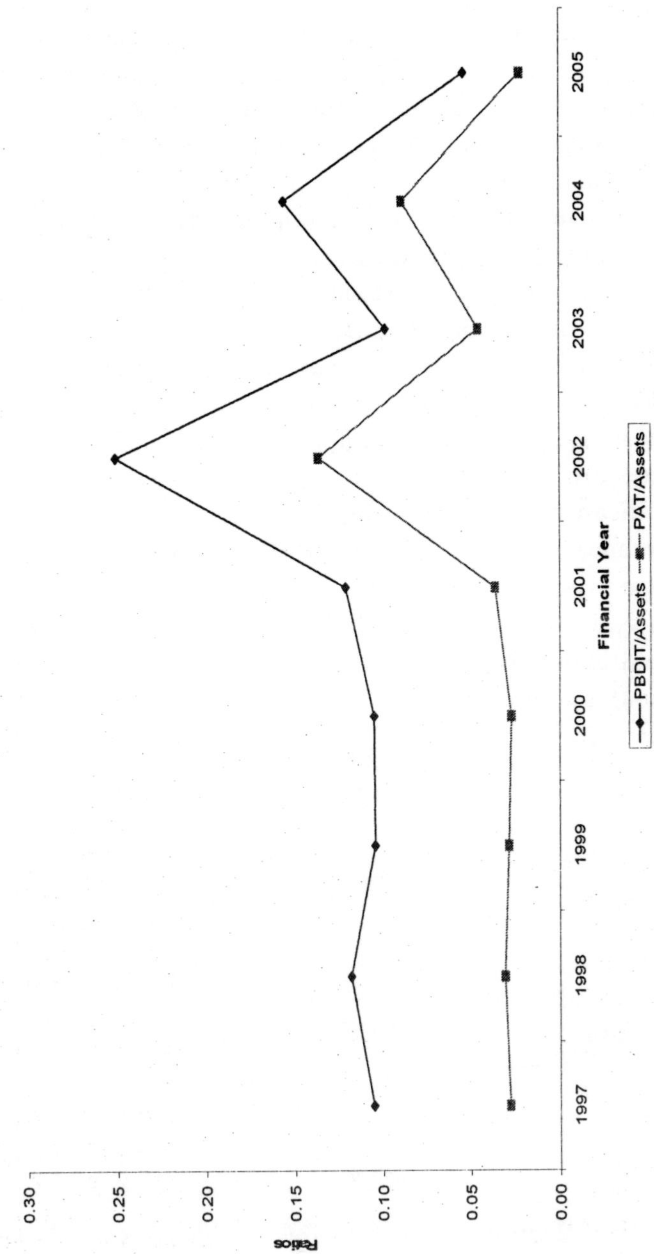

Return on Equity (ROE) Ratio

Return on Equity is a measure of an enterprise profitability that reveals how much profit an enterprise generates with the money that shareholders have invested. ROE is useful for comparing the profitability of an enterprise to that of other firms in the same industry.

Table 4 shows the paired samples t-test for PBDIT/Equity, PAT/Equity in pre-privatisation period and PBDIT/Equity, PAT/ Equity in the post-privatisation period. From the table it is observed that for pair 1&2 (Return on Equity (ROE)) the mean difference is -93.27 and -16.28 and standard deviation is 177.73 and 25.14 and standard error is 88.86 and 12.54 and t-values are -1.05 and -1.29 respectively and the corresponding significance values are .37 and 0.28 which are greater than 0.05 per cent significance level. This signifies that there is no significant difference in Return on Equity (PBDIT/Equity and PAT/Equity) in the pre-privatisation period and post-privatisation period. Hence the null hypothesis (Return on Equity in Per-privatisation period is equal to Return on Equity in the post-privatisation period) is accepted.

Table 4
Paired Samples T-Test

		Mean Difference	*Std. Deviation*	*Std. Error Mean*	*t*	*df*	*Sig (2-tailed)*
Pair 1 :	PBDIT/Equity pre PBDIT/Equity post	-93.27	177.73	88.86	-1.05	3	.37
Pair 2	PAT/Equity Pre PAT/Equity Post	-16.28	25.14	12.57	-1.29	3	.28

Graph.4
Return on Equity

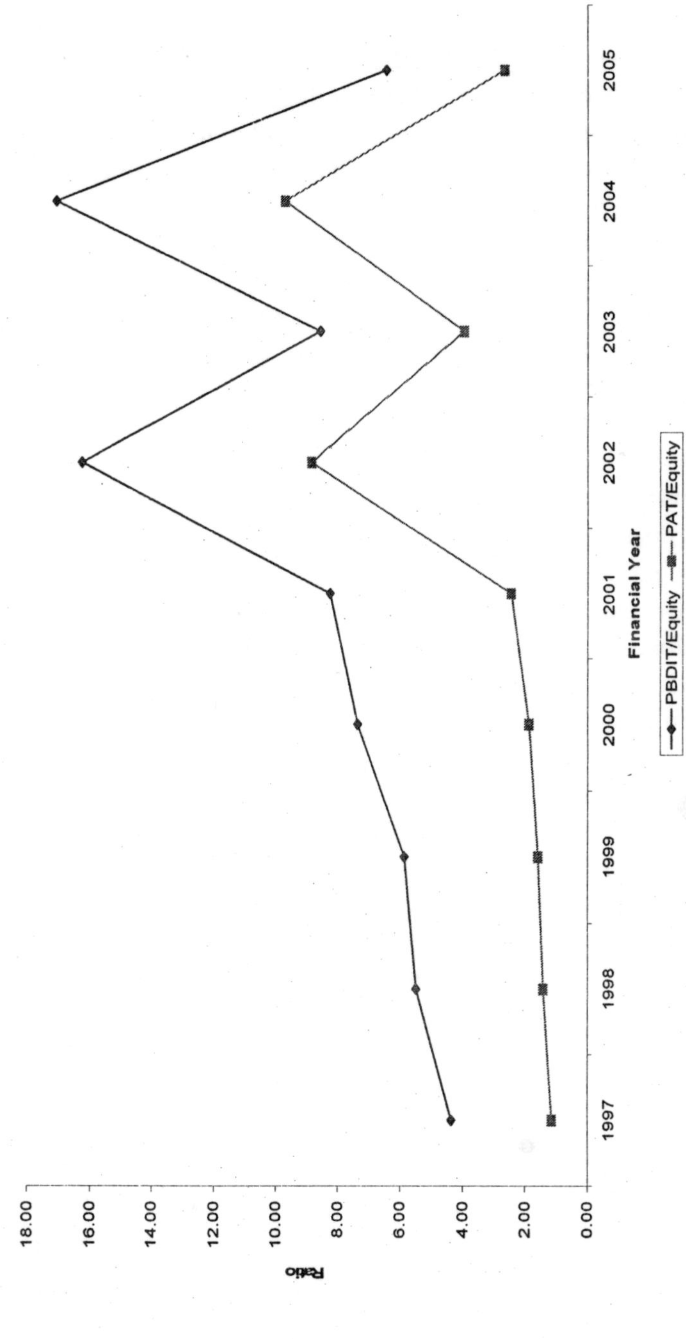

Graph 4 clearly shows that there are fluctuations in case of return on equity in the post-privatisation period. As the enterprise got merged with Indian Oil Corporation variety of changes have occurred in the shareholders pattern. This has influenced the return on equity to a considerable extent.

Asset Turnover Ratio

This ratio is useful to determine the amount of sales that are generated from each rupee of assets. Enterprises with low profit margins tend to have high asset turnover, those with high profit margins have low asset turnover.

Table 5 shows that paired sample test for Sales/Total Assets in pre-privatisation period and in the post-privatisation period is showed where in paired differences, t-test and significance are represented. From the table it is observed that for pair 1 (Asset Turn Over) the mean difference is -154.7 and standard deviation is 308.99 and standard error is 154.49 and t-value is -1.001 and the corresponding significance value is .39 which are greater than 0.05 per cent significance level. This signifies that there is no significant difference in Asset Turn Over in the pre-privatisation period and post-privatisation period. Hence the null hypothesis (Asset Turnover ratio in Per-privatisation period is equal to Asset Turnover ratio in the post-privatisation period) is accepted.

Table 5
Asset Turnover Ratio

		Mean	*Std. Deviation*	*Std. Error Mean*	*t*	*df*	*Sig (2-tailed)*
Pair 1	Sales/Total Assets Pre Sales/Total Assets Post	- 154.70	308.99	154.49	-1.001	3	.39

Graph 5
Asset Turnover Ratio

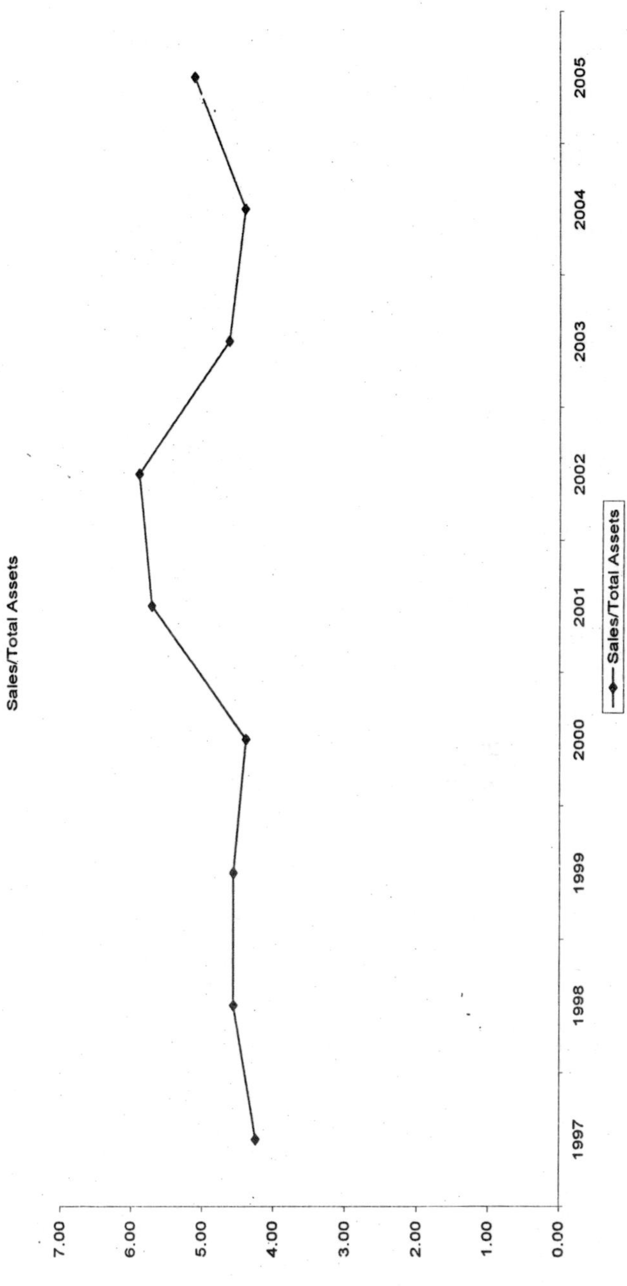

Graph 5 shows that the sales improved in the last two years after privatisation.

Debt Equity Ratio

The debt/asset ratio (Total liabilities divided by total assets) shows the proportion of enterprise assets which are financed through debt. If the ratio is less than one, most of the enterprise assets are financed through equity. If the ratio is greater than one, most of the enterprise assets are financed through debt. Enterprises with high debt/asset ratios are said to be "highly leveraged," and could be in danger if creditors start to demand repayment of debt.

Table 6 shows the paired samples t-test for Total Debt/ Total Assets in pre-privatisation period and in the post-privatisation period. From the table it is observed that for pair 1 (Debt Equity Ratio) the mean difference is -2.87 and standard deviation is 6.62 and standard error is 3.31 and t-value is -.86 and the corresponding significance value is .45 which is greater than 0.05 per cent significance level. This signifies that there is no significant difference in Debt-Equity ratio in the pre-privatisation period and post-privatisation period. Hence the null hypothesis (Debt-Equity ratio in Per-privatisation period is equal to Debt-Equity ratio in the post-privatisation period) is accepted.

Table 6
Paired Samples Test

		Mean Difference	*Std. Deviation*	*Std. Error Mean*	*t*	*df*	*Sig (2-tailed)*
Pair 1	Total Debt/Total Assets Pre Total Debt/Total Assets Post	-2.8	6.6	3.3	-.86	3	.45

Graph 6
Debt-Equity Ratio

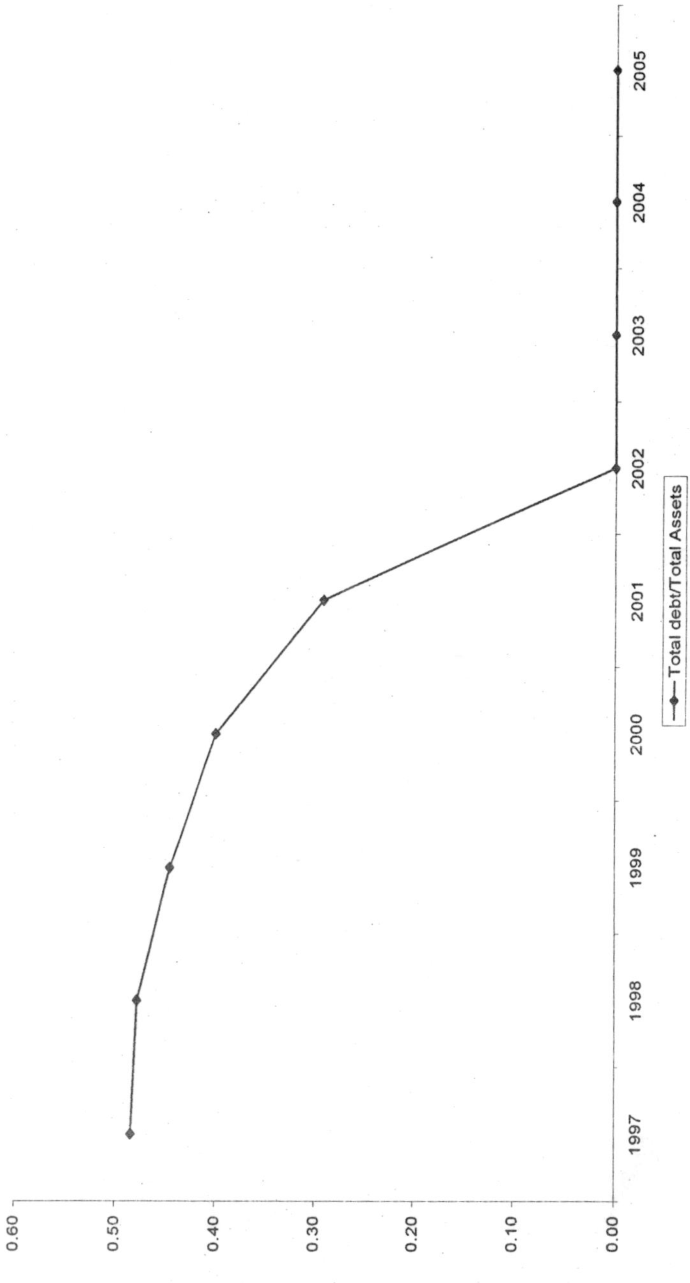

The graph on Debt-Equity in the pre and post privatisation period shows an decreasing trend in the post- privatisation period. This means that most of the enterprise assets are financed through equity because of new shareholders pattern.

Conclusion

The present case study explains that there is no much improvement in the post-privatisation period compared to pre-privatisation period. As the enterprise takes some more years to improve its performance with regard to improvement in the profit and assets. In case of sales and debt equity ratio the enterprise has showed positive sign. But statistically this improvement is not significant. On the whole the enterprise performance is not statistically significant.

Appendix 1 A
Financial Performance of IBP During Pre-Privatisation Period

(Rs. In crore)

	1997	*1998*	*1999*	*2000*	*2001*	*2002*
PBDIT	96.74	121.69	129.98	163.17	182.9	359.96
Sales	3906.16	4703.12	5686.45	6832.55	8637.51	8463.69
PAT	25.53	31.57	35.3	41.71	54.22	195.79
Assets	920.36	1031.53	1247.12	1558.29	1513.79	1438.6
Equity	22.15	22.15	22.15	22.15	22.15	22.15
No.of Employees	2689	2677	0	0	2626	2207
Total Debt	444.76	492.42	554.99	621.82	440.86	0
Dividend	5.29	6.09	10.57	12.43	24.41	22.15
Current Assets	497.52	528.2	594.28	774.51	813.58	773.49
Current Liabilities	233.7	280.64	401.09	639.05	772.82	910.13
Debt-Equity Ratio	1.71	1.73	1.79	1.83	1.19	0

Source: Annual Report of IBP, CMIE Prowess Data Base.

Appendix 1B
Financial Performance of IBP During Post-Privatisation Period

(Rs. In crore)

	2003	*2004*	*2005*
PBDIT	189.59	378.16	142.57
Sales	8964.54	10675.74	13633
PAT	87.75	214.66	58.87
Assets	1941.33	2429.92	2670.16
Equity	22.15	22.15	22.15
No.of Employees	0	0	0
Total Debt	0	0	0
Dividend	34.98	87.45	25.39
Current Assets	1212.12	1509.71	1561.64
Current Liabilities	1352.3	1699.77	1894.62
Debt-Equity Ratio	0	0	0

Source: Annual Report of IBP, CMIE Prowess Data Base.

Case 8
Hindustan Zinc Limited (HZL)

Background

Hindustan Zinc Limited (HZL) was incorporated in January 1966 as a public sector company after the takeover of the erstwhile Metal Corporation of India Limited, to develop mining and smelting capacities to substantially meet the domestic demand for zinc and lead metals. HZL's operations are broad based and its activities range from exploration, mining and ore processing to smelting and refining of lead and zinc, together with recovery of by-products like silver, cadmium, cobalt, sulphuric acid and copper. Its paid up capital is Rs.422.53 crore out of which Government of India holds 75.92% while Financial Institutions, other Corporate Bodies (including NRIs) and Indian nationals hold the balance equity. It is a profit making and listed company and its shares are traded on the Stock

Exchanges of Mumbai, Delhi and Jaipur. There has been a spurt in its share prices, especially after the successful disinvestment of VSNL, IBP etc. The weighted average price of shares over the six months is about Rs.25.30 and the average weekly high and low of closing price for the same period is over Rs.22 per share.

Disinvestment

On 29.8.2000 the Government of India has decided to disinvest 26% equity in Hindustan Zinc Limited in favour of Sterlite Opportunities and Ventures Limited, a Special Purpose Vehicle promoted by Sterlite Industries (India) Limited and Sterlite Optical Technologies Limited, at a price of Rs. 445 crore (amounting to Rs. 40.50 per share). This means a P/E (price/earning) ratio of about 21. The average dividend paid by the Company, calculated for 26% equity, over the last eight years till 2000, has been of the order of Rs. 3.50 crore per year Following due process, price bids were invited from all the Qualified Interested Parties (QIPs) to be received on 8.11.2001. Only one QIP submitted the price bid which was rejected since it was lower than the reserve price fixed.

Valuation

In pursuance of Government directions, a renewed exercise was undertaken involving the original exercise, as well as the Advisors/Legal Advisors to see how the value depleters in the transaction documents and bidding conditions could be modified to enhance the potential value of the company in order to make it more attractive to the bidders. M/s URS Corporation was appointed to conduct environmental, health and safety due diligence review of the company. Amongst the modifications made in the transaction documents are the sequencing of call and put options and their pricing, the provision to have the Chairman nominated by the Strategic Partner once it acquires 51% stake, unlimited environmental indemnity for a period of three years and a clear road map for the Government to exit from the company. Besides, sale price has been de-linked from Public offer price under the SEBI Takeover Code. Meanwhile, on 28.2.2002 it was announced that the customs duty will be reduced from 35% to 25%, which is likely to impact on the profitability of the company. Finally, price bids were invited from all the five QIP (Glencore International, Binani Industries, Indo-Gulf Corporation, Sterlite and Metdist).

Two financial bids were received from M/s Indo Gulf Corporation and M/s Sterlite Opportunities and Ventures Limited. The reserve price fixed was Rs.32.15 per share (Rs.353.17 crore for 26% stake). Both the price bids received were above the reserve price. The higher bid, that of M/s Sterlite Opportunities and Ventures Limited, for Rs.445 crore (translating to about Rs.40.50 per share) was accepted. The price offered by M/s Sterlite Opportunities & Ventures Limited is substantially higher than the offer made by Sterlite Industries in November, 2001.

The transaction was closed on 11.04.2002. An attractive ESOP scheme was offered to the employees and full-time functional directors of the Company. 1.46% shares were sold to employees @ Rs. 10/- per share in December 2002.

As part of the "Call Option' available to the Strategic Partner, Government parted with another 18.92% for Rs. 323.88 crore @ Rs. 40.50 per share in November, 2003.

Industry Overview

HZL is India's only integrated zinc producer and enjoys a 61% market share by volume in India in fiscal 2007. HZL's Rampura Agucha zinc mine is the third largest in the world in terms of contained zinc deposits on a production basis and the fourth largest on a reserve basis. It was estimated to have the third lowest cost of producing zinc concentrate in 2006, the new Chanderiya hydrometallurgical zinc smelter was in the lowest cost quartile in terms of all zinc smelting operations worldwide in 2006 and HZL was the world's fourth largest zinc mining company in 2006 based on mine production.

Internal Controls

The enterprise has well defined internal control systems with respect to different operational and managerial functions. Regular updation/modification of systems and procedure manuals is carried out keeping in view the changes in industrial and business scenarios. Total compliance with laid down systems is ensured along with integration of financial data with the controlling systems. Audit Committee meetings are convened regularly and attended by the Head of Internal Audit.

Audit is conducted in phases during the year covering various areas of business activities like purchase and stores, marketing, personnel, production, maintenance works, cost and budget, finance etc. The enterprise also conducted systems audit of its newly installed ERP system, SAP R/3. The audit observations have been implemented to further improve the effectiveness of the system. Important audit observations are reported to the Audit Committee and their directions are forwarded to the concerned units/ departments for compliance.

Human Resources

Human Resources have been playing a vital and positive role in the continued growth of the Company. The Company has undertaken many structured initiatives towards recruitment of the best talent as per well established norms, nurturing both fresh talent as well as internal talent through structured learning, creating a performance orientation with appropriate rewards and recognition and identifying talents and giving an opportunity to talented employees to take higher responsibilities in the organisation.

With a view to building competence at all levels and to strengthen the existing competence in many areas, the enterprise's employees are sponsored for various learning programmes both in-house and external. The external programmes are in partnership with reputed institutions like IIM Ahmedabad, IIT Mumbai, BITS Pilani, etc. Apart from this, the enterprise introduced the concept of 'Dronacharya' making one person responsible for learning and development in each of its Units, as a result of which the Company's performance towards training mandays per year has increased to 24633 mandays in 2004-05 from 8198 mandays in the year 2003-04.

The company has a policy of recruiting B.Sc. and other graduates from local areas, with special emphasis on increasing the ratio of female employees. Accordingly trainees for the new smelter have been taken on this basis. Special programmes are conducted for developing new talent with a view to providing better career opportunities for young aspirants.

The enterprise has a long and sustained tradition of cordial relationship with the Workers' Federation and Unions and the employee relations are also excellent. The participative approach of problem, solving at all levels, including at Company level, has continued to pay rich dividends not only towards continuing the cordial employee relations but also towards organization improvement in various areas and managing change with the times.

Environment Safety

HZL strives for continuous improvements, especially in the Environment, Health and Safety performance of its operations. The management of health and safety ("H&S") is a core activity for the enterprise. By its nature, the metal and mining industry brings with it H&S risks and the they ensures that these risks are monitored and mitigated through a variety of programmes and training within each of its Business. H&S performance is reported and discussed during internal meetings as well as at Board meetings. Each site has H&S managers and committees. All the units of HZL have achieved IS014001 (Environment) and OHSAS18001 (Health & Safety) certifications.

Corporate Social Responsibility

Corporate Social Responsibility (CSR) is an integral part of the enterprise business goals. The enterprise has been working in 65 villages, in its vicinity. The main thrust of interventions has been education, health and rural livelihood. The major focus on corporate social responsibility initiatives was further strengthened. The enterprise is initiating to set up an organization which would fortify the CSR performance in the coming years.

The enterprise outlay on CSR for the year 2005-06 was Rs 96.24 million. They are also partnered with various social agencies for some of our projects, like Kalyan Arogya Sadan, Sikar, Badhir Bal Kalyan Vikas Samiti, Bhilwara, Viklang Kalyan Samiti, Udaipur, Sterlite Matrimangal Kanya Mahavidyalaya, Ringas, Sikar, Rawal Mallinathji Foundation, Jodhpur, Ramanandacharya Sanskrit Vishwavidyalaya, Jaipur, mid-day meal programme among others.

Financial Performance

The total revenue earned from zinc production is more than doubled to Rs. 8,560 cr with a corresponding EBIDTA of Rs. 6,644 cr during 2006-07 compared to 2005-06, primarily due to higher metal volumes and LME zinc prices, which more than doubled over the year 2005-06

To analyse the performance of selected companies certain key ratios are taken into account. In the case of HZL there is an improvement in such ratios from pre-privatisation period to post-privatisation period. Profit Before Depreciation, Interest and Taxes (PBDIT)/Sales moved from 15.41 as an average to 37.27 in the post-privatisation period. On the other hand Profit After Tax (PAT)/Sales moved from 3.11 to 24.00, PBDIT/Assets moved from 10.01 to 30.79, PAT/Assets from 2.02 to 19.83, PBDIT/Equity from 35.45 to 240.87, PAT/Equity from 7.15 to 155.10. Sales/Total assets from 64.97 to 82.62. Total Debt/ Assets from 21.40 to 17.29 and Current Ratio from 239.74 to

265.89.The ratios explained that after privatization organization has given more importance to profitability as certain ratios indicating the same.

Table 1A
Financial Ratio Analysis HZL

	Pre-Privatisation					
	1997	*1998*	*1999*	*2000*	*2001*	*2002*
PBDIT/Sales	15.41	17.69	16.74	17.01	21.87	15.10
PAT/Sales	3.11	5.84	5.83	5.88	10.75	3.52
PBDIT/Assets	10.01	15.15	15.97	17.26	22.76	19.40
PAT/Assets	2.02	5.00	5.56	5.97	11.19	4.53
PBDIT/Equity	35.45	52.90	51.86	61.90	81.45	19.40
PAT/Equity	7.15	17.46	18.06	21.40	40.05	4.53
Sales/Total Assets	64.97	85.61	95.44	101.42	104.07	128.50
Total debt/Total Assets	21.40	6.33	6.84	0.99	0.37	0.25
CA/CL	239.74	170.84	240.06	180.21	220.80	235.18
employees	11771	11856	11851	11496	10235	8337

(Source: Compiled from Appendix 1.A)

Table 1B
Financial Ratio Analysis HZL

	post-privatisation		
	2003	*2004*	*2005*
PBDIT/Sales	15.40	31.08	37.27
PAT/Sales	7.28	17.17	24.00
PBDIT/Assets	18.69	27.39	30.79
PAT/Assets	8.84	15.13	19.83
PBDIT/Equity	71.11	173.33	240.87
PAT/Equity	33.64	95.75	155.10
Sales/Total Assets	121.39	88.13	82.62
Total debt/Total Assets	0.04	22.73	17.29
CA/CL	245.69	356.84	265.89
employees	6054	5762	5423

(Source: Compiled from Appendix 1B)

Graph 1

Financial Performance of HZL

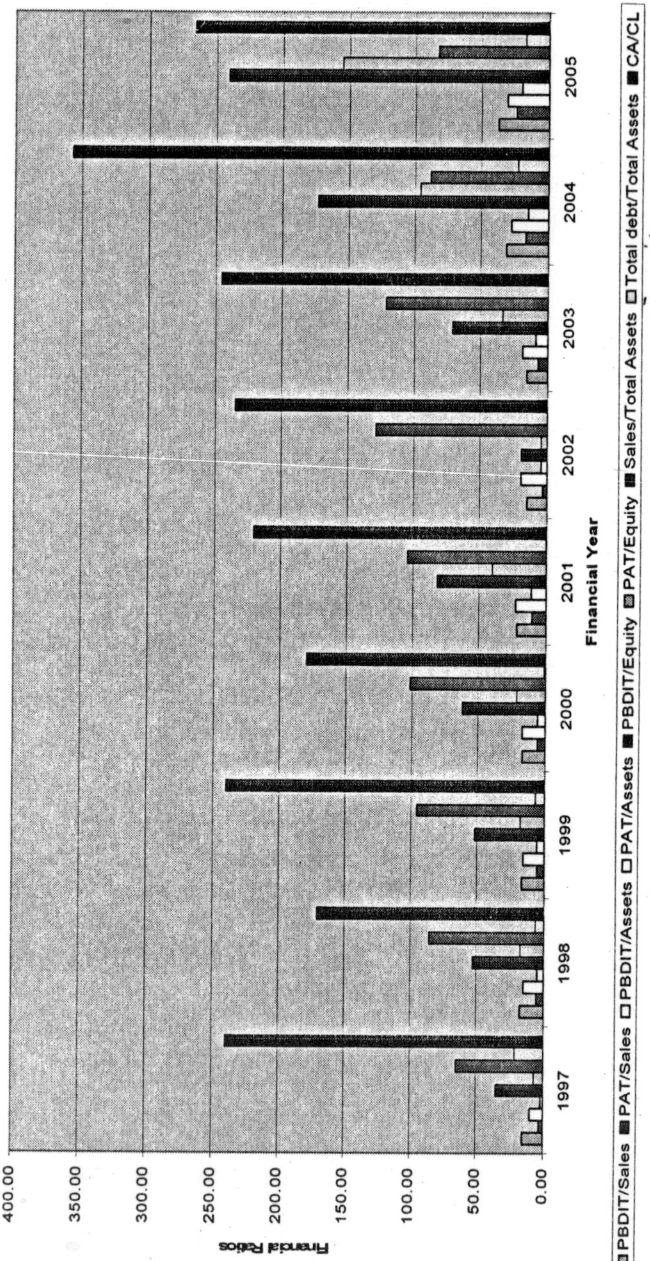

All the financial ratios shows a significant improvement in the post-privatisation period especially during 2005-06.

An attempt is being made to test the performance of HZL in Pre and Post Privatisation periods using paired samples t-statistics with reference to Return on Sales, Return on Equity and Return on Assets an Current Assets/Current Liabilities. The performance in case of each ratio is explained separately.

Return on Sales (ROS) Ratio

This ratio is widely used to evaluate an enterprise operational efficiency. ROS is also known as a firm's "operating profit margin". It is calculated using the formula Profit Before Depreciation Interest and Taxes/Sales. This measure is helpful to management, providing insight into how much profit is being produced per rupee of sales. As with many ratios, it is best to compare a Enterprise's ROS over time to look for trends, and compare it to other companies in the industry. An increasing ROS indicates the Enterprise is growing more efficient, while a decreasing ROS could signal looming financial troubles.

Table 2 shows the paired samples t-test for PBDIT/Sales, Pat/Sales in pre-privatisation period and post-privatisation

Table 2
Paired Samples T-Test

		Mean Difference	*Std. Deviation*	*Std. Error Mean*	*t*	*df*	*Sig (2-tailed)*
Pair 1	PBDIT/Sales pre PBDIT/Sales post	-16.49	14.91	7.45	-2.21	3	.11
Pair 2	PAT/Sales Pre PAT/Sales Post	-13.54	9.43	4.71	-2.87	3	.06

Graph 2
Return on Sales

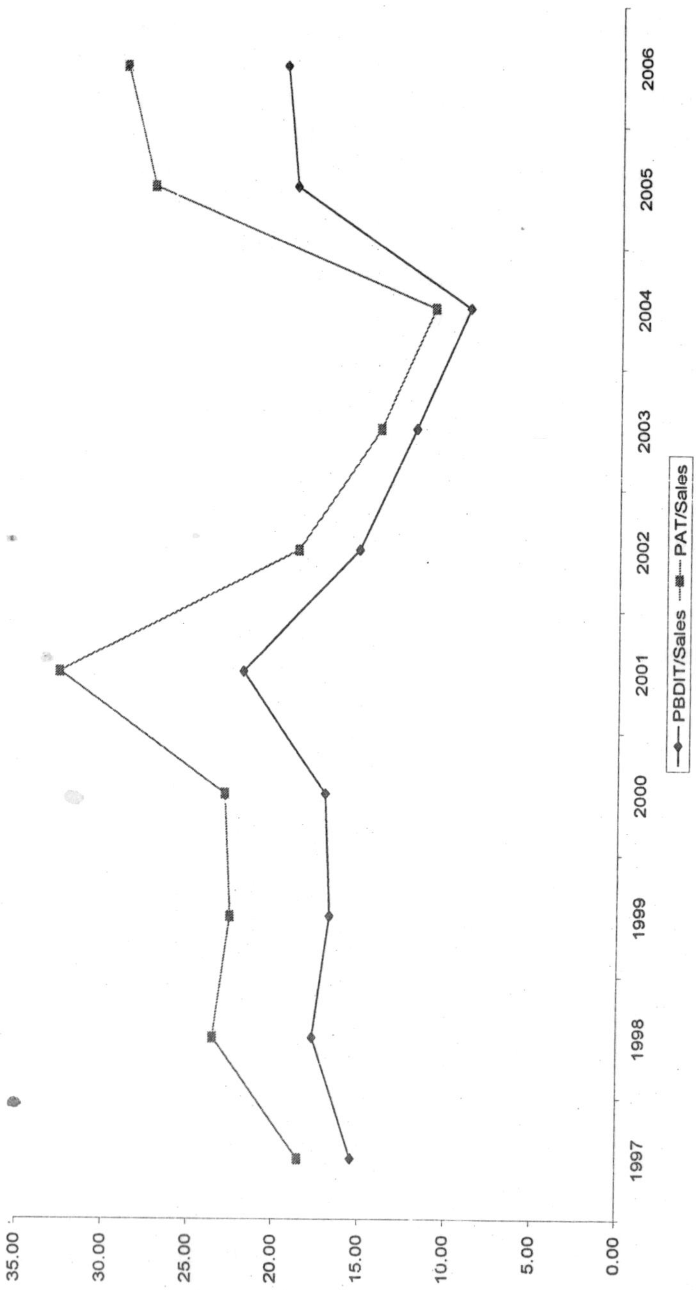

period. It is observed that for pair 1&2 (Return on Sales (ROS)) the mean difference is -16.49 and -13.54 and standard deviation is 14.9 and 9.43 and standard error is 7.45 and 4.71 and t-values are -2.21 and -2.87 respectively and the corresponding significance value is 0.11 and 0.06 which is lightly greater than 0.05 per cent significance level. This signifies that there is no significant difference in Return on Sales (PBDIT/Sales and PAT/Sales) in the pre-privatisation period and post-privatisation period. Hence the null hypothesis (Return on Sales in Per-privatisation period is equal to Return on Sales in the post-privatisation period) is accepted.

The graph on Return on Sales in the pre and post privatisation period shows a positive trend.

Return on Assets (ROA) Ratio

Return on Assets is an indicator of how profitable an enterprise is relative to its total assets. ROA gives an idea as to how efficient management is at using its assets to generate earnings. Calculated by dividing an enterprise's annual earnings by its total assets, ROA is displayed as a percentage. Sometimes this is referred to as "return on investment". ROA explains the earnings that were generated from invested capital (assets). ROA for public companies can vary substantially and will be highly dependent on the industry. This is why when using ROA as a comparative measure, it is best to compare it against a enterprise's previous ROA numbers or with the ROA of a similar enterprise. The assets of the enterprise are comprised of both debt and equity. Both these types of financing are used to fund the operations of the enterprise. The ROA figure gives investors an idea of how effectively the enterprise is converting the money it has to invest into net income. The higher the ROA number, the better, because the enterprise is earning more money on less investment.

Table 3 shows that paired samples t-test for PBDIT/Assets, PAT/Assets in pre-privatisation period and post-privatisation

Graph 3
Return on Assets

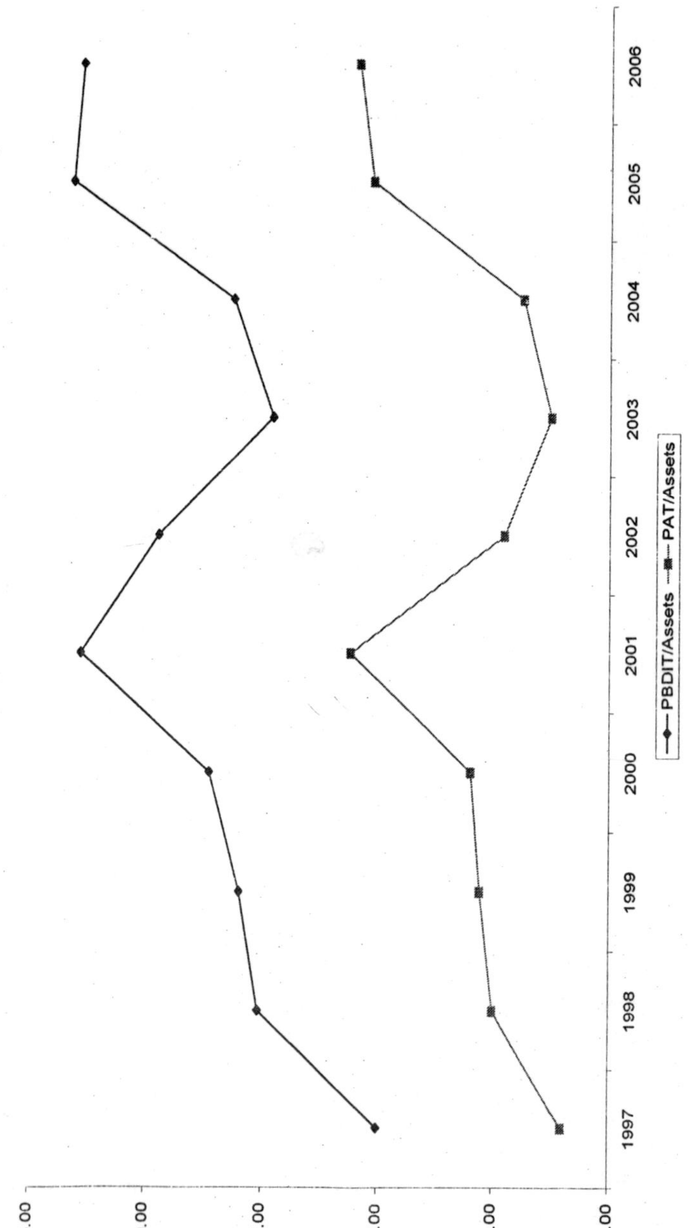

period. It is observed that for pair 1&2 (Return on Assets (ROA)) the mean difference is -13.83 and -11.61 and standard deviation is 9.67 and 6.50 and standard error is 4.83 and 3.25 and t-values are -2.85 and -3.57 respectively and the corresponding significance values are 0.06 and 0.03. Here PAT/Assets ratio is less than 0.05 per cent significance level and PBDIT/Assets ratio is slightly greater than 0.05 i.e., 0.06. This signifies that there is a significant difference in Return on Assets (PBDIT/Assets and PAT/Assets) in the pre-privatisation period and post-privatisation period. Hence the null hypothesis (Return on Assets in Per-privatisation period is equal to Return on Assets in the post-privatisation period) is rejected.

Table 3
Paired Samples T-Test

		Mean Difference	*Std. Deviation*	*Std. Error Mean*	*t*	*df*	*Sig (2-tailed)*
Pair 1	PBDIT/Assets pre PBDIT/Assets post	-13.54	9.43	4.71	-2.85	3	.06
Pair 2	PAT/Assets Pre PAT/Assets Post	-11.61	6.50	3.25	-3.57	3	.03

The graph on Return on Assets in the pre and post privatisation period shows a positive trend.

Return on Equity (ROE) Ratio

Return on Equity is a measure of an enterprise profitability that reveals how much profit an enterprise generates with the money that shareholders have invested. ROE is useful for comparing the profitability of an enterprise to that of other firms in the same industry.

Graph 4
Return on Equity

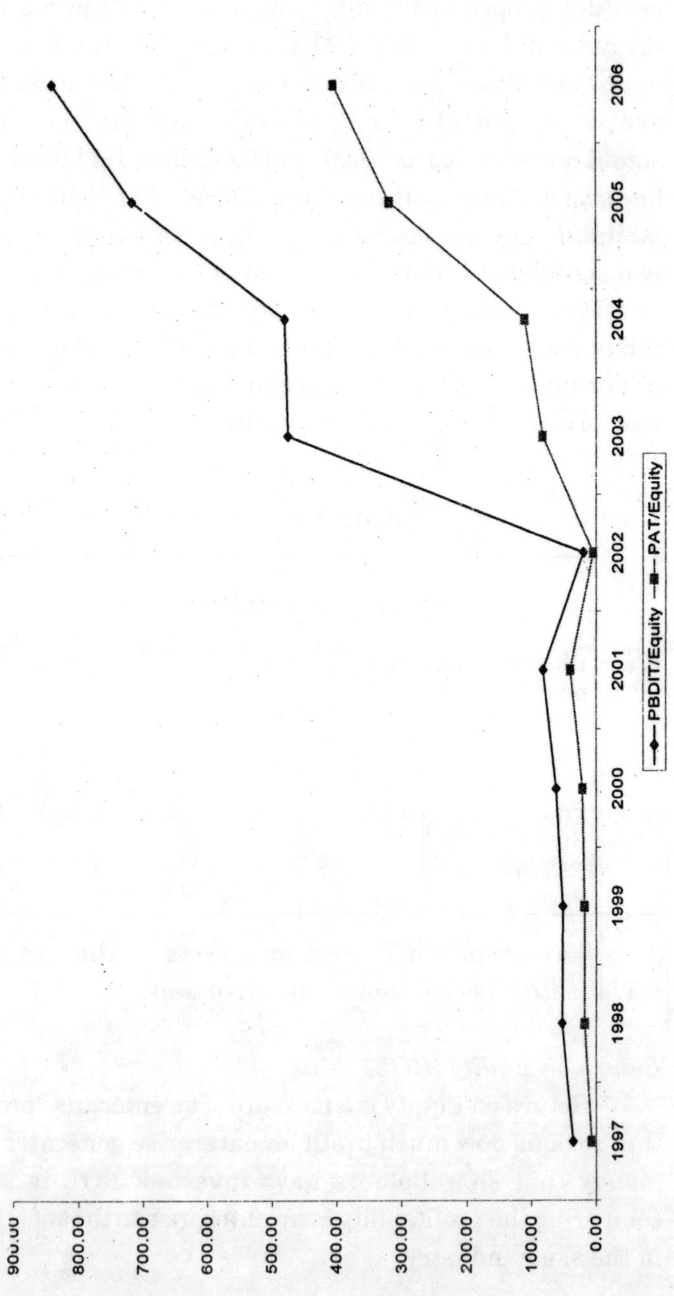

Table 4 shows that paired sample test for PBDIT/Equity, PAT/Equity in pre-privatisation period and PBDIT/Equity, PAT/ Equity in the post-privatisation period is showed where in paired differences, t-test and significance are represented. From the table it is observed that for pair 1&2 (Return on Equity (ROE)) the mean difference is -201.54 and -134.00 and standard deviation is 201.92 and 125.80 and standard error is 100.96 and 62.90 and t-values are -1.99 and -2.13 respectively and the corresponding significance values are 0.014 and 0.012 which are lesser than 0.05 per cent significance level. This signifies that there is a significant difference (i.e., financial improvement) in Return on Equity (PBDIT/Equity and PAT/Equity) in the pre-privatisation period and post-privatisation period. Hence the null hypothesis Return on Equity in Per-privatisation period is equal to Return on Equity in the post-privatisation period is rejected.

Table 4
Paired Samples T-Test

		Mean Difference	*Std. Deviation*	*Std. Error Mean*	*t*	*df*	*Sig (2-tailed)*
Pair 1	PBDIT/Equity pre PBDIT/Equity post	-201.54	201.92	100.96	-1.99	3	.014
Pair 2	PAT/Equity Pre PAT/Equity Post	-134.00	125.80	62.90	-2.13	3	.012

The graph on Return on Equity in the pre and post privatisation period shows a positive trend.

Asset Turn Over Ratio

This ratio is useful to determine the amount of sales that are generated from each rupee of assets. Enterprises with low

Graph 5

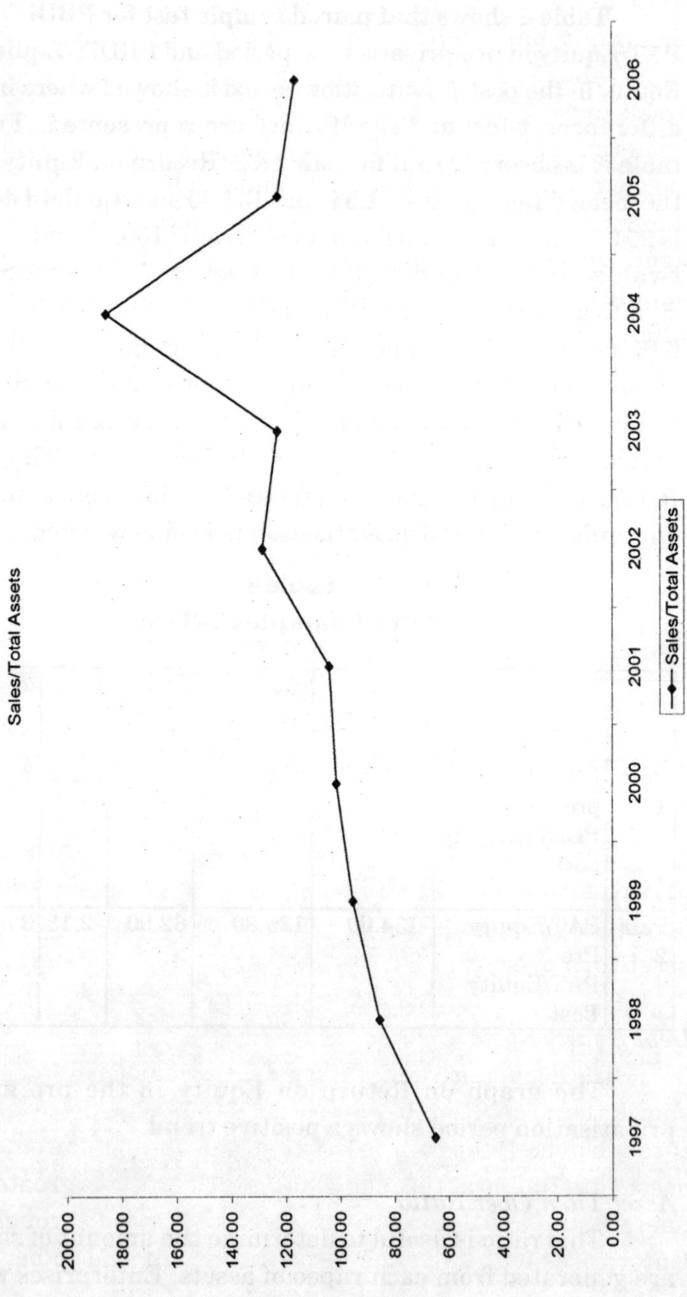
Sales/Total Assets
0.00
20.00
40.00
60.00
80.00
100.00
120.00
140.00
160.00
180.00
200.00
1997
1998
1999
2000
2001
2002
2003
2004
2005
2006
Sales/Total Assets

profit margins tend to have high asset turnover, those with high profit margins have low asset turnover.

Table 5 shows the paired samples t-test for Sales/Total Assets in pre-privatisation period and post-privatisation period. From the table it is observed that for pair 1 (Asset Turn Over) the mean difference is 1.28 and standard deviation is 25.16 and standard error is 12.58 and t-value is .1 and the corresponding significance value is 0.92 which are greater than 0.05 per cent significance level. This signifies that there is no significant difference in Asset Turn Over in the pre-privatisation period and post-privatisation period. Hence the null hypothesis (Asset Turnover ratio in Per-privatisation period is equal to Asset Turnover ratio in the post-privatisation period) is accepted.

Table 5
Paired Samples T-Test

		Mean Difference	*Std.Deviation*	*Std.Error Mean*	*t*	*df*	*Sig (2-tailed)*
Pair 1	Sales/Total Assets Pre Sales/Total Assets Post	1.28	25.16	12.58	.10	3	.92

The graph on Asset Turn Over in the pre and post privatisation period shows a positive trend in the post-privatisation period. The graph shows a declining trend in the asset turn over ratio.

Debt Equity Ratio

The debt/asset ratio (Total liabilities divided by total assets) shows the proportion of enterprise assets which are financed through debt. If the ratio is less than one, most of the enterprise assets are financed through equity. If the ratio is greater than one, most of the enterprise assets are financed through debt. Enterprises with high debt/asset ratios are said to be "highly

Graph 6

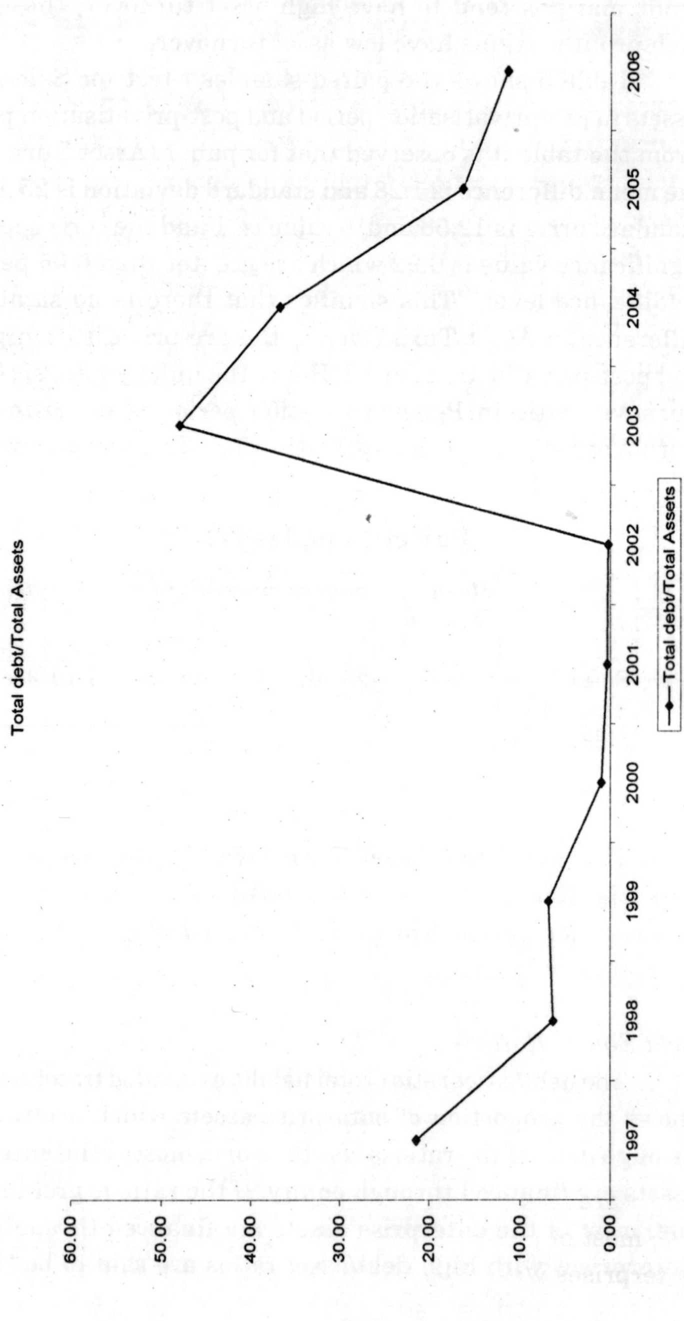
Total debt/Total Assets
60.00
50.00
40.00
30.00
20.00
10.00
0.00
1997
1998
1999
2000
2001
2002
2003
2004
2005
2006
Total debt/Total Assets

leveraged," and could be in danger if creditors start to demand repayment of debt.

Table 6 shows that paired sample test for Total Debt/Total Assets in pre-privatisation period and in the post-privatisation period is showed where in paired differences, t-test and significance are represented. From the table it is observed that for pair 1 (Debt Equity Ratio) the mean difference is -9.26 and standard deviation is 10.62 and standard error is 5.31 and t-value is -1.74 and the corresponding significance value is 0.18 which is greater than 0.05 per cent significance level. This signifies that there is no significant difference in Debt-Equity ratio in the pre-privatisation period and post-privatisation period. Hence the null hypothesis (Debt-Equity ratio in Per-privatisation period is equal to Debt-Equity ratio in the post-privatisation period) is accepted.

Table 6
Paired Samples Test

		Mean Difference	*Std. De-viation*	*Std. Error Mean*	*t*	*df*	*Sig (2-tailed)*
Pair 1	Total Debt/Total Assets Pre Total Debt/Total Assets Post	-9.2	10.62	5.31	-1.74	3	.18

The graph on Debt-Equity in the pre and post privatisation period shows an decreasing trend.

Conclusion

It is clearly evident from the analysis that, after privatisation a significant improvement has not taken place in the financial performance of an enterprise. But the year 2001 has experienced a lower performance and in the same year the government has marched towards disinvestment. In the successive years there is an improvement with respect to Return on Sales, Return on Equity, Return on Assets, Asset Turnover and Debt-Equity ratios. A detailed financial overview (given in appendix 1) makes it clear. But the growth rate is very low. That is why, the statistical results has not shown an significant improvement during the period 2003-04 to 2005-06. during the year 2006-07 the total revue of the enterprise increased by 119% from Rs. 40,006 cr to Rs. 8,791 cr. The PBDIT for the same period increased from Rs. 2418 cr to Rs.6,639 cr representing an increase of 175%. The net profit increased by 202% from Rs.1472 cr to Rs. 4442 cr.

Appendix 1 A
Financial Performance of HZL During Pre-Privatisation Period

(Rs. In crore)

	Mar-97	*1998*	*1999*	*2000*	*2001*	*2002*
PBDIT	149.77	223.52	219.13	261.55	344.17	291.26
Sales	971.7	1263.49	1309.39	1537.31	1573.99	1929.4
PAT	30.22	73.76	76.32	90.43	169.22	67.96
Assets	1495.59	1475.83	1371.99	1515.74	1512.39	1501.5
Equity	422.53	422.53	422.53	422.53	422.53	1501.5
No.of Employees	11771	11856	11851	11496	0	8337
Total Debt	320.03	93.46	93.91	15	5.62	3.72
Dividend	6.96	16.27	19.76	25.8	58.21	21.12
Current Assets	745.87	785.76	716.31	822.56	765.11	692.81
Current Liabilities	311.11	459.94	298.39	456.44	346.51	294.59
Debt-Equity Ratio	0.37	0.1	0.1	0.01	0	0

Source: Annual Report of HZLs, CMIE Prowess Data Base.

Appendix 1 B
Financial Performance of HZL During Post-Privatisation Period

(Rs. In crore)

	2003	*2004*	*2005*
PBDIT	300.46	732.37	1017.73
Sales	1951.43	2356.61	2730.6
PAT	142.15	404.59	655.33
Assets	1607.58	2674	3305.09
Equity	422.53	422.53	422.53
No.of Employees	6054	0	0
Total Debt	0.61	607.8	571.33
Dividend	38.13	66.74	84.46
Current Assets	735.85	1714.23	1424.6
Current Liabilities	299.5	480.39	535.78
Debt-Equity Ratio	0	0.4	0.27

Source: Annual Report of HZLs, CMIE Prowess Data Base.

References

1. This ratio is widely used to evaluate an enterprise operational efficiency. ROS is also known as a firm's "operating profit margin". It is calculated using this formula (Profit Before Depreciation Interest and Taxes/Sales). This measure is helpful to management, providing insight into how much profit is being produced per rupee of sales. As with many ratios, it is best to compare a Enterprise's ROS over time to look for trends, and compare it to other companies in the industry. An increasing ROS indicates the Enterprise is growing more efficient, while a decreasing ROS could signal looming financial troubles.
2. Return on Assets is an indicator of how profitable an enterprise is relative to its total assets. ROA gives an idea as to how efficient management is at using its assets to generate earnings. Calculated by dividing a Enterprise's annual earnings

by its total assets, ROA is displayed as a percentage. Sometimes this is referred to as "return on investment". ROA explains the earnings that were generated from invested capital (assets). ROA for public companies can vary substantially and will be highly dependent on the industry.

3. Return on Equity is a measure of an enterprise profitability that reveals how much profit an enterprise generates with the money that shareholders have invested. ROE is useful for comparing the profitability of an enterprise to that of other firms in the same industry.
4. This ratio is useful to determine the amount of sales that are generated from each rupee of assets. Enterprises with low profit margins tend to have high asset turnover, those with high profit margins have low asset turnover.
5. Total liabilities divided by total assets. The debt/asset ratio shows the proportion of a enterprise assets which are financed through debt. If the ratio is less than one, most of the enterprise assets are financed through equity. If the ratio is greater than one, most of the enterprise assets are financed through debt. Enterprises with high debt/asset ratios are said to be "highly leveraged," and could be in danger if creditors start to demand repayment of debt.
6. Bharat Aluminium Company Limited (BALCO), Computer Maintenance Centre (CMC), Hindustan Teleprinters Limited (HTPL), Videsh Sanchar Nigam Limited (VSNL), Maruti Udyog Limited (MUL), Indian Petroleum Corporation Limited (IPCL), Indo Burman Petroleum Limited (IBP), Hindustan Zinc Limited (HZL).
7. Sudir Naib (2003).
8. Mishra, Morton R Davies (2004).
9. Yarrow (1999).
10. Simrit Kaur, (2003).

13

Sikkim Nationalized Transport A Case Study

The State Level Public Enterprises (SLPEs) are an important component of the economy of the State of Sikkim. It is, however, important to note that the State of Sikkim continues to have its own Companies Act which was earlier promulgated by the Chogyal in 1961 titled as the Registration of Companies Act. The finances of the State of Sikkim need strengthening in terms of their allocation and productive deployment. The re-engineering of the state finances has been done with a human face. There are 22 SLPEs in the State of Sikkim and the total investment of these enterprises amounted to Rs. 726.06 crore as on March 31, 2004. The social and economic consequences of the re-engineering have to be kept in the backdrop while designing the strategies for this purpose and implementation of such strategies. The investments in the SLPEs in the State of Sikkim have been increasing over the years. The performance, however, has not kept pace with the expectations. This divergence has adversely affected the state finances.

Sikkim Nationalized Transport (SNT) and the Sikkim State Energy and Power Department are the major commercial activity enablers holding a predominant position in terms of investment, turnover, financial losses and manpower in the State. The paper deals with the organizational setup, financial profile, manpower, fleet strength, operational efficiency, vehicle productivity and fleet utilization in SNT. The paper analyses the strengths, weaknesses, opportunities and threats facing the organization and their impact on valuation of SNT. Finally, the paper suggests restructuring techniques and action plan for the turnaround of SNT.

Enterprise Profile

There was no public transportation system in Sikkim till 1944 when a Truck Department was created which was subsequently renamed Sikkim Nationalized Transport (SNT) in 1955. As most of the routes within the State were nationalized prior to 1975, all passengers and goods were exclusively transported by SNT buses and trucks or under its supervision. However, the system has been diluted after the extension of the Central Motor Vehicle Act, 1988 to Sikkim. Nevertheless, the bulk of passengers and the goods traffic in the State are being carried by SNT. SNT has 12 depots –cum-ticket booking officers for buses within the State one at Siliguri (West Bengal).

(See: Govt. of Sikkim, Report of the Comptroller and Auditor General of India, March 2003, p. 24).

In addition, there are four ticket booking agents at other places within the State and one at Kalimpong (West Bengal). SNT also operates three depots for trucks at Gangtok, Rangpo and Jorethang. It has one Central Workshop at Jalipool for major repairs and workshops at Gangtok, Rangpo, Jorethang and Rhenock for minor repairs. It has 100 buses, 54 trucks and 38 tankers. Its total fleet strength is 192.

Organisational Setup

The chart shows that the concept of line and staff is followed in the SNT. The concept has become outdated. The transport sector enterprises follow the Strategic Business Unit (SBU) approach in organising their activities. The functions such as Research and Development, job evaluation, performance measurement, training and management development, resource raising and bench marking find no place in the organisaitonal chart.

Organizational Chart

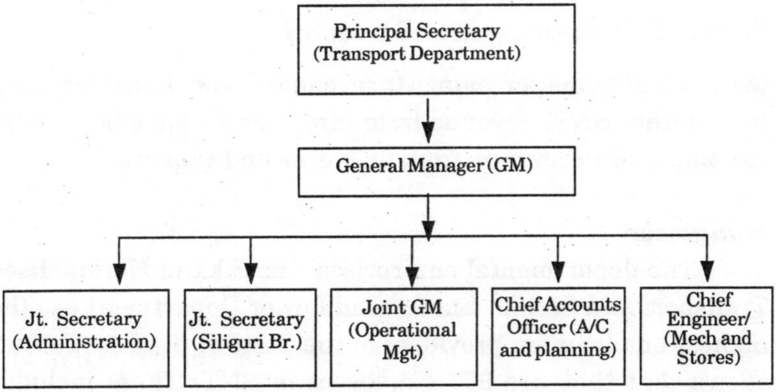

Financial Position and Working Results

Table 1 show that SNT has been a loss making organization. However, the operating deficit has declined over

Table 1 Financial Position and the working results

Particulars	*1998-99*	*1999-00*	*2001-02*	*2002-03*	*2003-04*
Operating Revenue	**9.53**	**10.10**	**11.91**	**15.41**	**17.46**
Passenger traffic	1.36	1.66	2.39	2.18	1.68
Goods traffic	4.50	4.76	4.65	8.13	10.42
Sale of POL	3.56	3.61	4.56	4.78	5.12

(Contd.)

(Contd. Table 1)

Particulars	*1998-99*	*1999-00*	*2001-02*	*2002-03*	*2003-04*
Miscellaneous	0.11	0.07	0.31	0.32	0.24
Operating Expenses	**17.92**	**20.38**	**19.47**	**22.49**	**22.15**
Passenger traffic	12.03	12.73	12.63	16.32	16.38
Goods traffic					
Purchase of POL	5.43	6.99	6.24	5.40	5.07
Miscellaneous	0.46	0.66	0.60	0.77	0.70
Operating deficit	-8.39	-10.28	-7.56	-7.08	-4.69
Percentage of deficit to revenue	**88**	**102**	**63**	**46**	**27**

Source: Information collected from SNT.

the years in terms percentage to revenue earned. It is interesting to note that SNTs revenue from hire charges have been more as compared to revenue from its trucks and tankers.

Manpower

The departmental enterprises, viz. Sikkim Nationalised Transport and Sikkim Energy and Power Department are the highest employment providers in the State of Sikkim. Table 2 shows that they are 957 employees in SNT. These includes regular, work charged and consolidated pay scale personnel.

Table 2 Manpower

Particulars	*Total no of employees*
No. of regular employees	824
No of Work charged employees	42
In consolidated pay	4
No. of M/R Employees	87
Total	**957**

Fleet Strength

Table 3 gives the fleet strength of SNT. The fleet strength is declining year after year. This is due to disposal of a part of the old fleet and restricted purchases as their replacement and new additions.

Table 3 Fleet Strength

Year	*Bus*	*Truck*	*Tanker*	*Total*
2001-02	110	70	45	225
2002-03	106	63	43	212
2003-04	100	54	38	192

Source: Information collected from SNT.

Acquisition of the Fleet

Table 4 shows during the period 2001-02 to 2003-04, 64 vehicles were disposed off. Against these numbers of disposed vehicles only 22 new vehicles were inducted in the fleet for the entire 3 years period. As per the norms of the Association of State Road Transport Undertaking (ASRTU), atleast 60 per cent of the fleet strength should comprise of vehicles aged not less than 4 years.

Table 4: Acquisition of Fleet

Financial Year	*No. of vehicles disposed off*	*No. of vehicle inducted in the fleet*	*Shortfall*
2001-02	Buses -9 Trucks – 13 Total 22	Buses -5 Trucks –6 Total 11	Buses -4 Trucks –7 Total 11
2002-03	Buses -8 Trucks – 12 Tankers -2 Total 22	Buses -4 Trucks – 5 Total 9	Buses -4 Trucks –7 Total 2
2003-04	Buses -6 Tankers - 5 Trucks –9 Total 20	Buses - Trucks – 2 Total 2	Buses -6 Tankers -5 Trucks –7 Total 18

Source: Information collected from SNT.

Fleet Utilization

Fleet Utilization is the ratio of the vehicles on road to the average number of vehicles held. According to the recommendation of the ASRTU, 92 percent of the fleet should be road worthy of which 90 percent shall be kept in operation and 2 per cent as reserve. In respect of buses, the fleet utilization of SNT ranged between 75 to 85 per cent during 1998-99 to 2002-03, falling short of the norm by 7 to 17 per cent. The fleet utilization of trucks ranged between 70 to 95 per cent during 1998-99 to 2002-03.

Vehicle Productivity (VP)

The vehicle productivity indicates the average revenue earnings per kilometer covered by each vehicle per day, for which SNT had not fixed any norm. The VP of SNT buses for the period 1998-99 to 2000-01 compared with that of other hill State's Road Transport Corporation is shown in Table 5.

Table 5 :Vehicle Productivity in Road Transport Corp in North East

State Road Transport Corp.	*1998-99*	*1999-00*	*2000-01*
SNT	85.64	81.90	80.72
Himachal RTC	215.10	224.80	223.40
Meghalaya RTC	186.10	121.10	136.90
Nagaland RTC	-	103.90	132.50
Mizoram RTC	118.40	119.60	118.80
All India Average	279.00	295.00	267.00

Source: Govt. of Sikkim, Report of the Comptroller and Auditor General of India, March 03.

Operational Efficiency

According to the latest fare formula adopted by SNT with effect from Feb 2002, the expenditure per kilometer per bus worked out to Rs 20.02 and RS 18.74. Out of 9,638 bus trips operated out of Gangtok during 2002-03, in the case of 2,923 and 6,715 long and short distance trips respectively the per kilometer earnings per bus was less than the cost. The loss on this account worked out to Rs 1.17 crore during 2002-03 for Gangtok depot alone.

It was also seen that SNT discontinued services, reasons for which were not record, from Gangtok, to Pelling and District Courts from August 2000 and September 2002 even though these services recorded high average earning of Rs.33.78 and Rs. 27.99 per kilometer. SNT resumed the Pelling service form October 2000 to November 2000 during which period the average earning came down to Rs 7.23 per kilometer. Thereafter these services were discontinued.

Fuel efficiency

SNT had fixed efficiency of buses at three kilometers per liter of HSD. However, the actual consumption was 1.82 kmpl, 2.41 kmpl, 2.19 kmpl, and 1.88 kmpl. The extra expenditure on

Table 6 Fuel Efficiency

State Road Transport Corp.	*1998-99*	*1999-00*	*2001-02*	*2002-03*
SNT	1.82	2.41	2.19	1.88
Meghalaya RTC	3.19	3.11	3.17	NA
Nagaland RTC	NA	3.5	3.5	3.5
Mizoram RTC	3.00	3.00	2.87	2.74
All India Average	3.68	3.67	3.53	4.59

Source: Govt. of Sikkim, Report of the Comptroller and Auditor General of India, March 2003.

HSD incurred by SNT due to the lower fuel efficiency being 27 to 37 per cent less than the norm and the consequent adverse impact on its profitability, SNT did not consider it necessary even once during the period under review to ascertain the reasons or take remedial measures. Further, the fuel efficiency of SNT buses for the period 1998-03 as the lowest compared to the Road Transport Corp. of other states with topographies similar to Sikkim, as evident from the table below in Table 6.

Strengths, Weaknesses, Opportunities and Threats (SWOT) Analysis

Strengths

The time proven strength of the Department is that it has consistently achieved its revenue as well as social obligations. In the last Financial Year 2004-05 alone, against the Government target of Rs. 21.50 crore the department not only achieved the target but also exceeded it by almost 8 crore.

- The existing law of land gives SNT the absolute transport market on all the domestic routes as well as the NH 31 A as these are nationalized routes. In principle, what this means is that SNT is the only recognized public transporter for the State. Here it may be noted that even the private trucks carrying public commodities have to run under the supervision of SNT. It implies that legally SNT has 100% control over the Transport business in the State of Sikkim.
- SNT has a very efficient and experienced work force both in the Operation Section as well as the mechanical section, which are the backbone of any transport organization. The department has also very good infrastructural setup like depots, workshops, godowns etc. all over the state as well as in the state of West Bengal.
- SNT has fully established its Brand name over the years. The number of accidents and fatalities is almost nil in the case of SNT. SNT is the sole official carrier of both the passengers and goods of important organizations and

departments as such the Army, General Reserve Engineering Force (**GREF**), all Oil Companies, FCI, all State government departments, etc.

Weaknesses

- The main weakness of the Department is that it has not been able to restructure its activities whereby the department has over the period of years lost the competitive edge to its competitors in private sector. Although, the freight business is almost 100% with the department, it has lost considerable grip over the passenger sector mainly because of its inability to modernise passenger carrier sector.
- Proper Manpower planning and optimum utilization of the workforce needs a serious review as the financial burden of maintaining the excess manpower can not be continued for long.
- The main weakness of the department is that it has not been able to hold an optimum number of fleet. The department is totally dependent on the Government for the funds required for its augmentation of fleet. Against the projected, optimum fleet of 400 - 500 vehicles the department has only 192 vehicles at its disposal.
- The present fleet of functional vehicles is over aged and consists of 66% of vehicles, which are over 10 to 14 years old. This factor adversely affects the important parameters such as vehicle productivity, load factor, etc.

Opportunity

- SNT has a great scope to increase its market share. With the increase in the flow of tourists, its market share is expected to increase further. The setting up of hydro electric projects, helipads, airports and opening up of the Nathulla Pass is expected to brighten the scenario further.

Threats

- The shrinking fleet is the biggest threat. The over manning is also causing a great stress. Too tight a departmental control is obstructing innovativeness and depriving the SNT of a healthy corporate culture. The corporation has become the dumping ground of un-required personnel who lack professional knowledge. The department has no vision. It does not have a corporate plan.

Valuation of SNT *(Annexure 1 shows the valuation of SNT)*

- LAND: The total valuation of land alone belonging to SNT is estimated at Rs. 69.42 Cores.
- BUILDINGS: SNT has well established office buildings, truck parking yards, guesthouses all over the state and at Siliguri, West Bengal. The net valuation of building alone is estimated at Rs. 15.36 crore.
- STOCKS: The net fast moving consumable, like fuel, oil, spare parts in possession of the department at any given time is estimated at Rs. 3 crore.
- VEHICLES: The present market valuation of the vehicles is estimated at Rs. 22 crore
- SUNDRY DEBTORS: The Sundry Debtors stand at Rs. 3.50 crore. This is the amount receivable from Army and Oil Companies.
- Miscellaneous: SNT has got substantial investment in plants and machinery in the various depots and workshops. The department also has major equipments or units such as Weighbridges (3 nos.), tyre rethreading plant, petrol pumps. The net valuation of these plants and machinery along with the total office equipments is estimated at Rs. 6.05 cores.

Restructuring Cost of SNT *(Annexure 2 shows the restructuring cost of SNT)*

- **Voluntary Retirement Scheme**: With the onset of the VRS introduced by the Government 88 numbers of staff of SNT had applied for VRS through the recommendation of the department. However, due to fund constraint only the case of 8 persons was considered. We still have old applications of 80 persons seeking VRS and in addition it is estimated that a minimum of 30 more applicants could likely submit applications for VR. The net fund requirement on VR @ 8 lakhs on average works out to Rs. 880/-Lakhs.

- **Renovation & Expansion**: Many depots including both the workshops and booking offices of SNT need to be renovated to improve working environment. The depot wise fund requirement for the renovation of booking offices, truck parking yards workshops, etc., is estimated at Rs. 60 lakhs.
- **Upgradation of Plant and Machinery** : With the advent of modern technology, the present day vehicles are much more sophisticated and therefore the cost of up gradation of the plant and machinery is estimated at Rs. 30 Lakhs
- **IT requirements**: In order to set up an efficient system of reimbursement of freight bills, the maintenance of stock inventory etc. It is necessary to introduce computers. The cost of IT requirement including both hardware and software is estimated to Rs 10 lakhs
- **Court Cases** : In variably, the nature of work is such that there will be court cases as result of accidents etc., the cost on accounts of this is estimate at Rs 10 lakhs.
- **Contingency liability** : In order to take care of the unforeseen rise in the cost of the operations, a contingency of 4 per cent on the total sundry creditors is estimated at Rs 8 lakhs
- **Operational deficit** : In spite of exceeding the revenue target, the department has a operational deficit of 400 lakhs This is maily attributed to the fact that SNT being a department, in the interest of the general public, is obliged to maintain the operations of bus services in almost 29 uneconomical routes. The department also gives concessions to the students, senior citizenship, Ex-

servicemen etc. Primary reason for deficit is that the department is excessively overstaffed whereby the present expenditure on salaries and wages alone exceeds 10 crore per annum. Therefore, the cost of restructuring cost in order to compensate the operational deficit i5 estimated at Rs. 400 lakhs.

- **Advertisement and Promotion**: The department needs to promote and advertise. Its businesses and activities so as to reach a larger section of the people. The restructuring cost on account of advertisement and promotion is estimated at Rs. 10 lakhs.
- **Sundry Creditors**: The restructuring cost on account of sundry creditors is estimated at Rs. 200 Lakhs.
- **Acquisition Of Fleet**: Perhaps, the most important action that the department has to take immediately is to augment its fleet. The restructuring cost for acquisition of 50 buses, 125 trucks and 25 nos. of tankers is estimated at Rs. 2237 lakhs.
- **Spare Parts**: The department needs to stock adequate quantities of spare parts. The restructuring cost for the requirement of spare parts is estimated at Rs. 2 crore.

Restructuring Process

- Restructuring SNT involves marketing, human resource, financial, commercial, material, and organisational change management. The restructured organization has to cope with the changing market needs, achieve the business goals and make the corporate vision a reality. Table depicts the restructuring costs SNT and vision, mission and passion to excel must become the watchwords of a new work culture. The restructuring approach is discussed below:

Marketing Restructuring

- Expand capacities to service all District Headquarters and neighbouring State capital cities.

- Broaden service facilities by way of Ordinary, Fast Service, Express, Luxury, Hi-Tech buses with different fare/stage structures to suit various needs and sections of the population.
- Strive for customer/passenger satisfaction by improving safety, regularity and punctuality of services.
- Tie up with Tourism Corporation/other public undertakings and meet their transport needs.
- Introduce Booking Agencies at all important traffic points.
- Organise regular traffic/opinion surveys to identify profitable routes.
- Conduct regular opinion surveys to refine operations to secure better passenger satisfaction.
- Introduction of marriage, personal, excursion tours to fill idle time of spare vehicles.
- Introduction of "Transport Cards".

Financial Restructuring

- Identify low cost fund sources.
- Reduce interest liabilities.
- Conversion of State/Central Government loans as equity.
- Conversion of interest due to State and Central Government as equity.
- Clearance of loans/interests of Finance Institutions/Banks by obtaining low cost
- funds.
- Rationalisation of MV tax system to improve operational viability.
- Waiver of MV taxes due to the State Government to set off the cost of services rendered by the Corporation by way of travel concession.
- Depreciation Fund provision of Rs. 20.00 lakhs may be waived.
- Rationalisation of internal accounts and audit system
- Obtain grants and budgeted subsidies from State Government towards bus pass
- concessions.

Human Resource Restructuring

- Lay down norms of staffing and reduce unproductive supporting staff.
- Improve the employee productivity by deploying required crew.
- Introduction of inter-functional transferability of supporting staff categories to Drivers/Conductors.
- Payment of employees' terminal benefits.
- Introduction of suitable VRS and offer to all willing supporting staff.
- Introduction of structured managerial and supervisory development training programmes for updating skills.
- Effective implementation of MOU system.
- Strengthening good employee-relation schemes.
- Introduction of suitable incentive schemes for all employees.

Commercial Restructuring

- Leasing and renting of Corporation infrastructure.
- Introduction of advertisements on bus stations, buses, bus shelters, tickets, CTV advertisement, etc.
- Introduction of parcel and courier services through Corporation buses.
- Maximise luggage revenues i.e. accompanied as well as unaccompanied luggage.
- Maximise the revenue on postal services.
- Maximise the revenue on paper parcel service.

Material Management Restructuring

- Introduction of integrated material management systems.
- Stocking of Depot spares inventory at 4 Zonal Headquarters.
- Standardizing stocking of spare parts with rationalized minimum and maximum limits as per the consumption pattern in order to reduce inventory carrying cost.

- Rationalisation of purchase policies to reduce inventory.
- Rationalisation of standardisation of disposal/auction activities of vehicles, scrap, tyres, batteries, etc.
- Tie up with oil companies to secure petrol, oil and lubricants (POL) at reasonable rates.

Operational Restructuring

- Scheduling of buses with minimum inputs of bus and crew for given traffic demand and design cost-effective transport systems.
- Structuring of operations with optimum service mix to have better return.
- Rationalisation of ticket system as per the service mix.
- Standardizations of various types of services with different stage structures.
- Rationalisation of fare structure.
- Identification of threats from competitors on each route and formulate strategies for effective encounter.
- Identification of opportunities in terms of change of timings, permit variations, etc.
- Strengthening of bus station management.
- Strengthening of quality of services by improving safety, regularity and punctual operations. Creation of passenger relation cells.xi) Strengthening passenger information system.
- Introduction of privately hired buses to improve profitability.
- Augmentation of services on all high density routes.
- Rescheduling of low density and vehicle utilisation services.
- Introduction of services on all approved routes.
- Take advantage of route pattern as 71% routes have length of more than 100 km.
- Strengthening of all inter-state routes.
- Restructuring 20 approved routes which have overlaps ranging from 5 to 56 km.

- Introduction of Hi-Tech buses to all District Headquarters with modern facilities.

Organisational Restructuring

- Smartsizing of Corporate Office with minimum staff. A lean Corporate Office is recommended.
- Closing of all Regional and Central Workshops to reduce cost of operation on
- Workshop repairs.
- Abolition of all Divisional and Sub-Depots to minimise the personnel cost on not very productive offices and staff.
- Creation of 4 self-contained near autonomous operational zones with appropriate delegation of powers.
- Establishing a strong one-tier system controlled by Zonal Office with supporting functions governed by federal administration from Corporate Office.
- Grouping of homogeneous functions to bring about economy.

Management Information Systems Restructuring

- Introduction of effective management information systems.
- Regular monitoring of Critical Successful Factors (CSF) to improve overall performance.
- Regular and timely exchange of information on few vital areas to focus managers' attention and bring about competitive spirit.
- Introduction of performance appraisal and review system.
- Introduction of computers.

Vehicle Maintenance Restructuring

- Introduction of preventive and breakdown maintenance systems.
- Enforcement of sound replacement policy.

- Strengthening of maintenance-operational systems and monitoring.
- Creation of Zonal Maintenance Engineers for this purpose.
- Introduction of technical, managerial and operational controls for fuel to improve use efficiency and performance.
- Introduction of technical controls in the area of tyres, lubes, batteries, springs, etc., to reduce the cost of operations.
- Scrapping of all vehicles over ten years age.
- Repairing of all vehicles which are less than ten years age.
- Rationalisation of fleet by making Bhopal, Indore as Leyland Comet bus and Jabalpur-Raipur as Tata bus zones.

Restructuring of Workshops

- Abolition of all Regional Workshops and Central Workshops to reduce Workshop repair costs.
- Establishment of Body Building Unit at Gwalior along with Printing Press and Training College.
- Establishment of four Zonal Workshops Co-terminus with Zonal operational Units along with Tyre Retreading Shop and Training Schools,.
- Control of Body Building Unit and Training College to be vested in Corporate Office.
- Modernisation of Zonal Workshop Body Building units with latest machinery.

Operational Restructuring

There is a need to corporatise SNT on a top priority basis. The organization should be restructured around the SBU concept. Excess manpower should be given VR. New rules of human resource development, financial management, marketing management should find place in the organization. The operational restructuring should be undertaken on war footing basis. The following are some of the suggestions:

- Preparation of a corporate plan
- Operational restructuring – renewal of fleet, re-organization of workshops, rethinking about the depots, acquisition of small sized buses to counter competition from private sector
- Human resources restructuring – rightsizing the corporation, abolition of practices of appointing handy boy, stopping the appointment of un-required personnel from government, management development and training, higher personnel productivity, induction of professionals.
- Financial restructuring – cost control and cost reduction, introduction of internal audit, low costs funding, fare revision and better cash flow management,
- Technological restructuring – computerization and Global Information System

Conclusions

The restructuring of SNT requires internal reforms paving the way for OPTIMA (Optimum Performance Through Interanl Management and Audit). This would require resources for extending voluntary retirement for surplus personnel, instituting management systems (eg., costing, budgeting, pricing, auditing, MIS, manpower planning and recruitment, training and management development, and performance evaluation). The renovation of old and outdated buses and machinery should be adopted. It is suggested that the GoS may provide a one-time restructuring grant to SNT which would continue to be in the state portfolio or should be retained in the long run. This grant could be disbursed over a period of three years in a ratio of 34:33:33 depending on the urgency, absorption capacity of the enterprise and the availability of the resources with the government.

Annexure 1

Valuation of SNT

(Rs in crore)

Land		*Building*	*Stocks of Machinery, oil, fuel etc*	*Vehicles (Functioning and non-functioning*	*Sundry Debtors*	*Others*	*Total*
Jorethang	12.00	01.40					13.40
Siliguri	20.00	05.00				Plant and Machinery 03.00	28.00
Gangtok	27.00	06.00				Office Equp. 02.00	35.00
Tadong	03.40	00.05				Pump 00.60	4.05
Rangpo	02.00	00.50				W.Bridge 00.45	2.95
Namchi	00.13	00.02					0.15
Mangan	00.80	00.04					1.20
Gyalsing	00.60	00.20					0.80
Melli	00.90	00.05					0.95
Jalipool	03.00	02.00					5.00
Rhenock	00.40	00.10					0.50
	69.42	**15.36**	**03.00**	**22.00**	**3.50**	**06.05**	**119.33**

Source: Computed by SNT.

Annexure 2

Restructuring Costs of SNT
(Rs in crore)

VRS	*Training*	*Renovation/ Expansion*	*IT Requirement*	*Contingent liability*	*Operational deficit*	*Advertisement*	*Sun. Creditors*	*Acquisition of fleet 200 nos. fleet*	*Forecast needs of spares for optimum fleet*	*Total*
80 Old + 30 New X 8 lakhs = 8.80		Jrt 0.65						Bus – 50 Rs @ 13.08 = 654.00 lakh Trucks 125 Rs @ 10.52 = 1315.00 lakh Tanker 25 Rs @10.72 = 268.00 lakh		
		Sng 0.40								
		Rpo 0.50								
		Jpl 0.14								
		Gtk 0.20								
		Nam 0.10								

VRS	*Training*	*Renovation/ Expansion*	*IT Requirement*	*Contingent liability*	*Operational deficit*	*Advertisement*	*Sun. Creditors*	*Acquisition of fleet 200 nos. fleet*	*Forecast needs of spares for optimum fleet*	*Total*
8.80	0.15	0.90 (includes upgradations of Rs 0.30 crore)	0.10	0.08	4.00	0.10	2.00	22.37	2.00	40.60

Source: Computed by SNT.

Index

F

G

H

I

J

K

L

M

W

Z